THE ECONOMIC MANAGEMENT OF THE FIRM

Edited by

J. F. Pickering & T. A. J. Cockerill

Philip Allan

Barnes & Noble Books

First published 1984 by

PHILIP ALLAN PUBLISHERS LIMITED
MARKET PLACE
DEDDINGTON
OXFORD OX5 4SE

First published in the USA 1984 by
BARNES & NOBLE BOOKS
81 ADAMS DRIVE
TOTOWA, NEW JERSEY, 07512

Library of Congress Cataloguing in Publication Data

Main entry under title: The economic management of
  the firm
  Includes indexes.
  1. Industrial management.
  2. Industrial organisation.
  3. Business enterprises. I. Pickering, J. F.
II. Cockerill, T. A. J.
HD31.E34D   1984   658   84-11098
ISBN   0-389-20495-1

Printed in Great Britain at The Pitman Press, Bath

Contents

Contributors

P. Buckley	Professor of Managerial Economics, University of Bradford
T. A. J. Cockerill	Senior Lecturer in Management Sciences, UMIST
P. Doyle	Professor of Marketing, University of Bradford Management Centre
Sir Douglas Hague	Chairman of the Economic and Social Research Council; Professorial Fellow, Oxford Management Centre; and Visiting Professor, Manchester Business School
C. W. L. Hill	Lecturer in Management Sciences, UMIST
T. T. Jones	Lecturer in Management Sciences, UMIST
H. Kinloch	Formerly Deputy Managing Director, Liberty Life Assurance Co. Ltd
D. A. Littler	Lecturer in Management Sciences, UMIST
B. J. Loasby	Professor of Management Economics, University of Stirling
B. J. McCormick	Reader in Economics, University of Sheffield
J. F. Pickering	Professor of Industrial Economics, UMIST
R. C. Stapleton	Professor of Business Finance (National Westminster Bank), Manchester Business School
D. Todd	Senior Economic Adviser, H. M. Treasury; and Directorate General for Economic and Financial Affairs, European Commission, Bruxelles

Preface

At all levels of management activity, decision taking involves, explicitly or implicitly, the use of economic tools and concepts. In this book we attempt to show how economic analysis and the insights from economic research can be used to guide and inform managerial decisions. We hope this will prove of interest and help not only to students in management, business studies and economics but also to those in managerial positions in business and commerce and public sector organisations.

Our contributors represent a wide array of scholarly and practical experience and expertise. We are grateful to them for their willing and expert contributions to this volume. We also wish to thank Mrs Christine Theobold for substantial secretarial assistance in preparing the text for publication and Miss Susan Edwards for preparing the index.

JFP
TAJC
February 1984

1
Introduction: The Firm in Economics

T. A. J. Cockerill and J. F. Pickering

1.1 Introduction

There is a tension between economics and management. While some tensions are creative and therefore achieve positive benefits, there are others whose effects are unhelpful since they tend to discourage communication where such communication ought to exist. All too often the latter seems to be the case where the possible contribution of economics to the process of management and to management education is concerned. Those individuals concerned with management tend to argue that economics and economists adopt too abstract and too generalised an approach to be useful where practical decision taking is required. Economists, on the other hand, tend to argue that much of management is based on *ad hoc* decision processes lacking a formal analytical input which indicates that the contribution of economics and economists is being ignored.

There may well be some grain of truth in both points of view. We do not believe that this separation is justified. Much good work—both analytically and in an advisory capacity—has been carried out on firms and industries by economists. We also believe that there is much more scope for recognition of the ways in which economics and the management process can interact effectively. This book is a reflection of this view. In it a number of different authors, all of them experienced in the application of economics to the management process, explore the ways in which economic concepts and techniques and empirical evidence contribute to strategic and functional management in the company.

1.2 The Nature of the Firm

Like Dr Johnson's elephant, the concept of the firm is elusive; it is hard to describe but you know it when you see it. There is a wide variety of types of

1

firms: they may be under the control of one person, or many; legally unincorporated or having limited liability, with or without publicly-subscribed share capital; assets may be financed from personal savings, share capital, long-term loans or by government money supplied out of general taxation or borrowing; they may produce a single product or service or many, from one place or many, to be sold predominantly in the domestic market or abroad.

Although the legal definitions of enterprises differ according to their method of formation, the fundamental characteristics of firms are clearly recognised in economics. The firm is, in essence, an input–output system in which inputs (resources) are transformed into, or used to produce, outputs (goods or services). The resources include raw or semi-finished materials, energy, labour and capital. These may be obtained directly from the basic source of supply by the firm itself, or obtained from other firms acting as intermediaries. The co-ordination of the various factor inputs and the identification of market opportunities from the sale of outputs is an important element in any organisation and this is the role of management or enterprise. The difference between the cost of the bought raw materials and the revenue obtained from the sale of the produce is the value added. This reflects the remuneration of the labour, capital and managerial enterprise achieved from the sale of the outputs of the firm. It is this which contributes to the gross domestic product.

The existence of a firm implies that there are advantages in bringing together these different resources and welding them into a team under a common system of control. Within the firm there is a linking of related activities and the application of opportunities to exercise the principles of division of labour that would not exist without the common organisational arrangements that characterise the firm. Thus a firm is characterised by an interdependency between factors of production and different units of the same factor (e.g. labour) within the team. It requires a management process within which basic decisions on outputs, factor mixes, and other aspects of resource allocation are handled. It involves a system for the collection, collation and dissemination of information.

While the logic for the existence of the firm may seem self-evident, it should be recognised that there is still scope for varying the extent to which different activities are brought within the control of a single organisation, rather than bought in from separate suppliers as and when required. This is a practical choice for many companies and, indeed, from time to time the boundary of a firm may be adjusted by either bringing particular activities under its own control or by obtaining them through the market. Thus the firm is a form of internal organisation which replaces the operation of an external market for those activities.

The choice between internalisation and use of the market was identified by Coase (1937) as basic to the nature of the firm. His work has more recently been developed in the discussion of markets and hierarchies by Williamson (1975, 1981). They both argue the case for internalising activities within the firm, rather than using the market, along the following lines. To use the market involves transactions costs (the cost of buying and selling, negotiation costs, middlemen's margins, legal contracts etc.), which can be avoided within the firm where decisions can be taken by managerial fiat. Markets cannot necessarily be assumed to be operating perfectly; information is not perfect within the market and to use the market as a source of information can be costly. Markets and market fluctuations impose a degree of uncertainty or partial ignorance which an internal administrative system can overcome by handling uncertainty and by forecasting (see Loasby 1976). Finally, internalisation of related processes offers economies of scale and the opportunity for division of labour that the separation of the activities through the market would not allow. Thus there are strong advantages in certain cases in internalising operations within the firm rather than using the market. On the other hand, internalisation involves possible disadvantages since organisational control may become more difficult as the firm grows larger, and the opportunity to purchase within a weak market on more favourable terms may well be lost.

1.3 The Firm in Reality

The main concern of economics has been with the most efficient allocation of society's scarce resources. To analyse the policies and problems associated with this, theoretical constructs of firms have been developed through which the effects of changing policies and assumptions on the performance of the economic system can be studied. There has been relatively little interest in seeking to understand how firms are formed, how they operate in reality, or how they may plan their strategy in order to serve their own interests more effectively and those of the society of which they are part.

The firm in the real world can have one of several different types of ownership: the sole proprietor, the partnership, the private company, the public limited company or the state corporation. It may be a unified organisation with a tier of top management supported by several line and functional departments, or it may have several divisions. It may have subsidiaries that are fully- or partly-owned or it may, itself, be a subsidiary of a larger enterprise. Moreover, its assets may be financed by retained profits, equity (share capital), long-term loans, short-term borrowing or loans, or grants and subsidies from government, and these could be in varying proportions. Unlike the firm in theory, the real-world enterprise will most probably produce a range of goods and services and operate a number of factories. Its output will span a number of the industry sectors identified in official production censuses.

Firms also exhibit a range of sizes as measured by turnover, capital employed, employment, or value added, and large, medium and small firms frequently coexist in the same industry. They may grow by expanding the scale of their present activities, extending into adjacent activities or moving into new, unrelated ones. These developments can be accomplished by raising additional capital and purchasing and building additional capacity, by the acquisition of other firms, or by some combination of the two.

Firms are not the largely autonomous, single-minded enterprises they are often assumed to be in theory. They comprise several interest groups whose objectives and standards for the assessment of corporate performance vary. The principal interest groups and their areas of interest are depicted in Table 1.1.

Table 1.1   Interest Groups and Performance Indicators

Interest group	Performance indicators
Owners	Profitability, growth, dividends, security, share price
Directors	Growth, market share, profitability, security
Managers	Growth, cash flow, discretionary expenditure, security
Employees	Earnings levels and growth, employment levels, security
Suppliers	Level, growth, variation and security of orders, payment period, prices
Customers	Prices, quality, after-sales service, efficiency of distribution channels, new product development, credit terms
Investors	Share price, dividends, asset composition and growth, financing of assets, return on capital (profitability)
Competitors	Growth, profitability, market share, non-price behaviour, advertising, investment rate
Government	Corporate taxation contribution, potential employment level, growth and regional distribution of output and employment, trading practices, balance of payments contribution

It is clear from this table that the expectations of the interest groups will vary considerably and may often conflict: for example in the drive for higher profits or higher earnings from employees, in the desire to raise price to improve profit margins and the pressure from consumers for lower prices, and to increase borrowings to finance growth but to avoid adversely affecting the share price and so running the risk of a takeover. As a result of the tension that exists within the firm, therefore, major decisions will reflect the influence of the main groups whose interests are affected and who have the power to influence the decision takers.

Another feature of firms is that they frequently interlock closely with other firms. It is rare that the entire transformation process from raw materials to finished product is accomplished entirely by a single enterprise. Some firms are major customers of, or suppliers to, other firms and their decisions on purchasing or on product specifications and quality may have significant effects on those firms with which they interact as well as on the final consumer. This relationship can extend across the boundaries of the private and public sectors of the economy (e.g. telecommunications; electricity). Interlocking relationships are also important when individual markets are supplied by a small number of firms, the output of each being a significant fraction of total demand. This is the market structure known as 'oligopoly' and may result in tacit or overt agreements between suppliers. These may reduce uncertainty and foster technological progress and risk taking or they may increase the power of the supplier in relation to the customer.

Lastly, firms' decisions and actions may have significant effects on the welfare of society. Technical progress may raise the growth rate of the firm and create more employment opportunities and give consumers a wider, better or cheaper range of output from which to choose. Decisions to make use of market power by raising prices or reducing output may increase profits and encourage investment by the firm, but may reduce consumers' welfare and distort the pattern of capital asset formation in the economy. Products that can generate profits may be thought to be undesirable in some way by significant interest groups in society. Waste materials resulting from the production process may pollute the environment or be thought to be a health hazard. Decisions to introduce new technology may reduce direct employment opportunities, and expansion of production activities in one country may reduce employment and the contribution to exports in another.

1.4   The Business Critique of the Economics of the Firm

It is often suggested that the economist's theory of the firm does not bear sufficient relation to the firm of the real world to be credible to those who actually have to manage firms. A summary of key points of difference between the two approaches that are commonly believed to exist is set out in Table 1.2. The economic position set out there reflects the neoclassical approach to the theory of the firm. As we shall see, however, there are other traditions and economic contributions which move economics closer to the stated realities of firms in the real world.

There are, however, respects in which the business criticism of the

Table 1.2   Comparison of Assumptions in the Neoclassical Theory of the Firm
with Reality

Neoclassical assumption about the firm	Reality concerning actual firms
Small	Multiproduct, often multinational
Profit the sole objective	Multiple objectives with growth and managerial utility important
Holistic	People are important
Passive response to market signals	Active management role is involved
Ignores internal organisation	Internal organisation is important
Leaves no role for enterprise	Entrepreneurship is important
Assumes costless transactions	Acquisition of information is important and costly
Equilibrium	Firm is involved in a dynamic process towards equilibrium
Assumes perfect knowledge	There is partial ignorance and limited capacity to consider the alternatives
Assumes economic rationality	Works under conditions of bounded rationality
Assumes the external environment is given	Works in an external environment that is complex and changing

economic approach to the firm is justified. Economic theory has been more
concerned with firms as agents within an economic system contributing to
resource allocation and growth. As a result, enterprises themselves have
largely been treated as 'black boxes' which absorb inputs and produce
outputs, and observation of the input–output relationship through time
and across a range of firms is then employed to postulate certain principles
about the way in which firms 'work'. This has tended to imply a high degree
of abstraction in the modelling of firm behaviour and, for a long period of
time, an undue emphasis on a single objective of profit maximisation in an
unrealistic situation where all the key parameters of cost, revenue, etc.,
were assumed to be known. This led to a failure to consider the actual basis
of decision taking within firms, and a failure to recognise that economics
here needs to be treated as a branch of behavioural and social science
(Boulding 1970). The general approach has tended to place emphasis on
the role of competitive markets in preventing the positive exercise of
managerial discretion. In this approach there is also little scope for the
dynamic aspects of innovation. In addition, it has had the effect of
emphasising the implications of allocative and distributive efficiency of the
economic system as a whole at the expense of the technical efficiency of the
individual organisation. There has until recently been little recognition of

the economic factors that serve to influence the internal organisation of firms or their range of activities.

While these are telling criticisms, though as we shall see they reflect an outmoded perception of the economic approach to the firm, there are defendants of that position. The 'black box' approach to the behaviour of the economic agents is defended by some (e.g. Friedman 1953) who argue that it is prediction, not explanation, that counts. This is, however, only a sound argument if it is safe to assume that the construction of a predictive model does not require a clear understanding of the various interactions that lie behind a decision in practice. It is also argued that critics of the neoclassical approach to the theory of the firm tend to misunderstand the profit-maximising approach that is implicit within it. They incorrectly treat this as a testable hypothesis rather than as it should be treated, namely as a paradigm from which testable hypotheses can be generated (Loasby 1971, 1976 ch. 11). Finally, it is argued that the firm of economic theory is not intended to represent a real firm. Rather, it is a theoretical construct used to predict how firms would behave, especially in making changes, as a result of a change in objective conditions (Machlup 1967). While the model does not accurately describe how changes are made, it is argued that it does predict effectively the direction in which prices are changed. This is attributed to the influence of competitive pressures and the way in which firms 'size up' a situation even if they do not have the detailed information prescribed by the theory.

There are, however, three quite different reasons for paying attention to the economic treatment of the firm. First, it is apparent that in recent years the discussion of the economics of the firm has moved well beyond the neoclassical paradigm and has many of the features built in that the critics say are omitted in the theory but are present in the real world. We consider this in the next section. Secondly, economic research on aspects of actual firm behaviour has developed extensively and there is now much research of an empirical nature that sheds light on such behaviour and on the implications for management of companies. We consider part of this material in the following section and many chapters in the rest of the book draw attention to other parts of this evidence. Finally, it is clear that there is much in the concepts adopted in economic analysis that directly contributes to the management process. This is reviewed in the final section of this chapter and is used extensively in the other chapters of this book.

1.5 The Development of the Economic View of the Firm

The emergence of economics as a separate branch of social philosophy is usually dated by the publication of Adam Smith's *Wealth of Nations* in

1776. This was a portentous year: it marked the beginning of the Age of Revolution and the Age of Industrialisation. Smith (1961) identified gains in efficiency and welfare that could arise from both the liberalisation of trade within and between countries and the growth of the factory system. His was thus the first coherent view of the role of the firm in the economic process. The advantages of the factory system, as he saw it, were increases in output and reductions in cost flowing from the division of labour and specialisation. The self-interest of merchants and employers in free markets would lead, through the operation of the 'hidden hand' of competition, to the best allocation of scarce resources and the best pattern of output to meet demand. Although Smith saw clearly the advantages of a market economy, it was left to the other leading economists of the classical school, namely Ricardo, Malthus, Mill and Marx, to debate how prices would be determined and income distributed.

Liberalism and individualism became the main themes of the dominant neoclassical economic analysis of the second half of the nineteenth century. Marshall (1920) saw prices and outputs being determined by the interplay of supply and demand in freely functioning markets. Purchases of goods or services are made on the basis of the utility derived from them by the consumer, and rational decisions made by comparing the marginal (or incremental) benefits with the marginal (or incremental) costs. Marshall also identified the different characteristics of the short and long periods and perceived a tendency for markets to adjust towards long-run equilibrium in which firms would earn just enough ('normal') profit to maintain themselves in business. The enterprise that is fully adjusted to long-run equilibrium was termed the 'representative' firm.

While this treatment introduced the concepts of the market, the distinction between the short and the long run, and the concept of equilibrium, there was also the concern with the equity of resource allocation, based upon the work of Pareto (1909) and drawing also upon notions of equilibrium. This sought to establish principles for the efficient allocation of scarce resources and to assess the welfare loss to society resulting from the failure to maximise allocative efficiency. It was founded upon the notions of consumer sovereignty in freely functioning and swiftly adjusting markets. A perfectly efficient system was regarded as having attained a 'Pareto optimum' in which it was impossible to make any one person better off without making someone else worse off. The key requirements for this to be attained are as follows:

(a) the rate at which each consumer is prepared to substitute one good for another while still maintaining the same level of satisfaction (the marginal rate of substitution (MRS)) must be equal to the ratio of the prices of the goods;

(b) the rate at which a producer can substitute the production of one good for another (the marginal rate of transformation) must likewise be equal to the ratio of their prices and, therefore, also equal to the consumer's MRS; and

(c) the rate at which one productive factor can be substituted (the marginal rate of technical substitution) for another must be equal to the ratio of the prices of the factors.

The main operational rule that emerges from this is that price should be equal to marginal cost in all markets. This will hold in perfectly competitive markets where individual firms are 'price takers' having to accept the market price established by the interaction of aggregate demand and aggregate supply, and when freedom of entry and exit to the industry means that in the long run only 'normal' profits (profits that are just sufficient to encourage the firm to stay in that business) are earned.

As societies, such as Britain and the USA, became industrialised, so it was acknowledged that the assumptions of the perfectly competitive system did not hold. It was recognised that firms were growing in size and often had some independence of market forces in determining their prices and outputs. The implications of this were analysed, almost simultaneously, by Joan Robinson in the UK (Robinson 1933) and E. H. Chamberlin in the USA (Chamberlin 1933). Mrs Robinson is normally credited with the standard monopoly model in which the firm is a price maker and is protected to varying degrees by barriers to entry. Price and output are determined by the equality of marginal cost and marginal revenue. Chamberlin's principal contribution was the monopolistic competition model in which product differentiation associated with relatively easy access to the market causes supra-normal profits to be competed away and the demand curve to move inwards towards the origin until it is tangential to the average cost curve, but at an output that does not employ fully the available capacity.

The use of marginal analysis to 'explain' the basis of firm price and output decisions and recognition of degrees of imperfection in the market was a very important development in the economic treatment of the firm. It was reinforced by developments in the understanding of the nature of consumer demand which, by emphasising the nature of income and substitution effects, confirmed the analytical basis of the downward-sloping demand, and hence marginal revenue, curves. At the same time attention was also being paid to the question of the structure of the firms' costs. If unit costs fell as firms became larger, then the only constraint on the size of the firm was given by the size of the market. However, work by Sraffa in particular established within economic analysis the concept of the U-shaped average cost curve (Sraffa 1926). Thus the approach to an equilibrium position for the firm was assisted both by falling marginal revenue and rising marginal cost in situations that were considered characteristic of many firms.

This form of marginal analysis was subsequently extended by Rothschild (1947) and Sweezy (1939) to markets in which a few sellers predominated and therefore each had a significant fraction of the total market. This form of market structure, known as oligopoly, has been recognised to be of considerable practical significance in many industrial sectors. It has served to build into economic analysis concepts of conjectural interdependence between suppliers and to draw attention to such phenomena as the apparent stability of price at times of changing demand and cost conditions, and the growth in emphasis on forms of non-price competition such as advertising, branding and after-sales service.

As firms grew larger and a managerial cadre became increasingly important to the overall success of the firm, so economists began to question the traditional assumption that the overriding objective of firms was the maximisation of profits. The implications of the separation of ownership (by shareholders) and control (by managers) seemed to point to the possibility that managers would pursue their own interests to quite a considerable degree. This incorporation of managerial elements into the debate has led to a number of interesting and fruitful developments.

Work arising from a more behavioural or organisational approach to economics (e.g. Simon 1966, Cyert and March 1963) drew attention to the importance of internal groups and coalitions of people within organisations who were likely to influence the nature of objectives and their actual achievement. From this it was argued that there were likely to be subsets of goals and targets within each department. The coalitions of interests which may emerge would be likely to transcend the formal organisation of the enterprise and lead to trade-offs within and between goal subsets and compensation of some interest groups by others through means of side-payments which may take several forms, for example an increase in personnel, increased research expenditures, new equipment, etc. From this insight into the nature of human behaviour within organisations arose a much clearer emphasis on the role of individual participation in goal setting and decision making and a greater emphasis on the notion that, in practice, it was unrealistic to expect the maximisation of any single target variable; rather, a multiplicity of objectives involving trading-off and satisficing (looking for an acceptable level of performance) was argued to be a more realistic statement of firm objectives and decision processes. Only 'bounded rationality' rather than full economic rationality could be assumed. However, some would argue that this approach tends to contain too many detailed and specific assumptions to make it easily applicable to broad problems (Marris and Mueller 1980).

The emphasis on managerial objectives and aspirations led another group of researchers (e.g. Baumol 1959, Williamson 1964) to explore in greater detail the notion that the objectives of firms were best expressed in terms of a managerial utility function comprising such considerations as sales volume, managerial expenses and perquisites. In each case it is argued that this specification of firm objectives is more consistent with the strength of the managerial position in modern organisations and therefore reflects their direct and indirect aspirations for prestige, security and remuneration (since size and remuneration are often held to go together).

Baumol's emphasis on sales revenue maximisation claims relevance in terms of such management aspirations. It is also interesting in that the predictive implications of this model point to a lower price and higher output than would arise under profit maximisation. However, Baumol saw that there was a minimum level of profit that would be required to keep shareholders satisfied and this would need to enter in as a constraint to the overall pursuit of sales revenue maximisation. Williamson's analysis (1964) also draws attention to the limits to the exercise of managerial discretion, since periods of poor trade will give rise to action to reduce the level of budgeted expenditure on managerial discretion items.

Drawing upon the analyses of both Simon and Williamson, Leibenstein (1966) has drawn attention to the manner in which inefficiencies and discretionary expenditures can grow within organisations, especially those that have some degree of market power and are therefore at least partially insulated from competitive threats. The 'organisational slack', or 'X-inefficiency', that emerges is wasteful of resources and indicative of an inadequate amount of competition. Cyert and George (1969), extending this approach, emphasised the impact of unexpected shocks on management attitudes and activities. This may come from sudden increases in the prices of essential factors of production, from sharp contractions in demand or from takeover threats. Crises stimulate responses on the part of management that, if successful, result in internal efficiency being improved. Alternatively, if the crisis overwhelms the firm, the assets will normally pass into different ownership and may be operated more efficiently.

Although the 'managerial' theories just reviewed draw attention to the issue of firm size, they remain essentially static in their approach. There are, however, other contributions which have emphasised more dynamic aspects of firm behaviour, particularly growth. A pioneering treatment of this subject was developed by Edith Penrose (1959).

In her analysis the spirit of enterprise (entrepreneurship) and the quality and amount of managerial talent are factors that both encourage and limit the direction and rate of growth of the firm. The drive, goals and ambition of the firm's owners and controllers influence the range and type of opportunities for expansion that are identified and the manner in which the obstacles to growth, such as the raising of finance, are overcome. Growth requires special managerial talents. These may become redundant or be difficult to redeploy once the firm approaches steady-state operation and may be a factor driving the firm on to further growth. But at the same time the supply of this managerial talent is limited. Continuing or accelerating growth involves the diversion of scarce managerial time from current issues to longer-term planning. The effectiveness of additional managerial resources in planning and controlling growth is likely to diminish as more is diverted from day-to-day administration. The firm may eventually exhaust its supply of effective human resources for expansion. This managerial limit to the extent and the rate of growth is known as the 'Penrose effect'.

This was followed by an important contribution by Marris (1964) in which he too placed emphasis on the growth of the firm as a managerial objective. In developing this theory he drew attention to the importance of marketing, innovation and finance as key influences on firm performance. He showed that the growth of the firm required investment in new products and in marketing. Growth of demand had to be balanced by growth of supply and this requires investment in new productive capacity and the raising of additional financial capital. This may be raised by increasing the proportion of profits retained in the business, issuing new equity or increasing long-term loans. Each method beyond some point is likely to have an adverse effect on the share price, so the firm has to balance its desire for growth with the potential costs of an undue emphasis on growth which may affect its stock market rating and so make it vulnerable to a takeover bid.

A further area of dynamic treatment of the theory of the firm is to be found in the work of such people as Schumpeter (1947), Clark (1961), Andrews (1949 and 1964) and Kirzner (1973), which may be grouped loosely under the heading 'Austrian' (see also Loasby 1976 and Hicks 1982). In this school of thought the concept of equilibrium, which is so central to the normative approach of the neoclassical school, is expressly discarded. Indeed, the emphasis is on the dynamic process of change, discovery and development. This therefore involves a process of information collection and acquisition to reduce uncertainty, though it is recognised that perfect knowledge is not attained. In this context, the role of the entrepreneur, which again hardly features in the neoclassical analysis, becomes important and, indeed, the role of the entrepreneur is seen as necessary and able to thrive precisely because there is a lack of perfect knowledge.

As firms have become larger, so their organisational structures have changed. The question as to which is cause and which effect is not necessarily readily resolved. Organisation structure is important to allow the development of business strategy, but it is equally the pursuit of business strategy that influences structure. The appropriateness of organisation structure may have an important bearing on overall performance of the firm. This too is an area that has received increasing attention from economists and those in related disciplines, commencing with the major study in the history of organisational change by Chandler (1962). It was Williamson (1970) who noted the particular implications of the development of divisionally based organisation structures for resource allocation and goal-oriented behaviour within the firm. He argued that the presence of a small, elitist head office without divisional responsibilities, but with an effective monitoring and control apparatus, was likely to encourage firms to pursue a much more profit-oriented approach than might be expected from managerially dominated organisations with other forms of structure. While this has significant elements which challenge other managerially oriented approaches to the firm, including Williamson's own earlier work (1964; see Williamson 1981), and while subsequent research evidence indicates that it cannot be assumed all firms do behave in the way that Williamson's theory suggests, this does offer further important linkage between business practice and economic analysis of the firm. In addition, by emphasising the importance of internal organisation and the possible operation of an internal capital market within the firm, Williamson brings us back to the whole question of the rationale of the firm reflected initially in the work of Coase (1937) and in Williamson's own work (1975, 1981).

There is one further approach that we should note in our review of economic contributions to the understanding of firm behaviour—this is that concerned with the industrial organisation school. This has its roots in the development of German economic thought during the period of industrialisation at the beginning of this century, but has been transplanted firmly into American analysis. The approach lays emphasis on the analysis of the structure and development of industrial markets and the connection with performance. The principal aspects of market structure are: the size and size distribution of plants and firms; the degree of horizontal and vertical integration and of diversification; demand and cost conditions; and the importance of any barriers to entry that might exist. Performance considerations lay stress on the rate of profit, price–cost margins, and technological progressiveness. Because of the development of the approach in relation to industrial markets, the analysis inevitably lays considerable stress on oligopolistic markets.

Some of the earliest of modern work in this area was undertaken by E. S. Mason (1939) who examined relationships between industrial structure and performance, indicating the dual relationship between the two: structure can affect performance and performance can affect structure so that the system is interactive and evolutionary. Bain (1956) extended this line of thought, examining in particular the influence of market entry barriers on structure and performance (predominantly profit rates). This work has been very valuable, but is deficient in terms of understanding the rationale of the organisation and the functioning of firms because it concentrates on the aggregation of firms operating in markets, and bases its analyses on markets defined in terms of the supply of particular categories of goods and (less frequently) services. The multi-product, multi-market firm is not adequately considered within this framework. Scherer (1970) has criticised the over-emphasis on deterministic relationship between structure and performance in this approach and has pointed to the important inter-mediating effect of conduct. This has introduced a necessary discretionary element into the system, taking account of the effect of firms' objectives and competitive strategies, both of a price and non-price nature. But still firms are often anticipated to react in terms of a set of stereotypes based largely on neoclassical constructs. An interesting development which seems likely to emphasise the potential contribution of the industrial organisation approach to analysis of firm strategies and conduct is reflected in the work of Porter (1980) which emphasises the possible contribution of the analysis of industrial structure to the development of competitive strategies within the firm.

Thus it should be apparent that the economic analysis of the firm has developed many facets over the years. It certainly is not restricted to the neoclassical view of the firm, though the nature of the prospective contribution of that particular paradigm needs to be more fully understood. Other contributions to the theory of the firm do take into account the characteristics of firms of the real world, concerning whose omission the neoclassical theory is most often criticised. That there is no unanimously agreed single theory of the firm should not be surprising since the very nature and structure of firms themselves are changing in material ways. There is, we believe, much to be said for an eclectic approach to the theory of the firm, recognising the different insights that different theories offer as they address different issues in different organisations. However, it is essential not to lose sight of the importance of the possibility of a degree of generalisation in a good theory.

1.6   Research on the Firm

As a social science, economics is a discipline that should place some emphasis on the empirical testing of its theories and hypotheses. This may be done in various ways, involving in-depth case study work of a limited range of circumstances to more quantitatively-oriented work using published data or specifically generated and collected information. The contributions in this book make extensive use, directly and indirectly, of the growing tradition of empirical study on the economics of the firm and so it is quite unnecessary to attempt to review this material here. The contribution of empirical studies will become clear to the reader of the individual chapters. There is, however, an area of research on aspects of the performance of the firm overall that does not find a ready place in individual chapters, so we may note the salient features here (for more extensive reviews of this literature see Hay and Morris 1979, Sawyer 1981).

We commence this review by considering the extent to which there really is a significant separation of ownership and control in companies. While this has long been held to be self-evident (e.g. Berle and Means 1932), recent work (Nyman and Silberston 1977) has cast doubt on the view and has emphasised that *de facto* control (in terms of the key ability to change the senior management) may be exercised by one person or a group holding as little as five or ten per cent of the shares of a company, especially where this is held by the founding family or the board of directors. On this basis, it is estimated that perhaps over half of major UK companies (and a similar proportion of US companies) are still subject to owner control. This suggests a possible limit on the scope for the exercise of managerial discretion and is reinforced when the growing influence of a relatively limited number of institutional shareholders (insurance companies, pension funds, etc.) is recognised.

The specification of variables and their measurement on a consistent and comparable basis for tests of the determinants of aspects of firm performance is not easy. For this, and no doubt for other reasons too, there is a lack of certainty about the key influences on firm performance. However, in an attempt to provide what seems likely to be a reasonable picture of empirical results obtained overall, we can offer the following pointers. Profitability of firms is particularly difficult to measure in an entirely satisfactory way and to compare between companies due to measurement problems (e.g. the effects of different policies regarding the valuation of capital employed on the calculated rate of return, and the problems of determining whether it is efficiency or market power that has really contributed to high profits). Nevertheless, there does seem to be a fair measure of agreement that profits tend to be higher in owner-controlled firms than in manager-controlled firms (as the theory would lead us to expect). There appears to be no clear relationship between size of firm and profitability, though profits are more stable in larger firms. There is a positive relation between growth and profits. It is not possible to say which is cause and which is effect; indeed, it seems the two are interdependent. There is, however, no clear relation between size of firm and growth rate. The level of remuneration of top executives is positively associated with both size and profits, though there are clearly many other influences upon remuneration of top management.

This brief review, together with other empirical discussion contained in the following chapters, should indicate that recent developments in the theory of the firm are amenable to empirical testing. In some cases the predictions of the theory are well supported; in others they are not so well upheld. There is a need for much more extensive work to relate both theory and empiricism to overall firm performance and to individual aspects of the management process within firms.

1.7   Economics and the Management Process

So far the discussion in this chapter has focused upon the economic overview of the firm as such. Hopefully, we have shown that there is a sufficient relation between the theoretical construct and firms of the real world to demand further and increased attention by those engaged on both sides—in economics and in management practice and education. However, there is another level at which economics contributes to the actual practice of management. This is in the identification and application of analytical concepts which are of importance to the manager's decision processes. These will be frequently encountered in subsequent chapters, and to help the reader we outline briefly here the essential ideas behind the main concepts.

(a)   Scarcity and Choice

A famous definition of economics is that it is the science of the allocation of scarce resources that have alternative uses. It is the finite limitation on resources—energy, water, goods, money—that obliges individuals, firms and nations to make choices. The management team of a firm is concerned with allocating its scarce financial resources between stock-building, wages, capital investment and profits in order to achieve the objectives that it has identified for the firm in the best possible way. To do this teams need to be able to appraise effectively the costs and benefits of alternative courses of action that are available to them. Rational decision making requires that, for any decision, the benefits should exceed the costs, thus yielding net benefits.

(b)   Marginality

If all the relevant costs and benefits associated with alternatives can be identified and measured, it follows that the choice to be selected should be that for which the benefits exceed the costs by the greatest amount. If there is no limitation on funds available and if there are no mutually exclusive schemes (such as alternative methods of making the same product), then a firm could undertake all activities for which the benefits are greater than the costs. Activity opportunities could be ranked in descending order of net benefits and undertaken until the point is reached at which the net benefit from the last opportunity undertaken approaches zero—i.e. the costs and the benefits are almost equal. In this way the net benefit to the organisation will be maximised. The principle illustrated is that for each non-exclusive decision, the benefit attributable to the decision should be equal to or greater than the attributable cost—$B \geq C$, where B represents the monetary value of benefits and C the monetary value of costs. For a sequence of decisions, net benefit will be maximised where, for the last decision made, the *change* in the attributable aggregate benefit (ΔB) is just equal to the *change* in the attributable aggregate cost (ΔC). This is the fundamental principle that underlies the well-known proposition in economics that profit is maximised where marginal revenue is equal to marginal cost. In practice, of course, decision making is rarely as simple as this: funds are limited, projects are to a greater or lesser degree substitutable for one another, a decision about one project will influence the net benefits anticipated from others and benefits and costs cannot always be fully measured in financial terms. Nevertheless, if any enterprise or economic system allocates its scarce resources so that aggregate net benefits are maximised, it can be regarded as having achieved an optimum.

(c) Avoidable and Sunk Cost

In calculating the net benefit associated with a decision, only the costs and benefits that are affected by the decision should be taken into account. Suppose I am considering making a journey for which it is only practicable to use my car because, say, the destination is a remote rural village. My decision to travel will involve me in the purchase and consumption of petrol and maybe oil. To the extent that the car will depreciate more rapidly and the tyres etc. require replacing sooner than would otherwise be the case, these too are costs incurred by the journey, although in reality I am unlikely to consider them because of the difficulty of measuring them. For most purposes, then, the cost of the petrol and oil will represent the avoidable costs of the journey. Insurance, taxation, financing costs and time-related depreciation are not relevant because I will incur them whether or not I use the car. The benefits of the journey may be pecuniary (if, say, I receive a fee for giving a lecture) or non-pecuniary (if I have the pleasure of the company of relatives or friends). Provided these exceed the avoidable cost, it will be in my interests to undertake the journey.

Similarly, a firm considering producing an additional product line in a factory with spare capacity should consider only the additional costs of labour, materials and energy, etc., that will be incurred and not the full costs including overheads, which at present are covered by the revenue from the existing products. Another aspect of the same concept refers to past investments in physical assets that are in current use (e.g. an electric

power-generating station). These have been built or purchased as a result
of past expenditures which represent a sunk cost. If the assets have no
resale or scrap value, the expenditures are entirely irrevocable; it is
irrelevant to production decisions now whether the past investment
decision was sound or foolhardy. Provided the revenue from the sale of the
output exceeds the avoidable cost of manufacture it is worth operating the
plant. The decision procedure is only slightly modified if resale or scrap
values are taken into account.

(d) Opportunity Cost

A comprehensive decision must take account of not only the costs directly
associated with the course of action chosen, but also the benefits foregone by choosing one alternative rather than another. Thus, to extend the
example above, I may calculate the avoidable cost of using my car, but
I should also take into account the costs and benefits of alternative
transport modes—bus, rail and possibly air. If the net costs of these, taking
account of convenience, stress, time, the opportunity to work, read, sleep,
etc., are less than those of driving, then the car should not be used.
Similarly, when a firm chooses between marketing two alternative products, the opportunity cost associated with the product selected is the net
revenue lost by not selecting the other. Plainly a rational decision maker
would choose the product with the higher net revenue. Thus the cost of
selecting any one of a number of options can be expressed in terms of the
benefits foregone from the next most attractive alternative.

(e) Time Cost

If the cost and benefit effects of decisions extend over time, the problem
arises of comparing revenues or expenditures received or incurred at
different times. This is because money has a time value: a pound received
today does not have the same value as a pound received in a year's time.
The relevant reason for this is that the pound received today could be
invested in an interest-bearing financial asset which would be worth more
than the pound in a year's time. If the initial amount (P) is invested at an
interest rate (r) of ten per cent for a period (t) of three years, the value of
the sum (S) at the end of the period will be given by $S = P(1 + r/100)^t$. One
pound invested will therefore have increased to a total of £1.331 after three
years. This is, of course, straightforward compound interest, but the
significance here lies in stating the reverse: the present value (PV) of a sum
(S) receivable at the end of period (t) with an interest rate (r) is:
$PV = S \cdot 1/(1 + r/100)^t$. Thus the present value of £1.331 receivable in

three years' time at an interest rate of ten per cent is £1. The reciprocal $1/(1 + r/100)^t$ is termed the discount factor and is used to standardise costs and revenues receivable at different times in terms of their present value, enabling an unbiased comparison to be made. This concept, it should be noted, is separate from the impact of changes in the general level of prices on the value of a unit of currency at different times, although in practice both influences of time have to be taken into account in appraising alternative decisions.

(f) Markets

A market is a forum in which interaction takes place between the potential buyers and sellers of relevant goods or services. The market may exist at particular times at a particular location (e.g. retail fruit and vegetable markets, wholesale fish markets, the stock exchange) or may be a network of physical and, increasingly, electronic communications between participants (e.g. foreign exchange markets, classified newspaper advertisements). The boundaries of a market are in theory determined by the cross-elasticities of demand (or ease of substitution) of one good or service for another. Where substitutability is easy (e.g. between butter and margarine) the products can be said to be in the same market; where the substitutability is difficult or impossible (e.g. typewriters for motor cars) the products are evidently in different markets. *Efficient* markets are those in which supply, demand and price all adjust quickly and smoothly to changes in each other. One condition for this is that there should be no undue power exercised by either buyers or sellers over the other.

(g) Elasticity

This refers to the responsiveness of one element (the dependent variable) to changes in another (the independent variable). A well-known application is the ratio of the proportional change in the quantity demanded $(\Delta Q/Q)$ to the proportional change in its price $(\Delta P/P)$ which gives the price elasticity of demand. This can be rearranged as $\Delta Q/\Delta P \cdot P/Q$ or in the limit as $dQ/dP \cdot P/Q$, that is the change in demand in response to a unit change in price weighted by the price/quantity ratio. This means that for the conventional demand curve of elementary theory possessing a constant negative slope, price elasticity varies over the length of the curve. Other common concepts of elasticity include demand changes in response to changes in income, advertising expenditure and the price of complementary goods or substitutes, and cost changes in response to changes in output.

(h)   Investment

Generally in economics this refers to the formation of physical assets to replace those that are exhausted or to increase the total stock of assets. This is distinct from the acquisition of financial instruments (shares, bonds, etc.) held in anticipation of future income from dividends or interest payments or from capital appreciation which is also described as investment. Physical capital assets have the characteristics that they provide a flow of output of goods or services over more than one decision period and that, generally, they are not desired for their own sake but for the assistance they provide in improving the efficiency of the production process or the quality of the final product. Increasing capital in relation to labour typically increases the complexity of the production process, making it 'roundabout' at the same time as increasing its overall efficiency. Capital investment thus involves diverting funds from current consumption to the formation of assets that it is anticipated will yield future benefits. Rational investment decisions in conditions in which the future is known perfectly will only accept investments in which the future benefits outweigh the costs of the present consumption foregone.

(i)   Rate of Return

This is a ratio, usually expressed as a percentage, that relates the profits generated in a period by a firm or an individual activity to the value of the relevant capital assets employed. Profits are the surplus of current income from trading activities or from financial investments over cost properly charged to income, i.e. operating costs, financial charges, depreciation and provisions for taxation. The value of the assets can be calculated either on the basis of their value when acquired or their cost of replacement at current prices, less the amount deemed to have been consumed in the production process and represented by the accumulated total of depreciation. It may be noted that this definition of profitability relates the surplus from production to only one factor input—capital.

(j)   Scale

The scale of a firm or economic activity refers to its overall size, a notion that may have several dimensions. The simplest and most commonly encountered is the rate of total output per period of time. It may also include the number of types of processes undertaken, the range of products produced and the number and size of plants or firms involved. If total costs of production increase more slowly than scale so that unit costs are reduced, economies of scale arise which derive from a more intensive use of productive factors or a reduction in their supply price, or a combination of the two. The typical pattern of the operation of economies of scale is that costs fall to some finite scale, thereafter remaining constant over a range of output. This is characterised by an L-shaped unit cost curve. The smallest scale at which least unit costs are first attained is termed the *minimum efficient scale*.

(k) Trade-Off

This term is derived from American economic literature and relates to the comparison of the net benefits or costs of one alternative with those of one or more others. Substitution between alternatives may be either continuous or discrete. Thus a firm may weigh the desirability of present profits against future growth; government may compare the rate of inflation with the level of unemployment. Rational decision makers will increase their consumption of the product, service or factor input that shows the highest net benefit or lowest net cost, reducing consumption of alternatives. Increasing consumption is likely to lower progressively net benefit or increase net cost, and will halt at the point where the marginal net benefits or costs are equal for all alternatives.

References

Andrews, P. W. S. (1949) *Manufacturing Business*, Macmillan.

Andrews, P. W. S. (1964) *On Competition in Economic Theory*, Macmillan.

Bain, J. S. (1956) *Barriers to New Competition*, Harvard University Press.

Baumol, W. J. (1959) *Business Behaviour, Value and Growth*, Harcourt Brace and World.

Berle, A. A. and Means, G. C. (1932) *The Modern Corporation and Private Property*, Macmillan.

Boulding, K. (1970) *Economics as a Science*, McGraw-Hill.

Chamberlin, E. H. (1933) *The Theory of Monopolistic Competition*, Harvard University Press.

Chandler, A. D. (1962) *Strategy and Structure*, MIT Press.

Clark, J. M. (1961) *Competition as a Dynamic Process*, Brookings Institution.

Coase, R. H. (1937) 'The nature of the firm', *Economica*, 4.

Cyert, R. M. and George, K. D. (1969) 'Competition, growth and efficiency', *Economic Journal*, 79.

Cyert, R. M. and March, J. G. (1963) *A Behavioural Theory of the Firm*, Prentice-Hall.

Friedman, M. (1953) 'The methodology of positive economics', in *Essays in Positive Economics*, University of Chicago Press.

Hay, D. A. and Morris, D. (1979) *Industrial Economics*, Oxford University Press.

Hicks, R. J. (1982) *The Firm, the Market and Knowledge: An Integration of Austrian Perspectives*, University of Manchester MSc Dissertation.

Kirzner, I. M. (1973) *Competition and Entrepreneurship*, University of Chicago Press.

Leibenstein, H. (1966) 'Allocative efficiency versus X-efficiency', *American Economic Review*, 58.

Loasby, B. J. (1971) 'Hypothesis and paradigm in the theory of the firm', *Economic Journal*, 81.

Loasby, B. J. (1976) *Choice, Ignorance and Complexity*, Cambridge University Press.

Machlup, F. (1967) 'Theories of the firm: marginalist, behavioural, managerial', *American Economic Review*, 57.

Marris, R. (1964) *The Economic Theory of 'Managerial' Capitalism*, Macmillan.

Marris, R. and Mueller, D. C. (1980) 'The corporation, competition and the invisible hand', *Journal of Economic Literature*, March.

Marshall, A. (1920) *Principles of Economics*, Macmillan.

Mason, E. S. (1939) 'Price and production policies of large-scale enterprises', *American Economic Review*.

Nyman, S. and Silberston, A. (1977) 'The ownership and control of industry', in A. P. Jacquemin and H. W. de Jong (eds), *Welfare Aspects of Industrial Markets*, Martinus Nijhof.

Pareto, V. (1909) *Manuel d'Economie Politique*, Giard and Briere.

Penrose, E. T. (1959) *The Theory of the Growth of the Firm*, Basil Blackwell.

Porter, M. E. (1980) *Competitive Strategy*, Free Press.

Robinson, J. (1933) *The Economics of Imperfect Competition*, Macmillan.

Rothschild, K. (1947) 'Price theory and oligopoly', *Economic Journal*, 57.

Sawyer, M. C. (1981) *The Economics of Firms and Industries*, Croom Helm.

Scherer, F. M. (1970) *Industrial Market Structure and Economic Performance*, Rand McNally.

Schumpeter, J. (1947) *Capitalism, Socialism and Democracy*, Allen and Unwin.

Simon, H. (1966) 'Decision making in economics and behavioural science', in A.E.A. *Surveys of Economic Theory*, Vol. III, Macmillan.

Smith, A. (1961) *An Inquiry into the Nature and Causes of the Wealth of Nations*, Methuen.

Sraffa, P. (1926) 'The laws of returns under competitive conditions', *Economic Journal*, 36.

Sweezy, P. M. (1939) 'Demand under conditions of oligopoly', *Journal of Political Economy*, 47.

Williamson, O. E. (1964) *The Economics of Discretionary Behaviour*, Prentice-Hall.

Williamson, O. E. (1970) *Corporate Control and Business Behaviour*, Prentice-Hall.

Williamson, O. E. (1975) *Markets and Hierarchies: Analysis and Anti-Trust Implications*, Free Press.

Williamson, O. E. (1981) 'The modern corporation: origins, evolution, attributes', *Journal of Economic Literature*, 19.

2
The Development of the Firm

J. F. Pickering

2.1 Introduction

There can be little doubt that planning the development of the firm is a major area of responsibility for senior management within any organisation. Indeed, given the difficult economic environment facing companies with low overall economic growth, severe competition in many sectors and a small number of areas where growth prospects are particularly favourable, it is even more important that the strategy for the development of the business should be clearly worked out.

We should note that nowadays 'development' of the business may not necessarily mean 'growth' since some companies may decide that their prospects are better enhanced if they trim down the overall scale of their operations. Others may require significant changes in the mix of their activities in order to retain their existing overall size. It is for this reason that we prefer to use the term 'development' rather than 'growth' in this chapter. While the theory of the firm has tended to distinguish between profit maximisation and growth maximisation subject to a profit constraint as alternative objectives of the firm, in the modern multiproduct, multi-activity organisation the choice in practice is less clear cut. Effective business development is an essential part of an overall profit strategy, just as the prospective profitability of the business must influence the development and growth choices that are made.

In the small firm it is possible to identify the traditional entrepreneurial role of selecting and developing business opportunities with the owner-manager. But what of this in the larger organisation? Here too, it seems important to emphasise the need for the entrepreneurial role to be exercised if the business is to develop (see Kirzner 1973). The commitment to the development of the business, the search for and identification of new opportunities and the implementation of these, are important entrepreneurial roles. In order to achieve these, it is clear that the entrepreneur needs to be someone with vision, foresight and flair who is willing to accept the need for change and to take risks. To do so successfully, however, he also needs to be someone with analytical skills and an ability to learn from the past and to win the confidence and commitment of others, such as workers, financial backers etc.

In the modern large organisation it may be argued that the entrepreneur does not and cannot exist as in the small company. Despite the persuasive arguments of Galbraith (1967) to this effect, it is not a view that stands up in the real world. For a large company to survive, the traditional entrepreneurial role as we have described it must still be exercised. The existence of bureaucracy and managerial conflict may threaten to crowd it out, but it still remains important. In many companies it is apparent that there is one senior member, perhaps the chairman or managing director, who is the human dynamo, driving things forward. In some instances he may have been the founder of the company who saw the firm become large as a result of his enterprise. In others it may be a member of the managerial cadre who exercises this role. For some companies the individual concerned may be readily identifiable and, indeed, difficulties may be feared for the company when he retires. In some companies the entrepreneurial role may be played by different people at different times and in relation to different developments. Indeed, in a decentralised, divisionalised organisation it is likely that at least part of the entrepreneurial role will be exercised within the divisions rather than at head-office level alone. It is relevant in this context to recognise that in the study of successful and unsuccessful innovations it was found that a key determinant of success was the presence of a senior manager who would take a full commitment for pushing through the project (Freeman 1974). A similar consideration applies to the achievement of success in export marketing (Turnbull and Cunningham 1981).

Thus, underlying this chapter is the view that enterpreneurship must exist in the large business organisation as in the small. The key features of the exercise of the entrepreneurial function will remain the same even if the location of this role may vary according to the type of business, the type of decision and through time. Some aspects of the entrepreneurial role may indeed be shared through a management committee or through a corporate planning or business strategy department. Whoever exercises the role, their commitment should be to the profitable development of the business based upon the exercise of good judgement and flair, drawing upon information and forecasts of present and future prospects, together with a process of learning from past experience.

2.2 The Analysis of Existing Performance

The starting point in the development of the business should be the assessment of performance and prospects of existing activities. This suggests the need for analysis at several different levels—product, market, corporate, the environmental level—and it will be conducted for each of the activities in which the company is currently engaged (see, for example, Porter 1980).

Product analysis will take account of the stage in its life cycle that the product has reached and its projected future growth potential. The relative attractiveness of different brands of the same product offered by competing suppliers may well be usefully analysed in this context. (The approach to the analysis of consumer choice advocated by Lancaster (1971), using a comparison of the relative degree to which competing brands have particular characteristics, seems applicable to supplier assessments of the competitive attractiveness of their own brands.)

Market analysis will consider the state of demand facing the product, the structure of the market (on both the supply and demand sides), conditions of entry and the degree of competition.

Competitive analysis will attempt, as far as information allows, a comparison of the relative performance of the company concerned against its major competitors in terms of efficiency and productivity in supply, profitability from this particular product and any interdependencies (e.g. vertical integration) between activities which may affect the relative competitive position of different suppliers. An assessment of their likely competitive strategies may also be undertaken.

Environmental analysis will take into account the impact of governmental policies (including macroeconomic developments) on the demand for particular products, the costs of supplying and the possibilities of competition policy intervention. It will also assess the impact of international economic and political phenomena (e.g. exchange risks, risk to overseas market and investment, etc.), consumerism pressures, etc.

The outcome of such an analysis is likely to indicate that the total array of products and services will be dispersed over some sort of continuum of relative performance and attractiveness for the company concerned. Consideration of existing performance and of future potential may well indicate some divergence between the two in the relative attractiveness of different products.

In an attempt to help companies in their product analysis, the use of portfolio matrices has been advocated. The best known is that of the Boston Consulting Group whose original matrix is shown in Figure 2.1. This suggests that companies have, and indeed to some extent need, a mix of different products analysed on this basis. The 'stars' are the leading business lines with high market shares and high growth potential. They are likely to be more or less self-sufficient in cash flow terms covering their

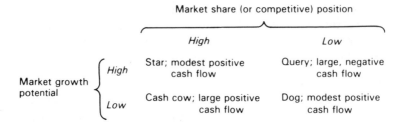

Figure 2.1   Boston Consulting Group Portfolio Matrix

operating and financing costs and meeting their investment needs, but clearly justifying every effort to ensure their full profitable development. The 'queries' represent products where the company is relatively weak in competitive terms yet, because of the high market potential, could well repay further investment expenditure to move them into the 'star' segment. 'Cash cows' remain of value to the company since although their overall market growth potential and, therefore, investment requirements are not substantial, the strong competitive position held ensures that there is a favourable cash flow which can be used elsewhere within the company on investments that may show a higher return. 'Dogs' are considered much less attractive since they offer neither the benefits of a strong market position nor favourable market growth potential. While their cash flow position may be reasonably balanced, great care is required to ensure that it does not become negative and drain resources from the company with very little benefit in return.

Though of interest and potential value, it is important to recognise some of the underlying assumptions of this analysis which may not always be valid. First, it is assumed that, via the concept of the experience curve (Boston Consulting Group 1968), there is a positive relation between market share and profits. While there is logic and empirical evidence to support this, it does not always hold. Economies of size and scale may not always be important influences on costs and profits. Undue expenditures may be incurred in building up or sustaining a high market share. Equally, a low market share may still be very profitable, especially if it reflects an effective segmentation strategy. This points to the importance of an appropriate identification of the relevant market before market share is established. In addition, it is important to take into account the strength of competition (both actual and potential) which will affect the profitability of a particular market, perhaps independent of the distribution of market shares within it.

More recently, the Boston Consulting Group has used a different matrix comparing the size of advantage open to a particular company in a market and the number of approaches that can be adopted in achieving this advantage (see Figure 2.2). The possible combinations indicate the ways in which advantages over competitors can be achieved. Thus a company with a substantial potential or actual advantage and many alternative ways of achieving this will be encouraged to specialise. Instances where there are few ways of achieving the advantage (which is, however, significant) will encourage volume production.

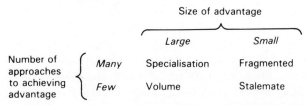

Figure 2.2   Boston Consulting Group Strategic Environment Matrix

		Business unit position – comparative advantage		
		High	Medium	Low
Industry attractiveness	High	1	4	7
	Medium	2	5	8
	Low	3	6	9

Figure 2.3   Directional Policy Matrix

An alternative approach—really a refinement of the Portfolio matrix shown in Figure 2.1—is that used by such companies as McKinsey, Shell, and General Electric (see Figure 2.3). This contrasts the comparative position of the particular business unit with the overall attractiveness of the industry it is in. By emphasising the comparative position of the business unit, this goes beyond the market share assessment used in the Boston matrix and allows other factors to be taken into account which may not be directly related to market share (e.g. relative efficiency). Similarly, the concept of 'industry attractiveness' seems likely to include a variety of influences over and above 'market growth potential' specified in the Boston matrix. For example, 'industry attractiveness' may be used to reflect technological influences, interdependence with other activities, the severity of competition, buyer power, overall elasticity of demand considerations, ease of entry, existence of government controls, as well as growth potential. In addition, the matrix is extended from 2×2 to 3×3

cells, so allowing a somewhat more incisive distinction between different situations (see also Sutton 1980).

The nine cells of this matrix indicate alternative business strategies that may be considered for particular products in a company's portfolio. Cell 1 indicates priority products which will repay considerable effort and attention. Cells 2 and 4 suggest that unless the product concerned can be moved into cell 1 through an increase in the brand's comparative position or because the industry becomes more attractive, the target should be at least to achieve a rate of growth in line with that of the industry as a whole. Products falling into cells 3 and 5 clearly have some attraction to the company. These are likely to be cash generators and, unless prospects can be considerably improved, they are unlikely to justify substantial commitment of new resources. Products in cells 6, 8 and 9 are unlikely to be viewed with great enthusiasm in a company (although those in cell 6 may be positive cash generators) and may well be products where a withdrawal may be appropriate, especially those in cell 9. The position of products classified within cell 7—a low relative position in the market but a highly attractive industry—would be likely to warrant particular attention in the hope that either by internal improvement or by acquisition the relative position of the company in the particular market might be improved.

While there is no entirely satisfactory form of analysis, it does seem that the matrix illustrated in Figure 2.3 above offers a useful framework against which the performance and prospects of a particular product can be assessed. The criteria underlying the assessment of the business unit position and the attractiveness of the market or industry concerned can be applied in such a way that the results of product, market, competitor and environmental analyses can all be built into this particular form of matrix.

However the analysis is carried out, it is likely to indicate that within the portfolio of products and activities of the modern company there will be some in strong and developing positions; some that are performing well and producing positive cash flows that can be redeployed elsewhere in the company, but do not require major new investments themselves; some that ought to receive attention with a view to raising performance or withdrawing from the market; and some where the performance and prospects are so unfavourable as to discourage further commitment and, therefore, to encourage a process of withdrawal either immediately or through a phased run down of the activity. However, in classifying all products it is clearly important to take into account the costs of getting or keeping a product in a particular cell. The chances are that the relative position of any product could be raised if the funds were available. The question is whether it would be a good use of scarce financial and managerial resources to work to that end. Equally, it may need to be asked whether a company can justifiably afford major expenditures which are, perhaps, helping to sustain the comparative advantage of a particular product in its market. In this, as in so many other areas of business decision taking, it is necessary to take into account the opportunity costs of choosing one course of action rather than another. In strategic terms it is also important to take into account the interdependencies that exist between different products and activities within a business. What effect will expansion or decline in one product field have on other activities within the company?

With its product's strengths and weaknesses established, the company will wish to build its developmental strategy in the light of its overall objectives of growth, profits, etc., and subject to possible constraints or choice criteria regarding the form or direction of growth, acceptable pay-off periods, sums of money available for new investments, acceptable degrees of risk, etc. In broad terms, the development of the business may take one or more of four different directions, as indicated in Ansoff's matrix (1968) in Figure 2.4.

Markets

		Existing	New
Products	Existing	1	3
	New	2	4

Figure 2.4 Possible Directions of Growth

Each of these four combinations may apply to either internal growth—development from within the company; or external growth—by acquisition. They do, however, have quite different implications for the growth path.

Cell 1—building on existing products and markets—may be described as *market penetration*. This emphasises the achievement of higher sales and, probably, higher market shares. It may be achieved through a horizontal acquisition of a competitor. If it is to be attained through internal growth it points to the importance of competition through the marketing mix—on price, distribution, packaging, promotion and product development. The requirements for expanded output may have implications for the organisation of the production process.

Cell 2—the development of new products for existing markets—may be described as *product development*. This may be a response to the decline in the life of existing products. It may point to the need for new product development, obtaining licences to produce or to market products of an overseas producer, or the acquisition of a supplier that has products that would meet the overall corporate and market requirements.

Cell 3 is concerned with *market development*, selling existing products in new markets. This may suggest an increased geographical spread of activities, the development of new export markets, joint ventures or foreign direct investment to establish production facilities in other markets. Mergers in this case are likely to be either for the purpose of acquiring additional plant capacity at home or abroad, or to acquire distribution outlets that will assist the penetration into new markets.

Cell 4—new products in new markets—implies a substantial degree of *diversification*. While such a strategy may flow from a company's internal research and development work opening up new opportunities, it is likely that if a company decides that this is the correct strategy to adopt it will seek to pursue it through acquisition since this is likely to be quicker and more certain in its effects.

Each strategy brings with it its own particular costs, problems and risks. As far as possible, the particular implications should be identified and spelled out as part of the final decision-making process. The choice between internal and external growth raises important issues which the next two sections consider in some detail. In comparing the two it seems that some distinctions can be identified. Internal growth may be preferable where an incremental growth is sought and where it is desirable to keep control within the existing organisation. It will be very dependent on the functional skills of the marketing, research and development and production staff. As such activities are likely to be capital deepening and employment creating, they are likely to be favoured by governments, may attract tax or other advantages and will, of course, avoid any possible problems from competition policy controls on mergers. Against this must be set the possibility that internal growth may well be slower, less certain and may provoke severe competitive responses from other companies active in the market.

Growth through acquisition is quicker, allows ready access to existing products, markets or know-how as required, and may offer lower risks of failure or of competitive response than may be associated with internal growth. A significant acquisition represents a step change in the size and corporate profile of the parent company. On the other hand, the evidence on the economic effects of mergers is not such as to generate confidence that mergers are generally likely to turn out well and there may be problems with the competition policy authorities. The financial effects of an acquisition in terms of the possible risk of dilution of shareholder equity, change in the pattern of share ownership in the company, together with the managerial costs of attempting to integrate the acquired company into its new parent, should all be taken into account before selecting external growth as the preferred route. In practice the actual choice will no doubt depend upon the direction of growth that is decided upon, the balancing of the different considerations mentioned above, the availability of potential takeover candidates, etc.

2.3   Internal Growth

The nature and implications of internal growth strategies have tended to be neglected by economists, for whom mergers represent a more significant means of growth. Even those studies that do focus on the overall growth of the firm (e.g. Penrose 1959, Barna 1962) do not get much beyond an explanation of the managerial and market influences on growth performance. They do not develop analysis in terms of possible internal growth strategies.

The essence of internal growth is that the firm has, or can readily obtain, the resource necessary for it to expand successfully its operations in existing or new markets with existing or new products. This points to the importance of successful product links, good management, effective production and marketing and the need for adequate funds to allow necessary investments in plant, research and development or marketing effort to achieve the desired growth. While external funding through rights issues has a part to play, the effective redeployment of internal positive cash flows is, therefore, an important aid to this process and serves to emphasise the importance of establishing an appropriate organisation structure (see below, Chapter 3).

Any internal growth in excess of the rate of growth of the market overall inevitably means that one company's gain will be another's loss of market share. Even slower rates of growth may still have to be achieved at the expense of a rival company's own growth targets. Thus internal growth strategies are very closely allied to competitive strategies and the choice of growth strategy must therefore take into account the competitive nature of the industry and market in which the firm wishes to expand. They require a good understanding of industrial structures and the nature of competitive behaviour in oligopolies and other industrial situations (for example, see Pickering 1974, Porter 1980, Shaw and Sutton 1976). In view of this, it is apparent that the choice of growth strategy will need to reflect the circumstances in the individual market, and will need to anticipate the likely responses of other competitors. A very careful analysis will be needed before the appropriate growth areas and strategies to be adopted can be determined. Careful search and appraisal techniques will be required to assist in the initial choice process and in monitoring the outcome.

A number of methods of achieving internal growth can be identified. They tend to relate to particular aspects of the tactical management of individual functional activities and as such are dealt with in more detail in other chapters. Consequently, we can draw attention to them here rather more briefly.

(a) New Plant Investment

This may be undertaken either to improve existing facilities (thereby raising productive potential and/or lowering unit costs and/or raising product quality) or to add to total capacity in an existing or new product market. Either way it is a basis for sales growth. Capacity increases tend inevitably to occur as step changes which may, at least in the short run, create a surplus of potential output in the industry over actual demand. The growth of the market may ultimately bring the two into balance, but in the short run there may be strong competitive responses from other suppliers anxious to sustain their own levels of capacity utilisation. A company planning a major new investment that increases the total capacity of the industry should satisfy itself that it is likely to get the projected sales increase it requires and at a profitable level of prices and costs in order to justify the investment. The most sophisticated investment appraisal is of little use if the basic research on market potential and likely competitor responses has not been undertaken. Investments in improvement to the existing plant may not create such a potential problem of under-utilisation of capacity, but one company's action here may also be met by response from others. This will depend upon the age of the plant, whether it has been fully depreciated and whether there has been technical progress that would encourage competitors to invest in a new generation of machines.

(b) Price Competition

Economists are sometimes accused of over-emphasising this form of competition to the exclusion of others that are more prevalent in business. This is not fully justified since economists do recognise the role of other forms of competition and it is clear that price competition does break out from time to time. It may well be used by a company wishing to expand sales, though care needs to be taken to distinguish between a short-run price reduction to clear stocks, especially where the price is not sufficient to cover the full costs of production, and price competition reflecting a long-term view about where the price level ought to be because of changes in costs of production, required profit margins, etc. The more homogeneous the product, the weaker is the overall level of demand; and the more price responsive is demand, the greater the impact a price reduction is likely to have. The initiator of such a move should, however, be prepared for a competitive response from his rivals. This may not necessarily be a matching reduction on the same product; it may involve other forms of competitive response, perhaps on other products. He will need to ensure that a lower price is not thought by consumers to indicate lower quality.

Especially in the case of consumer goods, in the absence of resale price maintenance the final selling price to the consumer is set by the retailer. Consequently, in such cases the manufacturer may need to make special efforts to ensure that any price reduction he makes is passed on to the final consumer. The emphasis here is, therefore, likely to be on the offer of additional discounts and other financial incentives to distributors to promote a particular brand.

There is little doubt that price competition is, in certain circumstances, a very powerful competitive weapon, though the company should certainly not assume that rivals will not respond to such a move. If the overall demand for the product is price inelastic, price cutting merely shifts market shares without boosting sales overall. In this case competitors may quickly come to the conclusion that price competition is too easily matched and is therefore not a very satisfactory means of achieving profitable growth. One exception to this, however, may be the case of a new entrant into an industry who, because of greater efficiency, a superior production technique or a different view of required profit margins, is prepared to sell generally at lower prices than have previously prevailed. If the market is sufficiently price responsive to reward such an action, price competition by a new entrant may be especially successful. However, it is sometimes the case that higher prices sell more units of a product than lower prices, so it does not necessarily follow that lower prices would be a preferred growth strategy.

(c)   Non-Price Competition

In contrast to price competition, non-price competition is much more product specific and less readily subject to direct imitation. A considerable variety of forms of non-price competition exist, such as advertising, promotions (including games and competitions), improved servicing and delivery, extended distribution points, improved packing and display, sponsorship, business lunches, special literature, trade fairs, etc. When correctly used they offer scope for increase in sales. However, it is important to monitor carefully the cost effectiveness of any particular non-price promotional activity in order to establish as far as possible that profitable sales are in fact being generated (see Chapter 6 below).

(d)   Product Innovation

This is a means of product development and also of diversification. There will probably be a spectrum of innovative activity, from product improvement aimed at improving the acceptability of existing products through to the development of entirely new products. The more fundamental is the innovation, the more important will be the scientific and technological input in the innovative process. Yet it is not always necessary to be a leader in the innovatory process; some firms are successful imitators. This latter strategy may be more attractive in that it reduces some of the risks of innovation, but it is likely to be less profitable. Indeed, there is always a risk, especially in some industries, that a successful innovation may be patented, so making a competitive response more difficult. Some companies may seek new products by acting as agents for the distribution of products developed by companies in other markets, or by obtaining licences to produce such items for their own market. These are likely to be less profitable than successful innovation by the company in its own right. If successfully handled, however, they may well make a very valuable and significant contribution to the overall development of the business.

Whatever the basis of product innovation, it is important to recognise the need to get both the design of the product and its marketing right. Not only are these of considerable importance separately, the coupling between the two is crucial. It is relevant to emphasise that successful research and development cannot necessarily be achieved on a short time-scale. The lead time will vary from industry to industry, but management must be realistic in its expectations. (On the whole question of innovation see Freeman 1974, Sutton 1980, Chapter 8, Pickering 1974, Chapter 10.)

(e)   The Development of Overseas Markets

So far, no distinction has been made betwen forms of business development in the home and overseas markets. However, given a relatively restricted home market, many companies will be forced to look to overseas markets for additional business growth. This may take a number of forms depending on the product, the product's life cycle position, the particular overseas market, the company concerned, etc.

This is a vast topic in itself and Chapter 12 below deals with these and other aspects of the management of multinational companies. Here we may briefly note that there are a variety of ways in which the business may be developed on an international scale.

Exporting will often be the first option considered. This is especially important where economies of scale and size are available which cannot be fully utilised by supplying the domestic market alone. It appears that all too often firms unwisely tend to treat exporting as a counter-cyclical activity, to be emphasised only when business in the domestic market is slack. If firms are to be successful in export markets, it seems they often require greater and more senior managerial emphasis on this activity, greater investment in the development of selected overseas markets on a long-term basis and the development of specialist skills and learning within the organisation (see Turnbull and Cunningham (eds) 1981). Companies should recognise that export efforts are likely to provoke a competitive response from others—local producers and foreign exporters—and the pattern of competition may therefore broaden and extend into other product and geographic markets as well.

The use of licensing, management contracts and joint ventures are all forms of involvement in overseas markets that allow the company to achieve some expansion without the full risks and involvement that foreign direct investment may incur. However, foreign direct investment—the ownership and operation of production plant abroad—is a significant feature of the overall operations of many companies. Companies should choose this route where the returns from foreign direct investment exceed those from other forms of overseas business development. The assessment of this will not be easy since there are often a greater number of unknowns and risk elements than in domestic investments. In general, however, it is likely that foreign production will take place where there are comparative advantages that are best exploited through overseas production and where there are particular incentives to produce locally, e.g. a sizeable local market, raw material availability, a favourable infrastructure, or opportunities to 'block' other possible producers.

2.4 Growth Through Acquisition

(a) Motives for Mergers

Mergers and acquisitions represent an important means of business growth, although their incidence tends to vary over time with greater merger intensity when business generally is booming, since this is the time when high stock market ratings make it easier for an acquirer to finance an acquisition by new share issues. It is also likely to be a time when business optimism is high, and this may encourage a more expansive outlook on the part of decision takers and their investors.

It is important to recognise that some mergers or acquisitions are readily agreed between the parties but others are not. While many mergers are instigated by the bidding company, others may originate from a suggestion by the target company or, indeed, by some third party (e.g. merchant banker, stockbroker, government agency, etc) which believes it can identify a benefit from promoting that particular merger.

A number of different reasons for merger can be identified and it is likely that the parties involved in a particular merger would have their own unique set of reasons to advance. The neoclassical emphasis in the theory of the firm would point to *profitability* as the main cause of mergers. Decision takers anticipate that the merger would increase overall profits due to the opportunity to release synergy, the benefits of greater size and scale of operations and the possibility that the target company is more valuable to its acquirer than to its present owners.

The managerial argument in the theory of the firm would point to the benefits of merger in terms of *growth and diversity*. A merger allows more rapid and less risky growth, easier entry into new markets and greater opportunity to diversify into new activities. It is interesting to consider whether there is an inevitable trade-off between growth and profitability. As some 'managerial' theories of the firm approach the question (e.g. Baumol 1958, Marris 1964) such a trade-off is postulated, suggesting that a growth oriented firm will expand beyond the profit-maximising position, though it will necessarily be subject to a minimum profit constraint. However, there are also respects in which there is a close positive association between growth and profitability, since growth is largely dependent upon profits as a means of internal and external financing and future profits will almost certainly be greater if past growth strategies have been successful. Thus, strategically, the firm requires both profits *and* growth. Furthermore, there is some evidence that diversification is an aid to a more stable level of profits which allows the company greater scope and confidence in planning and developing its future strategy.

Defensive reasons also encourage mergers. The purpose may be to buy up competitors in order to reduce competitive pressures, or ensure markets for the company's output by tying up customers. It may be that a merger may be sought by either the bidding or the target company as a means of avoiding another, less preferred, merger.

Finally, mergers may be seen as responses to particular *problems or opportunities*. They may be used to bring in more profitable product lines, to overcome constraints on internal growth, to bring in new assets, management or know-how or access to new markets. They may help to achieve a better balance in terms of asset structures, flows of profits through time, or a better balance between different types of shareholders, e.g. between institutional and individual shareholders. Mergers may represent the use of an opportunity to deploy liquid assets, to take advantage of unused tax relief or to respond to an unexpected opportunity to acquire a company that is for sale.

(b)   The Selection Process

Consideration of this process can be undertaken at two different levels—the way firms engage in a search for acquisition opportunities, and the statistical evidence concerning the sort of firms that make acquisitions or that are taken over.

The company's own search process is very important in the achievement of external growth. The identification of a suitable acquisition candidate may come as a result of an ongoing corporate planning exercise, from an offer by the target company or its shareholders to sell out, from an unexpected fall in the target's stock market rating or from the suggestion of a merger broker. Whatever the source of the opportunity and however much the need for haste in decision taking, it is important as far as possible to go through a disciplined search process.

This requires a consideration of such matters as: the type of business activity in which an acquisition is to be sought; the reasons for the desired acquisition; the use that the company intends to make of the acquired company; particular strengths that would be looked for in the acquired company; particular strengths that the acquiring company believes it has to enable it to manage, integrate and improve whatever company it acquires. It is then important to specify the size of acquisition that would be appropriate (companies may be too small, as well as too large, to be suitably acquired) and to indicate the sort of profit, market and asset profile that would be preferred. In the light of this information it then becomes possible to investigate various companies that might meet the requirements. This certainly implies a systematic approach to the external growth process, and it is clear that some companies have this as part of an ongoing process of corporate planning. Even where this is not the case, a systematic consideration and appraisal is important, even if the nature of an unexpected opportunity to acquire means that only a short period of time is available for the process to be completed.

As a good example of a well-developed, systematic approach to the identification of an acquisition opportunity, consider the documented approach adopted by Imperial Group in the steps it took leading up to the acquisition of Howard Johnson, the American hotel chain (*Financial Times* 1979). This search took more than two years. Imperial specified the area and scale of investment: it indicated that it wanted to make an acquisition in a sector with long-term growth prospects; it wished to acquire a company with a good track record that could be used as a springboard for further growth, which had a good management that would stay after the merger and which had 'corporate and personal integrity'; and it indicated that the USA was an attractive market for acquisition due to the size and stability of the economy. Imperial Group also pointed to certain sectors where it would not wish to consider making an acquisition. These were particularly industries that were intensive in their use of research and development or capital, where there were wide cyclical fluctuations, fragmented or competitive markets, complex distribution systems and where there was the prospect of government intervention. Clearly other companies would have different criteria, but this approach is indicative of a careful, analytical approach to such decision taking.

The statistical evidence on the companies involved in mergers is of particular interest to economists since it indicates how effectively the take-over market is working in disciplining poor performers by letting them be acquired and rewarding good performers by allowing them to make acquisitions. However, the evidence does have some prospective interest for management too in that it may offer pointers as to particular aspects of a company's performance that may have a bearing on its likely position should it be involved in merger activity. What follows draws heavily on the empirical work of Meeks (1977) and Singh (1971 and 1975).

Bidding companies were found to have been on average larger and faster growing than the general run of companies. They were also more profitable and more likely to have shown a profit increase over the previous two years. In addition, they tended to be more highly geared and more liquid. In contrast acquired firms, when compared with those that were not the subject of take-over bids, were smaller, less profitable, had more variable profits and a relative fall in their profits over the previous year. They tended to have a lower price/earnings ratio, a lower valuation ratio (the ratio of market value of the equity to the book value of the assets) and were under-geared.

While the statistical results can only paint a picture of an average situation, it does seem that certain generalisations can be made. First, it does appear that profitability, and especially recent changes in profitability, is relevant to identifying companies that will be involved in merger activity. This supports the traditional neoclassical emphasis on profits and has been shown by Meeks (1977) to apply especially where the two companies involved in a merger are of roughly equal size. There is, however, also quite strong support for the managerial emphasis on size of firm and, indeed, some studies have shown that size has an even greater bearing on the probability of being acquired than profitability. Thus neither size (and hence growth) nor profits can safely be ignored by management. These aspects of company performance will affect stock market rating which is also independently relevant in such analyses. Finally, it appears that the nature of financial management has a bearing on a company's prospects in takeover bid situations, since a more conservatively managed and, therefore, under-geared company is more likely to be acquired, while a more highly-geared company is more likely to make acquisitions. In both cases, it seems likely that there is a close association between high gearing, growth orientation and strong stock market rating.

(c)   Bidding and Defence Strategies

It is rare to find much consideration of this aspect of the merger process in economic discussions of the topic. This is surprising since the whole question of pricing and valuation strategy is one that involves a considerable economic assessment. Furthermore, the 'market' for the ownership of companies is one that would repay more extensive economic research and analysis. From those sources that are available some indicators can be identified concerning the key elements of effective bidding and defence strategies (see, for example, Newbould 1970, Pickering 1983, Wooldridge 1974, Weinberg 1979 and also Chia 1982).

(i) Bidders   They will find their attempts to make an acquisition much easier if they win the agreement of the target company's board to recommend to the shareholders that they accept the bid. Thus the nature of this initial approach to the target and the way discussions are handled about valuation, future plans and roles for the target's own staff in the new company are very important. Some aspects of the way the bid is approached will be influenced by such considerations as the target company's pattern of share ownership (e.g. how influential are institutional investors?) and the bidding company's own market position. However, there are a number of key issues that will generally need to be considered.

The price to be put on the target is clearly very important. Ideally it should be set to reflect the value of the target company to the bidder. This would take into account assets and past earnings, but should especially reflect the projected future earnings of the company if under the control of the bidder company. However, there is considerable uncertainty over such performance and, in practice, companies are likely to adopt a rule of thumb approach by offering a premium over the existing market price for the company. Often it seems the premium suggested is 20 per cent, but it may be as high as 40 per cent. The tactics involved in making an offer are also important. Some companies may choose to put in a fairly low initial offer so that they have something in reserve should they need to raise the offer later. However, others would argue that this may encourage opposition from the target's board and the entry of a possible further bidder, so a higher 'foreclosing' offer is sometimes preferred. Whatever the initial pricing strategy, companies should be anxious to avoid getting into a situation where a succession of ever higher offers is made without due consideration being given to the extent to which the price finally paid dilutes earnings and is well in excess of the true value of the acquisition to the bidding company.

The *type of offer* is also a potentially important influence on the success of a bid. Is it to be all cash, all shares or a mixture of the two? A cash offer is considered attactive to individual shareholders, though it can create a Capital Gains Tax liability. To the bidder it has beneficial effects on the measure of earnings per share, but it reduces liquidity. A share offer avoids the Capital Gains Tax problems for the target's shareholders and encourages them to retain an interest in the post-merger company. It avoids a loss of liquidity to the bidder, but it is dependent on the relative share prices of the bidder and the target remaining more or less in line for the duration of the bid, otherwise the value of the offer is less clearly defined.

Whether to build up a share stake before or during a bid is something that exercises many companies. The build up of a pre-bid stake may be attractive because it is cheaper and creates a springboard for a formal offer. On the other hand, it may raise the opposition of the target and may cause the share price to harden, thereby making the acquisition of further shares more expensive. 'Dawn raids' are sometimes used to establish a significant share stake quickly. For this to be possible it is necessary for the target company to have some significant institutional investors who are attracted to a cash offer and a stockbroker who is capable of carrying out the raid successfully. This is not, however, an easy task to accomplish. There may well be ethical questions over the failure to communicate with the target's board and the failure, necessarily, to make the same offer at that time to all shareholders. Some bidding companies have also had doubts as to whether they should attempt to build up a share stake once a bid battle is in process. Their doubts seem to reflect concern that if they are unsuccessful they will be left with a minority shareholding that could prove an embarrassment. Against this, it may be argued that a failure to buy up shares as they become available indicates a lack of commitment to the success of the bid or a lack of liquidity, both of which may be damaging in the eyes of other investors.

Communications play a very important part in the successful conduct of a takeover bid. Various interest groups will need to be won over—the target's board, management and workforce, institutional and private shareholders, the financial press. While the precise nature of the communication will no doubt vary according to the particular motivation of the interest group concerned, there will be a general need to emphasise the logic of the merger and the prospective benefits it will offer to all parties. Shareholders will no doubt be particularly interested in the comparative performance and prospects of the two companies; employees will be particularly anxious about the bidder's future plans for the target and about the prospects for job security, etc. The way in which communications are handled can have a significant influence on the overall success of a bid and on the longer-term standing of the bidding company.

Controls and regulations influence the operation of takeover bids. The Takeover Code specifies requirements regarding the conduct of parties to a bid. This Code, in its most up-to-date form, is clearly required reading for all involved in mergers (see also Johnston 1980). The larger mergers are also potentially subject to investigation by the Monopolies and Mergers Commission to establish whether the merger would be contrary to the public interest. This involves initial vetting by an interdepartmental civil service committee organised through the Office of Fair Trading (OFT), so contracts with OFT will be important in such cases (see Chapter 11).

(*ii*) *Target companies*   Their boards have a responsibility to consider the best interests of their shareholders and now also the company as a whole, not their own personal interests. There may well be circumstances where they conclude a particular offer should be resisted. Their defence strategies in such cases may involve a number of elements.

Financial and other direct action may be undertaken to raise the relative attractiveness of the company to its existing owners and to reduce its attractiveness to the bidder. This may be achieved by raising dividends, issuing bonus shares, revaluing the assets, selling off parts of the company, making an acquisition on its own account, seeking alternative bidders, giving service agreements to senior staff and directors or pressing for reference of the merger to the Monopolies and Mergers Commission.

Arguments against the bid will seek to emphasise the lack of industrial logic in the merger, demonstrate that the bid under-values the company, argue that the existing share price is too low, release favourable information, e.g. details of major new orders or new profit forecasts, or demonstrate employee opposition to the bid. Good communications with the institutions, smaller shareholders and the press are important. A defence is clearly helped if the existing board and management team is well respected and is seen to be united in resisting the bid.

(*iii*) *Competitive bids*   A fairly significant proportion of bids end up with more than one bidder. This may come about because more than one company is genuinely interested in acquiring the target, because the second bidder enters to disrupt the first bid or force up the price, or because the target company has brought in a preferred suitor—'the white knight gambit'. It seems the 'white knight' is likely to be a company from the same industry as the target and is often a response to a conglomerate takeover bid from a company in some quite disparate sector of the economy.

A competitive bid situation is likely to give rise to a greater number of separate offers as one bidder increases his offer above the previous bid from his rival (up to eight have been identified in some cases—Knight 1981). The nature of bidding and defence strategies will be similar to those outlined above. However, in this case the two bidders will now be concerned also to compare themselves against each other and convince investors of their rival virtues as acquirers of the target company. Especial attention in these circumstances will therefore focus not only on the performance and prospects of the bidders and the plans for the target, but also on the relative merits of the shape of the offers made by the two companies. An all-paper offer by a high risk company with a low market rating will be less attractive to shareholders than a blue chip equity or cash offer. In a competitive bid, the risks of paying over the odds for the target company are possibly even greater and it is important that bidders do have a clear view of the maximum price they are prepared to pay and do not go beyond that. In those circumstances, to be an unsuccessful bidder should be considered a virtue rather than a failing by investors and the financial press!

(*iv*) *Abandoned mergers*   Not all bids lead to mergers and at an earlier, less public stage in the consideration of possible mergers a high proportion of initial proposals fail to come to fruition. Often failure to agree on the valuation or on respective roles in a merged company are the cause of the breakdown of the proposals. Poor communications and personality conflicts are also contributory factors. Once a formal takeover bid has been made, research (Pickering 1983) shows that there are three main causes of the failure of the bid:

(a) *a good defence*, including support from major shareholders, and clear evidence that the target was recovering from its difficulties;
(b) *bidding errors/weaknesses in the bidder*, including tactical errors in the handling of the bid, adverse share price movements and a change of mind about the desirability of the acquisition; and
(c) *reference to the Monopolies and Mergers Commission*—where a ruling that the merger would be contrary to the public interest prevents the merger, but in other cases a bid has been abandoned simply because it was referred for investigation, or it has not proceeded even though the bid was cleared as not being likely to be contrary to the public interest.

It is interesting to note the reactions to the failure to merge, since this presumably indicates for bidding companies at least a serious rebuff to their planned strategy for the development of their business. My research shows that some bidders were very disappointed that their bid had failed, since it was a key part of a carefully planned strategy and they felt the logic for the merger was strong. Others exhibited a low degree of regret (which rather suggests the merger was not well planned in the first instance). The target companies were also generally pleased that they had avoided being taken over. However, some targets were left with a problem of a substantial minority shareholding which left some uncertainty about possible future developments.

The nature of the corporate response by companies involved in a takeover bid that had failed is also of interest. Both bidders and targets engaged in three alternative strategies—making other acquisitions, internal reorganisation and pursuit of internal growth. However, while other acquisitions appeared to be the most favoured response by unsuccessful bidders and internal growth the least favoured, target companies that had avoided being taken over were more likely to emphasise internal reorganisation as the main response, followed by internal growth. While this is not surprising, given the problems that often leave a company weak and vulnerable to a takeover bid, it does suggest that such companies had not fully appreciated the extent to which increasing size through acquisitions can, other things being equal, reduce the threat of takeover.

(d)   The Effects of Mergers

Considerable interest has been shown in recent years over the question of the economic effects of mergers. This is important because it has a bearing both on the question of whether economic efficiency generally is helped by encouraging mergers and, further, whether individual company managements are achieving the benefits from mergers that they claimed at the time of their takeover bids. Unfortunately, it is not easy to assess these matters with complete certainty since there are great problems in measuring accurately the effects and, indeed, in agreeing on the effects that should be measured.

There are perhaps four types of indicator that may be adopted for assessing the effects of merger. These are: the effect on profitability; the effect on share prices or other measures of shareholders interest; the effect on efficiency measured in terms of some form of factor productivity; and the qualitative assessment by management as to whether corporate objectives in the merger have been achieved. There is, of course, likely to be some similarity between the measures in terms of their identification as to which mergers have been successful and which not. However, different objectives and consideration of different interest groups may point to some variation in the results.

There are also methodological problems in carrying out this sort of analysis. There is an identification problem of distinguishing the effects of the merger from other influences that also acted on the company concerned. An acquisition intensive firm may be so active in mergers that the effects of any one merger may be difficult to unravel. There are several alternative sources of economic gain to the firm from a merger—e.g. increased market power, spreading overhead costs, tax advantages, benefits of rationalisation, risk pooling—so the actual source of any gain may be difficult to establish. There are questions about how to assess the extent to which the changes after the merger are due to general economic influences which would have been available to benefit the firm even without merger. This is normally dealt with by means of a comparison of merging companies with a control group of non-merging companies. Consideration also has to be given to the period of time over which the effects should be measured. Some may argue that a considerable period of time may be needed to achieve the benefits of merger. Others will point to the low net present value of future profits and argue for a short time horizon. There are also accounting and measurement problems, especially where the concern is the effect of the merger on profitability. Here varying accounting practices make inter-firm comparisons difficult; the use of historic cost valuation of capital makes reliable judgement difficult; and the inclusion of good will in post-merger asset values may cause the calculated rate of return on capital employed to be shown at a lower figure than is strictly justified.

Thus all empirical work has to be as careful as possible in its collection and use of data—it must recognise the caveats required in the work and in interpretation of the results. The surprising feature is the extent to which many studies based on different techniques, different data sets, etc., do yield similar conclusions (see, for example, Cowling *et al*. 1980, Firth 1979, Meeks 1977, Mueller (ed) 1980, Newbould 1970, Singh 1971, 1975, Utton 1974).

Here we cannot hope to review these studies in detail. However, the general conclusions may be summarised. Most studies conclude that on average mergers do not have a favourable effect on the relative profitability of a merged company with a control group or industry average, and this effect persists for a number of years after the merger. Thus, it is argued, if mergers increase market power but this still does not raise profits, it suggests that overall efficiency has fallen. Share price effects also tend to be considered unfavourable, with the shareholders in the target company more likely to benefit through the favourable terms on which they sell out than the shareholders of the acquiring company. Qualitative studies also tend to indicate that a significant majority of mergers are deemed to have been unsuccessful.

This is not to say that all mergers are unsuccessful. Many clearly do achieve their objectives and produce benefits of size or scale, solve particular managerial or growth problems and allow larger research and development or capital investment projects to be undertaken. It is also the case that most studies tend to show that merging firms grow faster than non-merging firms. The general implication of this brief review, however, is that firms which place considerable emphasis on merger may be trading off the benefits of growth against some other dimensions of performance such as profits or shareholder benefits. They may also need to recognise that, as Sutton (1980) has put it, 'merging is a high risk activity with a rather low probability of high pay-off.'

This does serve, then, to emphasise the importance of management, shareholders and financial markets taking a realistic and perhaps less 'bullish' view of mergers as a form of growth. A more careful and thorough search, planning and screening process would be likely to be helpful for this purpose. A realistic view of the true value of a potential acquisition might also help to avoid some of the subsequent difficulties. There is also much hard work once an acquisition has been made in order to ensure that the merger works. For an interesting case study of one merger in this respect see Erni (1979). Positive action will often be required to bring the two companies together. This will involve getting the organisation structure right (and ensuring that it is not too unwieldy), dealing with the human issues that arise, integrating activities on the basis of an agreed view of what the merged company should look like, standardising systems, strengthening areas that need it and working for the release of synergy. The view is widely accepted that stagnation and inactivity after the formal merger process must be avoided. This is the point at which the real management effort in mergers begins.

There is perhaps at the moment a lack of guidance for managers, on the basis of empirical research, as to the sort of mergers that are most likely to be successful. In an early study in the USA Kitching (1967) suggested that diversifying mergers were more likely to be successful than horizontal mergers. Meeks (1977) has shown that it is the more profitable acquiring companies before the merger that are more likely to make a success of a merger—thus a good 'track record' seems important. There is also some interesting evidence on the effects of foreign acquisitions (Baue and Neubauer 1980) which emphasises that it can be very difficult to make them work well. Differences in markets, problems of control and exchange rate fluctuations all make cross-national mergers very risky. Acquisitions into the USA have been found particularly difficult due, it is suggested, to onerous legal requirements, a lack of information on smaller companies and the strength of nationalistic feeling. The authors of the study suggest that success with foreign acquisitions is more likely to be achieved by those who already have wide experience of such mergers and already have diversified companies. This indicates that it is often better for a company to acquire another domestic company with its own foreign activities than to make foreign acquisitions on its own account.

2.5 Rationalising the Business

It is clearly important that companies should monitor and appraise the performance of their various activities. The basis of this appraisal will no doubt take into account the extent to which an activity or division is profitable, has achieved sales, growth or market targets, whether the activity 'fits' with the overall orientation and strategy of the company, etc. In some cases a poor performing activity may be the subject of a special injection of management or capital in order to turn it round. In others the decision may be taken that some more fundamental action may be required to close or sell off the particular activity. The reasons for this may be organisational, reflecting a change in the general strategy of the company. Frequently, however, it will be associated with the effects of general economic recession or with a specific decline in the market for the products concerned.

As with action to expand the business, steps taken to deal with particular problem areas must be based upon careful analysis of the situation and its causes. Is the problem a loss of relative competitiveness or an overall decline in demand faced by all firms in the industry? If it is a loss of competitiveness, why has that come about? Is it due to the product, its quality, the marketing or servicing it receives, low levels of efficiency and productivity, high price, etc? Whatever the reasons identified (and there may be multiple reasons), the underlying causes need to be established— e.g. overmanning or poor industrial relations, out of date production facilities or an out of date product due to failure to spend enough in the past on product development. Then consideration can be given to whether to attempt to retrieve the position or whether the situation is such that the company would be better advised to withdraw from the market rather than attempt to recapture its market position. If the difficulties are due to an overall decline in demand which all firms experience, it is clearly important to attempt to establish first whether the decline is temporary (cyclical) or permanent (secular). It is also important to explore what reactions competitors are making to the same situation and to assess whether there is sufficient comparative advantage to enable the company concerned to hold, or even increase, its own market share. Even in difficult trading conditions there can be scope for competitive gains by companies that act on the basis of analysis and their comparative advantages. However, there will be circumstances where some action is required to deal with an unprofitable situation. The literature on this is rather limited, but reference may be made to Singer (1981), *Financial Times* (1980) and Pickering and Jones (1979). Three different types of response may be identified.

(a)   Action to Restore the Competitive Position

This may be accomplished through pressure to reduce costs. Overhead costs may be saved by trimming down the size of head-office staff or by reducing perquisites that are offered. Operating costs may be reduced through pressure on raw materials and other input costs, through greater controls on wage increases and through improved manning and work practices. Control of stocks and work in progress, and action to stop any cross-subsidisation that may exist which may, in fact, make it difficult to establish the true performance of any particular activity in the company, are all relevant here. In short, tight financial discipline is important.

However, there will be circumstances in which the restoration of a competitive position will also require some expenditure. This may take the form of extra promotional expenses or price reductions. But the implications of such a strategy must be very carefully appraised, both in terms of the effect on corporate liquidity and also in terms of the likely response of competitors and, hence, on the chances of increasing profitable sales. Expenditure on new plant investments to raise operating efficiency or on product development may also be an appropriate course of action in certain circumstances, though again it must be emphasised that careful and realistic assessment of the likely effects of such expenditure is as important as it is difficult.

(b) Plant Closures and Rationalisation

There will be circumstances where analysis points to the conclusion that there is too much productive capacity in existence for the most realistically assessed level of demand. Here the decision may point clearly to the need for some plant closures. It may be that in the multiplant company the opportunity will be available to close one or more plants and to concentrate all production in the remaining plants. This would reduce plant overhead costs and may make for more intensive use of capacity and facilities in those plants that remain. There may also be disincentives to such action in terms of the human costs of redundancy and plant closure, especially in areas of high unemployment. Transport costs between the remaining plants and customers may increase and government and public pressure may add to the psychological, if not the financial, cost of plant closures.

The question arises as to which plants should be closed. Often it will be the oldest plants that are closed. However, this alone is not a sufficient basis for decision taking. Strictly speaking the whole of a company's productive capacity should be seen as a total productive system and closures organised in such a way that the total system costs of producing (and distributing) the required output are minimised. Similar considerations relate to some of the nationalised industries, e.g. electricity, railway workshops, etc., where, given that the industry is under single control, optimal decision taking on plant closures should be possible (see Pickering and Jones 1979). However, political pressures are even more likely to intervene in the case of public sector activities.

Where an industry is populated by a number of firms the question of the best means of rationalisation becomes more difficult. The preservation of all firms operating at sub-optimal capacity utilisation may be undesirable because it raises unit costs and reduces profits. The competitive process may help by driving out the least efficient firms, but this may not always work fast enough, and it may have the undesirable effect of causing firms to leave the industry who have lower overall financial resources rather than those who are less efficient. In some industries government may intervene to assist the process of contraction, as with the cotton industry rationalisation scheme in the late 1950s. In other cases, government policy on mergers permitting, individual firms may decide to buy out other firms in order to close their plants and so bring capacity back into line with predicted demand. This may be an attractive solution but, while the effects of closing a plant and so reducing competition may be to allow prices to strengthen and capacity utilisation to improve, the costs of the acquisition may represent a high price to pay.

When trading conditions become very difficult and profitability is greatly reduced, there may be grounds for considering complete withdrawal from that particular market. In terms of the portfolio matrices discussed earlier in this chapter, this would be most likely where both the relative position of the company in the market and the overall attractiveness of the market were unfavourable. While there will be costs involved in such a withdrawal, these are likely to be once-off and may be a small price to pay to avoid the financial and managerial costs of fighting a losing battle in a difficult market. However, such decisions are never as straightforward as they may seem initially. Withdrawal may lose access to customers or technical skills that are useful in other on-going areas of the business. Purchasing power in buying raw materials or components common to both the area of withdrawal and other continuing areas of the business may be lost. There may be vertical linkages between the abandoned activity and other company products or services where the loss of the linkage may weaken the remaining operations. There may be an inclination to withdraw from a particular market segment without realising that this will weaken the company's competitive position in other segments where it wishes to remain. This was considered to have been the problem of the so-called 'segment retreat' by the British motor cycle industry. This action actually allowed those competitors who remained in all segments the opportunity to benefit from higher overall volume and, hence, to achieve lower unit costs of components and to develop new products and technologies (on this see Boston Consulting Group 1975). Clearly it is important that the analysis on which any decision to withdraw from a market is taken should fully reflect the interdependencies between activities and the effects of any withdrawal on the relative position of competitors in other markets where the company still plans to be active.

(c) *Demergers*

Circumstances will arise where a strategic appraisal by a company will lead it to conclude that it no longer wishes to be involved with a particular activity at all. While this may apply most strongly to low growth, low profit activities, there may also be other types of situation which, although economically more attractive, still do not 'fit' the overall strategic plan the company has developed for itself. This lack of 'fit' may be in terms of the nature of the product supplied or market served, the volatility or cycle of earnings, the profit/risk profile of the activity concerned compared with that of the parent company, the capital intensity of the subsidiary, etc. It may be felt that there is an imbalance between the needs and resources of the subsidiary and those of the parent. A high technology subsidiary or one with substantial short-term capital requirements may not necessarily fit well with a fundamentally different type of parent company.

At the time of writing the significance of such demerger activity seems to be increasing. It reflects in some cases a decision by the parent to concentrate more on its 'core' activities. In other cases it reflects a decision to make more use of the external market rather than to internalise within the company services or products that could equally well be purchased in the open market (on the economics of this decision see Coase 1937, Williamson 1975). Some demergers may reflect a change of view about the strategic emphasis of the company or an attempt to rectify the past mistake of an unwise acquisition. Yet other instances may represent the results of an appraisal of the various activities obtained through a previous acquisition, some of which may well be quite peripheral to the new parent company's interests and requirements.

Thus there are many different reasons for individual corporate decisions to dispose of an activity. It certainly does not follow that they are all unprofitable at the time of their disposal or that under other ownership they would not be profitable. A managerial decision to dispose of an activity requires an assessment of the alternative costs and revenues of retaining the subsidiary or using the resources that would be released from its disposal in developing other activities within the company. In other words, a decision to dispose of a subsidiary should indicate a judgement that, in the light of the overall strategy of the company, the opportunity costs of retaining this particular activity are high relative to the available alternatives.

Where a decision to dispose of an activity has been taken, a number of alternative methods of demerger are available. The subsidiary may be sold to another company where the 'fit' would be more appropriate. Such sales and purchases now represent a significant proportion of all acquisitions (about 20–25 per cent by number and 10–12 per cent by value, see Lye and Silberston 1981, Chiplin and Wright 1980). Alternatively, the subsidiary may be sold to a group of employees—management or workers. The management or staff buy-out in particular represents an important development in recent years. It seems this may be especially associated with recession, where the absence of corporate purchasers and the threat of redundancy may encourage management to seek to acquire the company in which they work. The fact that some management buy-outs are occurring in high technology sectors perhaps reflects not only the particular problems of the 'fit' of such developments with many traditional companies, but also the desire of scientific and technical staff to exercise an entrepreneurial role and take a direct equity stake in their own activities. Such buy-outs may prove highly successful, but there can be exceptions. Any management team that wishes to acquire its own company will need to take very careful advice on the overall prospects of the company and will need to satisfy itself that it has adequate financial backing and management resources (see Coyne and Wright (1982) for the key issues to consider and the *Financial Times* (1982) for an interesting case study of such a buy-out).

A final form of demerger occurs where a parent chooses to float off a subsidiary as an entirely separate public company for quotation on the Stock Exchange. Such flotations have only been practicable since the Finance Act 1980 and, inevitably, they are likely to be relatively few in number and would probably involve only large subsidiaries of large public companies or of state-owned organisations where privatisation is desired.

References

Ansoff, H. I. (1968) *Corporate Strategy*, Penguin Books.
Barna, T. (1962) *Investment and Growth Policies in British Industrial Firms*, Cambridge University Press.
Baue, W. T. and Neubauer, F. F. (1980) 'Diversity and the failure of new foreign activities', Mimeo, Centre d'Etudes Industrielles, Geneva.
Baumol, W. J. (1958) *Business Behaviour, Value and Growth*, Harcourt Brace.
Chia, R. G. (1982) *Merchant Banks and Corporate Acquisitions*, City University PhD Thesis.
Chiplin, B. and Wright, M. (1980) 'Divestment and structural change in UK industry', *National Westminster Bank Review*, February.
Coase, R. H. (1937) 'The nature of the firm', *Economica*, 4.
Cowling, K. *et al.* (1980) *Mergers and Economic Performance*, Cambridge University Press.
Coyne, J. and Wright, M. (1982) 'Buy-outs and British industry', *Lloyds Bank Review*, No. 146, October.
Erni, P. (1979) *The Basel Marriage*, Naue Zurcher Zeitung.
Firth, M. (1979) 'The profitability of takeovers and mergers', *Economic Journal*, 89.
Freeman, C. (1974) *The Economics of Industrial Innovation*, Penguin Books.
Galbraith, J. R. (1967) *The New Industrial State*, André Deutsch.
Grinyer, P. H. and Spender, J. C. (1979) *Turnaround*, Associated Business Press.
Johnston, A. Sir (1980) *The City Takeover Code*, Oxford University Press.
Kirzner, I. (1973) *Competition and Entrepreneurship*, Chicago University Press.

Kitching, J. (1967) 'Why do mergers miscarry', Harvard Business Review, November/December, Vol. 45, No. 6.

Knight, P. C. (1981) *UK Competitive Mergers 1966–1981*, University of Manchester MSc Dissertation.

Lancaster, K. (1971) *Consumer Demand: A New Approach*, Columbia University Press.

Lye, S. and Silberston, A. (1981) 'Merger activity and sales of subsidiaries between company groups', *Oxford Bulletin of Economics and Statistics*, 43.

Marris, R. L. (1964) *The Economic Theory of 'Managerial' Capitalism*, Macmillan.

Meeks, G. (1977) *Disappointing Marriage*, Cambridge University Press.

Mueller, D. C. (ed) (1980) *The Determinants and Effects of Mergers*, Gunn and Hain.

Newbould, G. D. (1970) *Management and Merger Activity*, Guthstead.

Penrose, E. T. (1959) *The Theory of the Growth of the Firm*, Basil Blackwell.

Pickering, J. F. (1974) *Industrial Structure and Market Conduct*, Martin Robertson.

Pickering, J. F. (1983) 'The causes and consequences of abandoned mergers', *Journal of Industrial Economics*, 31.

Pickering, J. F. and Jones, T. T. (1979) 'Il problema dell'eccesso di capacita producttiva nell'industria inglese', *Rivista de Economia e Politica Industriale*; also available in English as 'The problem of excess capacity in British industry', UMIST, Department of Management Sciences, Occasional Paper No. 8104.

Porter, M. E. (1980) *Competitive Strategy*, Free Press.

Shaw, R. W. and Sutton, C. J. (1976) *Industry and Competition*, Macmillan.

Singer, F. A. (1981) *Strategies for Cut-back and Recovery in Manufacturing Industries*, Chesham Amalgamations and Investments Limited, Occasional Paper No. 6.

Singh, A. (1971) *Takeovers*, Cambridge University Press.

Singh, A. (1975) 'Takeovers, economic selection and the theory of the firm', *Economic Journal*, 85.

Sutton, C. J. (1980) *Economics and Corporate Strategy*, Cambridge University Press.

Turnbull, P. W. and Cunningham, M. T. (eds) (1981) *International Marketing and Purchasing*, Macmillan.

Utton, M. (1974) 'On measuring the effects of industrial mergers', *Scottish Journal of Political Economy*, 21.

Weinberg, M. A. (1979) *Takeovers and Mergers*, Sweet and Maxwell.

Williamson, O. E. (1975) *Markets and Hierarchies*, Free Press.

Wooldridge, F. (1974) 'Some defences to takeover bids', *Journal of Business Law*.

Boston Consulting Group (1968) *Perspectives on Experience*, HMSO.

Boston Consulting Group (1975) *Strategy Alternatives for the British Motor Cycle Industry*, HMSO.

Financial Times (1979) 'The long search that led to Howard Johnson's door', 17th December.

Financial Times (1980) A series of articles entitled 'Wrestling with recession'.

Financial Times (1982) 'Why a buy-out became a sell-out', 23rd March.

3
Organisational Structure, the Development of the Firm and Business Behaviour

C. W. L. Hill

3.1 Introduction

Many economists and no small number of businessmen have for too long ignored the economic implications of the different internal organisational arrangements that may be adopted by the evolving firm. Economists in particular have tended to overlook the significance of this aspect of the firm. Consequently, they have attached too much importance to the notion that the economic performance and competitive conduct of the firm is the product of its position in, and the competitive structure of, external markets, and not enough to the possibility that internal organisation may have a bearing upon these matters. A similar myopic attitude has resulted in many economists treating the development of the firm as being independent of internal structure, whereas in fact it is at least in part dependent upon internal structure.

The purpose of this chapter is to illustrate just how important a consideration of internal organisation is for both economists and businessmen alike. In order to achieve this we will discuss the nature of the link between the development of the firm and the adoption of different internal organisational structures. We will look at how different internal arrangements may have important economic implications. And finally, we will consider the empirical evidence which pertains to these areas.

3.2 The Development of the Firm and Organisational Structure

In the very small business no formal organisational structure as such exists. One man, the entrepreneur, often carries out most of the different business functions himself. As the firm grows within a single market, so this is no longer possible or desirable and a formal organisational structure based upon functional specialisms begins to emerge. Thus the firm is divided up into hierarchical functional departments dealing with buying, production, marketing, personnel, finance, and the like. Co-ordination of the different departments is achieved through a board of directors, the membership of which normally includes the heads of each functional department. This is reflected in the top part of an organisational chart such as that shown in Figure 3.1. This form of organisation is sometimes described by economists as being of a unitary or U-form (Williamson 1970).

Figure 3.1 Functional Organisation

So long as the firm confines itself to its original business area, then in general an organisational structure such as that depicted in Figure 3.1 will suffice. However, the functional organisational structure begins to show serious signs of weakness once the firm reaches that stage of corporate development where it begins to grow by diversifying into new business areas. The response to such strategic change has generally been to replace the original functional structure of the firm with a more decentralised organisational form.

The first to observe that the strategy of corporate diversification subsequently fosters a change in the internal organisation of the firm was Alfred Chandler (1962). In an historical examination of the organisational problems faced by some of the early diversified US corporations, such as Du Pont and General Motors, Chandler noted that diversification resulted in

> . . . problems of co-ordination, appraisal, and policy formulation too intricate for a small number of top officers to handle both long-run entrepreneurial, and short-run operational administrative activities. (Chandler, 1962, pp. 23)

In short, these problems arose because as firms like Du Pont began to diversify into new business areas, so single functional departments within the firm, such as the sales and finance departments, found themselves having to deal with several distinct businesses. This increased the workload of functional departments and made the co-ordination of individual business activities across departments difficult. The initial solution adopted to deal with this problem was often to expand further the existing functional hierarchies. This, in turn, resulted in a loss of information and control, necessitating that top officers, such as the sales and finance directors, become involved in the problems of running their own departments.

Furthermore, diversification within the framework of a functional organ-isational structure often meant that the contribution made by each distinct business to corporate profitability was difficult, if not impossible, to assess. This made for inefficient internal resource allocation. Typically, funds would be allocated within the firm according to considerations such as the 'political' strength of a particular department, or the persuasiveness of a departmental head, rather than according to the financial importance of each distinct business within the organisation.

As a consequence of the above, strategic considerations were often ignored by top officers, whose time was monopolised by short-run oper-ational administrative problems occurring within the firm. Moreover, even when top officers did turn their attention to strategic matters, the failure to isolate the performance of distinct businesses within the firm meant that they did not have the data necessary for effective strategic decision taking. Hence the likes of Du Pont and General Motors failed to react quickly enough to adverse changes in the external competitive environment, and both began to run into financial problems in the 1920s.

In addition, diversifying firms which encountered such organisational and strategic problems were in effect encountering fundamental mana-gerial limits to the continued growth of the firm. The functional structure proved ill-equipped to handle the combination of large size and diversity. It was too centralised with respect to day-to-day operational decision taking matters. Thus top officers would find themselves swamped with work and ultimately unable to control their own departments. Naturally enough, sooner or later such control loss would find expression in financial malaise which, in turn, would effectively limit further expansion.

The organisational response to these problems, pioneered by Alfred Sloan at General Motors, was to decompose the original functional hierarchies and reassemble the firm into a new decentralised form based upon product divisions. Each product division dealt with a conceptually distinct business and was basically self-contained, with its own functional hierarchies. The divisions were given the responsibility for taking day-to-day operational decisions (such as production, purchasing, pricing and promotional decisions) and were fully autonomous in this respect. The board of directors was superceded as the main co-ordinating body by a central office comprising the main directors and a small corporate staff of specialists. Its functions were primarily to determine the long-run strategic direction of the firm and to exercise ultimate financial control over the divisions. Thus the resultant organisational structure resembled that illustrated in Figure 3.2.

From a managerial point of view a number of important implications followed on from these changes. To begin with, the separating out of strategic and operational decision-taking responsibilities within the div-isional organisation resulted in General Motors and its followers becoming

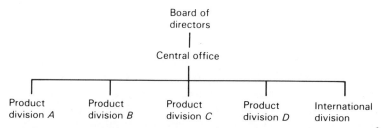

Figure 3.2   The Divisional Structure

more aware of the implications of developments taking place in the external competitive environment. These firms rediscovered their strategic direction, for top officers, freed of the need to take operating decisions, could turn their attention to the strategic development of the firm. Equally important, the financial contribution of each distinct business to corporate profitability was visible under the new structure. This was an invaluable aid to financial control, resource allocation and strategic planning. Direct comparisons between divisions could now be made which, strategic and allocative decisions apart, had the additional advantage of quickly stimulating managers of divisions performing below par to look for ways of improving performance. The decentralisation of short-run decision-taking responsibilities to the divisions also had beneficial motivation effects, encouraging initiative, responsibility, the taking of decisions close to the facts and flexibility from divisional personnel.

As for the organisational limits to growth posed by an overworked functional structure, the adoption of decentralised divisional structures overcame these. By reducing the problems of peak co-ordination to those of overall strategic and financial control, decentralisation enabled top officers to cope with a much greater spread of activities. Control loss was also attenuated by the visibility of each individual activity's performance which, in turn, allowed policies of management by exception to develop, with top officers only becoming involved in the affairs of operating divisions when performance was below par.

Furthermore, the problems of integrating new acquisitions into the existing corporate structure were greatly reduced within the divisional firm. Whereas within functional firms the problems of integration were essentially top management problems, within the divisional firm they became divisional problems or, in the case of a diversified acquisition, problems which were solved by the creation of a new division. Thus not only did the new decentralised management structures open up the possibility of much larger firms, they also enabled firms to overcome fundamental managerial limits to the rate of growth (such as those suggested by Penrose 1959).

Indeed, the significance that the decentralised, divisional, organisational innovation has had for the subsequent development of large firms should not be underestimated. Hannah (1976), for example, has argued that by solving the problems of large-scale organisation and the discontinuous digestion of acquisitions, decentralised management structures laid the foundations for the emergence of the modern corporate economy. Certainly it is true that 39 per cent of UK net manufacturing output in 1977 would not have been in the hands of the top 100 private UK manufacturing firms, had not most of these firms operated with decentralised management structures similar in concept to those originally introduced at General Motors and Du Pont (Pickering *et al.* 1982). Moreover, by decentralising production decisions away from the head office, and by concentrating top officers' attention upon financial aspects of the firm and strategic development, it is possible that the diffusion of divisional structures amongst large firms paved the way for the emergence of financial conglomerates.

In the UK both Hannah (1976) and Channon (1973) have noted that the adoption of a full divisional structure was often preceded by the adoption of an intermediate holding company structure (see Figure 3.3). This

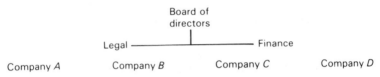

Figure 3.3   Holding Company Structure

decentralised structural form has a central legal and finance department serving the board and operating as a head office. There is, however, no formal linkage or interaction between the various subsidiaries. This structure implies a rather loose affiliation of subsidiary companies with no effective base for resource allocation decisions or scope for co-ordination and rationalisation. Indeed, one of the main differences between this structure and the divisional one is that similar companies are not grouped into product divisions but left to stand on their own, often to the extent that they compete with each other for business in the external market place. Thus there is a danger that the full benefits of divisionalisation are not obtained in a holding company structure. According to Channon, when competition increased as a result of the Restrictive Trade Practices legislation and the rise of international competition in the 1950s, many firms realised that this did not leave them strong to resist and they adopted the full divisional structure. Thus while the holding company structure, being decentralised, allows growth and diversification, it does not make for effective co-ordination of the full divisional form.

In a further refinement of Chandler's original analysis, Scott (1971) has developed a theory linking three different stages of organisational development to three different strategies. The three stages of development are associated with small businesses, vertically integrated businesses, and diversified businesses respectively. What is notable about Scott's formulation is that as we move from specialised Stage I organisations, through integrated Stage II organisations, to divisional Stage III organisations, so the key criteria for resource allocation move from being subjectively based to being objectively based. The measures of performance also become more objective, with personal subjective criteria in Stage I organisations giving way to abstract technical criteria in Stage II organisations and abstract profit-based criteria in Stage III organisations. In other words, as a firm moves towards the Stage III structure, so the tendency is for the firm to become more efficient in its internal allocation of resources. Following on from this is the prediction that divisionalisation will be associated with superior financial performance over time. We will return to consider this proposition in Section 3.3 of this chapter.

Under the direction of Scott, Wrigley (1970) in the US and Channon (1973) in the UK have both demonstrated that there is, indeed, a close match between the strategy of corporate diversification and the subsequent adoption of divisional management structures. Wrigley looked at the strategy and structure of the US Fortune 500. He found that all but 6 per cent of large US corporations had diversified by over 5 per cent of their sales, and that some 80 per cent had diversified by 30 per cent of sales or more. The 6 per cent that had diversified by less than 5 per cent of sales were organised along functional lines, while 91 per cent of the firms which had diversified by more than 5 per cent of sales were organised along divisional lines. Channon, who undertook a similar study based upon the top 100 UK manufacturing firms, found that the percentage of firms which were diversified by 30 per cent of sales or more rose from 25 per cent to 60 per cent between 1950 and 1970. The percentage that were diversified by more than 5 per cent of sales rose from 66 per cent to 94 per cent. During the same period usage of the divisional structure increased from 13 per cent to 72 per cent. A more recent UK study (Hill 1983) noted that in a sample of 144 firms drawn from the top 500 public quoted companies in 1982, 82.6 per cent operated with a divisional organisational form, 16 per cent with a holding company form, and only 1.4 per cent with the traditional functional structure.

The above figures largely speak for themselves. Fostered by the strategy of corporate diversification, it would seem that the divisional structure is now the dominant organisational form found amongst large enterprises. However, it would be a mistake to assume that all divisional firms operate with very similar structural arrangements. In reality there are wide variations between divisionalised firms as to the precise nature of their internal arrangements, differences which may well be reflected in variations in business and economic efficiency. Allen (1978), for example, attempted to classify the divisional structures of a sample of large

European firms. To achieve this he used three dimensions to measure basic organisational characteristics. These were the degree of divisional self-containment (including the degree to which strategic and operational decision making were separated out), the complexity of co-ordinating devices and the product scope of the divisions. In the event he found that six basic organisational types accounted for 66 per cent of the firms in his sample of divisionalised companies. He concluded that divisionalised organisations represent a more diverse family of institutional arrangements than has generally been recognised, with the general idealised view of the divisional organisation being used by less than half of the companies in his sample.

From another study (Hill 1983) comes the suggestion that it is not so much divisionalisation as decentralisation which should be the focus of those attempting to enhance efficiency and manage diversity with success. This is of particular relevance in the case of very large firms (such as those in the top 300 of the TIMES 1000). Within such firms each division is often a diverse and complex entity in its own right. Thus the engineering divisions of a large firm may contain a number of distinct operating subsidiaries, each of which may be involved in its own particular niche of the engineering industry. In such cases it is important that operating decision-taking responsibilities should be decentralised all the way down to the level of the individual operating subsidiaries within the divisions— rather than just to divisional offices. Similarly, it should be the operating subsidiaries, rather than the divisions, which are the main profit centres within the firm. Thus profit accountability should be pushed down the line to the level where the money is made. If this does not occur, and if the divisions are given too much power and are made the main profit centres, then the divisional office may encounter problems of peak co-ordination as it attempts to take operating decisions for a number of different subsidiaries, while an over-important divisional tier within the firm may blur profit accountability.

In fact, it is becoming apparent that in their initial enthusiasm for divisionalisation many firms attached too much importance to the role of divisional offices, giving them the responsibility for taking many operating decisions (typically those connected with marketing policy), and making the divisions the main profit centres. As a consequence they failed to recognise that it was at the level of individual operating subsidiaries within divisions where the money was made, and hence operating decision-taking responsibilities should be decentralised to that level. In effect, such firms were not decentralised enough. Often in such cases this began to have diverse effects upon profitability, primarily due to the blurring of profit accountability and the inefficiency inherent in taking operating decisions at a level removed from the operating facts.

In response, many of the largest firms are at present downgrading the importance of their divisions and, instead, are stressing the need to couple the decentralisation of operating decisions with centralised financial control and profit accountability. Hence within many firms the large divisional office has been replaced by a handful of personnel, or in some cases just one man (normally the divisional chief executive), whose function is to act as a communications channel, both between the head office and the operating subsidiaries, and between the different operating subsidiaries within the division.

A further development arising from the realisation that it is decentralisation (coupled with centralised financial control and profit accountability), rather than divisionalisation, which is the important factor in organisational design has been the creation of divisions within divisions. In effect, many firms are beginning to turn their original divisions into microcosms of the firm as a whole. Thus the arm's length relationship between the head office and divisional offices is being duplicated by an arm's length relationship between divisional offices and operating subsidiaries within the division. This is particularly the case amongst the most diversified of firms, for it is enabling them to manage their vast spread with some ease and, significantly for the future development of the corporate economy, further push back the limits to the growth of the firm. Typically, within such organisations a small divisional office may be given the responsibility for overseeing the strategic development of its division, a responsibility which previously resided at the head office. Thus the divisional office may initiate acquisitions within its area.

Finally, it should not be forgotten that many large firms are not only diversified, they are also international concerns. Again, when it comes to the effective management of domestic and international diversity, then adhering to the principle of coupling operational decentralisation with centralised financial control and profit accountability appears to offer the best organisational solution. Following this principle, many diversified international concerns have adopted the practice of splitting their operations up into geographical subsidiaries, and then splitting these subsidiaries down into divisions as shown for a hypothetical company in Figure 3.4. The divisions themselves may then be further split up into individual operating subsidiaries, with each division operating as a microcosm of the firm as a whole. The whole organisation may thus appear to be very complex on paper, but in practice the decentralisation of operating decisions means that intermediate levels in the organisation and the head office need only concern themselves with broad issues of financial control and strategic development. This, in turn, means that the effective management of such vast organisations is a practical proposition.

One problem with the kind of international structure depicted in Figure 3.4, however, is that generally it does not allow for the co-ordination of product strategy across international borders. When attempting to develop

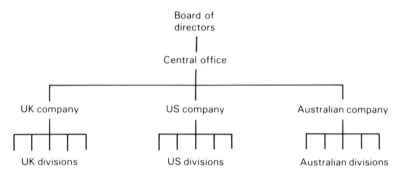

Figure 3.4   Typical Structure of an International Divisionalised Firm

a global strategy for a product several firms have experimented with a matrix structure. The concept behind this structure is the bringing together of product and geographically based elements in order that an overall global strategy for a product may be developed. Thus the matrix structure combines both product and geographic co-ordination, as shown in Figure 3.5 (see Channon 1982). A theoretical problem with this kind of structure is that each key person within the organisation has to report to two bosses—one for the region and one for the product—which can result in confusion. More generally, the development of a global strategy for a particular product requires that operating subsidiaries across the world give up some of their autonomy (and accountability) to a higher authority. It also envisages fairly complex co-ordination at an intermediate level. Hence there is a trade-off between decentralisation and the development of a global strategy. It may be for this reason that, to date, the matrix structure is more talked about in business school textbooks than used in practice.

To summarise, then, Chandler's historical analysis of US firms, supported by the work of Scott and the empirical work of Wrigley, Channon and Hill, indicates that the strategy of corporate diversification has resulted in wide-ranging organisational changes in the internal structural arrangements of the modern business corporation. The direction of causality appears to be from strategy to structure, although it is apparent that structure can aid the attainment of strategy. In the first instance, the organisational change for most firms was away from a structure based primarily upon functional departments, and towards one based upon self-contained and largely autonomous divisions. Latterly, many firms have begun to place more stress upon the concept of decentralisation in general, rather than divisionalisation in particular. This is a consequence of too much importance being attached to the role of divisions in the past, often to the detriment of the firm. As a rule, the guiding principle for successful

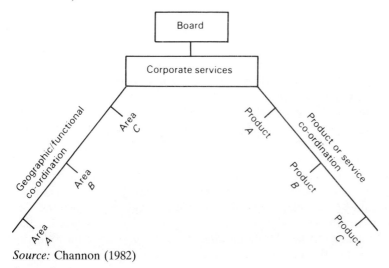

Source: Channon (1982)

Figure 3.5 The Matrix Structure

organisational design appears to be to couple the decentralisation of operating decisions to operating units with profit accountability and centralised financial control.

These structural changes have had several major implications for the development of the firm. One effect of the separation of strategic and operational decision taking within the decentralised firm has been to give top officers greater strategic control over the development of the firm. In addition, within the decentralised firm the financial contribution made by each distinct business to corporate profits is directly observable and measureable. Thus the performance of individual subsidiaries can be assessed and funds allocated by top officers in an objective arm's length manner, which aids financial control. Finally, and perhaps most significantly in the long run, the principles of decentralised organisational design have enabled large and diversified firms to overcome a major organisational limit to both the rate of growth of the firm, and its absolute size. Hence, as a result of recent organisational innovations, it is possible to envisage a society increasingly dominated by giant firms. Perhaps this is something that the appropriate public authorities might ponder upon.

3.3 Internal Organisation and Business Behaviour

In any discussion of how the internal organisational arrangements of a firm might influence business behaviour an acknowledgement must be made to the work of Oliver Williamson (1964, 1970, 1975) which is pathfinding in this respect. In his early work Williamson (1964) considered business behaviour within the traditional functionally organised or U-form firm. He noted that from the economist's point of view the U-form firm has a number of interesting characteristics. Foremost amongst these is the fact that within U-form firms the contribution of each functional department to corporate profits is neither directly observable nor measurable. As a result Williamson argued that in U-form firms resources would be allocated to different functional departments on the basis of a bargaining process between departmental heads. He also postulated that departmental heads derived considerable status from the size and importance of their department. Hence they were likely to take a partisan stand in the resource allocation bargaining process, with each departmental head attempting to maximise the funds allocated to his particular area. One consequence of this would be that each top officer would attempt to increase the size of his department beyond that strictly necessary. This envisaged a fair degree of managerial slack within each department and, in order to justify the excess staff, the creation of a number of discretionary investment projects.

Williamson placed this behavioural analysis within a market failure framework, arguing that the product and capital markets do not adequately discipline non-profit maximising firms. He also accepted the divorce of ownership and control thesis of Berle and Means (1932) and, in a style typical of the managerial discretion literature (see Baumol 1959 and Marris 1964), proposed that top officers would maximise a managerial utility function subject to the constraint that reported profits should not fall below the minimum level acceptable to shareholders. His proposed utility function had three main elements—expenditure on excess staff, some degree of managerial slack and some discretionary investment. It was argued that the maximisation of such a utility function was likely to produce an organisational presumption in favour of growth (a larger size allows a larger staff) and profit satisficing.

In later works (e.g. Williamson 1970) Williamson maintained that although growth is a major objective of the U-form firm, the U-form structure itself is a limit to diversified growth. The reasons he gave for this were those cited by Chandler (1962) and dealt with in the preceding section. Like Chandler, Williamson then noted that the most commonly adopted organisational solution has been to replace the U-form structure with a divisionalised, or what he preferred to call an 'M-form', structure. Unlike Chandler, he concentrated more upon the implications that this structural change has had for business behaviour.

The essence of his approach was in the resource allocation role of the central office. He saw it as operating as an internal capital market allocating resources between divisions on the basis of an objective analysis of actual and potential performance. It was suggested that the resource allocation decisions taken by such a unit may be more efficient than those which an external capital market would take since the central office has more, and better, information on divisional performance and prospects.

However, for this to occur certain organisational features must be present. The central office should be completely removed from operating decisions which should be decentralised to the divisions. Profits should be remitted back from the divisions to the central office for reallocation, and not left with the source divisions. The reallocation of funds between the competing claims of the different divisions should proceed according to objective and impersonal criteria such as return on investment, and the reward system within the company should be performance related.

If all of the above features are present, then within the M-form firm one finds a number of autonomous profit centres (divisions), each managed on an arm's length basis by the central office, and all having to compete with each other for resources on the basis of differential profit performance. In other words, within the M-form firm there is a mini-capital market for corporate funds. The central office itself is in a strong position to control the corporation. Utilising the elite staff, it can audit operating divisions in an objective and effective manner, it can 'reward' the most successful divisions by investing corporate funds in them, and it can use the promotion system within the firm to reward those executives who fulfil its wishes.

According to Williamson (1970, p. 134), the implications of these characteristics for business behaviour are that:

> The organisation and operation of the large enterprise along the lines of the M-form firm favours goal pursuit and least cost behaviour more nearly associated with the neoclassical profit maximisation hypothesis than does the U-form organisational alternative.

This is what has come to be known as the M-form hypothesis. It is saying that the shift from functional to divisional organisational structure amongst large diversified firms has been accompanied by a change in business behaviour. The discretionary behaviour which characterises functionally organised concerns has been superseded by least cost behaviour within divisional concerns, while the emphasis on goal pursuit has shifted away from profit-satisficing growth goals towards profit-maximising goals.

Now it can be argued that this change in business behaviour has further important implications for the economic efficiency and competitive conduct of the firm. Given that the performance of individual businesses within the divisional firm is visible, and so long as the central office reallocates funds according to objective profit-based criteria, then resource allocation decisions should be economically more efficient in M-form firms in terms of placing resources where returns are likely to be highest. This leads to the prediction that M-form firms will outperform U-form firms.

The M-form firm is also seen as being superior to the external capital market in allocating resources. This is because the central office of the firm has information advantages over the capital market and is not restricted to non-trivial displacement costs. A pertinent point here is that the central office of the M-form firm can use its internal control apparatus to intervene quickly in the operations of non-profit maximising divisions and enforce profit maximising behaviour. By way of contrast, the capital market is restricted to non-trivial displacement costs, such as takeovers or proxy battles. In addition, many studies have maintained that the capital market only imperfectly disciplines non-profit maximising firms (see, for example, Baumol 1965, Buckley 1972, Firth 1977, Kuehn 1975, and Singh 1971). Hence it is suggested that the greater the incidence of M-form firms in society, the greater the efficiency of resource allocation in society.

It is further suggested that the profit-oriented business behaviour which is characteristic of the M-form firm might influence its competitive conduct. This is of some relevance given that divisional M-form structures tended to be adopted by diversified firms. The emergence of large diversified firms in the post-war years, both in the UK and the US, has been the cause of some concern to the competition authorities. This is partly because there is always the fear that the diversified firm might subsidise one activity from the proceeds of another in order to gain a competitive advantage over smaller, single industry, firms (see Edwards 1955 and Blair 1972 for examples of such views). Williamson's work, however, denies that the cross-subsidisation of resources in order to monopolise markets is a serious possibility amongst diversified firms operating with M-form structures. The grounds for making this claim are that such an action would violate the autonomy of individual profit centres (divisions) within the firm, playing havoc with the idea that each operating division should be profit accountable. Thus the ethos of M-form firms, as determined by the structural attributes of the M-form type, is seen as being such that cross-subsidisation in pursuit of monopoly gain is unlikely to occur.

If one accepts the above arguments, then it is clear that the M-form innovation, fostered by the strategy of corporate diversification, has important implications for public policy. Williamson himself has proposed (Williamson 1975) that the authorities should adopt a permissive policy stance towards the emergence of large diversified firms on the grounds that such firms have M-form organisational structures. A hostile anti-trust attitude towards conglomerate mergers, for example, is in Williamson's view unjustified. M-form conglomerates increase the efficiency of resource allocation in society and do not behave in an anti-competitive manner due to the corporate ethos fostered by the M-form structure. To limit the emergence of such firms by restricting conglomerate mergers is, from this perspective, tantamount to restricting capitalism's creative response to the evident limits of the capital market.

Thus the theory of divisionalisation points to considerable benefits in terms of better resource allocation, greater profit orientation and a more effective planning and achievement of corporate growth, while aspects of this organisational structure are seen as attenuating anti-competitive behaviour. But we must ask whether all divisionalised firms behave in the manner implied above? Clearly they do not, and it appears from several studies that many operate according to principles which run contrary to those associated with the M-form model (see Williamson and Bhargava 1972, Steer and Cable 1978, Hill 1983). If this does occur in a firm, then as a consequence some of the benefits of the divisional structure may be either distorted or lost.

One common source of such distortion is to be found when the central office of a divisional firm involves itself in the operating affairs of individual divisions in an extensive and continuing way. This violates the arm's length philosophy which is supposed to characterise the divisional firm. It makes it possible that top officers who spend a good deal of their time involved in the operating affairs of certain divisions will develop loyalties towards those divisions. Top officers with personal loyalties might then influence resource allocation decisions in a harmful way and be unable to take strategic decisions in a non-emotive manner.

A potentially more serious distortion of M-form principles might occur if top corporate officers themselves do not have a profit orientation and, therefore, do not impose this upon operating divisions. Perhaps the major weakness in Williamson's work is that he assumed that top corporate officers in divisional firms will have a profit orientation as a matter of course—simply because the divisional structure fosters such an outlook. In reality though, it is conceivable that top officers might favour corporate goals associated with profit satisficing and the attainment of other objectives, such as the maximisation of the size of the firm or of its total market strength. In such cases resources may be allocated according to non-profit criteria. Deliberate action may be taken by the top officers to cross-subsidise resources in pursuit of market power gains or increasing the growth potential of the firm, while the adoption of other forms of anti-competitive practices within divisions may be encouraged. Such behaviour will disturb the overall pattern of performance and resource allocation in the firm, resulting in a less than optimal allocation of resources. Hence the economic efficiency benefits of the divisional structure may be lost while the firm may also use its aggregate economic power in order to pursue anti-competitive corporate goals.

Finally, if a firm is to achieve the full benefits of divisionalisation, then resources must be reallocated by the central office between the competing claims of the different divisions and not just returned to the source divisions. There must, in other words, be genuine competition for funds within the firm. If profits are left with the source divisions, then the full allocative benefits that normally ensue from the mini-capital market nature of the M-form firm are lost. It has been observed (Williamson and Bhargava 1972) that when this occurs the firm is behaving as a holding company rather than as an M-form firm.

Taking account of the above shortcomings, recent work by Hill (1983) has suggested that three broad types of internal economic system can be found within diversified firms which operate with decentralised management structures. Each of these systems is the product of top management choice and other 'political' considerations within the firm. Each has different implications for economic efficiency and competitive conduct.

The first of these is a *market internal economic system* within which there is genuine competition, based upon rates of return, for the funds distributed by the central office between the competing businesses of the firm. As such competition is profit based, it is likely to encourage least cost behaviour, economic efficiency and, due to the corporate ethos fostered by such competition, an aversion to anti-competitive conduct.

The second system is a *planned internal economic system* within which the internal competition for funds is limited by the imposition of a centrally devised corporate plan. This gives different sub-goals to different businesses within the firm and allocates resources accordingly. Thus while some businesses may receive funds on the basis of their projected rate of return, others will be given them in order to increase their growth rate or market share. In other words, funds are distributed according to the strategic goals assigned to individual businesses within the firm, and not solely according to profitability. In the absence of any genuine internal competition for funds, least cost behaviour is not enforced, economic efficiency may suffer, while the conscious use of corporate power by the head office, probably to achieve objectives stated in the plan, may result in anti-competitive conduct.

The third and final system is a *latent internal economic system* within which there is no general reallocation of funds by the head office and, hence, no basis for internal competition or planning which relies upon the pooling of corporate funds. The lack of internal competition may again have adverse implications for least cost behaviour and economic efficiency, while the lack of any mechanism for reallocating funds internally means that anti-competitive practices which involve the cross-subsidisation of resources in order to monopolise markets are unlikely to be employed.

These different systems are partly a reflection of different management styles. Thus the concept of strategic portfolio management popularised by the Boston Consulting Group (see Chapter 2) finds expression in a planned internal economic system, while 'bottom line' men are more likely to favour the idea of a market internal economic system. Firms appear to operate with latent internal economic systems either because top officers do not see the advantages of consolidating profits at the centre and then reallocating them, or because they lack the authority necessary to enforce such a policy upon reluctant and powerful divisions which argue that they should have first claim upon the profits they generate. Thus an essential difference between this approach and that of Williamson is that it takes into consideration top management choice and political considerations within the firm.

3.4   Internal Organisation and Economic Performance

It is clear from the preceding sections that different internal organisational arrangements will be associated with differences in financial performance. Thus we might expect to find firms organised into product divisional structures outperforming those organised along functional or holding company lines. Similarly, 'pure' M-form firms might be expected to outperform those, divisionalised or not, which do not have all the attributes of this organisational type. The studies which have concerned themselves with these issues can be divided into two types. There are those which are founded upon the strategy/structure theories of Chandler (1962) and Scott (1971) and seek to test for the impact of general organisational arrangements on financial performance. Secondly, there are those which focus directly upon the M-form hypothesis of Williamson (1970) and test for the impact that 'pure' M-form structures have on enterprise performance. It is important to understand here that although M-form firms are divisionalised, they also have all the special attributes described by Williamson. Thus not all divisionalised firms can be treated as being M-form. This is particularly the case for divisional firms where the top officers are over-involved in the affairs of operating divisions, or for divisional firms which do not reallocate profits. A hallmark of this second batch of studies, therefore, is that they all make the distinction between divisional firms which are M-form, and those which are not.

There have been four studies based upon the strategy/structure theories of Chandler and Scott. The first empirical study to concern itself with these issues was carried out by Rumelt (1974). He undertook a detailed analysis of the financial performance of different structural categories for a sample which amounted to 40 per cent of the United States Fortune 500 between 1950 and 1970. His three main organisational categories were the functional structure, a functional structure with subsidiaries and the product divisional structure. His results showed that product divisional companies scored higher on all the conventional measures of profitability and growth than either of the other two structural categories. Generally, his results were also statistically significant.

Channon (1978) repeated Rumelt's work for a sample of large United Kingdom companies which were active in the service industries. He recognised three main structural forms: the functional form, the holding company form and the divisional form. (The holding company form in this case was defined as being composed of a system of semi-autonomous subsidiaries, held together only as a corporate legal entity.) He found that the best rates of return were achieved by the functional companies (although these results were either not significant or significant only at the 10 per cent level), while the divisional firms exhibited statistically superior growth rates in absolute sales, assets and earnings per share. The holding company structure was clearly inferior on all counts.

Grinyer *et al.* (1980) carried out the third strategy/structure study on a sample of 48 large United Kingdom companies. This study found no evidence to support the proposition that companies with a divisional structure tend to outperform others. Indeed, it was observed that growth in both the return on investment and in net profits was significantly and negatively correlated with the degree of divisionalisation. Similarly, Hill (1983), in a study of the financial performance of 144 large United Kingdom companies, found that when significant differences in profitability between structural categories were observed, holding companies performed best of all while those organised into product divisions had the worst performance records. There were no significant differences in the growth rates of the various structural categories.

Taken together, then, the studies quoted above provide little support for the proposition that the divisional structure is a superior organisational form in terms of financial performance. Only Rumelt found evidence that divisional structures were associated with superior profitability, and only Rumelt and Channon found evidence to suggest that divisional structures were associated with superior growth rates. However, this failure to find consistently strong evidence in favour of divisional structures may be due to the lack of differentiation in the above studies between good and bad divisionalised organisational design.

The next batch of studies, which specifically tested Williamson's M-form hypothesis, do make this distinction. Only divisional firms which operate according to the principles outlined by Williamson are treated as M-form, while other divisional firms are treated as 'corrupt' M-form firms.

Five studies have attempted to test the M-form hypothesis to date. These were undertaken by Armour and Teece (1978), Steer and Cable (1978), Teece (1981), Thompson (1981) and Hill (1983). Armour and Teece (1978) linked the diffusion of the M-form structure throughout 29 firms in the United States petroleum industry between 1955 and 1973 to changes in profitability. According to their results, the adoption of pure M-form structures significantly influenced the rate of return on stockholders' equity, raising it by about 2 per cent above the 7.5 per cent level realised by the average firm. In another US study, Teece (1981) carried out a matched pairs comparison of the performance of principal firms in 15 major industries to test for the impact of the M-form innovation on profitability.

He found evidence at the 5 per cent level that the adoption of the M-form structure by principal firms increased their profitability.

Steer and Cable (1978) undertook a larger study using British data. Again they attempted to test for the effects of the M-form structure on profitability. They looked at the profitability of 82 large UK companies between 1967 and 1971. Their results indicated that an optimally organised firm could expect its rate of return to be 6–9 per cent higher than that of a non-optimally organised firm, and its profit margin 2–3 per cent higher, compared with means across the sample of 16.9 per cent and 6 per cent respectively. Thompson (1981) reworked Steer and Cable's data using share price returns as a measure of performance. The results generally substantiated Steer and Cable's finding of a large performance differential in favour of optimally organised firms. However, Thompson noted that much of the difference could be attributed to an abnormal short-term decline in the performance of the holding companies in Steer and Cable's sample. But, as he also noted, a greater susceptibility to such profit crises would appear to be consistent with the theoretical criticisms of the holding company structure as advanced by Williamson and Bhargava (1972) and Channon (1973) and, in particular, with the holding company's lack of appropriate internal control machinery.

Finally, Hill (1983) tested the M-form hypothesis using 144 large United Kingdom firms. He found that for 1978 to 1980 inclusive M-form firms had significantly higher profit margins and rates of return on capital employed than non-M-form firms. Hill, unlike the other researchers, also tested for the impact of the M-form structure on growth rates. No evidence was found, however, to indicate that M-form firms had significantly different growth rates in terms of sales growth and growth in earnings per share to non-M-form firms.

Thus it would appear that when allowances are made for poor organisational design, then divisionalised firms generally appear to be more profitable than non-divisional concerns. Clearly, then, organisational structure is important and it does influence profit. However, the mere adoption of a divisional structure is not enough. It is also necessary to develop appropriate relations between the central office and the divisions, to ensure that funds are returned from the divisions for reallocation by the centre, and to operate an effective internal market within which resource allocation decisions can be made properly.

3.5 Summary and Conclusion

In this chapter we have seen that as firms develop in terms of their strategic posture and, in particular, as they begin to diversify, their internal organisational arrangements go through a process of change, with a divisional structure replacing a functional structure. The appropriate structure, in turn, is a precondition for the attainment of strategy. Thus it is only through a decentralised (divisional) structure that a strategy of corporate diversification can be followed without encountering organisational limits to growth. Furthermore, decentralised management structures allow top officers the time to consider strategic alternatives and hence make better strategic choices.

The work of Oliver Williamson further suggests that the change from a functional to a divisional structure has been accompanied by a change in business behaviour. He sees the discretionary behaviour which characterised the functionally organised firm being replaced by least cost behaviour within the divisional firm. As the empirical work indicates, there is certainly something in this view. However, Williamson's M-form model also has its shortcomings. In particular, it ignores the critical role that top corporate officers might play in determining the principles by which resource might be allocated within the firm, as well as underestimating the impact that the countervailing power of important divisions might have on the patterns of resource allocation within the firm. It is in this area that the work of Hill on internal economic systems has something to offer.

Either way, it is clear that internal organisation has important implications not only for corporate strategy, but also for profitability and competitive behaviour. This being so, efficiency-seeking managers would be well advised to note the structural attributes consistent with the M-form idea. Similarly, the competition authorities would be well advised to consider more closely than hitherto the nature of internal organisation and resource allocation within firms which are seeking to expand by acquisition before they allow a particular bid to proceed. Thus the Monopolies and Mergers Commission might be justified in allowing a firm with a market internal economic system to make a substantial conglomerate acquisition, while forbidding a firm with a planned internal economic system from making a similar acquisition.

References

Allen, S. A. (1978) 'Organisational choices and general management influence networks in divisionalised companies', *Academy of Management Journal*, Vol. 16, pp. 341–365.

Armour, H. O. and Teece, D. J. (1978) 'Organisational structure and economic performance: a test of the multidivisional hypothesis', *Bell Journal of Economics*, Vol. 9, pp. 106–122.

Baumol, W. J. (1959) *Business Behaviour, Value and Growth*, Harcourt Brace.

Baumol, W. J. (1965) *The Stock Market and Economic Efficiency*, Fordham University Press.

Berle, A. A. and Means, S. G. (1932) *The Modern Corporation and Private Property*, Macmillan.

Blair, J. M. (1972) *Economic Concentration: Structure, Behaviour and Public Policy*, Harcourt Brace.

Buckley, A. (1972) 'A profile of industrial acquisitions in 1971', *Accounting and Business Research*, Vol. 2, pp. 243–252.

Chandler, A. D. (1962) *Strategy and Structure: Chapters in the History of the Industrial Enterprise*, MIT Press.

Channon, D. F. (1973) *The Strategy and Structure of British Enterprise*, Macmillan.

Channon, D. F. (1978) *The Service Industries: Strategy, Structure and Financial Performance*, Macmillan.

Channon, D. F. (1982) 'Industrial structure', *Long Range Planning*, 15, No. 5, p. 78.

Edwards, C. F. (1955) 'Conglomerate bigness as a source of business power in business concentration and price policy', *National Bureau of Economic Research*, Princeton University Press.

Firth, M. (1977) *The Valuation of Shares and the Efficient Market Theories*, Macmillan.

Grinyer, P. H., Yassai-Ardekani, M., Al-Bazza, S. (1980) 'Strategy, structure, the environment and financial performance in 48 United Kingdom companies', *Academy of Management Journal*, Vol. 23, pp. 193–220.

Hannah, L. (1976) *Concentration in Modern Industry*, Macmillan.

Hill, C. W. L. (1983) *Diversification: Internal Organisation, Economic Efficiency and Competitive Conduct*, Unpublished Ph.D Thesis, University of Manchester.

Kuehn, D. (1975) *Takeovers and the Theory of the Firm*, Macmillan.

Marris, R. (1964) *The Economic Theory of Managerial Capitalism*, Macmillan.

Penrose, E. T. (1959) *The Theory of the Growth of the Firm*, Macmillan.

Pickering, J. F., Hill, C. W. L. and Chaudhry, S. H. (1982) 'Concentration in British manufacturing industry into the 1970s', *Department of Management Sciences Occasional Paper*, No. 8207, UMIST.

Rumelt, R. P. (1974) *Strategy, Structure and Economic Performance*, Division of Research, Graduate School of Business Administration, Harvard University.

Scott, B. R. (1971) 'Stages of corporate development', *Harvard Business School*.

Singh, A. J. (1971) *Takeovers: Their Relevance to the Stock Market and the Theory of the Firm*, Cambridge University Press.

Steer, P. and Cable, J. (1978) 'Internal organisation and profit: an empirical analysis of large UK companies', *Journal of Industrial Economics*, Vol. 27, pp. 13–30.

Teece, D. J. (1981) 'Internal organisation and economic performance: an empirical analysis of the profitability of principal firms', *Journal of Industrial Economics*, Vol. 30, pp. 173–199.

Thompson, R. S. (1981) 'Internal organisation and profit: a note', *Journal of Industrial Economics*, Vol. 30, pp. 201–211.

Williamson, O. E. (1964) *The Economics of Discretionary Behaviour: Managerial Objectives in a Theory of the Firm*, Prentice-Hall.

Williamson, O. E. (1970) *Corporate Control and Business Behaviour*, Prentice-Hall.

Williamson, O. E. (1975) *Markets and Hierarchies: Analysis and Antitrust Implications*, Macmillan.

Williamson, O. E. and Bhargava, N. (1972) 'Assessing and classifying the internal structure and control apparatus of the modern corporation', in K. Cowling (ed), *Market Structure and Corporate Behaviour*, Gray Mills.

Wrigley, L. (1970) *Divisional Autonomy and Diversification*, Unpublished DBA Dissertation, Harvard Business School.

4

Organisational Control and Performance

B. J. Loasby

4.1 Objectives

It is impossible to appraise the performance of any individual or organisation without first deciding on the criteria to be used for that appraisal.
Those criteria should be related to the objectives of the individual or
organisation, but it is rarely immediately obvious what these are, or should
be. It is therefore necessary to begin this chapter with a discussion of
objectives—not only what but also whose objectives?

The Multiplicity of Objectives

In microeconomic theory the firm is almost always treated as a profit-maximising agent. Even in industrial economics this is the predominant model,
though students are likely to be introduced to alternative specifications of
the firm's objectives (most probably sales revenue maximisation or growth
maximisation) which, it is claimed, may generate results which differ from
those derived from profit maximisation. For the purposes of this chapter,
differences between such models are of secondary importance; their
similarities are far more striking.

The so-called 'managerial theories' of Baumol (1959) and Marris (1964)
are formally structured as constrained maximisation models of monopoly,
in which profit has been demoted from objective to constraint. Williamson
(1964) retains profit as an argument in an expanded objective function.
Although presented as theories of oligopolistic firms, there is no serious
attempt to cope with any of the standard problems of oligopolistic
interdependence. In all the models, both the objective function and the
choice set are assumed to be well specified; if there is any uncertainty, it

can be represented by a probability distribution and the objective modified to the maximisation of an expected value. In no model is any consideration given to the interior of the firm, except as a superficial justification for the choice of objective function, which is then treated as a group preference function; there is no consideration of either the structure of decisions within an organisation or the implications of multiple decision makers. These three issues—uncertainty, the structure of decisions, and the multiplicity of decision makers—provide the interconnected themes of this chapter.

Let us begin with the consequences of uncertainty and complexity. A firm of any size is a complex system, embedded in the larger complex system which we may call its environment. The environment is not too well understood; nor, in most organisinisations, is the internal system. Now as Simon (1964) has observed, in any complex system (even if it is perfectly understood) maximisation of the value of any decision variable must be subject to an extensive constraint set; it may therefore make very little difference if one of these constraints is exchanged for the maximand. (In standard models of competitive equilibrium, profit may be treated indifferently as objective or constraint.) Thus 'the choice of one of the constraints, from many, is to a large extent arbitrary. For many purposes it is more meaningful to refer to the whole set of requirements as the (complex) goal of the action' (Simon 1964, p. 7).

Simon accordingly suggests that the goal of an organisation should be defined (at least by organisational theorists) as the set of constraints which the organisation faces. This proposal has the advantage of generating a specification of the organisational goal which helps to define a set of organisational roles, for in any organisation a great deal of managerial activity has to be devoted to what, from a conventional economic perspective, appears as the management of constraints—most obviously costs and demand, but also such matters as conformity with both law and custom. Indeed, Pfeffer and Salancik (1978) have analysed the problem of management in terms of the organisation's continuing dependency on outside resources, and the various strategies and expedients which may be used to maintain the necessary flow of these resources in order to create, if possible, a usable choice space.

Ansoff (1965) advanced a different, but compatible, reason for the use of multiple goals—even for strategic decisions, and even if such decisions were to be taken by a single individual. After arguing in favour of profitability as the primary objective (pp. 39–42), he then insists on the need for a fairly elaborate system of objectives as a means to this apparently simple end. Long-run profit maximisation, though convenient (and often justifiable) as an analytical expedient for economists, is for managers a non-operational objective. The reason, in formal terms, is that although we may be able to list the arguments in the profit function, we do not know how to specify the functional form; therefore the best we can do is to use the arguments themselves as objectives.

> Exclusive concern with proximate profitability would be almost certain to leave the firm run down at the end of the period. Total emphasis would be on current products and markets . . . But to remain profitable into the long term, the firm must continue to renew itself . . . Therefore . . . commitments must be made to such long-term needs as research and development, management training, and new plant and equipment.
>   . . . It is essential, therefore, to establish long-term objectives aimed at maintaining and increasing profitability after the proximate period. The obstacle to setting these is that accurate ROI (return on investment) forecasts and measurements cannot be made for the long-term period.
>   A way around this obstacle is to abandon efforts to measure long-term profitability directly and to measure, instead, characteristics of the firm which contribute to it. (pp. 49–50)

He then suggests a structure of long-term objectives which is reproduced as Figure 4.1.

There are yet other influences on future profitability which (as G. L. S. Shackle has often reminded us) we may not even be able to list—unknown arguments in the function.

> The probable trends can be upset by unforeseeable events which may have relatively low probability of occurrence, but whose impact . . . on the firm as a whole would be major. The impact may be negative, with catastrophic consequences, or positive . . . opening wide vistas to the firm . . . A firm can effectively buy insurance against catastrophes and put itself in the way of potential discoveries . . . by adding a *flexibility objective*. (pp. 54–55)

Insurance premia or options on future prospects must be paid out of current income; flexibility is at the expense of present profits. It is no doubt still true that the way to maximise profitability is to specialise, but only if one is clever or lucky enough to specialise on the right things—many highly specialised firms have ceased to exist in the present recession. If flexibility is to be sought, then it is essential to provide some decision criteria which are quite distinct from those which might be regarded as more or less obvious contributors to profitability, either in the short or the long run. Thus Ansoff's discussion (pp. 55–59) leads to a set of objectives (reproduced here) which is designed actively to encourage, for example, research in areas outside the current business and a dispersion of sales effort over diverse markets.

The hierarchical structure of objectives suggested by Ansoff is a conventional device for organising ideas; it is not intended to denote a pattern of priorities. Ansoff's argument from partial ignorance leads to a similar conclusion to that of Simon: a single set of objectives/constraints of equal hierarchical status. This is not to deny that at any particular time some will require much more attention than others, or even that at times some may quite properly be disregarded; but any general judgement that, for

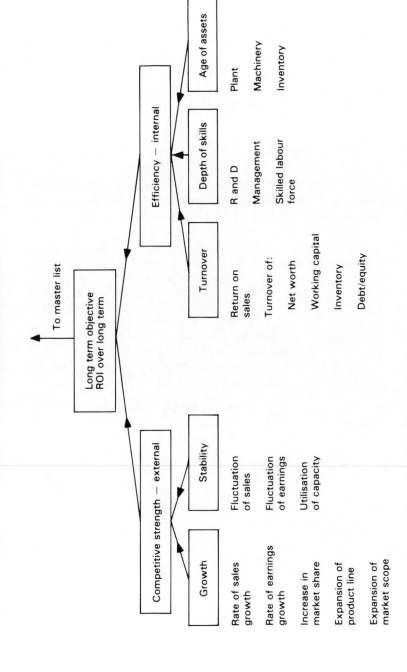

Source: Reproduced from Ansoff (1965)

Figure 4.1 Hierarchy of the Long-Term Objective

example, increasing market share is always more important than research into new areas—or *vice versa*— cannot be justified.

It is because there is no unequivocal hierarchy of objectives that the distinction between profit, sales revenue, growth, or any other prime objective is of secondary importance in this chapter. All will be included in the general set, and the differences will then appear as a matter of emphasis in decision taking, and in the relative attention paid to different aspects of performance. Such differences may be far from negligible, but they are not of primary concern in the present context.

Partial and Conflicting Objectives

Except for a major strategic review, it is impossible to expect any complete set of objectives to be consciously applied to decisions. Only a subset, and usually a very small subset, can be handled at a time, and the chosen subset will vary according to the way in which the decision is perceived—and by whom it is perceived. In an organisation of any size, the objectives will be distributed among the management. This distribution may be highly

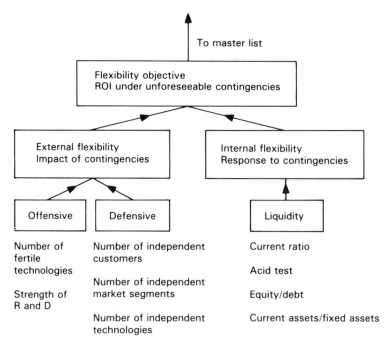

Source: Reproduced from Ansoff (1965)

Figure 4.2   Hierarchy of the Flexibility Objective

formal, very casual, or anywhere between, and it is not unusual for there to be substantial contrast between the precision with which areas of responsibility are defined and the definition of performance criteria. (In such instances it is usually the task which is clearly defined, perhaps with no mention of any objective or way of measuring success; but the opposite may also happen.)

Given the complexities of the organisation and its environment, it is inconceivable that the set of objectives—most of which are probably not well defined—could be neatly partitioned among the managers. In a complex interdependent system, the full set of constraints is always formally relevant; anyone trying to resolve what appear to be partial problems by the use of an incomplete set is always liable to error. That is why partial equilibrium analysis is formally inferior to general equilibrium analysis, and why piecemeal attempts to improve welfare may make matters worse. This is not, however, sufficient reason for eschewing partial equilibrium analysis, piecemeal welfare improvements, or the delegation of responsibility in organisations.

Any set of constraints or objectives describes a potential conflict. In much formal economic analysis this potential conflict is smoothly resolved by the application of choice theory. The conflict between buying a television set and taking a package holiday is resolved by applying a preference function to a budget constraint; the conflict between alternative input combinations is resolved by the application of relative prices to a production function; the conflict between alternative investment projects is resolved by a comparison of their net present values. Interpersonal conflicts too are resolved with no apparent difficulty in elementary market models. Indeed, we may not even notice that the familiar Edgeworth contract curve is more accurately described as a conflict curve, since the conflict over the terms of exchange is assumed to be resolved by perfect (i.e. impersonal) competition.

However, sooner or later in economics we come across situations in which the conflict is not neatly resolved—most obviously, perhaps, in oligopoly theory (where it is hard to find a generally plausible set of assumptions which will produce a conflict-resolving general equilibrium) or in applied welfare theory (where we may find it difficult to ensure that there are no uncompensated losers, even from changes which seem to be obviously beneficial). Both kinds of situations are fairly common inside organisations. Furthermore, standard choice procedures cannot be unambiguously applied, even in otherwise standard situations, if there is uncertainty about the specification of the objective function or the choice set —and that, we have just argued, is the usual situation within organisations.

To illustrate the problem areas we may consider briefly three kinds of conflict within organisations. First is the conflict between different aspects of performance in a limited sphere, as contained in such (actual) examples of statements of objectives as 'maximum output at minimum cost', 'quality at the cheapest price', 'increased productivity, but not at the expense of safety or customers' requirements', or 'to provide information in time at reasonable cost'. (This last statement was produced by an accounting department, but would serve almost as well for a research department.) If we know neither the trade-off between these objectives which is implied by the decision alternatives nor the value to be attached to the objectives, there is no guaranteed optimisation procedure.

Second (as Ansoff (1965) emphasises), there may be conflict between shorter- and longer-term objectives. Research effort may be devoted to the urgent improvement of a company's cash flow through reductions in current operating costs at the expense of future profits from new products, or expensive development work on new products may jeopardise present liquidity. Training for the future uses resources for no immediate benefit; indeed, if a particular department or a particular managerial position is used to train people for jobs elsewhere, then the immediate effect is likely to be reduced efficiency. For example, a trouble-shooting technical department may prove very effective for the induction of newly-recruited graduates, but they are not likely to be the most efficient trouble-shooters. More subtly, if a particular job, such as the managership of a specific branch or research establishment, is seen to be used as a staging-post for people on their way to senior positions, there is no great incentive for subordinates to accommodate themselves to the plans and incentives of the present temporary incumbent; nor need the incumbent concern himself with the consequences of his actions, which will not emerge until he is comfortably ensconced elsewhere and will then be difficult to attribute to him.

The third type of conflict is that between the objectives which are appropriate to various major activities, often represented by different departments. Efficient production management and cost control are facilitated by long runs of standard products, whereas in many markets sales revenue can be increased by tailoring products to the varying requirements of individual customers, and perhaps by producing special orders at short notice. Though research departments may share the salesmen's enthusiasm for new products—and both pay little heed to the production problems necessarily created by their introduction—they may be far from agreement on either the kind of new product or the time-scale for its introduction.

A major subclass of this type of conflict is that between line and service departments, particularly over the introduction of new services. Commonly, the line department knows best what its problems are, the service department what its potential is. Moreover, for reasons which will be considered later, the service department is often concerned to promote its role as the custodian of new techniques or of specialist information which its members believe will not be adequately or effectively used if the initiative remains with the line management. Accordingly, we may often observe a displacement of objectives from the provision of service to the attraction of custom, or even to the acquisition of control over some line functions.

This last type of conflict is normally associated with questions of power and status; indeed, personal factors can rarely be excluded from any comprehensive view of the problems of decision and control in organisations. However, it is important to recognise that these problems would not disappear even if all employees in an organisation were devoted to the success of that organisation, and even if they all agreed on a single overall measure of that success, whether it be profitability, growth, or whatever. The absence of any unique way of converting that overall measure into criteria for particular decisions based on uncertain information, and the necessity of allocating sub-objectives to those entrusted with the management of parts of the business, ensure that even if all personal preferences were to be transmuted into a single organisational objective, intraorganisational conflict would still be pervasive. Moreover, such conflict could not be resolved by any optimisation rule, but would need to be continuously managed.

Individual Objectives in Organisations

To these problems, individual preferences add further complications. In so far as conventional economics considers the relationship between individual preferences and organisational behaviour, it does so in terms of the supply price of inputs, implicitly assuming that the contract of employment requires employees to accept the authority (and therefore the objectives) of their superiors all the way up the hierarchy. This assumption is facilitated by two standard features of conventional theory. The first is that contracts are fully specified—with whatever contingent clauses are appropriate—so that the employee, at any level, has no discretion as an employee. The second feature helps to explain such a surrender of discretion: it is the conventional division of economic agents into households and firms.

Households are the spending units, firms the producing units; thus the supply of inputs from households to firms has significance for the supplier only as a source of income. The standard separation of production and consumption decisions, and the equivalent separation of investment and financing decisions—even in textbooks which are building up models of general equilibrium—reinforces this view. Production and investment are governed by the objective of maximising income; consumption and finance by the objective of maximising utility; the two sets of decisions can legitimately be treated separately provided that whatever maximises income makes possible the maximisation of utility. With conventional assumptions about preferences, this will be true provided that all objects of preference can be obtained in a perfect market.

Where markets are not perfect, utility maximisation may require production and consumption decisions to be made jointly; and it is characteristic of organisation membership that it provides some sources of utility at lower opportunity costs than is implied by pure market transactions. (They may, indeed, be joint products with cash income.) The general practice of defining preferences over commodities has helped economists to ignore this rather obvious fact; but as soon as one begins to think of goods and services as instruments of satisfaction rather than direct objects of preference, in the way that Lancaster (1966) and Marshall (1920) have done, the point becomes clear. A particular job may then offer one way, among others, of satisfying a desire for companionship, for the exercise of technical or professional skill, for recognition of achievement and for challenges which can be successfully (but perhaps not too easily) met.

Underlying motivations fall within the province of psychologists and will not be discussed here; but it is not difficult to suggest ways in which such motivations may affect behaviour in organisational roles. The wish to be accepted as a member of a group encourages acceptance of group norms which may be of very diverse kinds and standards; the desire to make full use of one's skills and to obtain recognition adds strength and, perhaps, bitterness to many intra-organisational conflicts of the kinds noted earlier. Practitioners of new techniques may be arrogant; practitioners of old techniques may be scornful and dismissive; and the line manager whom both are meant to serve may feel it inconsistent with his self-image to make use of any methods which he does not fully understand.

It is true that the concept of 'equal net advantages' is used within wage theory to allow for substitution between money income and satisfactions (or dissatisfactions) associated with particular jobs; however, this elaboration of theory is contained within the tradition of fully-specified contracts, and is not assumed to give rise to post-contract bargaining or to allow for post-contract discretion. The amount of prestige allotted to the Corporate Planning Manager, for example, is presumed to be specified at the time of his appointment (and presumably at the time of the appointment of anyone else, such as the Head of Management Services, Research Director, New Ventures Manager, or Finance Director, who might be rivals for some share of that prestige) and is not a matter of subsequent dispute. If there were no more uncertainty than could be accommodated in agreed probability distributions, and if the set of organisational objectives could be perfectly partitioned, then the effects of personal preferences might indeed be confined to the conditions of membership of an organisation; but as it is, the contracts cannot be perfectly specified, and formal structures and formal agreements are not sufficient to determine behaviour. Personal objectives influence organisational performance.

Recognition of the possible significance of personal preferences lies behind the introduction of 'managerial' theories of the firm, but, with the exception of the work of Simon (1964) and of Cyert and March (1963), such preferences have only been allowed to affect overall policy, and then only through consensus. It is not clear, however, that all the influential decision makers in the kind of firm modelled by Marris (1964) believe growth maximisation would conform to their own personal interest; and there is plenty of evidence that managers who wish their organisations to grow do not always agree on the direction or means of growth. Marris's analysis stops short of such organisational problems. So indeed does Williamson's (1964) more elaborate specification of a managerial utility function; but this specification has the unusual property of making the level of costs a choice variable. Firms pursuing growth maximisation or sales revenue maximisation incur costs beyond those incurred by a profit maximiser; but their costs are the lowest compatible with their sales and growth objectives. Williamson's firms, however, incur costs which are not necessary for sales or growth, but which contribute directly to the satisfactions of the decision makers. Moreover, these additional costs are not specified in the terms of their contracts; instead, they are created through the exercise of the discretion which those contracts (and a 'benign' environment) allow them.

Unnecessary costs are the focus of Leibenstein's (1976) analysis of X-inefficiency. His assumption is that all members of an organisation will try to use whatever discretion they possess to their own advantage. He gives most attention to the effects of discretion in the effort–payment bargain, claiming that people will tend to do as little work as the terms of their contract, the checks on their performance, their conscience and their willingness to take the risk of being fired will permit. It is, of course, critical to Leibenstein's argument that such organisational slack forms no part of the supply price of labour—that in a more constrained environment the same people would do more work for no more money or, indeed, any other kind of cost to the organisation. On these assumptions the identification and eradication of X-inefficiency becomes a plausible managerial task— though, since it is likely to require, at least for a time, more work by the managers (who will have to sacrifice some of their own organisational slack), they may not be keen to undertake it.

The most effective remedy for X-inefficiency, as for allocative inefficiency, appears to be competition. Indeed, the reaction of many organisations to hard times, which have tightened the constraints on both worker and managerial choice, has revealed the existence of substantial X-inefficiency at many levels in the organisation. This even seems to be true of universities.

4.2   Control of Performance

Problems of Control

Considered as a guide to organisational control, conventional micro-economic analysis is revealing, but not very helpful. The celebrated proposition that every Pareto optimum is a perfectly competitive equilibrium appears to demonstrate that in specific circumstances complete independence for every decision maker can produce ideal results for the total system. However, these specific circumstances actually allow no discretion whatever for any decision maker. Indeed, it is precisely because there is no room for discretion that we can be certain that the system will produce its ideal results. It is no accident that the perfectly competitive model can readily be turned into a perfect model of central planning.

As soon as anyone's actions are not completely determined by their situation we can no longer be certain that the performance of the system will be optimal. The standard reaction of conventional economists to suggestions of any such 'market failure' (or any other kind of market failure) is to frustrate independence by the imposition of the strictest rules in order to ensure the required outcomes. Neither monopolists nor the managers of public enterprises should be allowed any discretion whatever. The guiding principle is that every decision maker in the system should be constrained, by rules if it cannot be by circumstance, to take precisely those actions which would have been taken by the owner of the invisible hand, or the welfare-maximising central planner, if this benign despot had the knowledge and capacity to take them all. Transposed to the problem of delegation within a single organisation, this principle requires every subordinate to act as the managing director's proxy; it therefore implies a very precise set of rules. This is indeed the spirit in which economists using this approach have considered the problems of the nationalised industries.

From the earlier discussion it will be seen that there are two major sources of difficulty in devising and applying such rules. The first is the problem of the decomposability of decisions, which normally appears in welfare economics as the problem of the second best; the marginal cost pricing rule, for example, applied to one enterprise does not necessarily move the system towards Pareto efficiency if the same rule is not simultaneously applied in all other enterprises. Within a single organisation, the requirement for simultaneous optimisation is compounded by the need to specify decision rules in different forms for various activities; and it is rarely possible to organise these activities so as to avoid the kind of interdependencies which are such a threat to optimal decision making. What instructions can be given to a transport manager, the head of a research laboratory, or an industrial relations officer, which, if followed exactly, can be guaranteed to produce ideal decisions for the organisation which employs them all?

The problem of specifying the objective function is well recognised among welfare economists, but much less attention is paid to the problem of identifying the choice set. Any decision maker can only choose between those options of which he or she is aware, and according to his or her estimation of the likely consequences of each. What is of immediate relevance to the present theme is that any assessment of the decision maker's conformity to the prescribed rules must rest on the assessor's impression of the options, and these are by no means necessarily identifiable in the control data. Costs, to an economist, are defined in terms of opportunities forgone; so the marginal costs which are to be equated with price in the usual welfare economist's rule are not outlays, but the revenues which would have been generated by the best of the rejected options—revenues which, by definition, will never be recorded in the organisation's accounts. Unless those forgone revenues should turn out to be equal to the recorded costs, recorded profits are not equal to economic profits.

Now it is an inherent characteristic of full competitive equilibrium that the costs thrown up by the system do, indeed, measure the value placed on the most attractive of the forgone opportunities; in fact, this is an alternative way of demonstrating the optimality of such an equilibrium. Outside that equilibrium though, there is no reason to expect such a correspondence. It is a basic theorem of welfare economics that market imperfections produce discrepancies: in imperfect product markets (but perfect factor markets) inputs are valued at their marginal revenue product, not at the value of the marginal product itself. But more pervasive than the effects of market imperfections are probably those of partial ignorance. How are we to know what options were available to the decision maker? The options which have been rejected generate no revenues (or costs in the accounting sense, for that matter) to be observed.

In practice, there is no means whatever of deducing from the accounts of any organisation not totally constrained into competitive equilibrium whether it has been maximising its opportunities, however defined; the costs of the opportunities not taken are not the costs which appear in the accounts. Only if the supervisory agent or agency is as well informed and as perceptive as the decision maker is it possible for the performance of the latter to be accurately monitored; and that means that in such circumstances the only way to be sure that the decision maker is doing what we want is to duplicate his activities. It is the impossibility of control without duplication or detailed interference which accounts for much of the awkwardness of the relationships between many nationalised industries and their overseeing departments. Any economist who advocates pricing or investment rules for nationalised industries which are based on opportunity cost is implicitly, if unconsciously, calling for just such interference.

Control and Discretion

Similar problems arise within organisations wherever the person being monitored has better information about his situation than those doing the monitoring—and it is usually because he is expected to have better information that he is given the power to make decisions. Moreover, it is often the case that the person being monitored has some control over the information which is used for that purpose. As one might expect from the perfectly competitive model, monitoring is usually much easier if there are comparable organisations about which information is available. If other organisations, or departments within organisations, are seen to be taking attractive opportunities which are not being taken within the organisation under study, then there is a *prima facie* argument for believing that the decision makers have not been taking good decisions according to the objectives prescribed, or (what might be thought worse) that they have failed to recognise their opportunities. Of course, the *prima facie* case may later be rebutted—perhaps the objectives were different; the apparently attractive opportunity may turn out to be far from attractive after all; because of differences in skills, resources or market connections the opportunity may be much better suited to the rival—but at least the performance of competitors provides something to go on.

Within organisations, assessment of performance is likely to be most difficult for those activities which have no direct connection with revenue; such activities are likely nowadays to employ a large proportion of the staff, and they figure prominently in Ansoff's lists of objectives. For many of these activities no convincing optimisation procedures are available. There may be such guidelines as the average ratio of advertising or research expenditure to sales for particular industries, but in general the level of costs has to be chosen by someone. These are the areas in which uncertainty, the dispersion of objectives between managers and the possibilities of conflating personal with organisational objectives combine to leave a good deal of doubt about the level of costs which should be accepted, and sometimes no very clear idea, at least until much later, of what has been achieved by the acceptance of those costs.

One response to these difficulties is to recognise that managers are bound to retain some discretion, and to attempt to provide a framework within which they will be likely to use that discretion in ways which benefit the organisation. This means defining responsibilities and objectives so that their effective discharge is the most attractive means by which the manager can satisfy such personal preferences as the exercise of talents in effective performance. The freedom to make choices other than in accordance with specific rules may indeed be used as an inducement to join the organisation; and this inducement may prove particularly attractive to the more effective managers.

Such a strategy has been advocated by members of the 'human relations' school of management theorists, among whom McGregor (1960) was particularly influential, and formalised into the once-fashionable doctrine of 'management by objectives'. This doctrine required managers at each level to discuss with their subordinates the specific objectives which the latter should seek to achieve during the next planning period, to reach agreement on the ways in which the degree of success in reaching them should be measured, and at the end of the planning period (and possibly at more frequent intervals) to assess performance and set new objectives in the light of the experience gained. For McGregor and those who thought like him the procedure was intended to bring subordinates fully into the decision-making process; and agreement on objectives was expected to entail agreement on the kind of assistance to be given by each superior to his subordinates. However, it is not difficult to see that a programme labelled 'management by objectives' might be construed in a very different way, as McGregor (1960, p. 61) himself warned. At a conference designed to promote this system in the days of early British enthusiasm, one of its strongest advocates explained how effective it could be in inducing subordinates to accept full responsibility for meeting targets imposed on them by their superiors.

Its effect on organisational cohesion is also uncertain: open discussion of objectives (as distinct from activities) at all levels could result in greater congruence between them; but it could also reveal wide disparities of view about the purposes of some of these activities and seriously disturb the organisational coalition.

For these reasons, and because too much is expected of every new aid to management—for example, operational research, discounted cash flow analysis, or long-range planning—any mention of management by objectives nowadays is unlikely to evoke much support. Yet the ideas behind it, modestly applied in the right organisational environment, can be used to help managers to work together, to gain satisfaction through achieving their own targets, and to learn through a process of organised trial and error which has some of the attributes of good scientific procedure. We shall return to this theme at the end of the chapter.

Management Control Systems

A detailed consideration of the problems involved in the design and operation of a control system which would provide managers with adequate information and incentives to contribute effectively to overall system performance requires more knowledge of organisational behaviour and of accounting principles and practice than can be presumed here. Some insight into the issues may, however, be provided.

Economists may readily conceive of any activity within a firm, whether it be production, maintenance, selling, the construction of a forecasting model or the negotiation of a wages agreement, as a process in which inputs are converted into outputs according to some appropriately specified production function. A formal management control system identifies as 'responsibility centres' a set of activities which can—at least in part—be measured, and of which each is deemed to be within the control of a particular manager. Measurement and control are critical, but both are matters of degree.

Because the overall measures of company performance are primarily financial, and because the principal information gathering and processing facility in almost all firms of any size is the accounting system, control measurement is normally in financial terms. There are exceptions, some of them important—for example, process yield in a chemical plant, output per manshift in a colliery, hours between breakdown for a machine or vehicle—but when inputs or outputs are heterogeneous, money imposes a convenient homogeneity. That such conversions into scalar quantities may be misleading if the prices are not 'right' is a reservation that may occur to most readers; and it is often easier to assign values which are at least plausible to inputs rather than to outputs. That is one major reason why the most common type of responsibility centre—the cost, or expense, centre—is confined to inputs. The second major reason is that it is considered either impossible or undesirable to give the managers of such centres responsibility for outputs.

It is an elementary principle of management control systems that managers should be held responsible only for those elements of performance that they can control, but the application of that principle (as of many other principles of management) is not easy. It may not be difficult to identify some factors which are exogenously determined, such as all prices for a perfectly competitive firm; but where a manager does have discretion, that discretion is subject to many constraints which are external to his authority—though, for a junior manager, the great majority may be determined within the organisation.

'Influence' may be more accurate than 'control' as a characterisation of most managers' power to affect results. A production manager, for example, whose department is designated a cost centre, may find that wage rates are fixed by national negotiation and manning levels by a deal between the unions and the company personnel department. The time taken to complete a production run will be affected by the quality of the machinery at his disposal and the speed with which the maintenance department copes with breakdowns; and his success in organising the flow of production (and therefore his average unit cost) will be conditioned by the flow of orders into the department and their composition. The proportion of any recorded variation in costs (favourable or unfavourable) for which he should properly be held responsible is not beyond dispute. In particular, some variations may be partially attributable to other responsibility centres, such as (in this instance) the personnel or maintenance departments. The maintenance department, for instance, can cut its costs by reducing staffing to a level at which no one in that department is idle and at which defective machinery has to wait for attention.

The use of responsibility centres does not eliminate interdependencies and conflict, but it does help to clarify the issues—for example, whether on balance the organisation is likely to perform better if the production manager is made formally responsible for maintenance costs or for negotiating manning levels with the department shop stewards. One consequence of increased awareness of energy costs in recent years has been the redesignation in some companies of such costs, which were previously allocated overheads, as controllable costs of production. This has often entailed the installation of extra meters to provide control data hitherto thought unnecessary. Any control system creates costs and needs to be justified by the expectation of benefits.

The use of responsibility centres is a question of organisational design: what problems are to be tackled where, and on the basis of what information? Where it is thought both feasible and desirable to draw attention to output, responsibility for inputs and outputs may be combined in the creation of a profit centre. This comes close to creating a surrogate firm within the organisation, with its attendant advantages and disadvantages. The advantages, in terms of objectives, information and incentives, should be clear. The prime disadvantage is the danger that a profit centre may prosper through activities which damage the rest of the organisation. It is, however, possible that skilful manipulation of the costs and revenues which are attributed to a profit centre may achieve a satisfactory alignment of private and social costs and benefits—the latter being defined in terms of the parent organisation. The literature on transfer prices—the prices at which one profit centre sells to another within a single organisation—illustrates the problems in securing such alignment and the ways in which they may be tackled.

The creation of a surrogate firm is brought even closer if the profits attributed to a particular activity are related to the capital deemed to be employed in that activity, thus establishing an investment centre in which the summary measure of performance is not the amount of profit, but the rate of return. This process culminates in the M-form firm in which product divisions become investment centres; not only are these divisions surrogate firms, but the parent organisation in effect operates a surrogate capital market (Williamson 1975). Such organisations are likely to make extensive use of the performance measures discussed below.

4.3   Assessment of Performance

For any complex organisation there are many relevant objectives which may be used as a basis for assessing performance, either of the organisation as a whole or of particular departments or sections. In order to make any appraisal it is necessary to decide: first, what is to be measured; second, how it is to be measured; and third, against what standards performance is to be judged. It is probably true in most organisations that the question 'how' has a great influence on determining 'what': the great majority of measurements derive from accounting data, even though an increasing proportion of them may now be processed by some kind of management services department. It is a principle well recognised by writers on management control systems that action will be directed towards those results which are monitored, and especially those which can be measured with the greatest apparent precision. Consequently, it is by no means impossible that a management control system may have a perverse effect on performance. It is, indeed, to avoid such perverse effects that Ansoff insisted on enlarging his proposed system of objectives to include some which are in danger of neglect.

Budgets

No assessment is possible without reference to some standard, explicit or implicit. It should be clear from the earlier discussion that even if the formal objective of a firm is something as apparently simple as the maximisation of shareholders' wealth, the optimisation of any one of the many relevant objectives within the organisation is in general not to be desired; even if it were, it is not clear how one might decide whether it had been achieved. It is thus necessary to define some bench mark. The standard is usually derived from one of three sources: past experience, other organisations or plans. Plans are usually based on past experience, or on what other organisations are believed to have achieved (possibly with some allowance for subsequent progress); but they may be constructed, especially for new products, new processes, or other new activities, from estimates which are derived from engineering designs, laboratory experiments, statistical analyses or mathematical models (Loasby 1976, Chapter 6).

In principle, plans might seem to provide the most appropriate standards, since they allow for the incorporation of all relevant information which is provided by the other sources and anything else which is judged pertinent. In practice, they often seem to be the least regarded of the three. The probable reason is that the recorded results of one's own or of some other organisation appear to be severely factual, whereas a plan must necessarily be based on a set of assumptions or forecasts which are unlikely to prove entirely accurate. If the assumptions and forecasts are clearly stated, and the implications of error set down, then there should not be great difficulty in amending the plans to form a fair basis of comparison in the conditions which have actually been experienced. But organisations have generally been very reluctant to carry through whatever allowance they make for error and uncertainty during the planning process into the budgets with which outcomes are to be compared, preferring to make *ad hoc* allowances when the results are known. Shell's multiple scenarios are designed to help in the planning process; they do not seem to be used in the appraisal of outcomes (Jefferson 1983).

A possible cause and also a possible consequence of this preference for point-estimate budgets is the role which budgeting plays in the competition to modify the terms of the imperfectly specified contract of employment—or, in other language, in the attempt to expand one's own area of discretion and reduce those of other people. If budgets are seen (in the way that some managers saw management by objectives) as a means of constraining the behaviour of subordinates, then subordinates may be expected to attempt to loosen those constraints. Even with all the modern techniques of analysis, it is often impossible (for reasons outlined earlier) to establish more than a confidence interval for either the costs or the results of a subordinate's production function. Subordinates may be expected to use such uncertainties to enlarge their own scope for discretion. In many instances, especially towards the higher levels of the organisation, they will have substantial control over the information on which their budgets are based and on the information which is used to measure their performance. The difficulty of measuring such X-inefficiency or organisational slack both makes it easier to acquire and reduces the applicability of formal analysis of the phenomenon.

The use of budgets as instruments of control sits very uneasily with the use of the budgeting process as an instrument of learning. It may be argued that the process of constructing a set of budgets for an organisation is more valuable than the set of budgets which results from that process. To be effective the budgeting process requires a thorough exploration of alternative courses of action and careful working out of interdependencies between different aspects of the business—to take an obvious example, the cash flow implications of an attempt to build up sales. It is an instrument of learning. But little learning (at least of this kind) will take place if the participants are primarily concerned to protect their own future position.

The budget, once completed, can be an instrument of discovery too. Just as the competitive behaviour of the firm may be characterised as 'the testing of plans in the market' (Kirzner 1973, p. 10), so may a manager's actions be characterised as the testing of plans within his own particular sphere. Both are discovery processes. They are also control processes in the sense that the continued use of any hypothesis is controlled by the requirement that it be subjected to test and corroborated by the results of testing. But these processes are not likely to be very effective if the manager does not regard the plans as his own; and if failure to perform up to budget is to be judged as a managerial failure, then he will, quite rationally, try to avoid any risk of failure. If he succeeds, there will be no test, no control and no discovery.

Accounting Ratios: Return on Investment

Since performance is usually conceived as some kind of relationship between output and input or benefit and cost, it is not surprising to find that the most frequently used techniques for deriving performance measures from accounting data make use of ratios. Three kinds of ratios will be considered here, intended respectively to assess return on investment, financial status and operating success. The accounting categories employed are discussed in the chapter on financial management.

From the shareholders' point of view, the ratio of most immediate interest is the rate of profit (after tax) on shareholders' funds, which comprise capital raised by share issue and retained earnings. Since retained earnings represent past profit attributable to shareholders which has been reinvested in the business instead of being employed elsewhere, it is reasonable to assume that they have the same opportunity cost as subscribed capital and, therefore, require the same return to justify their continued employment. The rate of return on subscribed capital alone, or earnings per share, is not a reliable guide to management success in the use of the funds entrusted to them by the shareholders (though obviously relevant to the determination of current share prices). If, however, one wishes to appraise the efficiency with which an organisation has used the total resources under its control, then the appropriate measure is the total pre-tax surplus, before the deduction of interest payments on long-term loans, expressed as a ratio of the total of shareholders' funds and long-term capital. How this surplus is distributed between government, shareholders, and the holders of long-term debt, though significant for other purposes, is not relevant for this appraisal.

There are two possible limitations of this measure of return on capital employed, quite apart from the many practical difficulties which will be noted later. The first is that the 'capital employed' in the balance sheet is only equivalent to the net assets which are owned by the organisation and excludes any assets which are leased. These may be a significant fraction of the whole in some industries: at one time most of the machinery used in shoe manufacture was leased, and civil engineering contractors make much use of hired plant today. Custody, rather than ownership, is the proper economic criterion for determining what capital is currently 'employed' by an organisation.

More fundamental is the objection that many of the assets of the organisation are totally excluded—the assets represented by the skills of the people employed, the organisational forms, procedures, routines and understandings, many of which cannot be at all well expressed in blueprints, documents, or even computer programs—but all of which help to justify the existence of the organisation as a structured group of people, rather than a cluster of pure market relationships (Nelson and Winter 1982, Chapter 5). Organisations which are especially dependent on human skill, experience and interaction tend, if successful, to show very high rates of return on net assets, as these are defined by accounting convention. The objection to including human assets in the balance sheet, apart from the problems of valuing human capital, is that they can be withdrawn at any time and thus cannot, unlike conventional assets, be regarded as in the custody of the organisation; but it is not inconceivable that such assets might be included in an appraisal of past performance. It should perhaps be noted that human capital is not entirely excluded from accounting statements: such items as goodwill and capitalised research and development represent, however inadequately, some of the accumulated results of human effort, skill, and enterprise.

Accounting Ratios: Financial Status

Hitherto, the distinction between shareholders' funds and long-term debt has been considered only in relation to measures of return on resources commanded. However, the balance between the two sources of finance is important in determining the implications of variations in the overall rate of return; and this balance is measured by the debt ratio—the proportion of the total capital employed which is provided by long-term debt. Since the interest payments on this debt are a prior charge on profits, the higher this proportion is the more pronounced will be the effect on the return to shareholders' funds of a given change in the overall return on total capital employed. This effect, which is exemplified in Table 4.1, is commonly known as gearing.

As will be seen from the last row of the table, gearing can affect more than the amount of dividend payable to shareholders—it can affect solvency. That is why companies which seem liable to large fluctuations in profitability usually try to obtain a capital structure with a low proportion of debt. One notable exception to this association of low gearing with profit instability is the airline industry, which has generally either had difficulty in raising share capital or, being in many cases government owned, has not

Table 4.1 Effect of Gearing

Capital employed £10 million; interest rate on long-term debt 10%

Debt ratio	0		0.25		0.5		0.75	
Share capital (£000)	10,000		7,500		5,000		2,500	
Long-term debt (£000)	—		2,500		5,000		7,500	
Annual interest charge (£000)	—		250		500		750	
Operating profit (£000)	Share holder's profit (£000)	Rate of return (%)	Share holder's profit (£000)	Rate of return (%)	Share holder's profit (£000)	Rate of return (%)	Share holder's profit (£000)	Rate of return (%)
2,000	2,000	20	1,750	23.33	1,500	30	1.250	50
1,500	1,500	15	1,250	16.67	1,000	20	750	30
1,000	1,000	10	750	10	500	10	250	10
500	500	5	250	3.33	0	0	−250	−10

been allowed to; since airlines usually have a high proportion of fixed costs, quite modest declines in traffic are usually enough to precipitate losses. In general, not much thought seems to have been given to the consequences of varying fortune in devising the original capital structure for British nationalised industries; since they were entirely debt-financed, a year or two of bad trade has been enough in several instances to produce losses which, after charging interest on the accumulated debt, were sufficient to depress the chances of financial recovery and therefore, perhaps, any faith in and incentive for such recovery. Some experiments have fairly recently been made in the use of government share capital, but it is too soon to appraise the consequences. (Problems of capital structure are analysed in the chapter on financial management.)

As a measure of long-term solvency the debt ratio may be supplemented by the ratio of profit, before tax and interest, to the interest charge—usually known as the interest cover. This is an attempt to measure the size of the cushion protecting the company (and its debtholders) from the danger of not earning enough to meet its interest obligations. (Profit is taken before tax because interest on loans is tax-deductible.) But ability to pay interest, or indeed to make any other kind of payment, is directly related not to profitability, but to liquidity—it is a cardinal error to mistake profits for cash—and therefore financial appraisals always make use of some measures of liquidity. Two such ratios are routinely used: the current ratio, which is the ratio of total current assets to current liabilities, and the quick ratio (often known as the 'acid test') which excludes stock from current assets on the grounds that it might not be readily saleable just when the money is needed. Current liabilities include all charges which are due to be paid within the next twelve months, and current assets those items which are expected to turn into cash in the normal course of business (as well as cash itself). Since a substantial volume of current assets is required simply to keep the business in operation, it is widely assumed that the current ratio should not be allowed to fall much below 2:1, and it is normally thought prudent to ensure that cash and debtors alone should be equal to the total of current liabilities.

These ratios are not entirely reliable guides for two reasons. First, they do not allow for the time pattern of outflows or inflows: £1 million due to be received from customers in four months' time is not much use in paying a bill for £400,000 due next week. (It may be put to use by selling all or part of it to a debt factor, whose economic function is to bridge the gap between the sale of goods and the receipt of payment—a gap which is particularly likely to cause problems to small firms which are trying to grow without much financial support.) The second limitation is that the liabilities recorded are only those which have passed through the accounts—for instance, tax payable on past profits, and payment for goods already delivered. Approaching commitments—say for new equipment to be delivered next month—are not included. Therefore it is desirable to supplement the calculation of such ratios by the computation of a cash budget for the next few months; this may show an approaching cash crisis of which the liquidity ratios give no inkling, or reveal (more happily) that an apparently critical situation is about to be relieved by large cash inflows before any of the current charges have to be paid.

Accounting Ratios: Operating Success

The two kinds of ratios hitherto discussed may be calculated from published accounts; most of the ratios within the third group cannot. These are focused on operating performance and are commonly known as management ratios. The starting point is a measure very close to the rate of profit on shareholders' funds; but since the intention is to provide measures of performance in the organisation's chosen business, any returns which originate outside that business (such as investment income or dividends on shareholdings in other companies) are deducted from profit, and the capital value of the assets generating such excluded earnings is correspondingly deducted from capital employed. What remains is the ratio of operating profits to operating assets (but excluding leased assets unless a special adjustment is made). This ratio is then systematically decomposed in an attempt to identify the elements which have contributed to the overall result.

The accompanying chart (which is clearly related to Figure 8.3 and which might be substantially extended) indicates how this decomposition proceeds. The first step is to recognise that the overall return on assets depends partly on the volume of sales which those assets support and partly on the profit margin on these sales. Henceforward assets and operations are separately analysed.

The ratio of total costs to sales is simply the complement of the profit margin; this ratio may now be subdivided into major components such as manufacturing costs, distribution and selling costs, research and development costs and administrative costs, all expressed as a ratio of sales. (This division must, of course, be exhaustive; but there is no single correct classification—for example, depreciation charges may be included in each category or taken out as a separate item.) Each of these major components may be subdivided as required, manufacturing costs probably being separated into labour, materials, and other manufacturing costs. The process can continue as far as is thought useful, or as far as the available information allows: labour can be divided into direct and indirect, indirect labour into various skills and grades, and so on, every item of cost being expressed as a ratio of sales revenue.

The other half of the chart shows the decomposition of the turnover

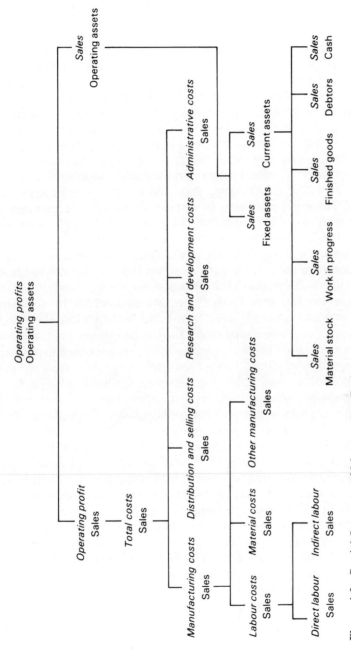

Figure 4.3 Partial Structure of Management Ratios

ratios. Operating assets are split into fixed and current, and each is then divided into its various components in as much detail as seems useful and feasible—figures may be produced, for example, for the turnover of different kinds of materials or different classes of debtors, or these categories may be left as aggregates. Many of the turnover figures may be expressed as reciprocals of the ratios shown for ease of comprehension: for example, a sales/debtors ratio of 7.5 may be more immediately understood if shown as a 48-day collection period. Occasionally the base may be varied for similar reasons: it is probably more helpful to know the relationship between material stocks and the cost of materials used in production, or between the stock of finished goods (valued at cost of production) and the total cost of goods sold, than the ratios shown in the chart. Similar adjustments may be made to the ratios used in the analysis of costs.

These records of performance also need to be matched against some standard. The usual practice is to make comparisons with past perform-ance, or with other organisations which are thought to be valid com-parators. It is not easy for most firms to do the latter accurately and in detail, except for other firms within the same group, since much of the information required and the basis on which it is calculated is not readily disclosed to outsiders; and so there has developed a specialist consultancy, the Centre for Interfirm Comparison, founded jointly by the British Institute of Management and the British Productivity Council, to under-take this task on a confidential basis. The Centre collects and standardises data from a group of firms which appear to be similar enough to provide an acceptable sample; each member of the group then receives a full specification of its own ratios together with summary statistics for the whole group—for example, median, first and third quartile and possibly, if the group is large enough to maintain confidentiality, first and ninth decile.

Whatever the reference model employed, it needs to be used with judgement. What values are attainable depends on circumstances; what values are desirable varies with the type of business. Supermarkets may be expected to show low profit margins, a high proportion of bought-in costs, high asset turnover and (since they sell little or nothing on credit) a minute debtors' ratio. Heavy chemical companies should have much higher profit margins, balanced by low turnover of assets (mainly plant, but probably including a substantial volume of debtors). They may have a fairly high value-added ratio, but very little of it will be attributed to direct labour. It is not always clear in what direction one might wish a particular ratio to move: the average collection period, for example, can be too short, indicating an unduly restrictive credit policy which is likely to hamper sales and profitability, or too long, indicating an expensive use of scarce cash or even a substantial risk of bad debts. It is similarly possible for research and development expenditure to be either inadequate or excessive.

Management ratios are commonly used as an instrument of management by exception, but there is some danger in this practice. In using this technique one begins by ascertaining whether the overall result is acceptable. If it is, enquiry stops; if not, one seeks to identify the specific element, or elements, which appear to be the cause of the shortfall—and therefore the manager who is responsible for remedial action. Thus one might be stimulated to search for failure by a comparison which shows a return of 8 per cent compared with an industry average of 10 per cent; if asset turnover is equal to the industry average (say at 2.0 per cent), attention is concentrated on the analysis of costs (at 96 per cent of sales, instead of 95 per cent). This analysis might perhaps reveal that direct labour is the element which is out of line: in this example it might appear, say, as 23 per cent of sales compared with the industry average of 22 per cent. The conclusion to be drawn would seem to be that everything is satisfactory except that there are too many workers or that these workers are too well paid. The analysis may be sufficiently detailed to determine which of these is the cause.

What an economist might find a little worrying about such a procedure, if applied unquestioningly, is the assumption of fixed proportions and separability—the notion that the optimum combination of inputs is the same for all firms, and that one element can be varied by the application of managerial effort without affecting any other part of the system. (X-inefficiency, however, is treated by economists as separable in this way.) It may be that the higher labour costs are attributable to some other element which the analysis appears to show as under control, such as poor quality materials or inferior equipment.

It may be much safer to use ratio analysis as a model of an interdependent system, not a separable system—to fit, that is, into the Ansoff/Simon conception of an organisation with a multiplicity of goals and constraints. In this model labour costs are not obviously less significant than the profit margin or the turnover of material stocks; nor should one assume that any can be treated in isolation, even from other ratios which formally appear in quite different parts of the structure depicted in the chart. By taking together particular groups of ratios it may be possible to identify possible problem areas: for example, high labour costs, low turnover of work in progress and a high turnover of machinery may indicate that the company has an unsatisfactory capital stock which is making the production process both slower and more expensive than it might be. But, however used, such an analysis should be treated as an indicator of possible problems, not as a sure guide to appropriate solutions.

Accounting Data: A Cautionary Note

Any measure of performance which relies, directly or indirectly, on accounting data should be handled with care; this is especially true when comparisons are made between different organisations. There is really no substitute for a basic understanding of the structure of the accounting system, the conventions employed and the particular interpretations which have been used to generate the data being used. (Reid and Myddleton (1982) have produced a workbook which should provide sufficient understanding to recognise the problems.) The principal difficulties are associated with asset valuations and the treatment of costs: one of the basic lessons of accounting is that the two are not independent. The effects of drastically writing-down the value of their aircraft on British Airways' reported profits for 1981/82 and the subsequent year provide a dramatic illustration of the connection.

The impact of inflation has caused much debate about the principles on which fixed assets should be valued and depreciation charged, but has not yet led to standard practice. Among the most striking variations are those between nationalised industries. Since it seems to be thought undesirable that such industries should make either large profits or large losses, it is not surprising to find the more profitable charging depreciation at much higher rates than the loss makers. (Control systems tend to provide incentives other than those intended.) Valuation of current assets also needs scrutiny: for example, stocks may be valued 'at cost' with the inclusion of all, some, or no overhead charges—with corresponding effects on the reported price–cost margins. The balance sheet date may also be important: a toy firm might reasonably be expected to have higher stocks on 30 September than on 31 December; a company about to complete a major contract will probably show a very high figure for work in progress and a very low figure for debtors, whereas on completion of the contract this balance will be reversed.

A major part of the work of the Centre for Interfirm Comparison is the adjustment of their clients' original data to a standard form. Outsiders may obtain guidance on some of the required adjustments from the notes to published accounts, but published information is not adequate for a detailed accurate appraisal, even on the assumption that the accounting categories correspond to the aspects of performance which it is desired to appraise.

4.4   Performance, Control and Learning

To conclude this chapter it may be helpful to summarise, at the risk of caricature, two distinct approaches to the control of organisations in order to improve performance. A more extended discussion will be found in Dunbar (1981). The first approach, which characterises older styles of organisation theory and earlier writing on management control systems, assumes that the purpose of control is to secure conformity to the rules prescribed by superiors, and the correction of deviations through the assignment of responsibility (implying blame) for such deviations to the holders of specific managerial positions. As has been suggested, this is an approach which seems close in spirit to the usual economists' discussions of the causes of market failure and the remedies for failure; it also comfortably accords with the notion of clearly-definable cost functions. The achievement of desired objectives, then, seems to depend on clear specification and the minimisation of managerial discretion.

However, the problem of organisational performance may be conceived in rather different terms. Instead of a single objective, or even a well-specified function of several arguments, the set of objectives may be imprecise and impossible to partition neatly among decision makers. Furthermore, these decision makers do not leave their own personal objectives at the office door in exchange for a salary and other benefits, but incorporate some of them into their managerial choices. Both of these characteristics are, in part, consequences of a third characteristic—a far from negligible degree of ignorance about system interactions, system capabilities, and the opportunities available.

On this set of assumptions attempts at control in the earlier sense will be partly frustrated by subordinates exploiting the ignorance of their superiors in order to maintain a degree of managerial independence to assist in the pursuit of their own objectives (indeed, managerial independence may well become an objective in itself); even where these attempts at control are successful, they may lead to perverse results because of failure to specify objectives correctly (an apparently sensible piece of cost cutting may cause the loss of valuable business). Successful performance on these assumptions requires discovery. Thus managerial discretion may be necessary in order to permit managers to search, and performance measures should be designed to check the adequacy of present operating routines and decision routines, and to provide clues for the discovery (or rather invention) of better routines.

This approach suggests the need for an evolutionary theory of organisational processes. A major contribution to such a theory has been made by Nelson and Winter (1982), but the theory still requires much more development before it can offer much specific guidance to managers.

References

Ansoff, H. I. (1965) *Corporate Strategy*, McGraw-Hill.

Baumol, W. M. (1959) *Business Behavior, Value and Growth*, Harcourt Brace and World.

Cyert, R. M. and March, J. G. (1963) *A Behavioral Theory of the Firm*, Prentice-Hall.

Dunbar, R. L. M. (1981) 'Designs for organizational control', in Paul C. Nystrom and William H. Starbuck, (eds), *Handbook of Organizational Design*, Oxford University Press.

Jefferson, M. (1983) 'Economic uncertainty and business decision making', in J. Wiseman (ed.), *Beyond Positive Economics?* Macmillan.

Kirzner, I. M. (1973) *Competition and Entrepreneurship*, University of Chicago Press.

Lancaster, K. J. (1966) 'A new approach to consumer theory', *Journal of Political Economy*, 174, pp. 132–157.

Leibenstein, H. (1976) *Beyond Economic Man*, Harvard University Press.

Loasby, B. J. (1976) *Choice, Ignorance and Complexity*, Cambridge University Press.

McGregor, D. H. (1960) *The Human Side of Enterprise*, McGraw-Hill.

Marris, R. L. (1964) *The Economic Theory of 'Managerial' Capitalism*, Macmillan.

Marshall, A. (1920) *Principles of Economics*, Macmillan.

Nelson, R. R. and Winter, S. G. (1982) *An Evolutionary Theory of Economic Change*, Harvard University Press.

Pfeffer, J. and Salancik, G. R. (1978) *The External Control of Organisations*, Harper and Row.

Reid, W. and Myddleton, D. R. (1982) *The Meaning of Company Accounts*, Gower Press.

Simon, H. A. (1964) 'On the concept of organizational goal', *Administrative Science Quarterly*, 9, pp. 1–22.

Williamson, O. E. (1964) *The Economics of Discretionary Behaviour*, Prentice-Hall.

Williamson, O. E. (1975) *Markets and Hierarchies: Analysis and Antitrust Implications*, Free Press.

5
Productive Performance in the Firm: The Economic Approach

Douglas Todd

5.1 Introduction

Perhaps the most important dimension of a firm's activities is its role as a production unit. This applies no matter what the sphere of activity might be. In its simplest terms one interpretation of the firm is that it purchases and co-ordinates inputs of various kinds of resource and transforms these into outputs of goods and services. At such a general level as this the notion of businesses as units which convert one set of things into something else is far too broad to have operational significance. It is therefore of value to go behind this notion and see what sort of economic interpretations might be feasible and useful. In particular, it is worth seeing the kinds of analysis and tools which economists and others have found to be of help when considering the operation and behaviour of firms.

This chapter is concerned mainly with the firm as a production agent, but a major problem is one of defining the boundaries of the subject. Clearly in a sophisticated business environment there can be few activities which do not, in some sense, influence a firm's production behaviour. As examples, the advertising, marketing and legal departments of large firms are all connected with and have an effect upon the ultimate productive efficiency of the enterprise. Since many of these other dimensions are covered elsewhere in this volume, this helps to narrow the focus. Thus, in order to keep the subject manageable, the discussion centres on the firm as an economic unit which organises its major resources or factors of production in order to produce a stream of outputs.

5.2   The Production Function[1]

Whilst there are many approaches to this problem, a natural starting point for the economist is to think conceptually of a firm or entrepreneur being faced initially with a spectrum of technical means by which he might produce his intended output. These available techniques are determined by the state of technical knowledge at the time. In some instances there may be only one generally recognised feasible way of producing a product or service. In other instances there may be several alternatives. Electricity, for example, can be produced from a number of alternative processes. It is common to express this technical aspect in the form of a production function:

$$X = F (V_1, V_2, \ldots V_k) \tag{1}$$

where X denotes the flow of output, with the V_i being inputs of factor services and hence also being flows.

It is important to note that the relationship equation (1) assumes in effect that the purely technical features of the production process or processes are known and solved. The precise technical association between inputs and outputs is described by the function F. The next question which arises therefore is what quantities of the factors V_i will be employed in order to produce output X. An obvious key determinant of choice here will be the relative prices or costs of the relevant inputs. Given this, one can envisage an entrepreneur making some considerable effort to ensure that he can maximise those returns he can obtain from employing his inputs. If, for convenience, we make the assumption that firms do try to maximise profits, then intuitively it may be seen that a factor input will be employed up to the point whereby the additional revenue generated is just balanced by the additional cost of doing so. That is to say, the marginal revenue (product price times the marginal increase in input usage) just equals marginal cost.

$$\pi = PX - \Sigma C_i V_i$$

where π = profits, P is the price of output and C_i the cost or price of the ith input. The object is to maximise profits π,

$$\text{Max. } \pi = PF(V_1, V_2, \ldots V_k) - \Sigma C_i V_i$$

with

$$F'_{V_1} = PF_1 - C_1$$
$$\vdots \qquad \vdots \qquad \vdots$$
$$F'_{V_k} = PF_k - C_k$$

1. The analysis here is much abbreviated and condensed. It concentrates on only those elements which are called upon at a later stage. An excellent textbook presentation is given in Layard and Walters (1978); a more advanced treatment is Chapter I of Varian (1978).

Thus the marginal contribution of factor V_i to revenue just equals the cost C_i of using additional units of that factor.

Returning to the production function as expressed by (1), we can decompose the technical and price or allocative effects in the following way. By differentiating (1) and setting the change in output equal to zero,

$$dX = F_1 dV_1 + F_1 dV_2 + \ldots + F_k dV_k = 0$$

$$\text{where} \quad F_i = \frac{dX}{dV_i}$$

$$\text{and} \quad \frac{F_i}{F_j} = -\frac{dV_j}{dV_i}$$

Figure 5.1 below illustrates this process by which the function (1) is now projected onto the factor input space for the case where two inputs are considered. The slope of X_o is given by the rate at which one input can be substituted for another, and its convex form suggests that as more of, say, V_2 is employed, increasingly larger amounts are required in order to compensate for the reduction in V_1. The line AB adds the cost dimension to the problem as stated. Its slope expresses the terms on which one input can be traded or substituted for another with output X held constant. At the point of tangency the rate of *technical* substitution is just equal to the terms on which V_2 can be substituted for V_1. That is to say, the ratio of input costs just equals this rate of substitution. If this were not so, then the position of the firm could always be improved by substituting one input for another up to the point where the marginal gain in revenue just equals the marginal cost of output. At the point E, therefore, the firm can be described as efficient in two senses, namely:

(a) a given output is being produced with the smallest number of inputs possible; and

(b) these inputs are being employed at least cost.

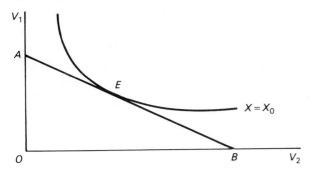

Figure 5.1

It must be stressed that the precise shape of the constant output curve or isoquant X_o is determined by the current technology.

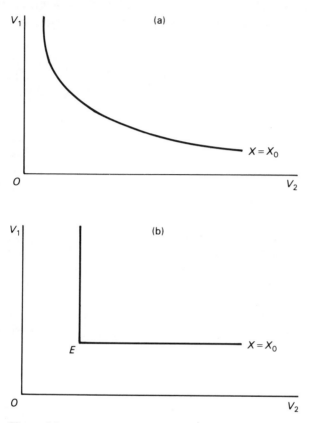

Figure 5.2

The isoquant in Figure 5.2 (a), for example, implies a very flexible technology whereby one input can be substituted for another with relative ease. Figure 5.2 (b), on the other hand, illustrates a situation where substitution is technically impossible. Indeed, the point E is consistent with an infinite set of relative input prices and hence we say that factor proportions are invariant to changes in these prices. It is hardly likely that there will be many practical instances of 5.2 (b) occurring over the very long run (the latter being defined usually as a situation where there are no fixed production factors). A topical illustration of this case is provided by the two very sharp rises in energy prices during the 1970s. In many important production processes the capital/energy input mix cannot be varied significantly even over a fairly long period, for example when switching from oil to nuclear generating plant. Nevertheless, over the longer period a persistent rise in the price of energy relative to capital would be expected to induce firms to use less energy intensive methods. For the purposes of this example the technology described by 5.2(b) would therefore be more suited to shorter-run situations, although in some circumstances 'shorter' here could mean perhaps some years.

Having said this, a situation where some factor substitution can occur is preferable to one where none is permitted. Figure 5.3 illustrates a situation where the cost of input V_1 rises with everything else remaining unchanged. This causes the ray or 'iso-cost' line OD to shift downwards to, say, OD_1. Assuming that costs are to be minimised, in fixed proportions technology, the 'L' shaped isoquant would have to move downwards along OD from A to, say, B. Total input costs would rise and the technology dictates that both inputs must be reduced in the same proportion. Comparing this with a situation in which substitution exists, we see that the production point would move to C on isoquant X_1. This indicates, *ceteris paribus*, that the loss in output is less in the substitutability case illustrated in Figure 5.3 because isoquant X_1 would be higher than the implied isoquant X_0 which passes through the fixed proportions point B.

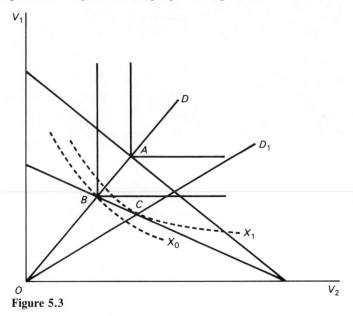

Figure 5.3

5.3 Productive Performance

The sort of considerations outlined briefly in the preceding section provide a starting point for analysing in more detail the ways in which an economist might begin to tackle the problem of analysing performance. Once again, because of the numerous aspects of this topic it is preferred to restrict the discussion broadly along the lines outlined already.

The notion of productive performance lends itself almost immediately to the transformation view of an enterprise as described. This is typified by one obvious and naturally popular interpretation which is often summarised as the 'engineering approach' to performance. In its simplest form this can be represented as either:

$$\frac{\text{input}}{\text{maximum output}} \quad \text{or} \quad \frac{\text{actual output}}{\text{capacity output}}$$

In place of maximum one could specify target or planned output, suggesting that current performance is being maintained against a production plan.

Returning to the production function given by equation (1), this defines the maximum stream of outputs which can be obtained from the inputs V_i. Alternatively, for a given value of the outputs the function defines the minimum amount of inputs required to achieve this. The similarity to the simple ratios above is now clear.

Figure 5.4 below provides an example for the single output–single input case.

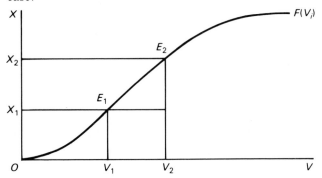

Figure 5.4

Holding output X constant, the measure of productive or technical efficiency is given by:

$$E_x = \frac{V_1}{X_1} \div \frac{V_2}{X_1} = \left(\frac{V_1}{V_2}\right) \tag{2}$$

where $X = $ constant

Holding input V constant and allowing output X to vary, we have the alternative measure:

$$E_v = \frac{V_2}{X_2} \div \frac{V_2}{X_1} = \left(\frac{X_1}{X_2}\right) \tag{3}$$

where $V = $ constant

Now it so happens that the two measures of productive or technical efficiency coincide under one rather important set of circumstances. This is when the production unit is operating under conditions of constant returns to scale. In terms of Figure 5.5 below, this is when a set or family of isoquants representing different output levels are spaced equally along a ray from the origin; $OA = AB = BC$, and so on.

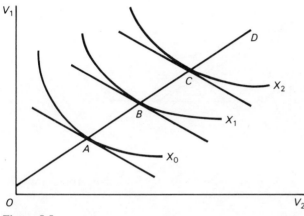

Figure 5.5

More formally, we can write our production function as:

$$F(\lambda V_i) = (V_i)\lambda^\eta \tag{4}$$

where λ is a scalar and η is the elasticity of scale showing the effects of proportional changes in inputs V_i on output.

If we maintain the assumption that a given percentage change in factor inputs results in the same percentage change in outputs, this leads to an illuminating interpretation of efficiency which was first proposed by Farrell (1957).

Figure 5.6 is drawn on the assumption also that all production units employ the same vector of factor inputs V. Both input and output prices are assumed to be given, and each production unit operates with the same basic technology.

If we transform the production function into a form in terms of input coefficiencies μ_i, where $\mu_i = V_i/X_i$, the isoquant XX_o can be regarded here as an efficient locus of points in the space. For given input prices (costs), the point of tangency at E indicates the optimum production combination of inputs, such as that suggested in Figure 5.1.

In order to simplify matters consider a single input case. In Figure 5.4 we can imagine input V_2 as being a scaled up value of input V_1 measured along

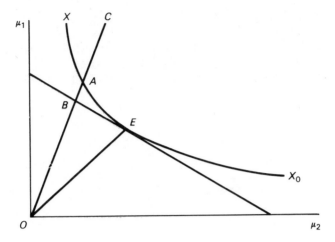

Figure 5.6

the same axis. That is, $V_2 = \lambda V_1$ with $\lambda > 0$. Then we can express our two outputs X_1 and X_2:

$$X_1 = f(V_1)$$
$$X_2 = f(\lambda V_1)$$

Hence the efficiency alternatives (2) and (3) can be written as:

$$E_x = \frac{V_1}{V_2} = \frac{V_1}{\lambda V_1} = \frac{1}{\lambda}$$

$$E_v = \frac{X_1}{X_2} = \frac{f(V_1)}{f(\lambda V_1)}$$

Now from (4), since $f(\lambda V) = f(V)\lambda^\eta$, then

$$\eta = \log \frac{f(\lambda V)}{f(V)} \div \log \lambda$$

and substituting E_x and E_v into this expression for η, we derive a relationship between the scale elasticity and the two alternative measures of productive efficiency, that is:

$$\eta = \frac{\log E_x}{\log E_v} \tag{5}$$

The significance of this somewhat laborious approach lies in the fact that, as equation (5) indicates, only when constant returns to scale apply ($\eta = 1$) are the two measures of productive efficiency E_x and E_v the same. Thus, holding output constant and looking at efficiency in terms of relative *input* usage is not necessarily the same as holding inputs constant and looking at relative *output* performance. In engineering economy terms this is a simple observation of some significance. Because of this the more familiar and obvious physical factor productivity indicators need handling with care, the interpretation depending on whether it is outputs or inputs on which one is standardising.

Returning to Figure 5.6, let us suppose that for some reason one production unit cannot succeed in producing at point E and instead produces at, say, point C. We now have a situation whereby one production unit is inefficient in two important senses.

Firstly, the ratio OA/OC shows how the same output could be produced, yet employing fewer inputs in the *same* proportions. Farrell described this as 'technical inefficiency'. Secondly, a production unit located at point A is not employing its inputs at a point which is optimal in terms of relative costs. This is indicated by the ratio OB/OA, an indicator of price or allocative efficiency which is a comparison of average production cost at A with that at the point of tangency E. Once again the comparison is in terms of what improvements mean under the fixed proportions assumption with measurement being along the ray OA.

The Farrell approach to productive performance leads quite naturally to an overall measure of efficiency which is given by combining the two ratios or radial measures of technical and price efficiency:

$$\frac{OA}{OC} \cdot \frac{OB}{OA} = \frac{OB}{OC}$$

Thus we have an index which incorporates an input/output component which is akin to the simple engineering ratio given earlier, but which also takes account of whether the factor proportions used reflect their relative costs.

We can generalise quite easily in the following way:

$$X = wL + rK \tag{6}$$

X is net output or value added, L numbers employed, w the wage rate, where r is the rental on capital K, with rK equal to gross profits. The object of the exercise, as suggested from the construction of Figure 5.6, is to compare a unit of net output X with that same unit valued at true opportunity cost prices, namely those prices indicated by the point of tangency at E, again in Figure 5.6. We therefore have a ratio of the following kind[2]:

$$e = w^*\left(\frac{L}{X}\right) + r^*\left(\frac{K}{X}\right) = \frac{X^*}{X} \tag{7}$$

---

2. This bears a strong resemblance to the efficiency criterion suggested by Downie in his original contribution (1958). Some applications using data at the firm level are given in Todd (1971).

where the asterisks denote opportunity cost prices. The aim is to find a practical expression of a movement from, say, C to E (Figure 5.6). The percentage change in efficiency e is derived by relating this to proportionate changes in (a) the input/output ratios and (b) factor input ratios. The first denotes a shift in technical efficiency, the second a shift in price or allocative efficiency; then we can derive the expression:

$$\frac{de}{e} = \frac{X}{X^*}\left(r^* \frac{a_k}{T} + w^* \frac{a_L}{T}\right) dT + \frac{X}{X^*}\left(r^* \frac{a_k}{P} + w^* \frac{a_L}{P}\right) dP \qquad (8)$$

where a_k and a_L are capital output and labour output ratios, with the terms T and P representing technical and price efficiency factors. P, for example, shows how a change in the capital/labour affects the coefficients a_k and a_L. Setting $dP = 0$ means that the ratio OA/OC in Figure 5.6 is being considered.

There are at least three other interpretations which can be placed on the isoquant or production frontier such as that in Figure 5.6. Let us suppose that a particular firm is operating with a number of plants of different ages, the newest being the more technologically advanced. The usual textbook isoquant diagrams represent technological improvements by a shifting inwards of the frontier towards the origin. We can therefore think of the locus $X X_0$ as a 'best practice' frontier which indicates the reduction in factor input ratios required if other plants were to reproduce the same technical performance as those of the newest vintage. This interpretation does, however, pose some special problems to which we will turn in due course.

Next, if our concern is with the long-run situation in an industry (when all production factors can be varied), the notion of an equilibrium here suggests that firms will tend to produce a unit of net output using broadly the same production technique and at optimal scale. Intuitively, this means no more than the fact that under competitive conditions in the long run it is always possible for one firm to imitate the activities of another. The question arises as to what is meant by optimal scale. If we look back to expression (5) it becomes clear that optimal scale in the input coefficient space—say Figure 5.6—means that the scale elasticity equals unity. If this were not the case, the production frontier $X X_0$ would be moving inwards or away from the origin. The constant returns to scale assumption, whilst extremely convenient for discussion such as that here, also has some justification as a longer-run concept. There remain, however, a number of important issues, some of which will be taken up in later sections of this chapter.

The third interpretation of this approach to productive efficiency is to regard the ratio OA/OC as a measure of what is popularly described as

X-inefficiency. This topic is covered more fully in the preceding chapter. Here it is sufficient to say that in the two input examples used for simple illustrative purposes, what X-inefficiency really implies is that inputs other than labour and capital are not being taken into account. In geometric terms, a multi-dimensional surface would be expected to eliminate some of the apparent discrepancy between unit C and unit A in Figure 5.6. There could remain, however, an element of organisational slack, for example, which remains unexplained by more conventional production factors (see Leibenstein 1966).

5.4 Cost and Returns

The above characterisations of productive performance focus attention in particular on physical inputs and the output which is produced. One can, however, approach this aspect of firm behaviour from a different direction by concentrating instead on the prices of these inputs and outputs.

An obvious and familiar starting point and one which is well known to business managers, plant operators and so on, is to use unit costs as one performance indicator. In discussions on costs per unit of output the economics textbook, as we have seen, distinguishes between the short- and longer-run situation. When some factors such as physical plant are considered as fixed over a given time horizon, the unit cost curve by definition refers to variable costs only. Over the long term, when all factors can in principle be adjusted to changing economic circumstances, the unit cost curve is inclusive of all factor outlays.

In conventional economic analysis, the long-run unit cost curve is of particular interest because it represents an analogue to the notions of productive efficiency outlined in the previous section. Before looking at this relationship in more detail, it is useful at this stage to consider the role of returns to scale. It was suggested earlier that returns to scale in an isoquant diagram such as Figure 5.5 could be represented by different spacing of the constant output level curves X_i. If we assume that relative factor prices are constant as output increases, the ray OD is the 'expansion path' for the production unit. As we move along the ray OD, both output and factor input quantities are changing. Given the relative costs of these inputs, the long-run unit cost curve can be derived from this expansion path. At each of the points A, B and C, we know output, quantities of inputs and their costs, and this information might yield a long-run unit cost curve such as $LRAC_1$ illustrated in Figure 5.7.

The scale curves shown are thus determined by the technical conditions embodied in the production function. $LRAC_1$ could be interpreted as

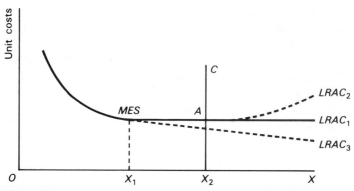

Figure 5.7

showing a schedule of cost minimising input choices for different levels of capacity output. Returns to scale, therefore, is just another way of characterising the transformation process between inputs and outputs. The curve $LRAC_3$ suggests that technical returns to scale are increasing, whereas $LRAC_2$ suggests that after a certain point of output they begin to decrease.[3]

It is at this point that one begins to run into one or two awkward problems. The questions arise as to what determines the extent of returns to scale, and what is implied if a production unit cannot achieve these in practical terms. It has been more or less a convention following Kaldor (1934) to suggest that the size of a firm measured by output is limited ultimately by its management capabilities. However, strictly speaking, and from the viewpoint of an operational manager or plant engineer, the long-run technical cost curve has an *ex ante* character. One may, for example, have firm views about what the shape of the LRAC curve happens to be for volume cars in the UK motor industry. This does, however, depend to a large extent on the size of the market, and beyond current market share it is largely unknown. Since management ability is a key determinant of overall corporate strategy, and hence a production factor in its own right, $LRAC_2$ must have its shape because managerial elements have been excluded from the production function.

Moreover, an argument expressed in this way implies that management is a fixed factor and what we are really observing is diminishing returns to

---

3. In the space available here one can hardly do justice to the subject of scale economies. The reader is referred to wide-ranging discussions of sources of scale economies, including many references in Silberston (1972), Pratten (1971), and Gold (1981). A warning is necessary, however. Typical textbook approaches such as that here assume single product returns. In a multi-product or multi-plant case, which many would find more relevant, the task of defining a unique scale curve is much more difficult and sometimes impossible. A recent treatment is that by Laitinen (1980); see also Beckenstein (1975).

this fixed input. It is at this point that a strong element of circularity appears because LRAC by definition is constructed from a situation where all factors are variable.

The second question raises a similar issue and can be treated by referring to point C in Figure 5.7. This unit is located some distance away from the technically efficient scale curves $LRAC_1$, $LRAC_2$ and $LRAC_3$. Its inefficiency is analogous to point C in the production frontier of Figure 5.6. Indeed, one could in principle propose an overall efficiency measure of the form $X_2A/X_2C < 1$ which is made at output X_2 and with reference to the efficient unit A. If the responsibility for this discrepancy in performance rests with managerial and organisational factors in business, we find ourselves in the same situation; namely, a more comprehensive definition of the underlying production function would appear to eliminate such differences. Obviously this cannot be so simple because differences in performance can be due to numerous factors concerned with the general business environment.[4] Nevertheless, the interest in X-efficiency analysis and, in particular, the growth of management science as a discipline emphasise the importance of factor input organisation. What the economist's highly simplified, two or three factor production approach does is to identify the relative importance and significance of these particular and more traditional factors in the production process.

Referring back to Figure 5.7, we note the point MES which is the point at which the $LRAC$ curves first attain their minimum points. This is usually referred to as the 'minimum efficient size' of the production unit. The long-run unit cost curve thus consists of a series of points being costs per unit of output for production units of different sizes. A multi-plant firm, for example, can find that increasing plant size yields scale economies from a variety of sources—spreading costs over indivisible or 'lumpy' machinery, allowing more scope for specialising functions, and so on.

The overall efficiency aim demands that a plant or firm at least achieves the point MES on the long-run unit cost curve. The smooth nature of the process implied by Figure 5.7 is, however, misleading. In any realistic situation we would expect to observe investment in, say, plant occurring in a series of discrete jumps. The $LRAC$ curves portrayed in Figure 5.7 suggest that a firm or industry can move and adjust more or less freely in order to achieve a desired scale of operations. In an *ex ante* formulation there may be some sense in this sort of interpretation. *Ex post*, however, a newly constructed plant which increases feasible operational capacity by, say, 25 per cent will constrain future decisions in several respects. Two of

---

4. Hall and Winston (1959) argue persuasively that environmental factors are of primary importance when making inter-firm efficiency comparisons. These act as a constraint on managerial choice. By way of example they ask the question: is it legitimate to compare two similar retail co-operatives when one is located in an urban and the other in a rural environment?

the more important are, firstly, the need to build up towards a capacity output before any further tranches of capital can be considered; secondly, and more importantly, the new plant is to all intents and purposes irreversible. One does, of course, hear of major mistakes whereby new plant is built in anticipation of a demand which is unrealised. One is then faced with a problem of sale, scrapping or mothballing. The major point is that for most purposes a firm will not be able to move back and forward along the expected scale curve without incurring severe and probably unacceptable penalties. The construction is therefore a useful tool of analysis which enables one to capture in a simple way some important structural characteristics of a process. A firm could choose a point or region on its notional scale curve and hope to attain such a point; it would not expect to adjust in the manner implied by its smooth construction.

5.5   Technical Progress and Learning

Within the terms of the simple analysis followed here, a technical improvement can be represented by a shift in the production function. In Figure 5.8 the isoquants could be relevant to the same output, say 100

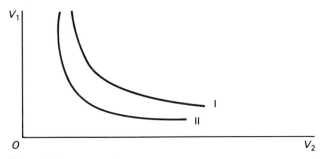

Figure 5.8

units. Curve II, however, is located close to the origin and describes a locus of points such that fewer units of inputs V_1 and V_2 are required in order to produce this same output. Technical change might favour one particular factor, capital for example, or it may be neutral in its impact. Quite apart from the purely technical improvements in, say, a new machine, such advances tend to cheapen the factor input itself. Thus there is some inducement to substitute the cheaper factor and become on average more intensive in production with that factor.

An alternative way of portraying this type of improvement is to see what happens to the long-run unit cost curve. As Figure 5.9 shows, a technical improvement will lead to a downwards shift in the whole curve. At all levels of output, the expectation is that unit costs will now be lower.

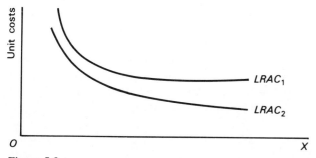

Figure 5.9

It is easy to see that the introduction of factors associated with technical advance change the essentially static nature of the analysis encountered so far. One interesting application of the more dynamic nature of the production process is seen in the analysis of learning and experience curves. In a wide range of production activities it has been found that labour costs per unit of net output tend to fall as *cumulative* output rises. The original idea here seems to have stemmed from observations on airframe manufacture in the United States in the early post-war period (Alchian 1953). There is now an impressive body of empirical information which lends support to the basic idea that as more units are produced, so labour and management organisation becomes more familiar with the process. As the job is repeated, experience eventually results in lower costs.

One could rationalise the learning and experience phenomena within the framework of analysis considered so far. It can be argued, for example, that improvements in labour skills over time are really just a form of technical improvement on the part of the labour factor input—a form of embodied technical change. At the same time, repetition and increasing specialisation result in economies of scale in the longer run. There are thus two effects which are captured by the one learning curve.

Figure 5.10 illustrates these possibilities where an observation made at two output levels leads to what can be interpreted as a learning curve

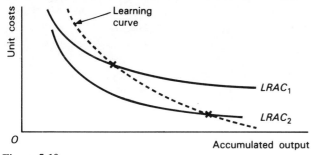

Figure 5.10

suggested by the dotted line. In fact the case here tells us that it is a hybrid composed of two effects—scale and technical progress. This should not, of course, detract from the fundamental ideas behind 'learning by doing' and the proven practical significance of the notion as a tool of economic analysis in production economics. Certainly many consultancy groups and business analysts have found the concept to be of considerable use as a starting point in analyses of business operations in a wide range of activities.

5.6   Theory and Evidence

So far as economic methodology is concerned, the various pieces of analysis outlined briefly above lead to numerous hypotheses about the behaviour of firms and industries. Moreover, they serve as a useful input for both private and public decision making—what the effects of a potential merger might be, the expected effects of capacity expansion, and so on. In all of the areas mentioned a considerable amount of effort has been devoted to putting quantitative flesh on those elements of the framework considered in this chapter. The following sections attempt to provide a flavour, albeit briefly, of what is known about some aspects of productive performance. The literature is growing and, inevitably, the approaches and the few examples given must to some extent represent the tastes of the author.

(a)   Efficiency Measurement

Efficiency of a production unit, be it plant, firm or industry, is, as we have observed, a multi-dimensional concept. Performance is meaningful only if reference is made to some standard, whether it is a budget plan, market share target, unit cost target, standard achieved by a competitor, or whatever.

By far the most common indicators of performance are output per head or labour productivity and the rate of return on capital and turnover. These much used measures are all of interest in their own right. The problem is that considered in isolation they tell one little if anything about how behaviour is affected if one of these measures is changed. The reason is that these and all other accounting ratios are based upon identities which must be satisfied *ex post*. To take one example we have:

$$\frac{\pi}{K} = \frac{\pi}{X} \cdot \frac{X}{K}$$

The rate of return on capital—the ratio of money profits to the value of capital employed K—is identically equal to the product of the profit output ratio and the ratio of output to capital. But net output X is identically equal to all employee costs plus gross profits, that is

$$X = wL + \pi$$

where w equals employee costs per head and L equals numbers employed; therefore

$$\frac{\pi}{K} = \frac{X - wL}{X} \cdot \left(\frac{X}{K}\right)$$

or $\quad \dfrac{\pi}{K} = \left[1 - w\left(\dfrac{L}{X}\right)\right] \cdot \left(\dfrac{X}{K}\right)$

In other words, this particular expression shows that the rate of return is composed of labour per unit of output and output per unit of capital. There are numerous other derivatives of this form depending on how far one wishes to disaggregate a given set of accounts. A good illustration is provided in Bela Gold (1975) and Teague and Eilon (1973). As a further example an interesting application, which tries to look at some of the more important factors determining output per head, is that by Harvey and Morris (1981). Here the authors undertake an intensive examination of twenty-one firms in the UK machine tool industry. Relating labour productivity to factors such as capital per unit of output and number of scientists employed, the authors conclude that these are significant contributing factors.

If we return to the view of the firm or production unit as a transformation process where the emphasis rests upon efficiency in utilisation of all resources, then clearly it makes little sense to maximise or strive for maximum efficiency in the use of a *single* factor input. Consider the following useful practical approach to the problem which rests on the ideas expressed earlier in Figure 5.6.

Observations on, say, individual plants are plotted in a factor input space with labour and capital being normalised for net output X. The innermost

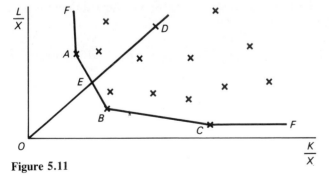

Figure 5.11

set of points are connected together by a hull or frontier FF. Thus plants A, B and C would be treated 'as if' they were technically efficient in their use of the two resources, labour and capital. Plant D, on the other hand, does not rest on the frontier. The implied technical efficiency given by the ratio OE/OD is measured relative to a hypothetical plant which is assumed to lie on the frontier FF at point E. Thus all plants which do not make up the frontier have a technical efficiency < 1 as measured by rays connecting them to the origin. Plant A has higher labour per unit of net output than, say, plant C, but both are technically efficient in the sense revealed here.

In other words, high output per head in plant C, which is a single factor productivity or performance indicator, does not necessarily guarantee that its efficiency in resource use is greater than some other plant with lower output per man, e.g. plants A or B.

This highly practical expression of some of the ideas set out earlier and used first by Farrell (1957) has been the source of a stream of empirical studies which have taken the form of direct applications or extensions and modifications of the basic Farrell suggestion. It is worth noting that this apparently simple suggestion is, in principle, much closer to the spirit of the basic theory than many of the more conventional statistical approaches. Typically, empirical production studies in economics are based upon fitted relationships which assume the existence of a random error term which has both positive and negative values. Strictly speaking, such a specification is incorrect since a production surface is defined as the maximum output which can be obtained from given inputs. Clearly the more usual 'average' production function relationships are rather different to those required by reference to the theory. In this respect the production frontier approach has a number of attractions.[5]

The frontier or reference standard can be defined in numerous ways. In the original approach the frontier is defined in terms of that performance which has been revealed by some of the production units. Implicitly, the question being asked is this: if some units can achieve this performance, then why and to what extent do others fail? The standard, therefore, is relative only to those observations used at a given time. One might wish to define the frontier in terms of some definition of capacity output or a more tightly specified set of technical engineering standards. Roll and Sachish (1981), for example, prefer this latter approach for establishing a reference standard in an analysis of multi-factor productivity indices in cargo handling at the port level.

Direct applications of the Farrell frontier method are given in Todd (1971 and 1977). The 1971 study investigated the relative technical

---

5. The literature on this subject has grown enormously in recent years. Two first-rate papers which cover many issues in a detailed but nevertheless readable fashion are those by Forsund and Hjalmarsson (1974) and Kopp (1981).

efficiency of small and large firms and concluded that, since both small and large firms made up the frontier for six broadly defined groups in UK manufacturing industry considered separately, there was little in the way of differences in technical efficiency between the size groups. The level of aggregation at the industry level in the survey material used was, however, extremely high and thus limits the degree of confidence in such comparisons. The second analysis was more narrowly defined, being based on an investigation by Ahmed (1976) of a sample of thirty small plastics producing firms in Ireland. No firm employed more than 130 persons and the product was reasonably homogeneous and produced under competitive conditions. The sample was split into three size groups with a number of efficiency or performance measures being computed for each.

Table 5.1   Mean Technical Efficiency Index

Size of firm	Overall frontier	Own frontier
Small	0.521	0.547
Medium	0.541	0.593
Large	0.538	0.733

Source: Todd (1977)

Relative to the frontier for all firms, the average efficiency of the very small firms is marginally less than for the other size groups. Measured with respect to each group's own frontier, the larger units came out last, which tells us that there is less variability in technical efficiency in the larger size class. The firms were ranked by the Farrell index and, for comparison, by rate of return on capital employed also. A simple rank correlation between the two suggested that in this instance the rate of return measure was as good as the efficiency index as a summary performance indicator. In a competitive industry it is reasonable to assume that cost conditions are broadly the same as between firms. Thus, referring to Figure 5.11, if firms A and C, for example, have identical costs per unit of output, it follows that any differences will be reflected in profits per unit of output. Since $\pi/X = (\pi/K) \cdot (K/X)$, a similar ranking between the conventional rate of return on capital and π/X implies similar capital/output ratios. This is not really surprising in an industry where the production technology is well known and widely diffused across producers. What this example does illustrate is the care which is necessary when attempting to identify differences in performances and what might be the reasons for such differences.

The apparent low average technical efficiency suggested by the figures given in Table 5.1 serves to highlight a particular problem and introduce another empirical feature of the analysis discussed previously. A low average relative to the boundary points suggests a large variance. In fact, in the illustrative example used here, the standard deviation typically is of the order of 20 per cent. The picture in terms of industry structure would therefore appear somewhat pessimistic. Another way of looking at this is in terms of Figure 5.12. Here the horizontal axis shows the percentage of plants or firms and the vertical axis shows the technical efficiency achieved, again in percentage terms. Thus, if all firms have efficiency equal to unity, they are all located on the boundary; the cumulative frequency collapses to a single point at the north-east corner of the box. The greater the departure from this point, the greater the efficiency dispersion in the industry.

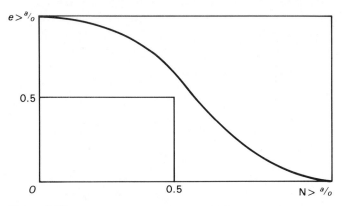

Figure 5.12

The actual cumulative efficiency distribution for the total number of firms in the investigation cited is given in Figure 5.13 below. Despite the small number of observations in the sample, the distribution function is seen to describe a profile which yields a 'bell-shaped' but skewed frequency distribution. The efficiency mode is around 45 per cent and well below the mean of about 55 per cent.

The obvious question which arises is why one should expect such a dispersion. The role which factors other than labour and capital might have has been discussed already, but another important reason is bound up with the place of technical progress in an approach of this kind. Two firms in an industry, or plants in a firm, can be rather different in terms of age of equipment and yet be efficient in economic terms. The static nature of the basic Farrell frontier methodology in effect tends to impose upon the production unit a somewhat unrealistic view as to what adjustment to alternative technical possibilities might be feasible. Firms are in the process of adjusting to a new or desired capital structure all the time. This may be an attempt to bring all plants up to the latest vintage; but even this is not necessarily optimal. Without some knowledge of optimal economic re-placement policy in a given market, the adjustment process must remain unknown. There is 'a deceptive appearance with existing structure which has no basis in a dynamic perspective . . . From a policy point of view the problem is not to bring the existing structure close to the best practice

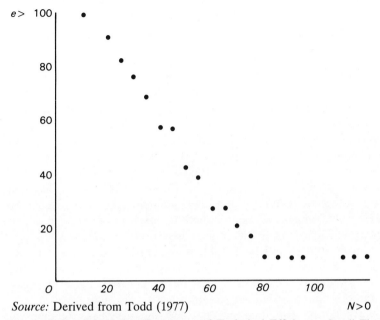

Source: Derived from Todd (1977) $N > 0$

Figure 5.13 Cumulative Frequency of Technical Efficiency: Small Firms in the Plastics Industry

structure, but consists in optimising a process that is going on the whole time' (Forsund and Hjalmarsson 1974).

Interesting and potentially fruitful attempts to incorporate the effects of technical progress within a frontier-based methodology have been made in a series of papers by Forsund *et al.* (see, for example, Forsund and Hjalmarsson 1976, Forsund and Janson 1977 and the Special Supplement of the Journal of Econometrics 1980).

The frontier approach concentrates upon input measures where ideally the specification of factor inputs is in the appropriate flow terms. More often than not, company accounts yield stock valuations only and these are taken as a somewhat rough and ready proxy for the flow of input services' counterpart.

An alternative, however, is to try and identify productive efficiency differences in terms of input prices or *costs*. One route, as we have seen, is to identify relative success in achieving scale economies, and more will be said about this later. The other route can be seen implicitly by referring again to Figure 5.6. A movement from the technically inefficient point C to points A or E is cost reducing. An interesting interpretation is provided by Cubbin and Hall (1979) in the following way.

The real unit cost of producing output X is defined as:

$$\overline{C} = \frac{\Sigma ci}{\overline{P}X} \tag{9}$$

where Σci is the total of all input costs ci, and $\overline{P}$ is an input price index.

Since total sales revenue S is composed of gross profits plus Σci, i.e. $S = PX = \pi + \Sigma\, ci$, with P being an output price index, we can combine this with (9) to yield the expression:

$$\bar{C} = \frac{P}{\bar{P}}\left(1 - \frac{\pi}{S}\right) \tag{10}$$

This is a real unit cost measure. In fact it can be seen readily that this measure is simply the cost dual of the Farrell frontier construction. A comparison of real unit costs made between two points in time and based on (10) assumes that factor proportions do not change. One is in effect moving along a fixed unit output ray such as OC in Figure 5.6.

When it comes to empirical work the Cubbin/Hall measure has one particularly attractive feature in that the information requirements can be met largely from company accounts. There remains the perennial problem of assessing efficiency on a divisional basis within a company because separate profit centres either do not exist, or the information is not collected in the appropriate form. With many qualifications Cubbin and Hall use their index as one means of assessing the efficiency performance of firms in the pre- and post-merger situation.

It is worth noting also that the dual cost measure has a number of possibilities for the monopoly and regulatory situations. Public enterprises, which in some cases exercise considerable market power in both product and input markets, can in principle be monitored in real cost performance terms on something like the above lines. The only criterion is that if real costs have been falling, then this is one indicator of improved efficiency. Judgements on pricing behaviour in this example can then be taken separately.

(b) Scale Economies

As an empirical subject this area of performance has attracted much attention and the literature is enormous. In rather general terms there are three approaches. The first, the so-called *'engineering'* approach, concentrates attention on the precise technical characteristics of the physical production process. What is probably the classic paper here is that by Chenery (1949), but there is also a wide range of examples and cases discussed in Smith (1966). More recent work has been conducted by Griffin in a series of papers (1977, 1978 and 1979). The engineering methodology is not so easy to apply in joint product technologies, and it is not surprising to find, therefore, that typical areas for investigation include attempts to identify the unit cost curve in electricity generation, dry bulk carriers, and so on.

From the company standpoint an outstanding work is that by Pratten (1971) in an investigation of individual companies operating in 28 industrial sectors in the UK manufacturing sector. The methodology combines the engineering approach with the second '*interview or questionnaire*' technique. A central conclusion which follows from Pratten's work is that 'there are substantial technical economies of scale for the production of many products' (Pratten 1971, p. 302). The studies do show, however, that a great deal of variability exists both within and between industries, with some sectors being able to achieve significant reductions in long-run unit costs through increases in plant size—steel, chemicals, motor vehicles. Other sectors have a relatively small minimum efficient size of production unit.

The 'review of monopolies and mergers policy' (Cmnd 7198, 1978) contains a useful and informative summary of evidence relating to scale economies at both plant and firm level. Again the conclusion overall is that in many industries only a small number of production units would be required if expected technical economies are to be realised. However, a related finding is that over a wide range of activities, plants are already large enough to take advantage of available cost reductions. That is to say, the minimum efficient size of plant is 'small' or has been achieved in many cases. As the review puts it, 'For only eight products (16 per cent of cases) did less than 25 per cent of output appear to be produced in such plants . . .' (Cmnd 7198, 1978, p. 79).

It is worth commenting briefly upon this kind of work since its strengths and advantages are not obtained in the absence of penalties. One clear attraction is that it strikes at the heart of the technical production process and helps one identify a technical scale curve. For any given size of plant, however, there is always a suspicion that engineering, questionnaire and survey data often yield an optimistic view of potential economies. Further, it is not easy to design control checks and make inferences about how right or wrong one might be.

It is for the above reasons that some researchers prefer the *statistical or econometric* approach. The advantages of being able to use formal statistical inference are clear and often it is easier to incorporate many different dimensions of unit costs in the chosen long-run unit cost relationship. On the other hand, it is not always easy to obtain data of sufficient quantity and variability for specific production processes.

The joint and multi-product firm cases are again difficult to handle and much work has tended to be concentrated on the output of public utilities. Notable exceptions are provided in Johnston (1960).

More conventional statistical approaches to the estimation of the technical scale curve encounter problems which are identical to those faced in the production frontier method. This is not surprising since, as we have indicated, for many purposes one can be regarded as the analogue or dual of the other. Fitting a regression plane to observations on costs and outputs will provide some idea of what an 'average' scale curve may look like. The technically optimal curve, however, is not really an average concept so that one really needs to know true minimum costs for each output. In other words, one would like to define a true scale curve which is consistent with its underlying production frontier. The engineering approaches are one possible means of dealing with this problem. The other, and in many ways more satisfactory, method is to use the fact that under certain conditions a cost function is indeed the dual of the production function. A frontier specification of one will imply a frontier specification of the other. More importantly, it can be shown that one need not specify the production relationship at all, but instead use the cost relationship directly. The references cited earlier in the previous part of this section may be consulted on this aspect of efficiency and scale estimation. It may be pointed out here that although it is not possible to develop these ideas further in this chapter,[6] the formal analysis and its empirical applications represent a potentially fruitful area for further research. As yet there are relatively few practical examples and most of these are at a highly aggregated industry or economy-wide level.

Possessing a knowledge of potential scale economies is useful for many purposes. Where policy is concerned, however, there remains an important problem of how one can use and interpret such information. To take an extreme example, if the technical scale curve for a product slopes downwards continuously, it follows that the optimum number of firms in a market such as the economy is one. On *technical* grounds then, one may wish to encourage mergers between existing production units.[7] But, as we have seen, this depends heavily upon whether the firm can actually succeed in achieving these *ex ante* economies. That is to say, can it operate on the scale curve?

Evidence in both the United States and the United Kingdom provides a rather unhappy view that this is not the case in practice. There is now a sufficiently long series of cases to make one doubt whether the alleged existence of technical scale economies is sufficient to warrant merger as a policy in many instances (see Meeks 1977 and Cmnd 7198, 1978).

Thus we raise again the issue of technical or productive efficiency and add to it now the possibility that increasing size of firm or enterprise is not a guarantee in itself that potential efficiency gains will be realised. There are of course many reasons for merger, but alleged economies of scale has been and still remains a popular justification in many instances.

---

6. A good introduction to the duality between production and cost functions is Varian (1978).
7. An interesting and, as far as the author is aware, rarely cited analysis with a good deal of policy content is that of Tisdell (1970).

(c)   *Learning Effects etc.*

In Section 5.4 it was suggested that the learning curve is something of a hybrid concept but that this should not detract from its usefulness in a practical situation. The Boston Consulting Group, for example, has made much use of the learning curve and has also collected a great deal of material on the subject (Boston Consulting Group 1970). From the empirical information assembled a fairly general observation which emerges is that as accumulated output is doubled, unit costs tend to fall by 20 to 30 per cent. Furthermore, this seems to continue as output is accumulated (see also Cmnd 7198, 1978, pp. 91–96, for several examples).

If this kind of result is of a general nature over many spheres of activity, there is a clear and obvious advantage in succeeding with a 'first in' strategy. By the time new entrants appear the initial producer is some way down the learning or production experience curve and has a more secure market position.

It is to be stressed, however, that the learning idea alone is not entirely satisfactory as a tool of analysis. Eventually one is driven back to the question 'why', and this leads once more to a consideration of those factors which determine relative efficiency. The application, therefore, serves as a useful first sift of information.

5.7   What Lessons?

We now turn to what is probably the most difficult part of the path followed so far; namely, to ask what has been learnt from the discussion here and what might be of economic significance for management in the firm.

Two things lie at the heart of just about everything which has been touched upon. The first is the notion of transforming a set of resource inputs into a stream or flow of output. The second is the idea that this activity should be pursued in an optimal fashion. Whilst these two points are at one and the same time appealing in terms of ordinary common sense, an obvious difficulty arises from the fact that success in business can be measured in a variety of ways—growth of profits, market share, cost reductions, productivity, product diversity, and so on. Any of these can be regarded as one aspect or dimension of performance in the market place. Ultimately, however, they are all reflections of the two broader aspects underlined above.

Let us consider briefly just a few examples of how a one-dimensional approach might be misleading. It is not unusual to read in, say, a Chairman's Annual Statement or in a *Financial Times* report that productivity in a plant or enterprise, measured as output per man, has changed by X per cent over the past year. Comparisons are made frequently on this

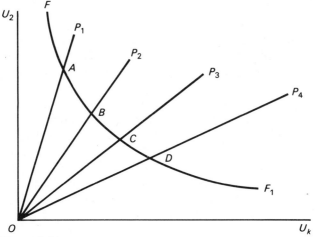

Figure 5.14

basis and there are sensible reasons why this widely used indicator is of interest in its own right. But consider Figure 5.14 where four plants P_1, P_2, etc. are looked at in terms of labour and capital employed per unit of output. Plant P_1 has high labour per unit of output (low labour productivity) as compared with P_2, P_3 and P_4. Productive efficiency, however, is greater in P_1 than in P_2, P_3, etc. That is:

$$\frac{OA}{OP_1} > \frac{OB}{OP_2} > \frac{OC}{OP_3} > \frac{OD}{OP_4} \tag{11}$$

In this deliberately exaggerated case, a ranking of productive performance in terms of output per man will be exactly the reverse of that where the two inputs are considered jointly. The main point, of course, is that productive performance depends on more things than labour usage and an excessive concentration on the latter alone can be misleading.

To illustrate this point further, the data on which the analysis of small firms by Ahmed (1976) is based and cited earlier reveals rather different conclusions according to which performance indicator is used. The close relationship by rank between the rate of return on capital and productive efficiency was noted. If, however, labour productivity is used and compared with an index of productive efficiency, the coefficient of rank correlation is only 43 per cent. Circumstances will vary enormously between individual firms and plants, but the basic point remains that a one factor input approach is not necessarily a satisfactory guide.

This leads us to a second illustration where performance is frequently analysed in terms of final sales revenue or turnover. If one is concerned with efficient utilisation of resources, however, there is much to be said for also paying attention to the *net* product of the firm, namely net output or value added.[8] This represents the actual work done using labour, capital, materials and other services. But on arriving at work done one must net out all bought-in materials and services since these are someone else's output; to include them would be double counting. Thus net output is the fund out of which primary factors of production are paid—gross employee compensation plus gross profits. It will have been observed that most of the approaches discussed in this chapter have been based on various notions associated with value added. Company accounts, however, tend to high-light the role of sales revenue and often it is difficult to extract a meaningful figure for work done over the accounting period. This does not imply that final sales is necessarily an inferior indicator. Once again, choice is deter-mined by the purpose in hand.

As a third illustration it is normal practice in many circumstances to compare performance between time periods or between firms on the basis of the return on capital employed, and it is useful to comment briefly on the relationship between this widely quoted indicator and the productivity based approaches.

Suppose two firms have the same labour charges per unit of value added, that is gross profits per unit of output are identical also. In these circumstances both will lie on a productive efficiency frontier such as that in Figure 5.11 used earlier, e.g. points A and B. Whether a rate of return on capital measure will lead to the same equality in performance now depends on how capital interest charges are treated. Taking Figure 5.11 at face value, it appears that firm A would be more efficient than B on a rate of return ranking. Profit per unit of capital is higher because it employs less capital than does firm B. On the other hand, capital costs in firm B will normally be expected to be higher than in firm A and since gross profits conventionally include interest charges, this conclusion is not so clear. One needs to know how capital interest charges relate to the rate of return before a final opinion can be made.

A slight modification of equation (7) reveals the issue clearly. Re-write the efficiency indicator as:

$$e = \frac{wL + r^*K}{wL + rK} = \frac{wL + r^*K}{V} \tag{12}$$

or $e = \dfrac{V - rK + r^*K}{V}$

$$= 1 - \beta(r - r^*) \tag{13}$$

---

8. The terms 'net output' and 'value added' are used interchangeably in this discussion. In the *Census of Production*, however, a distinction is drawn. Net output is defined as gross output less the cost of material purchases (adjusted for changes in stocks) and also the cost of industrial services. Gross value added, however, is derived by subtracting from net output other costs such as plant and equipment hire charges, advertising expenses, insurance charges, and so on.

where $\beta = K/V$ (the capital–output ratio) and $r^* =$ the interest 'cost' of capital to the firm. The form (13) is in fact almost identical to that used by Downie (1958) and discussed in Todd (1971). It is in effect a value added based index and suggests that the relationship between the index and the rate of return on capital, r, is likely to be fairly close. When comparing firms in the same industry or a firm between two time periods, for example, it is likely that K/V will not vary much and hence the correlation between e and r might be expected to be high.[9] There can, however, be substantial differences when the rate of return is zero, for example, or when the degree of capital intensity is relatively low.

These and other examples serve to illustrate the multi-dimensional nature of productive performance and explain why preoccupation with a one factor/output relationship can obscure other aspects of behaviour.

The desirability of an optimal use of resources in the production process has strong normative significance. At the same time, however, it carries with it an implicit idea that there is some absolute standard against which performance can be appraised. In one sense there is, since if a plant or firm can no longer gain an extra unit of output from an additional injection of inputs, this is a point on the production frontier and thus constitutes a maximal desired position.

On the other hand, the Hall and Winston view referred to earlier in Section 5.4 lends a lot of weight to the idea that local and other constraints on a firm's behaviour will limit performance in various ways. Thus within any plant or firm, whilst one can be ever vigilant in the quest for efficiency improvements on the basis of an estimated standard, inter-plant or inter-firm comparisons will be more difficult to make.[10] In these circumstances, to regard efficiency as a relative concept only sounds more reasonable. Indeed, one can interpret measures of productive efficiency as being relative to 'best practice' units as revealed by actual performance. This concentrates attention on the question raised in Section 5.6 (a), namely, if plants A, B, etc. can achieve a given productive performance, then why cannot plants W, X, Y, etc? Further, it induces one to consider in more detail exactly what the precise nature of any constraints or performance might be. The object could then be to bring production units closer to those best performers as revealed by actual behaviour. Once again, a multi-factor approach will be instructive here.

---

9. Todd (1977) found the rank correlation between firms ranked by r and the Farrell index to be 95 per cent.

10. Some analysts would seem to favour the view that efficiency comparisons should be restricted or can only be meaningful if assessments of performance are made within a business unit and with reference to a budget plan. See, for example, Amey (1969).

5.8 Concluding Comments

This chapter is in effect a quick tour of a few approaches to the economic assessment of productive performance. Even though the gaps are large, the breadth of subject matter still limits the discussion, but it does provide a brief flavour of some economic work in the general area. The references cited should, however, fill out many of the points raised.

Although the subject matter is part of what might be termed 'core economics' and central to any serious consideration of how resources are utilised by production units in a market economy, there is an unfortunate fact to be faced. All too few of the empirical studies undertaken are actually concerned with the behaviour of *firms*. With the exception of the public utilities, the great, or even overwhelming, majority of investigations are carried out at the industry level.

In part, this must be due to the well-known lack of quantitative material available on firms themselves. Since virtually all of the analytical material considered here is specified initially for the firm or plant as a *micro* unit, it is to be regretted that more effort is not devoted to making data available so that more direct testing of the various hypotheses suggested by the theory can be undertaken. Otherwise the suspicion must remain that many industry-based analyses which use the firm or plant concept as a starting point and then proceed to industry statistical sources conceal what may be a set of rather important aggregation problems. Somewhat mysteriously, these disappear by a sleight of hand which is rarely, if ever, discussed openly.

Yet having said this, the data requirements are very demanding if topics, such as best practice production frontiers, scale and technical progress, can be analysed at the micro level. The studies by Forsund and Hjalmarsson (1976, 1977) serve as examples of what can be achieved, but even to get this far the authors had access to very detailed information on factor input volumes, plants by age structure, precise depreciation practices, and so on. Such availability is rare and all too often one must resort to the use of accounting and other data which has been produced for many reasons; the economist's requirement is not necessarily the most important.

To a person engaged in day-to-day operations of, say, business management or to a plant engineer, for example, many if not all of the notions set out above may appear to have an air of unreality. The apparently rarified world of the professional economist seems all too remote. It is legitimate to ask, therefore, what economic analysis can contribute to the understanding of performance. Where purely technical and physical characteristics matter, the answer is probably nothing or at best very little. When one thinks in terms of opportunities foregone and the costs involved, then the ground becomes firmer. There is a distinct advantage in being able to analyse firms as units which transform inputs into saleable output and take account of the major inputs simultaneously.

There is still a proliferation of partial performance indicators produced which may or may not be useful. Most of these stem from expansion
of simple identities and say little about behaviour or the way in which
constraints might affect behaviour. Several of the topics touched upon here
help one to begin thinking about how input combinations can influence
relative performance and hence see beyond the more partial indicators.
Thus if they are not applicable on the shop floor, they can help in forming a
reasonable and intuitively sensible framework within which problems can
be appraised and the proper questions asked.

Finally, it is worth reminding the reader again that many of the empirical
techniques mentioned are still in something of an infancy stage in their
'product cycle' and many remain so for some time. But the subject matter
is evolving continuously so that one should anticipate that both improvements and more realism will be forthcoming.

References

Ahmed, M. (1976) 'Size and efficiency: the case of the Irish plastics industry',
    Economic and Social Review, Vol. 8, No. 1.
Alchian, A. (1953) 'Reliability of progress curves in airframe production',
    Econometrica, Vol. 31.
Amey, L. (1969) *The Efficiency of Business Enterprise*, Allen and Unwin.
Beckenstein, A. R. (1975) 'Scale economies in the multi-plant firm: theory and
    empirical evidence', *Bell Journal of Economics*, Vol. 6.
Chenery, H. (1949) 'Engineering production functions', *Quarterly Journal of
    Economics*, Vol. 63.
Cubbin, J. and Hall, G. (1979) 'The use of real cost as an efficiency measure: an
    application to merging firms', *Journal of Industrial Economics*, Vol. 28.
Downie, J. (1958) *The Competitive Process*, Duckworth.
Farrell, M. J. (1957) 'The measurement of productive efficiency', *Journal of the
    Royal Statistical Society*, Series A, Vol. 120.
Forsund, F. R. and Hjalmarsson, L. (1974) 'On the measurement of productive
    efficiency', *Swedish Journal of Economics*, Vol. 76, No. 2.
Forsund, F. R. and Hjalmarsson, L. (1976) 'Technical progress, best-practice
    production functions and average production functions in the Swedish dairy
    industry', paper presented at the *Econometric Society* European Meeting,
    Helsinki.
Forsund, F. R. and Janson, E. S. (1977) 'On estimating average and best-practice
    homothetic production functions via cost functions', *International Economic
    Review*, Vol. 18, No. 2.
Gold, B. (ed.) (1975) *Technological Change*, Pergamon Press.
Gold, B. (1981) 'Changing perspectives on size, scale and returns: an interpretive
    survey', *Journal of Economic literature*, Vol. 19.
Griffin, J. M. (1977) 'Long-run production modelling with pseudo data: electric
    power generation', *The Bell Journal of Economics*, Spring.
Griffin, J. M. (1978) 'Joint production technology: the case of petro-chemicals',
    Econometrica, Vol. 46.
Griffin, J. M. (1979) 'Statistical cost analysis revisited', *Quarterly Journal of
    Economics*, No. 1.

Hall, M. and Winston, C. B. (1959) 'The ambiguous notion of efficiency', *Economic Journal*, Vol. 69.

Harvey, R. A. and Morris, S. E. (1981) 'Pathways to productivity improvement', *Omega*, Vol. 9, No. 2.

Johnston, J. (1960) *Statistical Cost Analysis*, McGraw-Hill.

Kaldor, N. (1934) 'The equilibrium of the firm', *Economic Journal*, Vol. XLIV.

Kopp, R. (1981) 'The measurement of productive efficiency: a reconsideration', *Quarterly Journal of Economics*, August.

Laitinen, K. (1980) 'A theory of the multi-product firm', Vol. 28, in *Studies in Mathematical and Managerial Economics*, North Holland Publishing Company.

Layard, P. R. G. and Walters, A. A. (1978) *Microeconomic Theory*, McGraw-Hill.

Leibenstein, H. (1966) 'Allocative efficiency versus X-efficiency', *American Economic Review*, Vol. 56.

Meeks, G. (1977) *Disappointing Marriage: A Study of Gains from Merger*, Cambridge University Press.

Pratten, C. (1971) 'Economies of scale in manufacturing industry', Cambridge University, DAE Occasional Paper No. 28.

Roll, Y. and Sachish, A. (1981) 'Productivity measurement at the plant level', *Omega*, Vol. 9, No. 1.

Silberston, A. (1972) 'Economies of scale in theory and practice', *Economic Journal*, Vol. 82 Supplement.

Smith, V. L. (1966) *The Theory of Investment and Production*, Harvard University Press.

Teague, J. and Eilon, S. (1973) 'Productivity measurement: a brief survey', *Applied Economics*, Vol. 5.

Tisdell, C. (1970) 'Efficiency and decreasing cost industries', *Australian Economic Papers*, December.

Todd, D. (1971) 'The relative efficiency of small and large firms', *Committee of Inquiry on Small Firms*, Research Report No. 18, HMSO.

Todd, D. (1977) 'Efficiency and size: comments and extensions', *Economic and Social Review*, Vol. 8, No. 4.

Varian, H. (1978) *Microeconomic Analysis*, W. Norton and Company.

Boston Consulting Group (1970) *Perspectives on Experience*.

Cmnd 7198 (1978) *A Review of Monopolies and Mergers Policy*, HMSO.

6
Marketing Management

Peter Doyle

This chapter looks at the role of marketing in the modern firm and the key tasks of marketing management. How to be successful at marketing is a subject attracting increasing attention from companies, institutions and nations. Factors stimulating this focus are greater international competition, rapid social and technological change and shortening product life cycles. While the emphasis of this chapter has to be limited to the marketing activities of manufacturing businesses, it is worth noting that much is being written about marketing in service companies (e.g. Eiglier, Langeard *et al.* 1977) and non-profit organisations, such as universities and orchestral societies (e.g. Kotler 1975). Such organisations have many of the same problems as manufacturers. They must identify the groups they serve, determine their needs, develop offers to satisfy their needs, and communicate with their constituencies. Marketing provides a common discipline for approaching these problems.

6.1 Introduction

A major study by the National Economic Development Office found that lack of expertise in marketing was the single most important cause of the disappointing international performance of British companies in the last two decades (National Economic Development Office 1981). A survey of 21 top US companies concluded that chief executives in these companies believed that

> marketing is the most important management function in their businesses, and that they see it becoming more important in the future. Whether they come from a marketing background or not, they believe that the development and maintenance of an effective marketing organisation is the major requirement for success in the economic environment of increased competition and slow growth that will be the characteristic of most markets in the 1980s. (Webster 1981)

As a discipline marketing has drawn heavily on economics, especially microeconomics and econometrics. But it is misleading to think of market-ing as only a branch of applied economics. Marketing is a catholic discipline which utilises findings from several areas: its theory of buyer behaviour draws significantly on psychology (see, for example, Howard and Sheth 1969); sociological studies form the foundation for the theory of the diffusion of innovation (Rogers 1962); accounting and finance have provided key insights for market and product planning procedures (Hul-bert and Toy 1977); and statistics and psychometrics have contributed many of the tools used by market researchers (Green and Tull 1978).

Marketing, however, has become more than a mixed bag of findings from other disciplines. Its core is a unique approach to business strategy which proposes that firms will prosper to the extent that they can understand the needs and wants of buyers and adapt their production capabilities to matching these desires more effectively than competitor firms[1]. Marketing has borrowed from other disciplines where they can contribute to the study of buyers and to facilitating the adaptation of the firm to their desires. Economic theory has proved useful mainly because it has provided concepts for understanding how the firm should allocate marketing resources. Such concepts have proved especially important in pricing and advertising decisions. The real limitation of economics in contributing to marketing is the lack of insight economics provides into the motivation and product choices of consumers.

6.2 Marketing

Marketing, like economics, is concerned with the way resources are produced and allocated via the exchange process between buyers and sellers in a market. The perspective differs, however, in that the market means the group of actual or potential buyers to a marketer, and he looks at the exchange process primarily from the viewpoint of the seller. *Marketing* can be defined as the activity of satisfying the needs and wants of buyers through the exchange process in a manner which enables the firm (or other type of organisation) to achieve its objectives. The most obvious of such objectives is, of course, profit, but market share or growth may be additional ones.

Successful organisations now approach marketing in a professional, systematic manner and this has led to the recognition of marketing

---

1. It is sometimes useful to distinguish between needs and wants. Needs are not created by marketing, but are the basic requirements for human survival. Wants are the desires for specific products or services to satisfy these needs, e.g. a person needs food and wants a MacDonald's hamburger. Needs are few, wants are many and are continually reshaped by social forces and by the efforts of marketers to persuade people that their goods will satisfy a given need.

management as a primary business function on a par with finance and production. In an authoritative textbook Kotler defines *marketing management* as follows:

> The analysis, planning, implementation and control of programmes designed to build exchanges and relationships with target markets for the purpose of achieving organisation objectives. It relies on a disciplined analysis of the needs and wants of target customers as the basis for effective product design, pricing, communication and distribution. (Kotler 1980, p. 22)

6.3   The Marketing Concept

It is valuable to distinguish two related ways of thinking about marketing. One is the idea of marketing as a total business philosophy which affects all the different functional areas of the business. The second is a more specific, functional notion of marketing which defines the principal tasks of marketing management: identifying marketing opportunities, developing policies on price, advertising, product development and so on. The latter are the tasks which are usually led by the marketing department of the firm.

The former idea is called the *marketing concept* which states that the *raison d'être* of a business is to satisfy the desires of customers. It emphasises that failure to do this at least as effectively as competitors will mean that business cannot survive in a competitive world. Similarly, firms which are outstandingly successful are those which develop their analysis and planning capabilities to identify or anticipate customers' desires and match them with products and services more effectively than their rivals. Examples of companies which exhibit such a marketing orientation include Marks and Spencer, IBM, Procter and Gamble, Honda, and Cassio.

This marketing orientation is often contrasted with two earlier, but still prevalent, philosophies of business. One is the *production orientation*: the view that the product will find markets by itself if it is produced at a low enough cost or with a sufficiently advanced technical quality edge. Firms holding this philosophy tend to be dominated by engineers or production managers who pay little attention to the explicit study of prospective buyers. Such companies usually come to grief eventually by investing in goods which, while technically sound, turn out to be a poor match with the benefits buyers are actually seeking (for some good examples see Hartley 1976). Other companies are *sales oriented*, believing that success depends upon the effectiveness of the advertising, selling and promotional techniques used to stimulate the awareness and desires of buyers, rather than on any true differences in the offerings by competitors. The limitations of this philosophy lie in the assumptions about the gullibility of consumers to sales-stimulating devices and the unimportance of the attitudes and behaviour of dissatisfied customers.

The real distinction between the marketing and sales orientations was made in a classic article by Levitt:

> Selling tries to get the customer to want what the company has; marketing, on the other hand, tries to get the company to produce what the customer wants. (Levitt 1965)

This belief that marketing reverses the logic of these earlier philosophies of business was emphasised by Drucker:

> Selling and marketing are antithetical rather than synonymous or even complementary. There will always, one can assume, be a need for some selling. But the aim of marketing is to make selling superfluous. The aim of marketing is to know and understand the customer so well that the product or service fits him and sells itself. Ideally, marketing should result in a customer who is ready to buy. (Drucker 1974, p. 85)

Adopting the marketing concept implies totally reorienting the whole company such that its strategic planning starts by identifying opportunities created by the potential for more effectively satisfying customer wants. This then leads to the company's research, development, engineering and production capabilities being aligned to develop a product and a marketing mix which optimally matches the prior identified opportunity in the market. As Drucker observed, 'marketing is so basic that it cannot be considered a separate function . . . It is the whole business seen from the point of view of its final result, that is, from the customer's point of view' (Drucker 1974, p. 88).

6.4   The Marketing Function

There are two key decisions which are central to marketing management: the selection of target markets which determine where the firm will compete, and the design of the marketing mix (product, price, promotion and distribution method) which will determine its success in these markets.

(a)   Selection of Target Markets

A market is defined as the set of actual and potential buyers of a product. In today's rapidly changing environment products and markets have a limited life expectancy. A firm which does not update and change its products and markets is unlikely to be successful for long. A major job of management is to determine which markets offer the business opportunities for profit and growth in the future. Market research is the tool used to generate the information for reaching such decisions.

Three areas for research are particularly important. First, the firm will want to estimate the size and growth potential of alternative markets since in general it will prefer to operate in growth rather than mature or declining markets. Second, it will wish to judge the strength of competition in candidate markets. How tough is competition? Will it be possible to carve out a niche without strong reaction from existing competitors? Thirdly, choice of target market will be influenced by the fit of the market requirements with the firm's own strengths and weaknesses. A heavy engineering company, for example, is unlikely to be effective in switching to fast-moving consumer goods where it lacks technological or marketing expertise. In general, a company will seek product and market opportunities in areas where it has some expertise which can form the basis for a competitive edge.

After a broad market is identified comes the key task of *market segmentation. Undifferentiated marketing* (Figure 6.1)—a single marketing mix offered to the entire market—is rarely successful because markets are not homogeneous but made up of different types of buyers with diverse wants regarding product benefits, price, channels of distribution and service. A market segment is a group of buyers with similar purchasing characteristics. For example, the car market might be divided into an economy segment (buyers looking for a cheap form of car transportation), a status segment, a sporting-oriented segment, etc. In developing a marketing plan the marketer usually has to design appropriate offers for each segment if he is to compete. *Differentiated marketing* is the policy of attacking the market by tailoring separate product and marketing programmes for each segment. *Concentrated marketing* is often the best strategy for the smaller firm. This entails selecting to compete in one segment and developing the most effective marketing mix for this submarket. Ford, for example, now pursues a policy of differentiated marketing whereas Volkswagen has traditionally concentrated on the smaller car market.

(b)   Developing the Marketing Mix

The marketing mix is the set of choices which defines the firm's offer to its target market. McCarthy (1981) has popularised the '4 P's' definition of the marketing mix—product, place, promotion and price (Table 6.1). Buyers in the target segment have a set of wants and by research and successful

Table 6.1   Components of the Marketing Mix

Product	Price	Promotion	Place
Quality	List price	Advertising	Distributors
Features	Discounts	Personal selling	Retailers
Name	Allowances	Sales promotion	Locations
Packaging	Credit	Public relations	Inventory
Services			Transport
Guarantees			

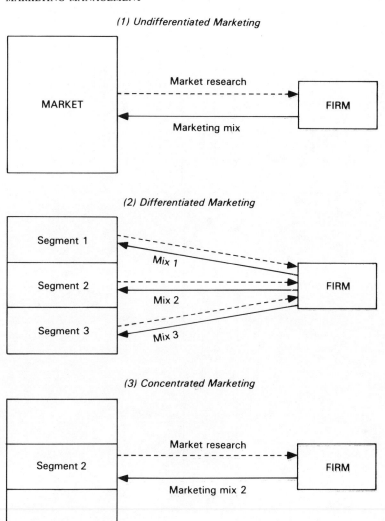

Figure 6.1 Marketing Segmentation and Alternative Marketing Strategies

adaptation the marketer will develop an offer to match them (Figure 6.2). 'Product' includes a number of decision elements, as do the other 'P's' shown in Table 6.1. As emphasised earlier, the marketing mix for one segment may need to be quite different from that of another. In tailoring its mix the firm will seek to offer one which target customers will see as superior to that offered by competition. This goal of offering a marketing mix superior to competition is termed the '*differential advantage*'.

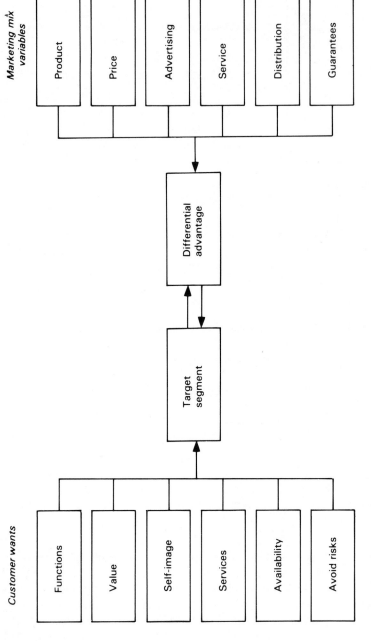

Figure 6.2   The Marketing Mix and Differential Advantage: Matching Customer Wants

6.5   Three Key Marketing Principles

In analysing marketing problems and developing marketing plans three concepts play a central role: marketing segmentation, the differential advantage and positioning strategy.

(a)   Market Segmentation

Pigou (1932), Robinson (1933) and Chamberlin (1938) developed the basic theory of market segmentation, showing that where different segments exist with separate demand functions the monopolist would maximise profits by charging different prices to the two segments. There are many practical examples of this type of price discrimination, e.g. a public utility charging different rates for business and domestic consumers. The concept of segmentation in marketing, however, is much more general. The marketer recognises that consumers differ not only in the price they will pay, but in a wide range of benefits they expect from the 'product' and its method of delivery. The firm can discriminate not only in price, but potentially in any of the 4 'P's'. For example, the market for electronic calculators is made up of a number of segments including a segment of 'scientific users', an 'office' segment and a 'general public' segment. Each segment is likely to have a different price elasticity, but in addition each desires different 'products' (the scientific segment requiring more sophisti- cated features and offices wanting greater robustness, for example). The channels utilised will also vary: scientific will be best reached via personal selling or specialist journals, offices via specific distributors and the general public through the major retail chains. Similarly, the advertising and promotional strategies will differ in media and message between each segment.

Segmentation is central to marketing because different customer groups imply different marketing mix strategies. The technique of segmenting a market also reveals profit opportunities and 'strategic windows' (Abell 1978) for new competitors to challenge established market leaders. As a market develops new segments open and older ones decline. Within most markets are a mix of fierce and relatively weak competitive segments, slow and high growth segments (e.g. the segment of people wanting large luxury cars has declined relative to the economy segment). The marketing strategist will be seeking to identify those dynamic segments offering the best growth and profit possibilities.

(b)   Differential Advantage

Target market segmentation is, however, insufficient for strategic planning since, in general, other companies will also be competing for any segment chosen. To be successful the marketer must also develop a differential advantage which will distinguish his offer from competitors in the segment. Only by creating such a differential advantage can the firm ordinarily obtain high profits. In a market where no firm has a differential advantage consumers choose on the basis of price, and such 'perfect' competition tends to eliminate supernormal profits.

The task of the modern business is to seek what may be termed a 'quasi-monopoly'—to make itself unique to consumers so that they will not switch to competitors for minor price advantages. High profit firms such as IBM, Marks and Spencer, Avon Cosmetics, Kodak, Yamaha and Procter and Gamble are generally those which have succeeded in creating such consumer preferences. These differential advantages may be obtained potentially via any element of the marketing mix—creating a superior product to competition, more attractive designs, better service, more effective distribution, better advertising or selling, and so on. The keys are understanding that an 'advantage' is based upon research into what customers really value and that a 'differential' is derived from an evaluation of competitive strategies and offers.

(c)   Positioning Strategy

Positioning is the amalgam of these two earlier principles. Positioning strategy refers to the choice of target market segment which describes the customers the business will seek to serve, and the choice of differential advantage which defines how it will compete with rivals in the segment. Thus Porsche is positioned in the prestige segment of the car market with a differential advantage based on technical performance. The Mothercare store is positioned to serve mothers with young children with a differential advantage based on breadth of merchandise assortment for that target segment. The appropriateness and effectiveness of the positioning strategy is the major determinant of a business' growth and profit performance.

6.6   Key Analyses for Developing Marketing Strategy

In formulating its choice of target market segment, marketing mix and differential advantage, the firm will focus its research in six major areas:

(a)   Market Analysis

As described earlier, before committing itself further the company should assess the growth and profit opportunities likely to be open to it in the candidate market.

(b)   Customer Analysis

The firm will need to research how the market is segmented, which of these segments are the most attractive and what are the benefits desired by customers within each of these segments. Knowledge of such factors will be central to designing its product and offer. In addition, in order to develop its promotional and distribution strategy it will need to determine who are the key people affecting product choice in the buying unit (the household or buying organisation) and what type of buying process occurs before a decision is reached (e.g. how information is sought, how alternatives are compared).

(c)   Competitive Analysis

Developing a differential advantage means making target buyers an offer superior to that of the competition. Clearly, therefore, this strategy requires identifying who the competitors are now and whether new ones may emerge in the future. The marketer needs to judge what their strategic objectives are, how their offer is perceived by buyers and how it may change in the future. Finally, it is crucial to estimate how competitors are likely to react to any strategic initiative. If a new product is introduced or prices are cut in an effort to gain market share, is this initiative likely to be nullified by speedy retaliation from competition? (For a thorough discussion of competitive analysis see Porter 1980.)

(d)   Trade Analysis

Most companies do not sell all their goods directly to the final consumer but use trade intermediaries (wholesalers, distributors, agents and retailers) to do this for them. Such an arrangement offers the company economies in marketing and distribution and the opportunity to sell to wider markets. On the other hand, these intermediaries are normally independent and their commercial goals will not be identical to those of the individual manufacturers they buy from. Thus the company will need to consider how to motivate the trade to give its product preferential treatment in their presentations to the public.

Star, Davis *et al.* (1977) suggest the manufacturer's trade analysis should be focused around the following questions:

1. What role does the product play in the trade's merchandise mix (e.g. traffic generation or margin generation)?
2. How does the trade merchandise the product (e.g. self-service versus personal selling)?

3. How satisfied is the trade with the marketing and trade strategies of competitors?
4. What differential advantage might be obtained through actions such as generous trade terms, extensive advertising, improved delivery, etc?

(e) Environmental Analysis

Strategy formulation also needs to consider the changing environment of the business. Success will be affected by broad changes in the economic, demographic socio-political and technological environment. The major US car companies, for example, which concentrated on large, heavy-petrol consuming vehicles, were severely hit by the Middle East Crisis and the rapid rise in oil prices after 1973. In the more immediate marketing environment management must study the problems and opportunities being created by new consumer tastes, changing patterns of distribution (e.g. from independent shops to multiple grocery-type shops) and emerging products. Such forces curtail the product life cycle of existing products and necessitate continual strategic innovation and repositioning if the firm is to maintain its viability.

(f) Economic and Stakeholder Analysis

In assessing a strategy the firm will want to assess the financial implications and its impact on those stakeholder groups of importance to the firm. For the business, the strategy will need to generate an adequate level of profit to satisfy shareholders and provide for the firm's continuing investment requirements. Since investment generally anticipates profit return, the cash requirements will also have to be considered—can the business finance the marketing strategy? Other stakeholder or interest groups that may constrain the policy include consumerist organisations, the local community, government regulatory bodies, unions and suppliers. The well-designed strategy will have considered the impacts on all relevant parties.

6.7 Marketing Mix Decisions

Market research and business appraisal (to complete the six analyses considered in the previous sections), together with judgements about how the company is to position itself against potential target market segments and to develop a differential advantage, are implemented by management decisions on the marketing mix. Important normative rules for optimising the marketing mix have been developed by economists. These rules stem from the classical model of the firm in which output and price are the only decision variables and where sales are optimised at the point at which marginal revenue equals marginal cost. Dorfman and Steiner (1954) extended this to include other 'marketing mix' variables, namely advertising and product quality. The Dorfman–Steiner theorem showed that short-run profits are maximised where the company balances lower prices, increased advertising expenditure and higher quality products in such a way as to equate:

$$\xi_q \frac{P}{C} = \xi = \mu$$

where $\xi_q P/C$ is the elasticity of demand with respect to quality improvement multiplied by price over average unit cost; ξ is the price elasticity of demand; and μ is the marginal revenue product of advertising.

The Dorfman–Steiner theorem provides an important insight for designing the marketing mix, and several studies have tried to estimate and apply this rule (e.g. Lambin 1969; Corstjens and Doyle 1981). In practice, however, its use is limited for a number of important reasons. In particular, it is extremely difficult to estimate these marginal effects, especially in oligopolistic markets where competitive reaction is a major dilemma and where many variables (advertising, intensity of distributing and price) interact with one another. Also, the firm is generally not seeking solely to maximise profits, but may have a range of strategic goals (growth, risk avoidance, supporting complementary products in the firm's range, etc). Some of these issues become clearer when the elements of the marketing mix are considered.

(a) Product Policy

Economic theory has little to say about product policy because the theory of consumer behaviour treats the products themselves, rather than the benefits or characteristics they possess, as the direct objects of utility. Under such an assumption little can be said about the key questions of how one product competes with another or how one can develop a superior product. Recently economists have tried to fill this gap by developing a new theory of consumer behaviour which defines a product as a bundle of characteristics which are the ultimate goal of the buyer. As Lancaster (1966) has shown, this opens up the possibility of a much more fruitful set of insights into consumer behaviour.

Paradoxically, this notion that consumers are interested in the benefits provided by a marketer's offer rather than the product itself has always been central to marketing theory. The 'new economics' mirrors an approach which has long been applied in marketing to the study of brand preferences (for a discussion see Ratchford 1975). To a marketing manager a product is the constellation of benefits generated by the physical product, namely its design, features, packaging, style and service support, which together provide satisfaction to the consumer. It is often said that much of IBM's success was based on its recognition that their cost and complexity make computers unattractive to industry executives. At the same time, IBM knew that these executives increasingly needed more effective systems for efficiently and rapidly handling and manipulating information. IBM's offer was not a computer but a 'management information system' made up of not only the hardware, but software, attractive input/output and related peripherals, technical support, training, installation, operational back-up and easy financial arrangements. The founder of Revlon Cosmetics, one of the most successful consumer goods companies, put the distinction between products and benefits more colourfully when he said, 'In the factory we make cosmetics, in the store we sell hope!'

For marketing it is crucial to see how the product's benefits are perceived by consumers rather than how they are defined by production experts. *Product positioning* is a market research technique which seeks to elicit from buyers a description or 'map' of how alternative brands are perceived. Figure 6.3 shows a positioning study by Johnson (1971) of the US beer market. The dimensions (characteristics) buyers appear to use when judging beers are lightness and mildness. The circles show the preference of buyers. Since, of course, different segments have differing tastes, these are spread, while the radius of the circle indicates the estimated size of each consumer segment. Positioning studies have obvious uses in product planning: they show the strengths and weaknesses of the manufacturers' brands along the dimensions which are important to consumers; they show how closely competitive brands are seen; and they indicate where different segment preferences are. Such insights have obvious implications for repositioning the product by quality changes, design, packaging or advertising modifications and also for new product development.

Product positioning models suggest a marketer can pursue seven alternative strategies by modifying his product or persuasive communications (Boyd, Ray and Strong 1972):

(1) Developing a new brand
(2) Modifying the existing brand
(3) Altering beliefs about the company's brand
(4) Altering beliefs about the competitors' brands
(5) Altering the importance attached to the individual characteristics
(6) Calling attention to neglected characteristics
(7) Shifting consumer preferences

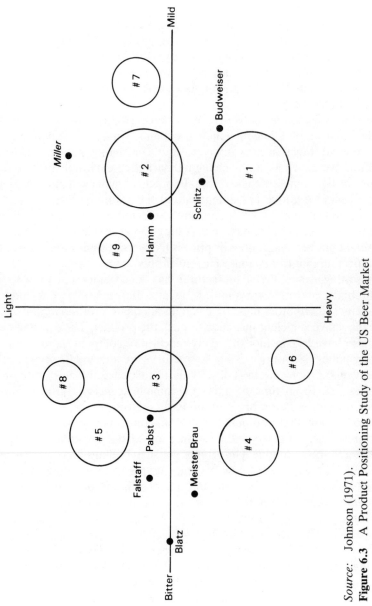

Source: Johnson (1971).
Figure 6.3 A Product Positioning Study of the US Beer Market

(b)   *Pricing Policy*

The economic theory of price shows that profits are maximised when prices are set to equate marginal revenue and marginal cost. An obvious practical problem is that other variables usually affect demand both independently and interactively with price, e.g. some studies have shown that advertising reduces price elasticity (Frank, Massy and Wind 1972). In principle modern econometrics provides methods of estimation in such circumstances, and there have been a number of successful empirical applications published (see Palda 1969).

Generally speaking, however, few firms explicitly follow the economic model in developing pricing policy. Most find estimating the parameters of the demand function too difficult, time-consuming and expensive. In addition, with such a rapidly changing marketing environment, few would expect such parameters to be stable. In practice, management prices on the basis of more intuitive judgements about the nature of cost, demand and competition. Pricing is also significantly affected by the firm's objectives. Where the firm has, for example, a long-run strategic goal of winning a dominant market share, then its price is likely to be significantly lower than for a firm aiming to maximise current profits.

In setting prices the manufacturer has to consider not only its own profitability and the reaction of buyers, but other parties too. The company's distributors must be given an adequate profit margin to ensure that they have sufficient incentive to push the product. The decision maker will also have to consider the likely reaction of competitors to a switch in pricing policy. Not only existing competitors are affected by pricing policy; the level of profit margin is also likely to influence the entry rate of new competitors. From time to time government agencies also affect pricing policy for anti-inflation or anti-monopoly reasons.

Studies show that in practice almost all companies price on the basis of cost-plus. Price is determined by adding some fixed percentage to unit total cost at a 'normal' output. Unfortunately, such findings do not really tell us much without a theory of how the mark-up percentage is determined. The major determinant of the potential mark-up is the product's differential advantage—the greater the perceived value it has over competitive products the more the consumer will pay. The most sophisticated marketing companies, like Hewlett-Packard and 3M Corporation, calculate this perceived value to the consumer in considerable detail before making a pricing decision (Shapiro and Jackson 1978). The McKinsey management consulting firm advocates calculating this value by comparing the product's total costs and benefits with those of a 'reference product', e.g. the market leader.

For example, consider a company seeking to price a new industrial product, X, in a market where the brand leader is product Y. Users of Y

pay £3,000 for the product, another £2,000 to set up the product (e.g. transportation, engineering, installation), and over the life of the product spend another £5,000 in maintenance and operating costs, making a total life cycle cost of £10,000. Suppose the new product X has features which lower set-up and post-purchase costs to £4,000, yielding a £3,000 life cycle saving. Then the economic value to the buyer of product X is £6,000. That is, the consumer should be willing to pay a price of up to £6,000 for the new product. At £6,000 there would be no incentive to switch from the brand leader. Hence, the supplier might decide to price it at £4,000 to produce a £2,000 'customer savings incentive'.

In practice the most common types of pricing policies pursued by firms are the following:

Market penetration pricing   Here the firm prices low, sacrificing short-term profits, to aim at a dominant market share. Circumstances favouring this policy are: (1) where the market is highly price elastic; (2) where total unit costs will decline substantially with production experience; and (3) where a low price will discourage new competitors entering the market.

Market skimming pricing   This entails setting high initial prices which yield high profit margins over a relatively small volume and generally for a short period of time. It is a viable option where (1) a segment of significant size exists which will buy at the high initial price; (2) the firm has limited production capacity or resources with which to expand; (3) the high initial price will not attract an immediate competitive takeover of the market; and (4) the high price creates an image of a superior product.

Cost oriented pricing   Most firms, as noted, set prices largely on the basis of product costs. *Mark-up pricing* and cost-plus pricing set price by adding some fixed percentage to the unit cost. *Target pricing* is another cost oriented pricing approach that sets prices to achieve a certain target return on investment.

Perceived value pricing   Unlike the cost oriented policies, this approach, as described earlier, bases price on demand considerations—on how the buyers perceive the value of the product relative to competition. To be effective this approach requires market research to obtain an accurate picture of the market's perceptions.

Price discrimination   This is another common form of demand pricing whereby the firm seeks to charge different types of customer with different prices for the same or similar product. Where segments exist with different price elasticities, this type of discrimination allows the firm to achieve higher profits. To be successful, customers in the higher price segment must not be allowed to buy from the lower price segment. In addition, the practice should not lead to serious customer resentment.

Companies change their prices and strategies over time. The most common stimuli to price increases are rising costs or increased demand for the firm's product. Price cutting can be initiated from excess capacity in the industry, the loss of market share or because the company decides to strengthen its position in the market.

(c) Promotional Policy

After a company has designed a product and an offer to match the wants of its target market segment, it needs to communicate this offer to buyers and persuade them to try it. There are four main tools which are used to achieve these goals—advertising, personal selling, sales promotion and public relations. In general, before purchasing a product the buyer has to be brought through various stages of the communications process. First, he has to be made *aware* of the product's existence; second, he has to *comprehend* the benefits the product offers; third, he needs to become *convinced* that it will meet his wants; and finally, he has to be brought to the point of making a positive *purchase* decision (Aaker and Myers 1982).

The different communications tools are frequently used to achieve specific communications goals. Advertising is particularly good at making the market aware of a new product, but it is usually far less effective than personal selling at closing the sale. Personal selling is usually a very costly means of creating awareness and comprehension, but more efficient at stimulating conviction and purchase. There are also differences between consumer and industrial goods. Sales promotion and publicity tend to be used for both types of marketing, but because of the larger number of buyers which characterise consumer marketing mass media advertising is more important there, whereas personal selling is usually the major selling medium in industrial marketing.

Here we shall note the key decision areas in advertising. In planning advertising the marketer, usually in conjunction with his advertising agency, will need to make five decisions. First, he will need a clear definition of the target market segment to which the advertising is to be directed. Next, he will need to determine the most effective media (newspapers, journals, TV, radio, posters, etc.) for getting his message to these people. Agencies are increasingly using a computer programme to seek an optimum combination of media which will deliver the desired number of exposures to the target audience (Broadbent 1977). Linear programming, heuristic programming and simulation models have all been used as aids to help the planner determine the media mix which maximises effective exposures subject to budget and other company constraints. The third area for decision is on the form and content of the message or copy to be expressed in the advertising. In general, the advertising agency will try to create a message which will express the differential advantage of the product in a manner which makes it believable, desirable and exclusive. The other two decisión areas concern determining how much should be spent on advertising and how the investment should be subsequently evaluated and controlled.

Econometric studies have been widely used to estimate the payoff of advertising and determine the optimum advertising budget. For example, in a study for a major alcoholic drink product, Corstjens and Doyle (1981) used time series data to estimate the demand function of the brand as:

$$q_t = 4.27 - 0.004B_t + 0.245A_t - 1.20P_t + 0.672q_{t-1}$$

where

q_t = sales of the brands at time t in units
B_t = industry sales of the product class
A_t = brand advertising expenditure (in logs)
P_t = price (in logs) of the brand at time t

This equation explained 85 per cent of the variation in sales of the brand. From this it was possible to calculate the short- and long-term advertising elasticities for the brand as 0.14 and 0.43 respectively. Then, using the Dorfman–Steiner theorem (which shows that at the optimal level of advertising, the marginal revenue product of advertising equals the price elasticity of demand), it was shown that the optimal long-term advertising ratio was 13 per cent of sales revenue for this brand.

(d) Distribution Policy

Distribution management is concerned with decisions on moving goods from the producer to the target consumers. Decisions about distribution channels are very important because they intimately affect all other marketing mix choices and because once made they are not easily changed. In principle, a manufacturer can choose between selling the goods directly to the consumer and using a variety of distributors and retailers.

The marketing distribution channel undertakes a number of tasks besides the physical transportation and storing of goods. Middlemen may also undertake market research for the manufacturer in the areas of promotion, pricing and negotiation with the customer, and financing the sale and purchase of the goods. Manufacturers use middlemen to perform some or all of these functions, as this often leads to superior efficiency in marketing the goods to the customers. Intermediaries, through their experience, specialisation and contacts, can often offer the manufacturer more than can be achieved by going direct.

In developing a distribution strategy the manufacturer will make choices about the types of intermediary to use (e.g. agencies, distributors, retailers, etc.), the number to use, the specific tasks they are to undertake (e.g. storage, advertising, pricing, transport) and the terms (profit margins, teritorial rights, etc.) under which the intermediary will undertake these tasks. Central to the problem of channel management is the recognition that distributors are independent businesses with goals that are at least partially conflicting with those of the manufacturer. Whether the manufacturer can design the channel to meet his own goals depends upon the power he has and his ability to motivate the intermediaries to co-operate.

Knowledge of these marketing issues has been enriched by a considerable number of research studies by behavioural scientists (e.g. Stern and El-Ansary 1977). One of the remarkable changes in the last two decades has been the growth in power of the major retail chains at the expense of grocery manufacturers. Increasing concentration in grocery retailing has meant that manufacturers depend on the major chains to give them effective distribution, and the retailers have not been slow to utilise this power in demanding higher margins and better terms from their suppliers in exchange for co-operation.

In choosing distribution channels the manufacturer will seek intermediaries which meet four criteria. First, they should be oriented to serving his target market. A manufacturer of fashionwear for upper income women will need to get his product into retail outlets effectively serving such a clientèle. Second, the firm will want distributors which help it to exploit its differential advantage. If the product's competitive edge is in sophisticated technology features offering cost savings to buyers, then the manufacturer will need dealers capable of explaining these benefits to prospective buyers. Thirdly, working with a particular channel must be economically rational for the manufacturer. Direct selling with a company sales force is a powerful channel, but it is too expensive for companies without a significant market share. Finally, the manufacturer will be influenced by the control and motivation of prospective intermediaries. A distributor selling a wide range of successful competitive products might give insufficient attention to a newcomer's product.

Distribution channels once established are not easy to change. Yet as the manufacturer's circumstances or the market evolves, it often becomes necessary to adapt or even radically revise existing distribution channels. When starting out a manufacturer may choose distributors to market his product because this will reduce his overhead costs. But if the company grows, it is likely to become increasingly financially attractive to switch from distributors to direct selling because the higher overheads can now be spread over a larger volume. In addition, channels like products are subject to life cycles. Yesterday's highly successful forms of distribution give way to new forms more effectively geared to today's markets. Variety stores and small supermarkets have lost ground to superstores, catalogue showrooms and discount stores (see Davidson, Bates and Bass 1976). Such forces mean that the firm must be continually monitoring the performance and prospects of its distribution arrangements and be prepared to adapt them when conditions change.

6.8   Conclusion

In today's rapidly changing and highly competitive international environment a business can be successful only if its offer matches the wants of buyers at least as effectively as its best competitors. Marketing management is the task of planning this match. It is based upon the analysis of customers, competitors and distributors, the selection of target market segments, and the design of marketing mixes which will provide the firm with a differential advantage. An organisation's success in creating a differential advantage is never secure. Change requires the firm to con-profit performance.

The changing environment—changing wants, new competitors and technologies, different stakeholder pressures on the firm—means that a differential advantage is never secure. Change requires the firm to continually reposition itself by shifting from declining to emerging market segments, and renewing its differential advantage by such measures as improving its product features, adapting new technologies or higher levels of service. Businesses which fail to develop such repositioning strategies gradually lose contact with buyers and give way to firms which are more successfully marketing oriented.

References

Aaker, D. A. and Myers, J. G. (1982) *Advertising Management*, Prentice-Hall.

Abell, D. F. (1978) 'Strategic windows', *Journal of Marketing*, Vol. 42, No. 2, April, pp. 21–26.

Boyd, H. W., Ray, M. L. and Strong, E. C. (1972) 'An attitudinal framework for advertising strategy', *Journal of Marketing*, Vol. 36, No. 2, April, pp. 27–33.

Broadbent, S. (1977) *Spending Advertising Money*, Business Books.

Chamberlin, E. H. (1938) *The Theory of Monopolistic Competition*, Harvard University Press.

Corstjens, M. and Doyle, P. (1981) 'Evaluating the profitability of advertising for heavily advertised brands', *European Journal of Operational Research*, Vol. 8, No. 3, November, pp. 249–255.

Davidson, W. R., Bates, A. D. and Bass, S. J. (1976) 'The retail life cycle', *Harvard Business Review*, Vol. 54, No. 6, November, pp. 94–105.

Dorfman, R. and Steiner, P. O. (1954) 'Optimal advertising and optimal quality', *American Economic Review*, Vol. 59, June, pp. 817–831.

Drucker, P. F. (1974) *Management: Tasks, Responsibilities, Practices*, Heinemann.

Eiglier, P., Langeard, E. *et al.* (1977) *Marketing Consumer Services: New Insights*, Marketing Science Institute.

Frank, R. E., Massy, W. F. and Wind, Y. (1972) *Market Segmentation*, Prentice-Hall.

Green, P. E. and Tull, D. S. (1978) *Research for Marketing Decisions*, Prentice-Hall.

Hartley, R. F. (1976) *Marketing Mistakes*, Columbus: Grid Inc.

Howard, J. A. and Sheth, J. N. (1969) *The Theory of Buyer Behaviour*, Prentice-Hall.

Hulbert, J. M. and Toy, N. E. (1977) 'A strategic framework for marketing control', *Journal of Marketing*, Vol. 41, April, pp. 12–20.

Johnson, R. M. (1971) 'Market segmentation: a strategic management tool', *Journal of Marketing Research*, Vol. 8, No. 1, February, pp. 15–23.

Kotler, P. (1975) *Marketing for Non-Profit Organisations*, Prenctice-Hall.

Kotler, P. (1980) *Marketing Management*, Prentice-Hall.

Lambin, J. J. (1969) 'Measuring the profitability of advertising: an empirical study', *Journal of Industrial Economics*, Vol. 17, No. 2, April, pp. 86–103.

Lancaster, K. J. (1966) 'A new approach to consumer theory', *Journal of Political Economy*, Vol. 74, No. 2, April, pp. 132–157.

Levitt, T. (1965) 'Marketing myopia', *Harvard Business Review*, Vol. 43, No. 5, September, pp. 26–44.

McCarthy, E. J. (1981) *Basic Marketing*, Irwin.

Palda, K. S. (1969) *Economic Analysis for Marketing Decisions*, Prentice-Hall.

Pigou, A. C. (1932) *The Economics of Welfare*, Macmillan.

Porter, M. E. (1980) *Competitive Strategy*, Macmillan.

Ratchford, B. T. (1975) 'The new economic theory of consumer behaviour: an interpretive essay', *Journal of Consumer Research*, Vol. 2, September, pp. 65–75.

Robinson, J. (1933) *The Economics of Imperfect Competition*, Macmillan.

Rogers, E. M. (1962) *Diffusion of Innovations*, Free Press.

Shapiro, B. P. and Jackson, B. B. (1978) 'Industrial pricing to meet consumer needs', *Harvard Business Review*, Vol. 56, No. 6, November, pp. 119–127.

Star, S. H., Davis, N. J. *et al.* (1977) *Problems in Marketing*, McGraw-Hill.

Stern, L. W. and El-Ansary, A. I. (1977) *Marketing Channels*, Prentice-Hall.

Webster, F. E. (1981) 'Top management's concerns about marketing: issues for the 1980s', *Journal of Marketing*, Vol. 45, Summer, pp. 9–16.

National Economic Development Office (1981) *Industrial Performance: Trade Performance and Marketing*, London.

7
Financial Management

R. C. Stapleton

7.1 Introduction

The financial management of a firm has many aspects in common with the financial management of a household. Expenditures have to be budgeted and then monitored as they occur. If cash deficits are predicted, plans for financing them have to be made. For large companies these tasks, which are simple in concept and carried out effectively by any good housekeeper, are complex and often crucial to the success or failure of the organisation. Just as a household has to decide whether or not to build an extension onto the house or to replace the car, so the firm has its expansion and replacement decisions to make and the associated financing to arrange. At a more mundane, but no less vital, level the firm, like the household, has to decide when to pay its bills, how much stock to hold and how to reinvest any surplus cash it generates.

Broadly, we can distinguish between the planning and control functions of financial management and the decision-making function. Take, for example, replacement capital expenditure. The financial manager will normally prepare an annual budget for replacement expenditures based on plans from departments, divisions and companies in the group. After approval of the budgets he will then monitor actual expenditure against budget during the financial year. These important activities of planning and control of expenditure are different in principle from the decisions involved in replacement expenditures. Typical decisions required are: How long should cars be kept before they are replaced? What should be the total replacement expenditure for the year? How should the expenditure be financed?

Figure 7.1 distinguishes between planning and control and decision making, and outlines the main types of decision problems that we are concerned with here in this chapter. The decisions can be classified under three headings: capital investment, working capital and capital structure. Figure 7.2, which is an outline Balance Sheet, helps to describe these three

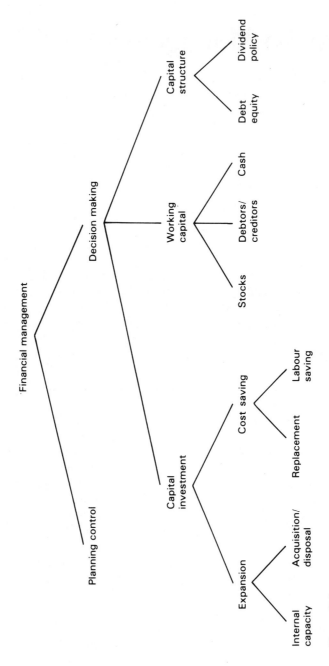

Figure 7.1

Balance Sheet as at

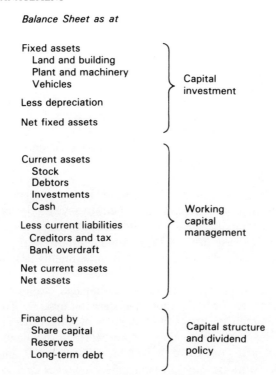

Figure 7.2

types of decision. Capital Investment refers to the purchase of fixed assets, i.e. assets which are expected to have a life of more than one year. These assets may be land or buildings, plant and machinery of various types or vehicles depending on the type of business the firm engages in. Alternatively, they may be intangible assets, as in the case of the purchase of the goodwill of another business by merger or acquisition. The second area where decisions are required is in the use of current assets and current liabilities. Current assets minus current liabilities is referred to as net working capital by accountants; hence the management of all these items is referred to as working capital management. The third major area of decision making concerns the long-term financing or capital structure of the firm. For example, the firm has to decide between issuing more shares, i.e. raising equity capital from existing and new shareholders, and raising money from non-owners in the form of long-term debt.

Figure 7.1 further classifies the decisions in these three major areas. Note that investment decisions are about the purchase of assets for production. Hence these decisions are either about the level of output or about exactly how to produce a given level of output. On the other hand, capital structure decisions are about liabilities; they are pure financial decisions and do not directly affect the physical assets and production of the firm. Working capital decisions usually involve a balance of assets and liabilities. However, as we will see, these are essentially financial as opposed to production decisions since many of the assets purchased—debtors, investments, cash, for example—are financial as opposed to physical assets.

Capital investment may be made in order to expand production capacity or to produce existing output more cost effectively. For example, output can be expanded by investing in buildings, plant, etc., and increasing the capacity of the firm. Alternatively, the firm could acquire another firm or the assets of another firm. These decisions are usually referred to as mergers, acquisitions and disposals. On the cost saving side, investment may involve the replacement of machines with more efficient machines or simply the installation of capital equipment to save labour costs.

Working capital management also involves decisions to purchase assets. The assets in this case are stocks of raw materials, work in progress or finished goods, trade debtors, short-term investments in financial instruments, such as treasury bills, and holding of cash. However, as far as stocks and debtors are concerned the financial manager's role is more one of setting policies and control rather than decision making. The problem is normally to minimise stocks and debtors without adversely affecting production and sales respectively. Short-term investments do involve decisions of course, but these are of a purely financial nature. On the liabilities side, working capital management involves decisions to extend trade creditors as well as choices between bank and other short-term loans.

Undoubtedly the most interesting, if not the most important, decisions concern the long-term financing of the firm. Under the general heading of capital structure, decisions have to be made between long-term debt and equity financing and between equity financing from new issues and retained earnings. This latter choice is determined by the firm's dividend policy. These issues are of interest because of the richness of the theory that surrounds them and because of the contrast between the thinking of financial economists and practitioners concerning them.

Although we have tried to dichotomise the decisions involved in the three areas of financial management, the connections between them should be appreciated. For example, any expansion investment decision requires that the sub-optimisation decisions on working capital have been taken. In addition, the capital structure decisions are designed to minimise the cost of long-term capital to the firm, and this cost is the standard against which the profitability of investments has to be judged.

7.2 Economic Theory and Financial Decisions

The vast proportion of the literature on the theory of financial management has assumed that the goal of the firm is to maximise the wealth of its shareholders. Capital investments should be made if they are worth more than they cost; the capital structure should be changed if, as a result, the value of the firm can be increased. The focus is on the present value of the future profits from investment; and this value can be observed by looking at the market value of shares. What will be the market value of a set of distant and risky cash flows from an investment? How does the value change if debt rather than equity is used to finance the investment? How far does the value of a company's shares depend on its dividend payout policy? Because of this focus on market value the contribution of economic theory has been fundamental. The price of a company's shares, like the price of anything else, depends on the supply and demand for them and crucially on the price of close substitutes, such as bonds and other companies' shares.

The central role of share value in the theory of financial management is illustrated in Figure 7.3. Here the basic financial decisions and the goal of wealth maximisation are related using financial ratios familiar in the financial analysis of company accounts. Shareholder wealth at any point in time is constituted by the value of the shares in issue plus any dividend paid minus any money that has to be contributed by way of a rights issue.[1] The value of the shares, i.e. the number of shares in issue multiplied by the price per share, is of course determined by supply and demand in the stock market. However, at a more fundamental level it represents the value of the net assets of the firm less the value of long-term debt, preference stock and any other claims against those assets. The first two lines of Figure 7.3 illustrate the central importance of share value for the capital structure decisions. Dividend policy involves a balance between increasing cash payments to shareholders and a corresponding increase in either long-term debt or rights issues, or a reduction in the value of depleted net assets. The debt–equity ratio decision, known as the gearing decision, involves a balance between increasing long-term debt and either increasing rights issues or reducing dividends.

As we will appreciate in a later section, the objective of capital structure management, i.e. of dividend policy and gearing policy, is to maximise the value of net assets given the firm's investment in net assets. In line III of Figure 7.3 this objective can be stated as maximising the value over book ratio given the book value of net assets. In contrast, the capital investment decision involves a change in the size of net assets. If the goal is wealth maximisation it is necessary for any expansion in net assets to increase the value of net assets by more than the cost of financing. The capital cost of

---

1. A rights issue is a new issue of ordinary shares made to the existing share-holders. Shareholders are given rights to apply for new shares in proportion to their existing holdings. Most equity issues by existing companies are rights issues. The major exception occurs when companies make acquisition issues directly to a company's shareholders.

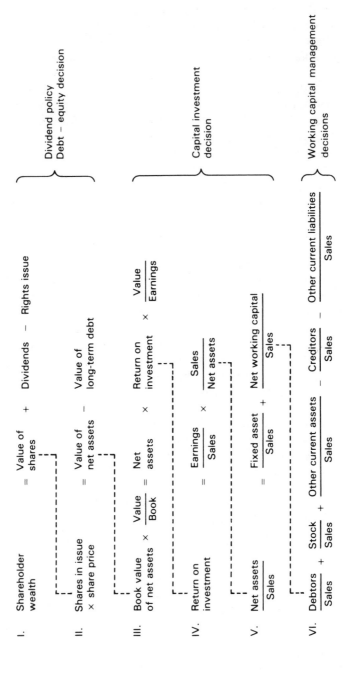

Figure 7.3 Shareholder Wealth and Financial Decisions

financing involves either an increase in rights issues or long-term debt, or a reduction in dividends below the level at which they would otherwise be. This is the foundation of the Net Present Value rule for capital investment decisions. One important point to note is that wealth maximisation implies that if the firm is faced with two mutually exclusive investment projects, it will pick the one with the largest absolute difference between value and cost. It will not necessarily pick individual projects with the highest value to book ratios.

Line III analyses the value to book ratio into the return on investment times the value to earnings ratio. The ROI is defined conventionally:

$$\text{Return on investment} = \frac{\text{Profit before long-term interest, after tax}}{\text{Net assets}}$$

and the value to earnings ratio is akin to a price to earnings ratio used in the stock market. It is defined:

$$\frac{\text{Value}}{\text{Earnings}} = \frac{\text{Value of net assets}}{\text{Profit before long-term interest, after tax}}$$

A profitable, acceptable investment is one with a value to book ratio greater than one. So if we compute the ROI for a proposed investment, and if we know the appropriate value to earnings ratio (or capitalisation rate), the investment decision can be determined. Readers should be warned that the accounting definition of profit has many flaws for investment decision-making purposes; also that much of the theory of financial management has surrounded the determination of the capitalisation rate. However, basically if an investment of the sort under consideration is typically valued at ten times earnings and if the ROI is 12 per cent, the value to book ratio is 1.2 and the investment will add to the wealth of the shareholders. The discounted cash flow (DCF) methods of investment appraisal which will be discussed below are basically a more sophisticated version of the ROI analysis.[2]

The value to earnings ratio is basically market determined. The most important determinant is the interest rate which obviously influences the required rate of return on investments. However, the return on investment is something that management can influence. Line IV in Figure 7.3 analyses the ROI in a manner that has become known as a 'Dupont Analysis'. This simple equation reveals that ROI is equal to the margin on sales times what is known as the asset turnover. Since the sales margin is

---

2. If profit before interest, after tax, equals cash flow (i.e. if depreciation = replacement investment) and if profit is constant and perpetual, then the ROI equals the DCF rate of return. The cost of capital is simply one over the capitalisation rate in this case, and a comparison of the DCF rate of return with the cost of capital yields the same result as that discussed in the text.

normally determined by the type of business the firm is engaged in, the ROI, and ultimately the value of an investment, is dependent on the sales to assets ratio known as asset turnover. This ratio reflects the economy of capital expenditure on final assets and working capital. This is shown by the further analysis of the inverse of asset turnover in line V. One of the crucial roles of the financial manager is to question every last bit of capital expenditure in order to improve this ratio, the resulting ROI and the wealth of shareholders. Difficult decisions may be involved when a trade-off exists between the level of profit or its timing and the amount of capital expenditure. Usually the quicker the investment project has to be completed, the more expensive it will be.

The final aspect of investment profitability concerns economy of net working capital. Line VI analyses net working capital into its constituent parts. It shows clearly that the capital investment decision depends partly on sub-optimisation of working capital.

Recent bouts of high inflation and interest rates have reminded management sharply of the need to control and optimise their working capital. High interest rates mean that the cost of giving credit to customers increases and, unless stock values keep pace with inflation, the cost of holding stock also rises. Bank overdrafts rise to finance the working capital and even if the net working capital to sales ratio is therefore not affected, interest costs affect the ROI directly through the effect on profits. Given the level of sales, working capital management aims at minimising the net working capital to sales ratio without adversely affecting profits. The key ratios are the debtors to sales ratio, which is often expressed as:

$$\frac{\text{Debtors}}{\text{Sales per day}} = \text{Number of days of debtors}$$

and the stock to sales ratio, often expressed as:

$$\frac{\text{Sales}}{\text{Stock}} = \text{Stock turnover.}$$

Similarly, on the liabilities side, creditors over daily purchases is often more appropriate than the creditors to sales ratio.

Before we launch into a detailed analysis of the three areas of financial management described so far, readers who have studied microeconomic theory should note that the concepts of opportunity cost and the marginal principle are used extensively in financial theory. For example, the idea of the cost of capital to a company is used extensively both as a standard against which to judge the rate of return on investment and as a cost to be minimised when capital is raised. However, the cost of retained profits, for example, is not an explicit cost. It is an opportunity cost to the shareholders of not receiving the dividends that could have been paid out if the investment had not been made.

Optimal investment by the firm can be determined by comparing the marginal rate of return on investment, known as the marginal efficiency of capital in macroeconomics, with the marginal cost of capital. Also, throughout the theory of financial decisions it is incremental costs and benefits that are relevant. In many respects the theory of investment that underlies capital project analysis is merely a multiperiod extension of the single period analysis of cost and output in the theory of the firm.

7.3   The Management of the Capital Structure

The capital structure of a firm does not require continuous management. By its nature, long-term capital needs to be raised occasionally. The dividend policy of the firm and its debt–equity ratio tend to be decided upon and then left to run for a number of years. However, the occasional nature of the decision problem belies its importance. If a non-wealth maximising capital structure is allowed to persist, the company leaves itself open to the threat of a take-over bid from another which is prepared to change the policy.

The Goal

The goal of the firm is to maximise the wealth of its shareholders. This goal can be sought in two ways. First, we could say that in choosing between debt, new issues of equity, and retained profits, the firm should minimise the cost of capital. This view regards the firm as buying capital and paying for it with future payments. The common-sense view is that capital, like any other resource, should be bought at the lowest cost. Unfortunately, this common-sense view is very misleading and can result in disastrous policies. The problem is that different types of long-term finance appear to have different costs because of differential risk to investors. Debt may appear cheaper than preference capital or equity because it involves the promise of relatively secure returns. It is also very hard for managers to understand the concept of the 'cost of new equity' or the 'cost of retained earnings' where the cost in these cases is not a legal obligation but rather an opportunity cost.

The alternative is to regard the firm as selling its future income stream to different security holders and the objective is to sell it for the highest price. In terms of the variables in Figure 7.3 the objective of capital structure policy is to maximise the value of net assets, given the book value of net assets, i.e. to maximise the value to book ratio. We will first establish that maximisation of this value leads to a maximisation of shareholder wealth.

Assume that by raising £20 million debt rather than making a £20 million rights issue the value of net assets would be £105 million as against £100 million. In other words, by selling off more of the future income stream to bond holders the market value of the assets rises. If this were the result of the policy switch, who would benefit? Ignoring costs of issuing the debt and equity, if the debt is issued at current market rates of interest its value will also be £20 million. Moreover, if the debt issue has no effect on the value of existing debts, the value of the long-term debt of the firm will rise by £20 million. Looking at line II in Figure 7.3, the value of net assets is £5 million higher and the value of the shares is £15 million lower than under the alternative policy. However, since shareholders have not had to contribute £20 million to a rights issue, they are £5 million better off with the policy shift.

In the above example the £5 million increase in the value of net assets has gone to the shareholders in increased wealth. This is because the debt was issued at current market rates and also did not affect the value of existing debts. With these two provisos we can conclude that an increase in the value to book ratio will increase shareholder (and not bondholder) wealth and take as the objective of capital structure management the maximisation of the value of net assets, given their book value.[3]

The Theory

(*a*) *Gearing Policy*   Perhaps the most well-known names in the theory of finance are those of Franco Modigliani and Merton Miller. Their 1958 article on the effect of the debt–equity ratio on the value of the firm and its cost of capital was one of the first serious attempts to apply the reasoning of economic theory to financial problems.[4] In essence the theorem says that in the absence of market imperfections, and in particular of taxes, the value of the net assets of a firm is independent of the gearing (debt–equity) ratio. While no attempt will be made here to prove any of the basic theorems of finance, we will try each time to explain the intuition behind the propositions. The 'MM theorem', as it is usually referred to, states that the way the income stream from an asset is divided between debtholders and shareholders will not affect its total value. Any advantage that the shareholders of a geared firm might gain from selling a prior claim to debtholders could be obtained equally well by the shareholders of an ungeared firm borrow-

---

3. Interesting issues arise when these conditions are not satisfied. For example, if significant default risk exists on a firm's debt, it may be selling below par value. In these circumstances an equity issue, by giving the debts more security, may increase the value of debt and leave shareholders worse off despite an increase in the value of net assets. It is usually difficult, however, to reduce the value of existing debts because of legal covenants in debt contracts.
4. Modigliani and Miller (1958).

ing on their personal account. This idea of home-made gearing is a fundamental one that runs through the theory of financial management. Firms cannot benefit by simply replicating transactions that shareholders could indulge in.[5]

The MM theorem states that the value of net assets depends on what the firm does with them, not on their financing. As such it is in line with much of economics which sees money as a veil and real factors as the long-run determinants of economic welfare. However, the corollary of the theorem is not so intuitively obvious and appealing. The corollary is that the cost of capital to the firm (reflected in the value to earnings ratio in Figure 7.3) is independent of the debt ratio. As relatively cheap debt is added to the capital structure the average cost of capital from debt and equity remains constant. However, this constant overall cost of capital is consistent with the increasing cost of equity capital which, in turn, is the consequence of higher equity risk as gearing increases.

(b) *Dividend Policy* Just as the gearing decision involves different ways of distributing the income generated from assets between debt and equity holders, the dividend decision is about different ways of giving share-holders their own money back. The main contribution of the article by Miller and Modigliani (1961) was to define dividend policy clearly in these terms. A dividend policy change is defined as a change in payout to shareholders while holding investment constant. With dividend policy defined in this way it was a short step to showing that, given perfect markets and no taxes, dividend policy merely determined the division of the shareholder's return between dividends and capital gains and not the size of that return. Hence future dividend policy has no effect at all on the value of the shares or its net assets.

Like most fundamental ideas, the MM definition of dividend policy is a simple one. The sources and uses of funds identity from accounting states:

$$\begin{matrix} \text{Cash flow from} \\ \text{operations in year } t \end{matrix} + \begin{matrix} \text{Net new long-} \\ \text{term debt in } t \end{matrix} + \begin{matrix} \text{New equity} \\ \text{in } t \end{matrix} =$$

$$\begin{matrix} \text{Investment in fixed} \\ \text{assets in } t \end{matrix} + \begin{matrix} \text{Investment in} \\ \text{working capital in } t \end{matrix} + \begin{matrix} \text{Dividend} \\ \text{paid in } t \end{matrix} + \text{Interest}$$

Given that cash flow from operations is fixed and interest is determined by debt outstanding at the beginning of the period, an increase in dividends must come from either new debt, equity or a reduction of investment in fixed assets or working capital. Miller and Modigliani define a change in dividend policy as a change in dividend payout while investment is given. From the sources and uses equation this is then a pure financial policy

5. The principle applies, for example, to the case of mergers undertaken to achieve diversification, and to the effect of certain foreign exchange transactions.

change. Its mirror image is an increase in new debt or newly issued equity.

In the long term, if investment policy is taken as given, more payout means more outside finance is required. Further, if the debt ratio is fixed by other considerations, more dividends means more new equity issues. It is then fairly clear to see that if these equity issues are by way of 'rights', the firm is simply giving money out to shareholders with one hand and taking it back with the other. It is not hard to see that shareholders will be indifferent between high dividend and low dividend payouts and the value of net assets unaffected by the choice of policy.

(c) *Some Provisos, Especially Taxation*   The two papers by Miller and Modigliani, provide a foundation for the theory of capital structure. In a sense they are negative, saying that nothing in capital structure management matters. However, they do warn managers against certain policies that might otherwise seem logical. For example, the raising of apparently cheap debt is unlikely to lower the overall cost of capital and an increase in dividend payout is unlikely to have the desired effect on share price. The papers form only a foundation for thinking about capital structure issues because there are many complications in the real world that are relevant to policy.

Tax systems are rarely neutral when it comes to financial policy.[6] Under most systems debt interest is allowable against corporate tax, whereas dividends are not. Also the personal tax rate on dividends tends to be different from that on capital gains. One fruitful way of looking at capital structure management is to think of it as minimising the tax take of the government from the firm and its security holders (it is no good minimising the firm's tax if the shareholders finish up with high tax burdens). Minimisation of tax will then imply maximisation of the value of net assets. This view is really a modification of the basic MM propositions. Although the value of the net assets of the firm to shareholders, bondholders and the government is unaffected by financial policies, the distribution between the government and the other interest groups is affected.

There are constraints on the minimisation of taxes via the capital structure. Some of these are imposed by the tax authority and may, for example, force dividends to be paid or debt to be treated as equity. However, the main constraint on gearing is perhaps the fear of bankruptcy and the associated costs and disruption involved. This is reinforced by constraints placed by financial institutions who have great problems controlling loans to risky companies. In practice the goal of gearing policy becomes one of minimising taxes subject to these constraints. In addition, recent high interest rates due to high inflation expectations has led to

---

6. For a comprehensive look at the effect of taxes on the two MM propositions see Stapleton (1972), and for the post-1973 UK tax system, Stapleton and Burke (1975).

increased uncertainty as to the real cost of long-term borrowing and a reluctance to issue long-term debt.

In practice the dividend policy decision is also complicated by a number of constraints. Sudden changes in policy can have severe information effects on the price of shares since they are taken as indications of management's view of earnings prospects. Furthermore, institutional investors often use dividend policy as an indication of management's determination to produce the profits from which they are paid. In effect dividend payment is used as a control mechanism by owners.

(d) *Relevant Empirical Evidence* Like much of economics, the theory of finance suffers from a surfeit of elegant theory and a lack of convincing evidence. Most of the direct tests of the two MM hypotheses have used US data. Recent sophisticated tests of the dividend policy proposition adjusted for taxes have been consistent with the theory.[7] However, the evidence for the debt–equity propositions is largely circumstantial.[8] The circumstantial evidence is provided by the evidence for the 'Efficient Markets Hypothesis'.[9] This hypothesis essentially states that stock and bond markets are competitive and reflect all available information. If markets are competitive and liquid, the essential preconditions for the MM propositions are established. Of course it does not confirm that gearing policy never affects the value of net assets (apart from tax effects). However, it does lend considerable circumstantial evidence to that proposition. Managers should have respect for the market and not expect to be able to make money out of thin air by switching capital structure policies. Any gains are likely to be hard won at the expense of the tax authorities.

7.4 Management of Capital Investment

Output and Technology Alternatives

In Figure 7.4 capital investment decisions are classified into expansion and cost-saving decisions and, further, into internal capacity and acquisition,

---

7. Litzenberger and Ramaswamy (1979) show that share price tends to be a declining function of payout as would be expected, given the higher taxation on dividend income than on capital gains. A previous study by Black and Scholes (1974) found no effect at all of dividend payout. A recent study of dividend cuts in the UK by Miskin and Stapleton (1982) showed that share prices tended to rise, again as predicted by the tax-adjusted MM theory.

8. The most detailed tests are by Miller and Modigliani (1966) and are consistent with the tax-adjusted MM proposition.

9. For a summary of the EMH and the evidence for it in the UK see, for example, Henfrey *et al.* (1977).

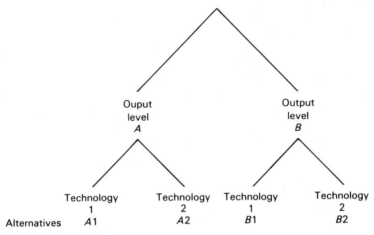

Figure 7.4   Alternatives and Decision Making

and replacement and labour-saving decisions. At a more fundamental level investment concerns the level of output and how to produce a given output. The first basic principle of good decision making is to sort out clearly the alternatives open to the firm. This allows the appropriate incremental benefits associated with a project to be identified. Figure 7.4 illustrates the importance of this process.

The firm has a choice between the existing level of output A and a higher level B. It also has to choose between the existing technology (1) and a new technology (2). There are clearly four alternatives open to the firm and the cost and profitability of each needs to be investigated. However, it is always possible to separate the technology and output decisions. First we decide the optimal technology for each output level and then the output decision is taken. For example, it could be that with the existing level of output technology 1 is the best. However, at the higher level of output technology 2 is more economic. Hence the output level involves a choice between A1 and B2. It is important to go through the logical process of Figure 7.4 and clearly distinguish output level and technology decisions. A capital project may well be presented as A1 compared to B2 when either A2 or B1 is superior. Comparing A1 and B2 involves crediting the higher output with the advantages of the new technology. But if the new technology is also more economic for the existing output (A2 better than A1) the correct output decision depends on a comparison of A2 and B2.

Two Principles: Relevant and Incremental Costs and Benefits

The above example is an illustration of a more general principle. Only those costs and benefits which uniquely result from the decision are relevant and should be considered. Projects should not be credited with advantages which would accrue whether or not they were accepted. This general principle might be obvious to an economist, but it is often difficult to interpret in practice. If a project to expand output will lead to future profitable expansion opportunities, then these should be credited to the project, providing that they would otherwise not be open to the firm. However, if the project produces benefits which can be reinvested at a high rate of return, these future excess returns should not be credited to the project if they would be available to the firm whether or not it invested in the project. Money could always be raised in the future to finance high return projects. Similarly, the tax benefits of financing a project with debt should not be credited to the project if they could be gained by financing other projects with debt.

The incremental principle states that the additional benefits from an investment should be compared with the additional costs. The fact that past expenditures have been sunk into the project is irrelevant to the present decision. However, the incremental or marginal principle must not be taken too far. If only the short-run incremental costs of a project are taken into consideration, the impact of the project on future costs (for example on head office costs) may be ignored. A particular project may have no direct impact on central costs but have a long-run indirect impact in conjunction with other projects.

Cash Flows rather than Accounting Profits

In Figure 7.2 it was shown that the objective of capital investment management was to choose projects with a value to book ratio greater than unity. In that diagram the value to book (or cost) ratio was analysed into the ROI and the value to earnings (or capitalisation) ratio. Now, of course, if the capitalisation ratio is a known constant across all projects, the ROI would be sufficient indication of project profitability. But the accountant's definition of earnings is such an unreliable measure of future profitability that the capitalisation rate will vary widely according to the exact timing of future cash receipts and the risk associated with them.

A more accurate valuation of an investment project may follow from an estimation of its cash flow. Cash flow is defined as follows:

$$\begin{aligned}
\text{Cash flow (year } t) &= \text{Cash receipts } (t) - \text{Cash costs } (t) \\
&= \text{Profit after tax before interest } (t) \\
&\quad + \text{Depreciation } (t) - \text{Capital expenditure } (t) \\
&\quad - \text{Change in working capital } (t)
\end{aligned}$$

Cash flow is quite simply the difference between cash received and cash paid out as a result of the project. It is more relevant than profit for project valuation because it is the cash outflows of a project that have to be financed and it is the cash inflows that allow that finance to be repaid. The equation shows the precise difference between cash flow and profit. First of all cash flow in year t reflects actual capital expenditures rather than the time allocation of depreciation. An accurate assessment of a project should account for the exact timing of replacement capital expenditure. The second main difference is the deduction of working capital. If stocks have to be built up in the early years of a project or credit has to be extended to customers, cash flow can be negative while profits are positive. Again, an accurate valuation requires a calculation of the effect of working capital on financing charges.

Discounted Cash Flow Methods: Timing and Value

The theory of the value of an investment consists of a theory of the effect of cash flow timing on value and a theory of the effect of riskiness on value. The discounted cash flow (DCF) methods are closely associated with the theory of timing and valuation. We will talk about investments, initially assuming that their cash flows are certain and hence known for each year of the project's life. We will also assume initially that they are financed 100 per cent with equity capital and that the cash flows are paid out to shareholders in the form of dividends.

The wealth generated for shareholders by accepting an investment project is the difference between its value and its book cost. The net present value (NPV) of a project is an estimate of this excess of value over cost. If i is the rate of interest assumed constant over time (for convenience only), the NPV is defined as:

$$\text{NPV} = \frac{X_1}{1+i} + \frac{X_2}{(1+i)^2} + \ldots + \frac{X_n}{(1+i)^n} - C_0 \tag{1}$$

where X_t is cash flow in year t, C_0 is the capital cost of the project at year 0 and n is the project life.

The NPV as defined in Equation (1) can be justified as an estimate of the excess of value to book by recourse to share valuation theory. Miller and Modigliani (1961) showed that if the following assumptions were made:

(a) cash flows are certain;
(b) the capital market is perfect;
(c) investors are rational;
(d) there are no taxes;

then the value of the company would be equal to discounted value of cash flows. Hence the effect of a project on shareholder wealth would be accurately estimated by the NPV. Clearly the assumptions, especially (a) and (d), do not hold true in reality. However, if (b) and (c) are retained, a theory of value can be constructed which justifies a modified version of equation (1).

$$\text{NPV} = \frac{\bar{X}_1}{1+r} + \frac{\bar{X}_2}{(1+r)^2} + \ldots + \frac{\bar{X}_n}{(1+r)^n} - C_0 \qquad (1')$$

In (1′) the certain cash flows are replaced by the (mathematical) expected cash flows and the interest rate by a discount rate r. This discount rate covers a multitude of sins. It includes a risk premium reflecting the risk aversion of investors. It also accounts for the various taxes imposed on investors and the impact of the firm's capital structure (and dividend policy) upon these.

Risk and Value: The Capital Asset Pricing Model (CAPM)

One of the major developments in the theory of finance and perhaps in economic theory of the past two decades has been the CAPM. This is a theory of valuation under uncertainty. The theory is attributed to Sharpe (1964), Lintner (1965) and Mossin (1966) and was built on the portfolio theory of investors' demand for securities pioneered by Markowitz (1952). Although there have been many extensions, the essential hypothesis is that the risk premium $r - i$ depends on the 'beta' of shares.[10]

Figure 7.5(a) states the basic CAPM proposition. The required return on a risky share (and hence on a new investment in the company) is a linear function of its β. Beta is the appropriate measure of risk because it represents the risk that cannot be diversified away by holding the shares in a portfolio. An appreciation of what the risk measure is and how it can be estimated is given in Figure 7.5(b). This shows the relationship between the achieved rate of return from holding the shares of firm j (a high β share) and firm k (a low β share) in comparison to the rate of return on an index of market performance (such as the FT Index).

Although it is impossible to outline a complex theory in a paragraph, the essential rationale behind the CAPM can be readily appreciated. If the regression relationship illustrated in Figure 7.5(b) is

$$\bar{r}_j = \alpha_j + \beta_j \bar{r}_m + \bar{\varepsilon}_j$$

then the total risk of holding the shares of firm j can be split into two elements:

$$\text{variance } (\bar{r}_j) = \beta_j^2 \text{ variance } (\bar{r}_m) + \text{variance } (\bar{\varepsilon}_j).$$

---

10. For a summary and examples of the many extensions see Stapleton and Subrahmanyam (1980).

(a) *The security market line*

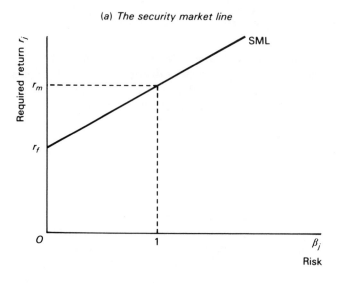

(b) *The beta of a share*

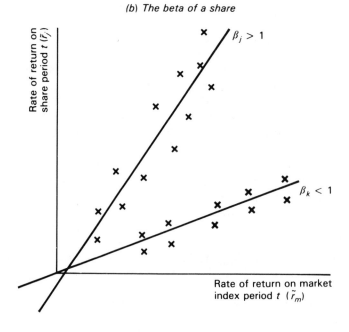

Figure 7.5 The CAPM Proposition

Now if the shares of firm j are held in a large portfolio, the law of large numbers ensures that only the first element β_j^2 variance $(\tilde{r}_m)$ affects the portfolio risk since the remaining risk is washed away. Hence β_j is the only relevant measure of risk in a portfolio context. In equilibrium, then, investors will only be rewarded for bearing non-diversifiable risk and this depends on the beta of the firm.

DCF Methods: Some Practical Considerations

Alternative Methods Capital investment management requires a sound grasp of NPV as an estimate of the wealth created by a project and of the theory of time and risk effects. However, NPV is rarely used directly as a method of investment appraisal. This is because it is hard to understand at 'shop floor' level and because other DCF methods can be used which give the same answer as NPV while being more intuitively appealing. The most common of these is the Internal Rate of Return (IRR) or DCF rate of return.

The IRR of a project is given by R in the equation below:

$$0 = \frac{\bar{X}_1}{1+R} + \frac{\bar{X}_2}{(1+R)^2} + \ldots + \frac{\bar{X}_n}{(1+R)^n} - C_0 \qquad (2)$$

The IRR is none other than Keynes's marginal efficiency of capital applied at the micro-level. As long as the expected cash flows are positive it is clear that NPV > 0 in (1') implies R in (2) greater than i. Hence the simple decision rule is to accept projects with an IRR greater than the 'cost of capital' or required rate or return, i. Although some care has to be exercised when mutually exclusive projects are analysed and where some expected cash flows are negative, the IRR method is essentially the same as NPV.[11]

Coping with Inflation

Recent bouts of high inflation have concentrated minds on the difference between the 'real' rate of interest and the 'money' or 'nominal' rate which includes an inflation premium. Investment decisions can be taken either by comparing nominal cash flows (including inflation-assisted growth) with the nominal cost of capital or by comparing real cash flows with the real cost of capital. A great problem arises if managers project cash flows conservatively in real terms, but compare the resulting IRR with the nominal cost of capital. This is tempting because the gains from inflation

---

11. See Stapleton (1970) for a thorough comparison and discussion.

are uncertain and in the future, whereas the costs (in terms of interest) are immediate and relatively certain.

Although the two methods, using real and nominal cash flows, are alternatives, major projects should be analysed at least once in nominal terms. The reason is that inflation can have major effects on a project's profitability. The reasons are twofold. First fiscal drag has the effect of increasing the real tax burden during periods of inflation, caused by non-indexation of depreciation allowances and working capital. The second cause is the effect of increasing working capital required to finance debtors and stocks in inflationary periods. The effect of inflation on tax and working capital should be worked out carefully.

Risk Analysis

Capital investment decision making is not usually a mechanical process of calculating NPVs and IRRs and drawing the appropriate conclusion. Under uncertainty the estimate of the value of the project is so subject to error that the decision maker must obtain information from as many sources as possible. One very useful tool is sensitivity analysis. This involves repeated calculations of the profitability measure (say IRR) under different assumptions regarding the outcome of the factors determining project cash flows. Computers are especially useful in this process since they enable huge amounts of information to be digested and processed. The final output should be a series of answers to 'what if . . .?' questions. What will be the IRR if sales increase by five per cent per annum? Although the aim of decision making is to accept wealth-increasing, positive NPV projects, the identification of these is a matter of feel and intuition rather than direct calculation. However, this intuition can be helped by the right kind of calculations from a risk analysis.

7.5   Management of Working Capital

The management of working capital is an area where planning and control is often a far more important activity than decision making. Notwithstanding this, we will isolate the major working capital decisions and discuss their economic content.

Figure 7.6 lists the broad categories of working capital items—both assets and liabilities—and the associated decisions. The first two items, namely stock and debtors, require independent decisions on long-term policy. After these policies are set, the overall size of the resulting assets is largely beyond the control of the financial manager. In the case of stocks it will normally depend on production and sales out-turn, whereas with

Assets		Decision
Stocks	-	Days*
Debtors	-	Terms of payment*
		Creditworthiness
Short investments	-	When, how much, to buy or sell?
Cash	-	How much to hold?
Liabilities		
Creditors	-	When to pay?
Bank	-	How much to borrow?

Note: * Independent decisions on policy

Figure 7.6 Working Capital Management Decisions

debtors it depends on sales and on customer reaction to the credit terms which have been set.[12]

When the overall policy on debtors has been established (for example, five per cent discount to customers if payment is made within 10 days; 30 days maximum credit) credit decisions are largely made by the customers themselves. Should they take the discounts and pay within 10 days or take the maximum credit period? One area of decision the financial manager may have to advise on is the assessment of credit worthiness. Especially where the firm's customers are themselves limited liability companies this decision requires careful, professional analysis. Important as they are, these decisions are not designed to determine the overall size of trade debtors. This working capital item has to be forecast *given* the overall credit policy, and then the required finance has to be found.

In contrast to stocks and debtors, daily, weekly or monthly decisions have to be made which directly determine the other items in Figure 7.6. Also, these decisions are highly interdependent. For example, if finance is short because of unexpected delays in customer payment, investments could be sold, creditors could be extended (by foregoing discounts), the bank overdraft could be increased or the cash balance run down. Given the forecast level of sales, purchases, debtors and capital expenditures, the financial manager has the job of financing deficits and reinvesting positive balances. The treasury function is in fact much more complicated than this in major companies. The company will have many bank accounts with different overdraft limits; it will hold a portfolio of short-term investments

12. The main policy decision on stocks is the number of days of stock to hold of particular items. The economic order quantity (EOQ) model, which balances holding costs against ordering costs, can be used to determine policy. See, for example, Wagner (1969).

of different maturities in different currencies; it can hold cash on deposit on various terms (overnight, seven days, etc.) and will have many different suppliers offering varying credit terms.

The balancing of these four items of working capital is referred to as cash management. A number of approaches to the problem of cash management have been suggested in the literature. The cash balance, for example, can be regarded as an inventory of liquidity, and an EOQ model could be applied.[13] Also the decision to accept or refuse credit extensions can be judged by calculating the effective rate of interest that is being paid by foregoing discounts. Another useful idea is to try to match maturities of liabilities with those of assets. In practice, however, this is an area where good rules of thumb, professional forecasting and quick action can lead to near optimal decisions and efficient management. Perhaps the two most important ideas contributed by financial theory are the use of deterministic linear programming to capture the interrelationships between the short-term assets and liabilities and the constraints imposed on the manager and the use of hedging and forward contracts to minimise risk exposure.

Cash Management: A Linear Programming (LP) Model

Linear programming models have been suggested by Robichek and Myers (1965) and by Orgler (1969). This brief description follows the latter author's model.

The objective of cash management is to minimise the cost of financing short-term assets over a specified period. This sub-optimisation objective is consistent with overall wealth maximisation for the firm. The cost of financing is basically the interest cost of loans, plus any discounts lost by not paying suppliers on time, minus interest and capital gains on investments. The objective, the variables and the constraints under which cash management normally has to operate are summarised in Figure 7.7.

Perhaps the most obvious constraints of the model concern payments on suppliers' bills and on sales of investments. Normally suppliers cannot be paid more than they are owed. These constraints also have to include the latest time period in which a supplier can be paid. The essence of this LP problem is that it is multiperiod. There are constraints on the amount that can be paid for each period. Similarly, sales of investments cannot normally exceed the amount of investments held at the beginning of the period. In addition to bank overdraft limits and cash balance constraints a number of discretionary limits may be placed. The firm may well wish to ensure that certain ratios are maintained—for example, the quick ratio of current assets less stocks to current liabilities may be constrained.

---

13. See, for example, Baumol (1952) or for a more sophisticated stochastic version of the same idea see Miller and Orr (1966).

Objective

Minimise cost of financing =
interest costs + lost discounts −
interest and gains on investments

Variables

Payments to suppliers

Loans

Sales and purchases
of investments

Constraints

Bank overdraft limits

Payments on bills

Sales of investments

Cash balance

Accounting: cash period t =
cash period $t − 1$ + receipts −
payments + loans −
net purchase of investments

Solution

Optimal values of variables
for each period

Dual prices — reflecting
the cost of imposing
the constraints or the
profitability of easing them

Figure 7.7 Cash Management: An LP Formulation

Setting up the cash management problem as an LP problem may well be a good way of learning about it. An LP does not actually have to be solved to be useful. One of the most significant outputs of an LP solution, however, is the size of the dual prices which reflect the profitability of easing the constraints of the model. Nevertheless, in setting up the problem as an LP the analyst can appreciate feasible policies and in particular the dynamics of the problem. What one does in one period affects the possibilities of action in the next. This is all captured by the accounting constraint shown in Figure 7.7. The books must balance! Hence the investments that can be sold in period t depend on how many were inherited in $t - 1$ and how many were sold in that period. This simple idea, which in the LP is reflected by the accounting constraints, is the essence of the multiperiod cash management problem. Whether the problem is solved by rule of thumb or by LP, the constraints must be satisfied.

Hedging, Forward Contracts and Financial Markets

Treasury or cash management is an unglamourous and largely unnoticed activity. Moreover, as an academic subject it lacks the depth and subtlety of capital structure theory or the logic of capital budgeting. Unfortunately it is only when things go wrong that the treasury function is noticed. If the safe is empty when money is required to pay bills or, more likely, if the firm is left holding long-term securities (financed by short-term ones) when interest rates rise, or is left with dollars or Deutsche Marks as the pound rises, then a real crisis can occur which may threaten the whole existence of the firm to say nothing of the job of the treasurer. A crucial feature of cash management is thus the avoidance of risk. More precisely, it is the minimisation or limiting of exposure to major risks.

Risk exposure is limited by good financial forecasting and planning together with sensible *matching* and *hedging* policies. Forecasting is required so that plans can be made to arrange overdraft facilities and avoid financial embarrassment. Matching refers to both the maturity and currency of assets and liabilities. Risk of exposure to interest-rate and exchange-rate changes can be almost eliminated if assets and liabilities can be matched. For example, if the firm has a tax bill to pay in six months' time, it could hold a six-month Treasury Bill investment to cover it. If it has sales revenue accruing in dollars, it can raise short-term loans in dollars to match the future revenue.

Exact matching is desirable but will usually be either impossible or prohibitively expensive. Firms will normally have short-term assets in excess of liabilities and also be long in particular loan maturities and currencies. However, it can still reduce exposure by hedging. Hedging involves the purchase of forward contracts on foreign currency or financial futures as a form of insurance against shifts in the value of money. The recently opened London Financial Futures Exchange paves the way for more efficient hedging of financial risks. But it has long been the practice for a firm receiving foreign currency to sell the currency forward for a fixed future sterling price. This type of transaction is increasingly part of the treasury management function of large international companies (see Chapter 10). It requires a knowledge of finance and financial markets which is outside the scope of this chapter.

7.6 Conclusions and Reflections

In this brief chapter we have tried to outline the economics behind a whole range of financial management decisions. Students of financial management should bear two things in mind when reflecting on the material contained here and in the references at the end of this chapter. First, the practice of financial management is in many ways more complicated than portrayed here. Fiscal and legal aspects of corporate finance are extremely complex and the alternatives open to the manager extensive. Also the manager has to act within the constraints of his organisation. Capital budgeting, for example, is not simply a matter of computing NPVs or IRRs, it always involves the overall business strategy of the firm. Furthermore, the firm has to recognise that its employees, customers, bankers and management are stakeholders as well as shareholders. It cannot pursue policies of unbridled wealth maximisation. However, when it comes to management of working capital and the capital structure the interests of these groups are usually congruent.

The second point concerns the theory of finance, or rather the theory of the valuation of assets. This branch of economic theory has developed to an extraordinary degree since the path-breaking works of Modigliani–Miller and Sharpe–Lintner–Mossin. Only the tip of the iceberg has been covered in this chapter. Many fascinating hours can be spent delving into this literature published in the *Journal of Finance*, the *Journal of Financial Economics* and the *Journal of Financial and Quantitative Analysis* over the last two decades. However, much of this literature is relevant to the positive questions of why investment takes place and why financial structures are as they are. It is not intended to help financial managers directly in their jobs. There are and will always be excellent financial managers who are largely ignorant of the theory of finance, but who are well versed in the practice.

References

Baumol, W. J. (1952) 'The transactions demand for cash: an inventory theoretic approach', *Quarterly Journal of Economics*, November.

Black, F. and Scholes, M. (1974) 'The effects of dividend yield and dividend policy on common stock prices and returns', *Journal of Financial Economics*, May.

Henfrey, A. W., Albrecht, B. and Richards, P. (1977) 'The UK stockmarket and the efficient market model: a review', *The Investment Analyst*, December.

Lintner, J. (1965) 'The valuation of risk assets and the selection of risky investments in stock portfolios and capital budgets', *Review of Economics and Statistics*, 47, pp. 13–37.

Litzenberger, R. H. and Ramaswamy, K. (1979) 'The effect of personal taxes and dividends on capital asset prices: theory and evidence', *Journal of Financial Economics*, June.

Markowitz (1952) 'Portfolio selection', *Journal of Finance*, Edition vii, March, pp. 77–91.

Miller, M. H. and Modigliani, F. (1961) 'Dividend policy, growth and valuation of shares', *Journal of Business*, October.

Miller, M. H. and Modigliani, F. (1966) 'Some estimates of the cost of capital to the electric utility industry 1954–57', *American Economic Review*, 56, pp. 333–391.

Miller, M. H. and Orr, D. (1966) 'A model of the demand for money by firms', *Quarterly Journal of Economics*, August.

Miskin, A. and Stapleton, R. C. (1982) 'Dividend cuts, share prices and market efficiency', *Manchester Business School Working Paper*.

Modigliani, F. and Miller, M. H. (1958) 'The cost of capital, corporation finance and the theory of investment', *American Economic Review*, June.

Mossin, J. (1966) 'Equilibrium in a capital asset market', *Econometrica*, 34, October, pp. 768–783.

Orgler, Y. (1969) 'An unequal-period model for cash management decisions', *Management Science*, October.

Robichek, A. A. and Myers, S. C. (1965) *Optimal Financing Decisions*, Prentice-Hall.

Sharpe, W. F. (1964) 'Capital asset prices: a theory of market equilibrium under conditions of risk', *Journal of Finance*, 19, September, pp. 425–442.

Stapleton, R. C. (1970) *The Theory of Corporate Finance*, Harrap.

Stapleton, R. C. (1972) 'Taxes, the cost of capital and the theory of investment', *Economic Journal*, December.

Stapleton, R. C. and Burke, C. (1975) 'Taxes, the cost of capital and the theory of investment: a generalisation to the imputation system of taxation', *Economic Journal*, December.

Stapleton, R. C. and Subrahmanyam, M. G. (1980) *Capital Markets and Corporate Financial Decisions*, JAI Press.

Wagner, H. M. (1969) *Principles of Operational Research*, Prentice-Hall.

8
Personnel Management

B. J. McCormick

8.1 Introduction

Personnel management may be defined as the development of a highly motivated and efficient labour force. In the pursuit of this objective management has to take into account the possibilities presented by the external labour market and the gains which may be achieved through co-ordination and control within the internal labour market known as the firm. What the external labour market offers is both possibilities and constraints. The constraints are the size and composition of the working population, social and cultural values, legal restrictions on the form and content of employment contracts, and rules laid down by trade unions and employers' associations. In total the rules form the industrial relations system of the external labour market. Management is therefore confronted by choices. The external labour market may provide a source of labour, but an employer may find it cheaper to train his own workers. Such a decision could involve variations in the employment contract and, if followed by other employers, could lead to changes in the external industrial relations systems.

In the first part of this chapter we shall examine some aspects of the environment which confront management, and how changes in the environment alter the scope and content of personnel management. The emphasis will be upon Britain, but since solutions to problems similar to those of Britain have been sought elsewhere, international comparisons will be drawn. In the second part we shall concentrate upon the decision rules for hiring, training and paying employees and the problems created by organisational change.

8.2 The External Industrial Relations System

The most striking feature of the British economy has been its low productivity. The causes of low productivity are obscure and have been variously attributed to the effects of industrialisation (Lewis 1978). Productivity is much lower than that achieved by Japan, West Germany, the United States and even by smaller countries such as Sweden. Low productivity and high aspirations helped to produce creeping inflation in the fifties and sixties and, shaken by oil price rises and large increases in the money supply, there was stagflation (high unemployment and inflation) in the seventies.

Although the low level of productivity had many causes, there is no doubt that the industrial relations system has been a contributory factor. The emphasis upon industry-wide agreements coupled with restrictions upon picketing served to keep unions off the shop floor, and the fact that national agreements did not deal with productivity was of little consequence during the interwar years. But national agreements were ill-suited to the full employment of the fifties and sixties—a period in which individual employers were willing to break national agreements in order to get workers, and in which there was an upsurge of shop-floor unionism and militancy. In the mid-sixties some employers negotiated successful productivity agreements (Flanders 1970), but these endeavours were later wrecked by inflation. Despite their failings, productivity agreements did have the merit of forcing a recognition of shop-floor unionism.

By 1968 a Royal Commission on Trade Unions and Employers' Associations noted that Britain had a dual system of industrial relations—a system of national agreements and an increasingly important system of workplace agreements. The Commission based most of its conclusions upon conditions prevailing in the engineering industry. During the seventies the dual system began to crumble and was increasingly replaced by single employer agreements which, by the end of the decade, covered two-thirds of the employees in manufacturing; national agreements came to be used more and more to police low wage firms. Furthermore, because of merger movements some 50 per cent of these workers were in firms employing over 200,000 employees (Brown 1981).

Beyond manufacturing, industry-wide agreements persist in industries such as clothing, catering and retail distribution—industries characterised by small firms, high labour turnover, little unionism and a reliance upon statutory wage regulation. The other group, loosely called the public sector, has always tended to use the single employer/national agreement—although some, such as the National Coal Board, have oscillated between national and local agreements.

A striking feature of personnel management in the seventies was the growth of professionalism. This had its origins in three factors. First, there was the mass of legislation introduced by successive governments and covering employment security, industrial training, health and safety and discrimination. Secondly, there was the changing nature of firms. Family ownership tended to give way to institutional ownership by pension funds and insurance companies (prompting a need for more efficient managerial control systems). The growth of firms, especially by mergers, led to the adoption of multi-divisional structures with an emphasis upon corporate strategy and manpower planning. Thirdly, the plant agreements of the sixties and seventies brought a shift from informal, *ad hoc* agreements to written agreements. Job evaluation spread and in the late seventies there was a return to incentive payments schemes. The growth of professionalism led to a decline in employers' associations.

Finally, we may note that successive governments were driven to cope with inflation, to introduce training and mobility programmes and to use legislation to deal with discrimination. The total effect of the legislation and controls was to undermine the doctrine of voluntarism (or collective *laissez-faire*) which had left employers and unions to their own devices. Indeed, it is possible to go further and argue that in the light of the massive government training programmes and the use of the educational system to absorb the potential young worker, the labour market has almost disappeared under a welter of legislation.

The disappearance of the labour market threatens to have serious political and social consequences if, as most forecasters suggest, heavy unemployment persists throughout the 1980s. Paradoxically, the resolution of the unemployment problem may require more state intervention (in the form of a negative income tax) to break the dependence upon wages as the sole source of income, and the introduction of a wealth tax to correct property distribution. These proposals put forward by Meade during the automation scare of the late fifties have acquired a greater relevance for the eighties (Meade 1964).

8.3   Other Countries: Other Solutions

The British disease of low productivity, inflation and niggling disputes led to an examination of the industrial relations systems of other countries. In the sixties there was a flirtation with manpower policies along the lines of those pursued by Sweden. But Sweden had a much simpler union structure, more sophisticated union leaders and thirty years of socialist rule (Turvey 1952). There was also an attempt, via the 1971 Industrial Relations Act, to reduce the power of unions along the lines pioneered by the American Taft–Hartley Act. But the reduction in the power of American unions owed more to the abundance of natural resources and the greater mobility of American workers and firms. And whereas the passing of the Taft–Hartley Act coincided with the Cold War, British legislation was crushed in an upsurge of inflation.

There was also an interest in worker participation and industrial democracy. The Yugoslavian experiments attracted attention, but it seemed doubtful whether a system nurtured in a developing country could be transplanted into a mature economy (Meade 1972). The German system of *mitbestimmung* was appraised and worker directors were appointed in the steel industry. But worker directors were ignored by unions which wished to avoid having to choose between the pursuit of efficiency and the possibilities of redundancies, and they were also ostracised by management (Brannen *et al.* 1976). The attempts to foster a national move towards industrial democracy via the Bullock Report also foundered in a sea of hostility from unions which preferred the collective bargaining solution to democracy. There were also other aspects of the German system which were conspicuously absent from the British scene; management was more professional, vocational training was well developed and unionism was weak.

The Japanese system was also investigated. Japan had a dual industrial structure, with large firms offering employment security to able workers up to the age of 55, and a sector of small firms which gave casual employment. Within the large firms, moreover, the use of bonuses (deferred wages) gave rise to an element of profit-sharing. But Britain also had a dual structure and between 1940 and the mid-seventies there had been full employment. Finally, there were studies of the Australian system of wage regulation which seemed to divorce wages from politics, but drove many would-be workers to enforced leisure on Bondi Beach.

The catalogue of comparisons makes for dismal reading, but it does serve the useful purpose of drawing attention to possible non-economic factors operating in different countries.

8.4   Law, Property Rights and the Theory of the State

Industrial relations systems cannot be divorced from the theory of the state which inspires them and which confers the system of property rights. And parallelling the investigations and speculations discussed in the two previous sections, there have been considerable developments in labour law. Twenty five years ago a textbook on labour law would have contained sections on the contract of employment, industrial safety and accident compensation and trade unions. The discussion of the employment contract would have been based upon common law decisions concerning the relations between master and servant (thereby betraying its pre-industrial origins); the analysis of accidents would have been based upon common law as amended by the factory acts; and the discussion of trade unions would have been devoted to their legality and to disputes. There would have been no recognition of collective agreements.

Today the divisions of the subject matter remain the same, but the emphasis has changed and may be in the process of changing again. A knowledge of common law is required to determine wrongful dismissal, as opposed to the statutory determinants of unfair dismissal, and the conciliation and arbitration services of the state, established around the turn of the century, now masquerade in new guises. But a good argument could be advanced for commencing a discussion of labour law with trade unions and industrial relations because most issues are now regulated by the collective agreements of employers and trade unions which become implicit or explicit terms of the individual contract of employment. There is also a good case for starting with statute law rather than common law on the grounds that between 1959 and 1982 some 28 pieces of legislation devoted to labour problems were enacted.

Yet despite the emphasis upon the collective as opposed to the individual contract, we shall begin with the latter. Our reason for so doing is that during the 1980s there has been an attempt to reduce the importance of collective agreements and return to a world of individualism. The kind of individualism sought clearly depends upon what degree of individualism already exists.

(a) The Individual Contract of Employment

The distinction between a contract of employment and a contract for services rests upon a concept of control. An employee is one whose activities are directed and controlled by another, whereas a self-employed person is someone who is paid for a job but given complete freedom to perform that job. The increasing sub-division of labour and the growth of specialist knowledge have sometimes made this concept of control difficult to apply and so multiple control tests have tended to be introduced. Thus an employee is one who is an integral part of a firm's activities, who may be supplied with tools and equipment, who may not bear the risks of the firm's failure, and from whose income, tax on a PAYE basis (Schedule E as opposed to Schedule D) and insurance contributions are deducted. In contrast, a self-employed person may enjoy tax allowances under the more favourable Schedule D provisions, but will not be eligible for compensation for unfair dismissal or redundancy.

Given the definition of an employee, we can now observe the common law requirements concerning hiring and dismissal. Thus an employer is expected to pay wages (but not necessarily to provide work) and to exercise care in the selection of his employees, whilst an employee is expected to exhibit obedience, show due care and attention and not divulge trade secrets. These common law requirements have, however, been overlain by the following statutory obligations.

Guaranteed work　Although most collective agreements contain arrangements for the payment of a guaranteed amount in any week in which work is not available, there is also statutory provision which entitles an employee to a guaranteed daily payment for up to five days in any three month period in which work is not available. The guarantee does not apply if reasonable alternative work is provided or if there is a trade dispute (unless that dispute is in another firm which is a buyer or supplier to the employee's firm).

Length of notice   The statutory minimum notice to be given by an employer to an employee who has been employed continuously for four weeks or more rises from one week's to twelve weeks' notice according to length of service. What constitutes the period of continuous service is also important in determining the amount of compensation for redundancy or unfair dismissal, and breaks in continuity are ignored if they are due to strikes, sickness or pregnancy.

Redundancy   An employee who is made redundant has a right to compensation, with the amount being determined by his rate of pay and length of continuous service; but it can be withheld if the employer offers reasonable alternative employment.

Unfair dismissal   An employer may be deemed to have unfairly dismissed an employee if his reasons include: pregnancy or confinement, a past criminal offence which has already been spent, belonging to a trade union or refusing to join a trade union under the employer's control. Reasonable grounds for dismissal include: serious misconduct, incapacity for the job, redundancy, national security, statutory requirements (e.g. driving disqualification) or an unwillingness to accept a change in working conditions agreed between an employer and a trade union. The 1980 Employment Act exempted small firms employing less than 20 workers during the first two years of their operations. The 1982 Act provided for compensation to individuals who had been dimissed for failure to be members of a union and gave employers greater freedom to dismiss striking workers.

Equal pay   An equality clause is automatically incorporated into the contract of every person employed and the clause can be operated if it can be demonstrated that a person is being paid less than someone else doing 'like work' or 'work rated as equivalent'.

Discrimination   The 1975 Sex Discrimination Act was copied by the framers of the 1976 Race Relations Act. The legislation seeks to establish whether conduct amounts to discrimination and whether the discrimination is lawful.

In addition, there are statutory provisions governing the employment of women and young persons, pregnancy, confinement and maternity.

We shall now turn to the legislation covering collective agreements.

(b)   The Legal Position of Trade Unions

A trade union which is deemed to be an independent trade union, that is not subject to control by an employer, can apply for certification under the 1974 Trade Union and Labour Relations Act. If the Certification Officer is satisfied that the union is independent, then it can obtain relief from income tax for its provident funds. Recognition as an independent trade union, however, does not mean automatic recognition by an employer. Before the passing of the 1980 Employment Act it was possible for a union to achieve such recognition by appealing to the Advisory, Conciliation and Arbitration Service (ACAS) and the Central Arbitration Committee (CAC), and a recommendation could be made determining which union should represent a group of workers for bargaining purposes. If an employer rejected the recommendation, then a compulsory arbitration award could be issued. This provision was repealed by the 1980 Act and had, in fact, been undermined by the Grunwick Dispute (Elias *et al.* 1980) in which an employer refused to recognise a union despite massive picketing of his factory and an arbitration award in favour of a union.

The closed shop   Most trade unions operate a closed shop. Under a *pre-entry shop agreement* an employer can only hire those workers who are already members of the relevant union. In the newspaper industry a pre-entry closed shop exists whereby the unions are responsible for supplying labour, especially the casual labour required for Sunday newspapers and emergencies. The alternative closed shop arrangement is the *post-entry closed shop* in which an employer is free to hire a worker, whether he is a unionist or not, provided that that worker joins a union when he is employed. Between 1964 and 1980 there appears to have been a increase in the number of closed shop agreements (Gennard 1981).

The existence of closed shop agreements poses problems not only with respect to employers, but also with employees. If all unions were voluntary societies, then union efficiency (or 'democracy' as it is sometimes called) could be ensured by the ability of dissatisfied members to join another union. And the problem of union democracy has been increased by the decline in the number of unions as a result of amalgamations.

The 1980 Employment Act introduced some control over the operation of pre-entry closed shops. First, it extended the protection given to those who were dismissed for not joining a union from the narrow category of those who had a religious conviction to those who had a deeply held personal conviction. Secondly, an employer could no longer be protected from the charge of unfair dismissal if the worker had been in his employment before the closed shop was introduced. Thirdly, an employer could only be protected against a charge of unfair dismissal if the closed shop were set up after an 80 per cent affirmative vote *of all those who would be covered by the agreement.* Fourthly, a worker who is excluded from a trade union which operates a closed shop can appeal to an industrial tribunal (as well as to the courts or the TUC review body) on the grounds that his expulsion was unreasonable, and the trade union would be liable to pay compensation if this were found to be so. The 1982 Act extended the grounds for unfair dismissal by making it automatically unfair to dismiss an employee because of non-union membership where there is no union membership agreement, and also where there has not been an appropriate level of support for the union membership agreement in a secret ballot within the five years preceding the dismissal of either 80 per cent of those entitled to vote or 85 per cent of those voting.

Immunity from damages   As a result of the 1906 Trade Disputes Act trade unions became exempt from all actions for damages arising out of *the contemplation or furtherance of a trade dispute.* This meant that the actions of a union could not be held wrongful because they hurt someone else by restricting their activities to buy and sell and engage in gainful activity. But although no action for damages could be taken against a union for damages, the 1980 Employment Act made it possible to sue individual members of a union in three cases:

(1) where the act resulted from someone picketing at some place other than where he was employed;
(2) where the act resulted from action in a trade dispute which had been taken against an employer who was not a party to the trade dispute, and was not a direct supplier or customer of the employer who was a party to the dispute;
(3) where a person induces an employee of one employer to break his contract of employment in order to persuade an employee of another firm to join a particular trade union.

Because the definition of a trade dispute also covers inter-union disputes, an employer cannot recover damages from either union, and the only machinery to resolve inter-union disputes is a TUC committee. The 1980 Act also removed immunity from tertiary boycotts; that is, where workers on strike at A induce workers at C not to supply goods to B who, in turn, sells to A.

The 1982 Act further restricted the range of actions which could claim protection under the 1906 formula 'in contemplation or furtherance of trade dispute'. The old definition of a dispute embraced disputes between workers and between employers and workers. The 1982 Act confines the definition of dispute to those between an employer and his workers. Hence, a protest against a government's incomes policies might not be deemed a trade dispute. And a union taking action against an employer without the support of his employees will not have immunity. The final contribution to the narrowing of union immunities comes by enabling actions in tort to be available for acts not protected by the 1982 Act. Limits, however, have been placed on the amount of damages that can be awarded.

Picketing Peaceful picketing means the attempt to peacefully persuade others not to work, and it *is* lawful. However, problems arose in the 1970s from the sheer size of picket barriers and the difficulties that pickets had in attempting to communicate with lorry drivers or bus drivers bringing suppliers or strike breakers. The 1980 Employment Act attempted to control the scale of picketing by outlawing tertiary and secondary picketing, but the onus of proving that such activities are taking place is placed upon the employer and not the police. The control of picket lines *is* left to the police, however, who have wide ranging powers in such matters as obstruction of the highway or breach of the peace, and it remains difficult to devise rules to govern picketing short of abolition.

Contracts for the supply of goods and services The 1982 Act attempts to outlaw union membership or union exclusion practices by commercial contractors engaged on government tasks; that is, the insistence that contractors use union (or non-union) labour. Any such terms in a contract are declared to be void and not enforceable in law.

(c) Substitutes for Collective Bargaining

In some trades, such as catering and retail distribution, there exists statutory minimum wage regulation by which councils of employers and workers' representatives (usually union representatives) plus three independent members determine rates of pay. In addition, there is the Fair Wages Resolution of 1946 which stipulates that government contractors should observe the wages and conditions of employment determined by collective bargaining. In order to implement the various statutory provisions, and to intervene in voluntary arrangements when there is a breakdown, there are some special judicial or quasi-judicial bodies as well as the regular courts of law. Thus industrial tribunals deal with breaches of statutory provisions in individual contracts, such as discrimination and equal pay. There is also the official service, the Advisory Conciliation and Arbitration Service (ACAS), whose function is to improve industrial relations by acting as a conciliator in disputes and by encouraging, extending and reforming collective bargaining machinery. ACAS has no enforcement powers, but the Central Advisory Committee (CAC) does.

(*d*)   *The Effects of the Legislation and Some Alternatives*

We shall now attempt to assess some of the effects of the legislation of the last two decades and consider whether there might be more efficient alternatives. The legal changes attempted to redefine property rights against a background of Britain's poor economic performance due to an inefficient use of labour arising out of labour immobility, restrictive practices, lack of skilled labour, too many strikes and cost–push inflation. In addition, there was a desire to harmonise UK legislation with the provisions of the Treaty of Rome and the prevailing practices of the EEC countries. Hence, skills were to be increased through taxing firms which did not train labour. Compensation was to be given to those made redundant, barriers to the employment of women and minority groups were to be removed and equal pay introduced. Accident prevention was to be achieved through a comprehensive system of factory safety officers. The structure and organisation of trade unions were to be improved through the encouragement of amalgamations. The position of the individual member *vis-à-vis* his officials was to be strengthened and union officials were to be compelled to control their shop stewards and not allow unofficial strikes to occur.

To conduct a thorough review of the effects of all the legislation would require more space than is available and could not be attempted without carrying out research into many neglected aspects. Comment will therefore be brief.

The 1964 Industrial Training Act proved unsuccessful and was subsequently repealed. Its place has been taken by a vast programme of training and retraining under the aegis of the Manpower Services Commission. But the root causes of the lack of skilled labour have not been tackled. Thus a major reason for the introduction of the 1964 Act was the alleged poaching of trained workers by employers who did not train workers, and it was felt that the poaching problem could be overcome if a tax were placed on all firms in an industry and the proceeds paid out to those firms which trained workers. The poaching argument, however, rested upon the assumption that employers should normally pay for the acquisition of skills. But since workers cannot be owned by employers, the argument seems dubious. Lack of skilled labour might therefore arise because *workers* could not afford to pay for skills—an argument which could be countered by the assertion that if employers wanted skilled labour, then they would raise wages.

A more compelling reason for the lack of skilled labour, however, lies in the extremely narrow wage differential which exists between apprentices and skilled workers, and union work rules. During the 1970s the age at which the adult wage came to be paid was lowered to 18 years and the average differential between the wages of young and adult workers wás less than 50 per cent. In Western Europe the differential is much wider. Hence, with a narrow wage differential there is a reluctance by employers to train labour. Government policy in the early eighties has been to expand the scope of government training schemes through the Manpower Services Commission, but without adequate wage signals in the labour market there is a danger of investment in the wrong skills. The success of the German training programme of the sixties and seventies may have been due to the fact that mistakes could be corrected by means of the buffer stock of guest workers. Britain does not operate a guest worker system and to use the young and married women as a buffer stock may create political problems.

The 1965 Redundancy Payments Act may have enabled firms to dispense with older workers, but may have increased the numbers of long-term unemployed (Fryer 1973). It may also have led to a rise in short-term unemployment by enabling workers to search longer for satisfactory jobs (although it is difficult to disentangle the effects of the Act from those resulting from the sharp rise in unemployment benefits in 1966). But it is extremely difficult to generalise about the effects of unemployment benefits because household circumstances differ considerably (Creedy 1981).

The Equal Pay Act resulted in a narrowing of differentials in the mid-seventies, but since then there has been a widening as well as a sharper rise in unemployment amongst women and minority groups. It is possible that the Equal Pay legislation may be repealed, although the anti-discrimination legislation would still stand (Snell et al. 1981; Chiplin and Sloane 1976).

It has been argued that the legislation on unfair dismissal has not been successful in obtaining reinstatement of workers because there is no provision for employees to be retained until after a tribunal hearing. Once severed, the employment contract is difficult to re-establish. Only unions can provide adequate protection against unfair dismissal; unfortunately, unions have been reluctant to organise the unorganised.

In addition to its recommendations enacted in the Health and Safety at Work Act, the Robens Committee suggested an examination of the possibilities of abolishing common law claims for accidents and moving to a system of statutory income payments, as practised in New Zealand and certain Canadian provinces. However, the Pearson Committee on Personal Injuries and Liabilities failed to recommend change. The common law system is still, therefore, in an unsatisfactory state. Administrative costs are extremely high due to the monopoly position of the lawyers in the conduct of claims. Most settlements are made out of court, the payments to injured and dependents are very low and the price mechanism (premiums plus compensation) does not control the level of accidents, nor provide adequate income maintenance. What effects the Health and Safety Act has had upon accidents has not yet been assessed.

Minimum wage legislation is still in an unsatisfactory state and there have been proposals to abolish it and the Fair Wages Resolution was not renewed in 1983. Some sectors of the retail trade are not covered by the machinery, e.g. butchers' shops and pet stores. Only a small percentage of establishments are investigated each year and underpayment can, on occasions, be considerable. Studies of trades (such as cutlery and toy-making) where the legislation has been withdrawn suggest that voluntary machinery does not fill the vacuum speedily and effectively (Craig *et al.* 1982).

There has been an increase in union mergers since the 1964 Act, but mainly amongst the smaller and medium-sized trade unions. There has been little rationalisation within the unions involved in mergers, and most of them remain federations.

Legislation on the closed shop, picketing and union immunity from damages is still in an unsatisfactory state. Meade (1981) has proposed the retention of a decentralised system of collective bargaining, but also that there should be a norm for increases in the general level of wages. Departures from the norm might then be conceded as a result of local demand and supply conditions. But should a dispute occur, then the issue could be referred to an arbitration body. Should the arbitrator's award not be accepted, the union could lose its immunities and strikers could lose their social security benefits.

Meade's proposals have been criticised on three grounds: first, that social security benefits do not appear to play an important role in strike activity (Gennard 1981); secondly, that the determination of the norm would still leave wages as a political issue; and thirdly, that the proposal would give too much power to the arbitrator. Since his decision will be binding, both employers and unions will attempt to guess what he will offer and agree to settle for that amount. This would be acceptable if he were always to award the market clearing wage, but if he did not, then a poor allocation of resources could result. Thus an arbitrator might seek to maximise employment by setting a low wage, but that low wage might then cause the supply of labour to contract. An alternative proposal put forward by Lerner (1980) and Layard (1982) is for a wage inflation tax which would tax wage increases above the norm, and would sacrifice any effects upon local demands and supplies for overall stability.

The problem posed by Meade and others is how to find the most appropriate method of implementing an optimal tax solution for a second best situation. The essence of an optimal tax is that it leaves the allocation of resources undisturbed and, preferably, achieves a first best solution. Thus a tax on income (work) must be matched by a tax on goods complementary to leisure, such as ice cream and football matches. And the same reasoning can be applied to trade unions and the labour market. Thus, in Figure 8.1 we measure the total labour supply along the horizontal axis, the demand for labour in sector A along the right-hand side and the

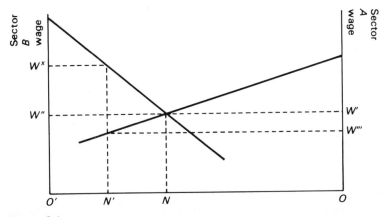

Figure 8.1

demand for labour in sector B along the left-hand side. In the absence of unions and assuming competitive conditions, the wage levels in both markets would be OW' and $O'W''$ respectively and the amounts of labour employed in each sector would be ON and $O'N$.

Assume that the B sector becomes unionised by a monopoly union which raises the wage to $O'W^x$ and displaces NN' labour to the non-union sector where the wage is depressed to OW'''. Now the essence of all schemes is to remove W^xW'' either by arbitration, taxation or anti-union legislation. In the case of a negative income tax the monopoly wage would be taxed away and paid as a subsidy to workers in the non-union sector. However, Figure 8.1 glosses over the problem of whether unions perform any function other than acting as monopolists. Thus, if unions were to increase productivity, then the demand curve in sector B would shift upwards. This problem of what unions do also besets the case for anti-union legislation. It is easy to suggest that instead of introducing second best schemes, such as Meade's 'not quite compulsory' arbitration and Layard's wage tax, the state should legislate against trade union immunities, especially those contained in the 1906 Act, but that would depend upon whether there are aspects of unions which increase efficiency.

8.5 Trade Unions and Collective Bargaining

(a) The Demand for Trade Unions

The interdependence of the activities of resource owners, especially workers, in the production process suggests that there might be a need for some monitoring agency to protect the interests of workers against adverse management decisions. Furthermore, we should expect that this demand for trade unionism would be greatest where production processes were difficult to monitor by individual workers—hence the tendency for unionism to be concentrated amongst manual workers and in large plants. In the latter, moreover, not only may workers demand trade unions, but management may also desire some form of workers' organisation because it eliminates the problem of dealing with too many workers on an individual basis (this would be a form of sub-contracting).

Given the possibilities of gains from unionisation, we might expect the demand for unionism to vary with the relevant benefits and costs. Over the period 1880 to 1970 Bain and Elsheikh (1982) found that the following factors gave a good explanation of changes in the overall level of union membership:

(1) the existing level of unionism;
(2) the behaviour of money wages;
(3) the behaviour of retail prices;
(4) the movement of unemployment;
(5) political and legal changes.

The correlations between unionism and the isolated variables were in some instances non-linear. Thus, when prices increased by more than four per cent per annum, the rate of increase in membership slackened. Severe inflation, however, only occurred in wartime when men replaced women in factories and some unions refused to admit women.

In other studies Bain and Elsheikh (1982) have examined the factors influencing the sizes of individual unions. Their findings are compatible with an earlier study of Phelps Brown and Hart (1957) which suggested that the size distribution of unions was lognormal. Thus, if unions did not deviate much from their industrial bases through, for example, mergers with unions in other industries, then a major factor affecting their sizes would be random variations in demand.

(b)   The Supply of Unionism

Externalities can give rise to a demand for unionism, and legislation may nurture unionism as well as creating the possibilities of monopoly rents through the exploitation of legal immunities. Hence, a union may be able to increase the wages of its members without reducing their employment if the following factors affecting the employer's elasticity of demand for labour are favourable:

(1) the price elasticity of demand for the product;
(2) the elasticity of substitution between union labour and other resources;

(3) the elasticity of supply of complementary factors;
(4) the percentage of total costs constituted by union labour (Hicks 1963).

Given the existence of legal immunities and the nature of the employer's demand curve, however, what will a union attempt to maximise? There have been many attempts to produce an economic model of a trade union and numerous goals have been suggested. During the 1950s there was a difference of opinion between those who followed Dunlop (1950) and argued that a trade union was an economic agency with goals which might vary with time and circumstance; and those who followed Ross and argued that a trade union was a political agency operating in an economic environment. Thus, Dunlop produced models of union behaviour in which the maximand was respectively the wage per member, the wage bill, the wage plus unemployment benefits and so on. In contrast, Ross argued that unions frequently struck for wage increases that bore no relationship to the economic conditions confronting their members, but which were provoked by increases obtained by members of other unions (Ross 1948).

In retrospect the arguments of both sides had merit. Thus, there is no reason to suppose that all unions have the same objective which they persistently pursue. Economists do not make a singular assumption for firms and, indeed, it may be argued that the debate over union goals foreshadowed the debate over the goals of corporations. For the trouble with the conventional models of unions was that they ignored the point that union members do not obtain saleable property rights; they cannot sell the rights to future earnings or sell the jobs they possess, whereas financial shareholders do have the right to sell their shares. And it is this lack of a market in trade union property rights which accounts for the low level of trade union subscriptions.

A trade union is a member of a large group of firms which have no saleable property rights. Thus charities, consumers' co-operatives and above all the state are other examples of firms which do not issue saleable property rights. Furthermore, the analogy with the state is strengthened by the fact that people refer to the presence or absence of democracy in trade unions and not to their efficiency (Magrath 1959).

The absence of saleable property rights imposes particular features on the supply curve of union members. Thus, if we consider a union in equilibrium, with wages per member being maximised, then an increase in the demand for union labour need not result in an increase in the supply of union labour. If the union admits more members, then the marginal product of members will fall; but if all members must be treated equally, then new members must also be paid the average product. Hence, there may be losses and not gains for existing members by admitting newcomers. Indeed, the potential gains may be increased by reducing membership.

Only if the potential members threaten to form another rival union will the existing union member admit newcomers. Hence, the supply of union members may depend upon whether the union is closed or open (Turner 1962).

Now consider a fall in the demand for union labour. If the union accepts a fall in wages, then there will be a redistribution of income from older members to newer members. Given the absence of saleable property rights, the analogy with the state becomes apposite because union policy will tend to be determined by the median voter. And faced with a fall in demand, the median union member will be in favour of redundancy or temporary lay-off in order of seniority. Thus the ethics of the queue will be observed. The apparent rigidity of money wages and the use of redundancies rather than voluntary wastage may therefore owe their origins to trade unions, although we should not ignore the fact that employers may also be interested in a policy which maintains good will.

Absence of property rights provides a possible explanation of union wage rigidity, but what determines the median voter's preferences between wages and employment? There are several solutions to this question, some of which can be illustrated by means of Figure 8.2. Given the average and marginal product curves of labour, several bilateral monopoly situations can be distinguished. Below are three examples:

(1) the union sets the wage at OY and ignores the employment consequences;

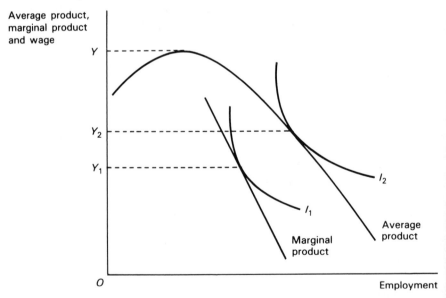

Figure 8.2

(2) the union pays attention to employment effects and seeks wage OY_1 at which its indifference curve is tangent to the marginal product curve;

(3) the union may seek an all-or-nothing contract (sometimes called an efficient contract) which fixes both the wage and employment. At wage OY_2 the union's indifference curve is tangent to the employer's average product curve and also to an unmarked iso-profit curve. Note that in this case the union increases both the wage and employment.

The union's indifference curves depict the union's trade-off between wages and employment, and their location will be determined by such factors as the wages obtained by other unions or the non-union wage, unemployment benefits, employment subsidies, etc. These can be more formally expressed in terms of an expected utility function or the more restricted forms, such as the Stone–Geary function, which have been employed in econometric work (Dertouzos and Pencavel 1980). Thus a union member may envisage himself in a lottery in which the prizes are the union wage or unemployment benefit and if unemployment benefits rise, then the union wage might be pushed higher. Similarly, a union in the public sector might push up wages and allow employment to be maintained by government subsidies. In this latter case wages in the private sector fall not as a result of labour migration, but because the net of the tax demand curve shifts downwards (which is an amendment to Figure 8.1).

(c)   The Effects of Unions

Any assessment of the effects of unions must await detailed studies of their effects on wage costs. Unfortunately, few studies exist. What we have are some analyses of the effects of unions on money wages, but the study of the effects of unions on productivity is still in its infancy. We begin therefore with wages.

Wages   Given the nature of the employer's demand curve, a union may increase wages without reducing employment. If it does cause unemployment, then the unemployed may drift into unorganised trades and reduce wages there. This result was illustrated earlier in Figure 8.1. It follows from that analysis that the unions may affect the wages of workers in the organised trade and the wages of workers in the unorganised trade. Usually only the first effect is measured and the spillover effect is ignored. Furthermore, we need to consider whether the union effect should be measured in terms of the hourly wage or the weekly or annual wage. Since a union may comprise both income-preferrers and leisure-preferrers, a measurement in terms of weekly earnings might not capture any gains resulting from a reduction in hours worked.

Finally, we need to take account of the quality of the available statistical material. In Britain there have been no studies of the effects of individual unions, and given the very high union density, it is difficult to obtain information on non-union wages. What is available is the proportion of workers covered by collective agreements at national and local level. Such data may, of course, overlook the possibility that non-union workers may

Table 8.1 Trade Union Wage Differential in Britain, 1964–73

Author	Time period	Subject of study (by occupation, type of collective agreement, or sex)	Union differential	Comments
Pencavel	1964	Industrial manual workers:		The dual nature of UK industrial relations system is important.
		Overall collective agreement	0–10	
		With a local collective agreement	14	
		Without a local collective agreement	0	
Mulvey	1973	Industrial manual workers:		
		Overall collective agreement	26–35	
		National agreement only	0	
		National plus supplementary	41–46	
		Local agreement only	46–48	
Mulvey and Foster	1973	Overall collective agreement	22–31	
		Manual occupations: men	36–60	
Stewart	1971	Manufacturing manual workers: men	40–47	
Nickell		Manufacturing manual workers:	Men	Women
		Overall effect of		
	1966	unionism	5	14
		Overall collective		
	1972	agreements	18–21	19–26
		National only	10.5–14	19.5–23
		National & local	22	9–21
		Local only	20–28	44–49

Source: Parsley 1980

be paid union wages as a result of the operation of the fair wages clause because of arbitration awards or because employers pay union wages in order to keep unions out of their factories. Bearing in mind these qualifications, Table 8.1 presents a range of estimates of unionism which suggest that national agreements may yield a differential ranging from zero to 10 per cent and that local agreements give much higher differentials. American results, which are based on better data, are contained in Table 8.2.

Table 8.2   Trade Union Wage Differential in the USA, 1923–75

Author	Time period	Subject of study (by industry, occupation, or race/sex)	Union differential	Comments
Lewis	1923–29	Industrial	15–20	Inadequate data a major constraint.
	1931–33		25+	
	1939–41		10–20	
	1945–49		0–5	
	1957–58		10–15	
Throop	1950	Selected	25.0	
	1960	Industries	29.7	
Freund	1965–71	Municipal employees	Average weekly earnings inc. $7	Major explanatory factors were market forces.
Personick	1972	Construction industry:		Differential varied widely between regions.
		Carpenters	35–50	
		Laborers	40–65	
		Electricians/Plumbers	55–70	
		Cement masons	35–50	
Personick and Schwenk	1971	Shirt manufacturing:		
		All production workers	12.5–16	
		Sewing machine operators (women)	10–13	
		Sewing machine repair (men)	7–9	
Ashenfelter	1961–66	Firemen	6–16	Composed of: (i) reduction in hours: 3–9 (ii) increase in salaries: 0–10

Author	Time period	Subject of study	1967	1973	1975
	1967	All workers	12.0	15.0	17.0
	1973	White men	10.0	15.5	16.0
	1975	Black men	21.5	22.5	22.5
		White women	14.0	13.0	17.0
		Black women	6.0	13.0	17.0

Author	Time period	Subject of study	Union differential	Comments
Schmenner 1962–70		Teachers	12–14	Unionisation important, but
		Fireman/Police (in eleven cities)	15	not as significant as other factors.

Source: Parsley 1980

All the results shown in Tables 8.1 and 8.2 have been obtained from single equation estimates; that is, they have been obtained from regressing wages on a variety of variables, such as age, sex, skill, education, etc., and inferring that the residual was due to unionism. But instead of the relationship running from unionism to wages, it may run in the reverse direction from wages to unionism. Thus the early unions used to determine their membership by admitting only those who could earn a particular rate of wage. Hence, a union could push up wages and then experience an increase in membership which would then consolidate the union bargaining position. Estimates using simultaneous equations are only available from the United States and give much lower estimates of a union effect than those contained in Table 8.2.

Finally, we may note that some studies suggest that unions may have reduced the dispersion of wages within occupations, but may have pre-served inter-occupational and inter-industry wage differentials. This is consistent with the earlier view of the Webbs (1902) that the imposition by unions of a standard rate eliminates discrimination.

Productivity But even if union members obtain a differential over non-unionists, it is still possible that wage costs remain unchanged simply because union workers are more productive. Thus, the effect of unions pushing up wages may be that employers hire more productive workers or reorganise their plants. There may, in fact, be several reasons why union members do not get a free lunch and employers get benefits from paying higher wages. Unions may substitute Voice (negotiation, strike) for Exit (labour turnover) and so reduce cost and increase productivity. There have been a few studies in the United States of the impact of unions upon productivity, but they are the subject of considerable controversy (Addison and Barnett 1982). Of course, any conclusion drawn on this subject would still meet with the industrial relations experts' view that unions attempt to create a system of industrial jurisprudence in which the rights of the worker are respected. In other words, the issue is social costs and not private costs (Slichter 1937; Flanders 1970).

Strikes The notion that unions attempt to introduce a system of industrial jurisprudence leads us to consider the part played by strikes in industrial relations. The standard treatment is by Hicks (1963). In Figure 8.3 we measure time along the horizontal axis and wages along the vertical axis. Suppose that a union starts with a wage claim of OW which is greater than the employer's offer of OW_1, then a process of bargaining takes place which depends upon the expected length of a strike. Thus the union can be viewed as having a resistance curve which shows the minimum wage it would accept, rather than undergo a strike of a given length. The resistance curve is assumed to slope downwards, suggesting that the union would accept a lower wage the longer the expected strike. Similarly, the employer

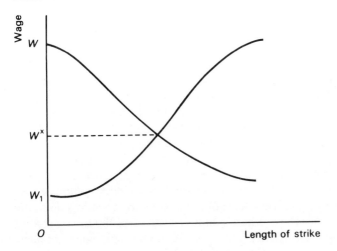

Figure 8.3

will have a concession curve which slopes upward, indicating that he will be prepared to offer a higher wage the longer is the expected strike. And if both the union and the employer correctly estimate the length of the strike, they would both readily agree to a wage of OW^x. Hence strikes are accidents in the sense that both parties fail to produce a contract which anticipates all contingencies (Addison and Siebert 1982; Reder and Neuman 1980).

Empirical studies tend to support an accident theory of strikes, but also draw attention to a number of non-economic factors.

(1) Strike activity is associated with changes in real wages, the demand for labour (usually measured in terms of the behaviour of unemployment), productivity and relative wages (Smith *et al.* 1978).

(2) The thesis that the larger the plant the greater the probability of bumping into someone is debatable (Revans 1958; Prais 1982; McCormick 1979; Turner *et al.* 1971) because the official statistics do not cover small plants.

(3) There is some evidence that some industries may be strike prone in the sense that contracts cannot be framed for all possible states of the world (e.g. coal mining, vehicles, docks).

(4) There is evidence that some regions are strike prone which may point to differences in regional temperaments.

(5) Concentrated industries are less likely to have strikes.

(6) Most strikes occur in a few plants in a few regions which suggests that wide sweeping legislation may be less efficient than the use of a body of specialist arbitrators.

8.6   What Kind of Labour Law? What Kind of Monopoly Law?

We return to the question of the appropriate individual and trade union law. One solution is to recognise that unions internalise an externality, but seek to disentangle that benefit from legislation which gives unions monopoly privileges. Thus unionism might be permitted at plant level, but national unions and collusion between plant unions might be outlawed. The objection is that it would still leave the distribution unresolved if, as some observers maintain, product markets are oligopolistic.

Whether oligopoly is prevalent is debatable. Some writers, such as Andrews and Brunner (1975), and latterly Baumol (1982), maintain that cross entry from one industry to another renders oligopoly unimportant. Some economists take the view that foreign competition renders domestic oligopolies impotent, whilst others maintain that since the emergence of multinational corporations the problem is one of international oligopolies. If oligopoly is important, then union legislation may be irrelevant. Hence the solution might be price ceilings which would, of course, fix the exchange rate. And in the case of the public sector there might have to be either an incomes policy or denationalisation.

Further changes in trade union legislation must remain a matter of conjecture, although there are straws in the wind. Thus, it has been suggested that unions should conduct secret postal ballots for all union posts and ballots before all strikes. And a proposal with much deeper implications is the substitution of 'contracting-in' for 'contracting-out' for the political levy—a proposal which would remove the Labour Party's political base. There may, in fact, be a movement towards the creation of a non-political unionism, a form of company unionism, devoted to improving wages and productivity at plant level. Such a unionism would be shorn of its political power of calling sympathetic strikes. But such a unionism would raise two problems. First, it would be difficult to maintain plant level unionism in the face of industrial relations policy determined at corporate level; there would be a vacuum to fill. Secondly, a non-political union movement would bring to the surface all those issues of income and wealth distribution which have lain dormant under a blanket belief that collective bargaining is the main vehicle for income redistribution.

8.7   The Firm's Decision

Hiring efficient workers is not only a requirement for private efficiency but, as our discussion of labour indicates, it is also a social obligation. How, then, can or should an employer find efficient workers? The standard treatment of labour demand envisages an optimising employer hiring workers up to the point at which the wage offered measures the marginal revenue product of labour. Unfortunately, this theory of labour demand is a long-run theory; it assumes that labour productivity is known, that productivity is independent of the wage offered and that management is free to vary factor proportions. In a nutshell, it assumes away all the interesting and difficult managerial problems. Hence, we must re-appraise the personnel problem in terms of jobs, the supply of possible workers to do those jobs and the demands for those possible workers.

(a)   Job Evaluation

The tasks of the personnel manager involve his interaction with marketing, production and financial managers. Marketing dictates the types of goods to be produced; production determines how they are to be produced; financial management attempts to cost the production of those goods; the problem for personnel managers, however, is to find the workers to do the jobs at the wages which financial considerations suggest are feasible. Hence the first task is to have a clear idea of the nature of the jobs.

Job evaluation attempts to provide a systematic and detailed analysis of the content of jobs which can be presented in a written form as distinct from an informal, *ad hoc* treatment. At one pole job evaluation may take the form of simply ranking all jobs in terms of overall content. At the other pole there may be an attempt to dissect jobs into their components—skill, mental and physical requirements, etc.—and then award points to each component. The points awarded for each element in a job can then be aggregated to obtain the total score for a job, and the scores for different jobs can then be compared. The process of awarding points and then aggregating them is, of course, open to criticism on the grounds that the various components of a job are qualities, and it is absurd to attempt to add together qualities. Hence, the only way to tackle the problem is to see what the market is prepared to pay for those bundles of characteristics. But this criticism overlooks the point that the rankings of jobs obtained by job evaluation are tied to the market by the selection of certain key jobs which have recognisable market counterparts, and the market rates for these key jobs are then used to interpolate or extrapolate the pay for jobs which may have no recognisable market counterparts. This is an important point to consider when firms are operating job hierarchies and on-the-job training in specific skills. In such circumstances only jobs at ports of entry may have market counterparts.

Job evaluation has also become important since the 1970s because firms have had to adapt to a changed economic climate in which traditional skills and their associated market rates have become anachronisms. In this changed world so-called market equilibrium rates cannot be announced until firms have discovered what the new market clearing rates should be, and this process of search involves the analysis of jobs and the analysis of the most efficient methods of doing those jobs.

8.8   Motivation and Labour Supply

The second step in the task of filling jobs is to have some understanding of the determinants of labour supply. This is not just a matter of heads and possible hours of work, but a more detailed understanding of workers' motivation.

(a)   Motivation

Our discussion of motivation is based upon utility theory as modified by the concept of a hierarchy of wants (Georgescu Roegen 1966; Alderfer 1972). An individual is assumed to have a hierarchy of wants. Basic wants will comprise such things as food and shelter; lower order wants may include such things as prestige. An individual will first attempt to satisfy his high order wants before attempting to satisfy his low order wants. It is possible that more than one commodity will satisfy a given want (e.g. water and beer), and it is also possible that one commodity may satisfy more than one want (e.g. a motor car may satisfy the want for travel and also ostentation). But no one will attempt to purchase a good or indulge in an activity which satisfies a low order want until a high order want has been satisfied.

The foregoing propositions can now be translated into an indifference map as follows. In Figure 8.4 we measure job characteristics along the two axes—say, skill and autonomy (Hackman and Oldham 1980; Wall, Clegg and Jackson 1978). The solid curve *aa* is an indifference curve which traces out the varying combinations of skill variety and autonomy which yield the same level of utility and satisfy the want for, say, nutrition. Thus the combinations denoted by *L* and *M* yield the same utility. Greater quantities of skill variety and autonomy can lift the individual on to the higher indifference curve *a'a'* and increase his ability to satisfy the want for nutrition. Now consider the curve *bb*. Points on *bb* will satisfy the want for prestige.

Returning to the curve *aa*, we observe that the individual will be indifferent between *L* and *M*, but he will not be indifferent between *M* and *R* because *R* also satisfies his requirement for prestige.

The concept of a hierarchy of wants taken in conjunction with the distinction between income and substitution effects enables us to understand why the problem of selecting suitable motivators may be difficult. In

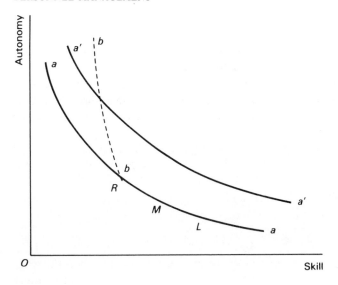

Figure 8.4

the standard treatment of utility theory an increase in the motivator (for instance pay) will give rise to an income and substitution effect. The substitution effect will operate in the desired direction by inducing the individual to trade more effort for pay, but the income effect can operate either to increase or decrease his effort. Thus, if the higher rate of pay enables him to satisfy a given want (e.g. nutrition) with a lower input of effort, then the motivator may be inefficient. Only if the motivator opens up the possibility of satisfying a lower want may it be effective. But the satisfaction of a lower want may require a different motivator. This is the essence of Herzberg's distinction between hygiene and motivating factors, and it is also to be found in those theories which argue for job redesign and job enlargement as the only motivating factors once basic wants have been satisfied (Herzberg 1959; Wall and Stephenson 1970). Finally, we should note that the theory may need to be extended to include the mode of want fulfilment. If A thinks that he is being paid too much relative to B, then he may increase his efforts. This point is stressed in equity theory (Adams 1963).

Empirical studies on job satisfaction by sociologists and psychologists are considerable. Amongst economists there has been a tendency to confine attention to the effects upon hours of work of changes in real income which have usually been brought about by tax changes. What the available studies tend to suggest is that the supply curve for men is slightly backward sloping (increases in pay cause a fall in hours worked), whereas increases in pay tend to bring a rise in that supply of labour from married women.

(b)   Investment in training

In a competitive economy wages in different jobs would tend towards equality. (Strictly speaking, it would be the net advantages—the sum of monetary and non-monetary factors—which would be equalised.) Such equality does not exist; clean jobs tend to pay more than dirty jobs. One reason for the differences in benefits is that some jobs require considerable investment in training.

Workers will invest in training as long as the net present value of investment in skills is positive. Neglecting non-pecuniary advantages accruing to jobs, the stream of monetary benefits discounted to the decision date will be

$$PV = \frac{W_1}{(1+r)} + \frac{W_2}{(1+r)^2} + \ldots + \frac{W_n}{(1+r)^n}$$

where *PV* is the present value of the future earnings stream, *W* is the wage earned in each period, and *r* is the discount rate used to discount the future earnings stream to the point of decision making.

From the present value is deducted the cost of the investment in skills which may be approximated by the highest earnings stream foregone (i.e. the opportunity cost of the investment).

(c)   Search

The labour market provides no costless way of revealing where the best jobs are, and workers have to spend some time searching for and assessing jobs. They invest in knowledge about job opportunities and will continue to search until the marginal benefit from search is equal to the marginal cost of search.

8.9   Employers' Hiring Policies

(a)   Search

Given some ideas on the factors which may motivate workers and their method of finding jobs, we can now consider the optimal hiring strategies. Because knowledge of workers' abilities is not ascertained easily, managements pursue a variety of strategies for obtaining the most efficient workers. Thus, they can either set a high wage and attempt to cream the market; advertise or use the services of government or private employment agencies; ask their existing workers to recommend new employees; indulge in intensive or extensive interviewing; pursue strategies which 'make workers transfer information about themselves through various signalling devices; or alternatively, they can seek to accumulate information through hiring and training.

Since there are many methods of obtaining workers, an optimum strategy for management to pursue would be to equate the ratios of the marginal products of their employees with the marginal costs of the different procedures used to hire them:

$$\frac{MP_1}{w} = \frac{MP_2}{MC_2} = \frac{MP_3}{MC_3} = \ldots = \frac{MP_n}{MC_n}$$

where MP is the marginal product of employees hired by the procedures 1,2,3 . . . n, w is the change in the starting wage (the market creaming strategy), and MC_1, MC_2 . . . MC_n are the marginal costs of hiring labour by methods other than by simply raising the starting wage.

(b)   Screening, Filtering and Discrimination

Confronted by the complexities of selecting efficient workers, management may fall back upon proxy indicators, such as age, sex, martital status, education, etc. Thus, men may be preferred to women because they have had more work experience and hence have been better graded and sorted; and those with jobs may be preferred to those who are unemployed. The use of such indicators is analogous to fixing a high starting wage and has the effect of dividing applicants into distinct groups, especially when wages are inflexible. Thus, in Figure 8.5 we assume that there are two groups of workers with different educational attainments (and presumably abilities). The effect of placing the hiring standard at X is to discriminate against group A. Such discrimination arises from lack of information and not from prejudice; it would disappear if workers in group A offered to work for lower wages than those in group B and employers believed that it would be worth taking the risk at the lower wage. But the problem could be

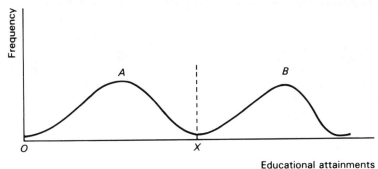

Figure 8.5

exacerbated if governments attempted to impose equal pay and employment quotas for different groups.

(c)   Human Capital Theory and Signalling

There is a link between employers' filtering techniques and workers' investment decisions. If workers think that employers are using particular indicators, then they will invest in acquiring those indicators. Hence, there will be *self-selection*.

Human capital theory, however, can be applied to both workers' and employers' investment decisions, but a distinction needs to be borne in mind between *general skills* and *specific skills* (Becker 1964). General skills are those which are relevant to jobs in many firms and industries, whereas specific skills apply to one firm or industry. General skills will therefore tend to be paid for by workers because of their widespread saleability and the inability of employers to own workers (making them reluctant to invest in their acquisition).

Specific skills will be paid for by employers, but because of the problem of protecting their investment employers will have to pay wages which will control the level of labour turnover.

(d)   Hiring Standards and the Labour Market

Indicators are known as hiring standards, and their use will vary with the state of the external labour market (McCormick 1959). If the labour market is tight, then job specifications will be revised downwards and hiring standards will consequently be lowered. If the labour market is slack, then hiring standards will be raised.

(e)   Information Networks: Casual and Regular Trades and Trust

The problem of finding good workers (or good employers) accounts for the emergence of information-gathering institutions in the labour market. The existence of vacancies may be transmitted by the existing workforce to friends, by local union branches, newspapers and job centres. And because information once released becomes a public good, various methods are taken to ensure that its acquisition is paid for.

Differences in information networks enable us to classify external labour markets as either *casual* or *regular* (Hicks 1963). Casual markets are characterised by relative absence of skills, high labour turnover, little capital equipment and simple management systems. They may be further sub-divided into those characterised by demand instability and those exhibiting supply instability. Demand instability may give rise to a pool of idle labour if the peaks of individual employers' demands do not coincide. Dock labour markets tended to exhibit this state of affairs. A worker who failed to get a job with one employer might find that all jobs had been filled once he had resumed his search. Although some workers accepted the life-style offered by dock markets, there has been a tendency to replace casual hiring in docks by permanent hirings.

Supply instability is usually characteristic of markets for services. The total demand for taxi-drivers and waitresses may be constant, but customers may trade with different suppliers. In regular trades there may be low labour turnover and implicit long-term contracts may be established so that investment in trust and fairness reinforce the cash nexus.

8.10   The Internal Labour Market

Instead of incurring heavy external search costs to find suitable workers, management may substitute on-the-job training. Such a procedure is common where skills are specific to the firm and where the firm operates a job hierarchy, the ascent of which involves workers moving to jobs of ever increasing complexity. Within such an internal market, management can conduct controlled experiments in which workers are trained and their skills are assessed.

In contemplating investment in specific skills, management has three problems to consider:

(1) How much internal training should a new employee be given?
(2) Should an existing employee be trained and promoted or should an experienced outsider be recruited?
(3) Should an existing employee be trained and promoted or should an outsider be recruited *and* trained?

Consider the first problem. Management will be willing to invest in training a worker if (a) the sums of the expected present values of the marginal productivity of the worker increases and (b) there is any increase in the marginal productivities of complementary resources.

The *direct return* to a firm from training will be larger the more specific is the training, the greater the monopsony power of the employer and the longer the period over which the employment contract is expected to last. The *indirect return* will increase with the amount of complementary factors employed and the extent to which the training affects marginal productivities. Costs will comprise finding and training workers and any losses of output incurred from diverting staff from production to training workers. In the second case management will train and promote an insider if the net revenue on insiders is greater than on outsiders. Similar considerations apply in the third case.

(a)   Labour and Plant Utilisation: Inventories of Goods, Machines and Workers

The provision of skills and the question of who pays for them provide an introduction to the problems of plant and labour utilisation. Casual, as well as detailed, empirical evidence points to the following phenomena which need explanation:

(1) the tendency for plant and machinery to be idle for considerable periods, especially at night and weekends;
(2) the tendency for output to fluctuate more than employment over the business cycle;
(3) the tendency for output to fluctuate less than inventories of goods;
(4) The tendency for money wages to be inflexible downwards.

The four stylised facts involve long-run and short-run decisions by consumers, employers and workers. Specifically, the economic problem over the long run is to maximise the sum of consumers' and producers' surpluses subject to the preferences of consumers, employers and workers. In the short run there may be fluctuations, anticipated or otherwise, in consumers' demands, and the problem is to determine whether these variations should be met by changes in current output or by changes in the levels of stocks (including stock-outs). The choice will depend upon relative costs. But we begin with the long-run decision on shift working.

(b)   Shift working

One of the most striking features of the British economy, and even of the economies of most countries, is the low level of plant utilisation. Most plant and machinery is idle at weekends and even night work is infrequent. This problem of low levels of plant utilisation was the subject of a National Board for Prices and Incomes report on overtime and shift working in the late 1960s. The main determinants of shift working appear to be the following:

(1) the capital intensity of production;
(2) the wage–rental ratio;
(3) the size of the shift premium;
(4) the elasticity of substitution between capital and labour.

The prevailing state of technology may determine the potential capital intensity of production and incline a firm towards greater capital utilisation. But whether shift working will be adopted may depend crucially upon the size of the shift premium. If workers dislike the disruption of domestic and social life which shift working can produce, then they may demand a prohibitive shift premium. Economic factors are therefore important in determining the amount of shift working and may underscore any legislation. Thus, the factory acts have traditionally prohibited the employment of women and young people on night work.

(c)   Short-Run Variations in Hours of Work, Employment and Stocks

The tendency for output to fluctuate more than employment over the course of the business cycle has been well documented and its causes have been attributed to the high costs of hiring and training labour. Thus, within the production function we must distinguish between the number of employees and the hours they work. What is then observed in time series analysis is that the numbers employed fluctuate less than hours worked and output. If we start from a situation at the lower turning point of the cycle with a given number of employees, then the early stages of the upswing are characterised by a reduction in idle time and a greater utilisation of plant and labour, with the result that output increases and real and money wages may rise together. In the later stages of the upswing, bottlenecks may occur and more labour may be employed, overtime working may be introduced and productivity may decline; real and money wages may therefore move in opposite directions. With the collapse of the boom, output and hours of work will fall, but productivity may also fall if the numbers employed are not reduced; real and money wages may therefore continue to move in opposite directions (Sargeant and Wallace 1968).

Oi (1962) attempted to explain the phenomenon of labour hoarding in recessions by an extension of human capital theory. Thus, the costs of employing labour may be written as follows:

$$C = W_t(1 + r)^{-t} + H + K$$

where the first term on the right-hand side is the sum of discounted wage payments, and H and K are hiring and training costs respectively.

The discounted marginal revenue product stream is:

$$MRP = (VMP + \Delta VMP)(1 + r)^{-t}$$

where VMP is the value of the workers' marginal product before training and ΔVMP is the addition due to training.

Profit maximisation requires that the discounted cost of an additional worker is just equal to his discounted revenue:

$$H + K = (VMP + \Delta VMP - W_t)(1 - r)^{-t}$$

with periodic rent

$$R = \frac{H + K}{(1 - r)^{-t}}$$

Hence, a worker will only be laid off if his periodic rent falls below the value of his marginal product. If the value of the marginal product falls below the rent, then the firm will find that it pays to dispense workers to save on current costs, i.e. wage payments. But as long as workers are bringing in some rent, it pays to retain them because the costs of hiring workers when the boom begins will include a new outlay on hiring and training costs.

Labour hoarding, however, will not be practised if employers know that they can temporarily dismiss workers with the knowledge that they will return when demand picks up. Temporary lay-offs (Feldstein 1976) may be possible when there are state unemployment benefits available and when there are no alternative jobs.

Labour hoarding represents one possible response to changing demand conditions. Another possibility is to keep the labour fully employed by manufacturing for stock purposes during slack periods. Whether that is feasible depends upon the costs of holding the stock of finished goods.

(d) Labour Turnover and Monopsony

Manpower planning is concerned with maintaining an efficient stock of labour; it therefore involves an analysis of flows into and out of the labour force and the implications of long-run and short-run changes in demand for labour. So far we have been concerned with inflows and now we must turn to the outflows.

Wastage can be divided into voluntary and involuntary quits, although the distinction should not be pressed too sharply. Voluntary quits may rise in anticipation of a fall off in trade; some workers may decide to leave whilst the prospects of employment elsewhere are good.

Statistical studies suggest that labour wastage can be approximated by a lognormal distribution in which most wastage takes place within the first few weeks of hiring. Wastage tends to be highest for young workers and for unskilled workers, turnover tends to vary with the state of the labour market, and involuntary quits become more pronounced under trade unionism (Shorey 1980; Medoff 1979). Such findings are consistent with an investment-search model of worker behaviour in which firms simultaneously determine their wages and labour turnover. But note: a given quit rate is compatible with the payment of different amounts of wages if monopsony is present. Hence in periods of considerable unemployment we may observe wage increases which seem to bear no relationship to the state of the labour market.

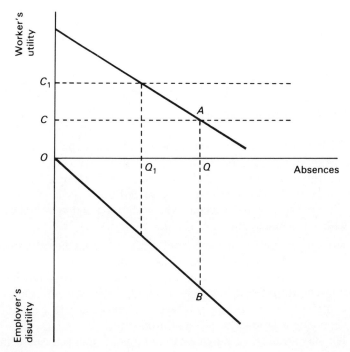

Figure 8.6

(e)   Labour Absenteeism

Not only may a firm simultaneously determine its wages and labour turnover, it may also determine its wages and absenteeism. Thus, in Figure 8.6 we measure a worker's demand for absences (leisure) in the top half of the diagram. He will equate his demand for absences with the opportunity cost of those absences (i.e. at wage OC he will demand OQ absences). In the bottom half of the diagram we measure the disutility to the employer of those absences (in other words, his demand to reduce absences). When OQ absences occur, the disutility to the employer is QB, and since QB is greater than QA, it would be profitable to the employer to increase the cost to the worker of absences either by threats or bribes, which shift the cost to OC_1. At cost OC_1, OQ_1 absences are produced and marginal benefits and disutilities are equal. OQ_1 absences are therefore Pareto optimal.

Could absenteeism be eliminated? If the employer were a discriminating monopsonist, then he might remove absenteeism. But in most employment situations transaction costs preclude negotiating with each worker and a standard wage is paid. At that wage, self-selection may take place; only those willing to offer a given number of hours will offer their services. Hence, absenteeism within the labour force may exhibit little variance; there may be a group norm. That norm may be acceptable to both sides because, as in the case of coal mining, workers may be attempting to maximise their time spent working and employers may be interested in minimising the costs of hiring new workers. Absenteeism therefore tells us nothing about job satisfaction.

8.11 The Employment Contract

So far we have discussed: (1) some aspects of labour supply; and (2) some determinants of the demand for labour. What we have not considered is the employment contract which binds employer and employee together. This is an omission which we must now remedy.

Consider the case of an individual who wishes to purchase a house. He is faced with three main courses of action.

(1) He can purchase each component separately from different specialist suppliers. Thus he will buy bricks, timber, the services of a brick-layer, joiner, plumber, etc. In this case the distinction between household and firm becomes blurred; there are no employment contracts, but there are contracts for services, with each supplier supplying a product or piece of product.

(2) He may arrange the purchase from a middleman who sub-contracts the various tasks, as in case (1). In this case there are contracts for service between the householder and the middleman and between the middleman and the various sub-contractors.

(3) Finally, he can arrange to purchase from another individual who supervises the work of others and who may have a permanent staff who produce houses.

Where does the distinction between (1), (2) and (3) lie? The usual argument is that the distinction between a contract for services and an employment contract lies in the fact that there is an element of control and direction in an employment contract which is absent from a contract for services. Hence, in case (3) an employment contract would exist between one individual and his permanent staff. This is the distinction which we observed being made in the law earlier. But if a householder purchases bricks and asks for them to be delivered to the site, is there not control and direction? And if he specifies the layout of the kitchen, is he an employer? Nor should we seize upon the element of permanency in case (3) because not all workers are permanently employed. What we have in the three cases is a variety of contracts (contract of sale, contract for services and contract of employment), the choice of which depends upon the following factors.

(1) The costs of arranging all the contracts—only the unemployed and the under-employed have the time to arrange a large number of

different contracts. Most people have an opportunity price tag on their time.

(2) Identifying a product also requires expertise and time, especially when the problem is one of specifying the quality of a component which may have no obvious substitute or market price.

(3) It may not always be possible to measure all the dimensions of a job and an all-in contract or delegation to an expert may have to be conceded.

(4) There may be interdependence in some activities. This is an aspect of work which has been emphasised by Alchian and Demsetz. One person's output may be conditional on the efforts of others and safety considerations may be important. If an externality exists between workers, then there will be a need to monitor the performance of others. Thus, one solution for our would-be house owner is to act as labourer to the craftsmen. But the general point remains— shirking can only be reduced by some form of monitoring and that monitoring is what Alchian and Demsetz (Alchian 1977) consider to form the essence of a firm. In some instances, such as group piece-work, the problem is minimised through self-selection by members of the group, as in coal mining.

(a)   Time-Rates, Piece-Rates and Jousts

Contracts for service are for products, whereas employment contracts are either for units of time or products. But the distinction in employment contracts may be apparent rather than real. Most time-rates imply an output and most piece-rates imply some period of production. The distinction tends, in fact, to turn upon whether output can be measured and what form supervision takes. If tasks are divisible and outputs can be measured, then payment by product or piece will be used; supervision will take the form of monitoring the quality of the output and ensuring a constant flow of materials and a reduction of extraneous interruptions to a worker's performance. Management's task is essentially that of the consumer—checking the quality of the product. If tasks are not divisible and not measurable, then an all-in contract will be used and management's task will be to monitor the effort of the worker as well as the quality of the product. An obvious disadvantage of time-rates is that there is no link between output and payment; if pay is doubled then output might not be doubled. Hence the attraction of piece-rates. But simple piece-rates have the disadvantage that they do not compensate for the rising cost of effort. Hence, the attraction of premium bonus systems in which the bonus rises as output rises, although sometimes at a diminishing rate in order to correct for incorrect rate fixing and learning effects.

Piece-rates became popular around the turn of the century and were associated with the pioneers of scientific management, such as F. W. Taylor. They were used extensively in the First and Second World Wars, but declined in popularity in the 1950s in America and in the 1960s in Britain. Their wartime popularity was undoubtedly due to the shortage of labour for monitoring, the influx of women who were less concerned with challenging wages systems, and the existence of large numbers of repetitive jobs. Their postwar decline owed a great deal to the dissemination of the writings of industrial sociologists, such as Roy (1954) in America and later Lupton (1963) in Britain. There was also the impact of that great work, *Management and the Worker*, by Roethlisberger and Dickson. The thrust of their writings may be summarised as follows.

(1) The assumption that workers may only be interested in monetary rewards may be false.
(2) The assumption that effort can be harnessed by an incentive scheme may be false.
(3) There may be no connection between effort and output.
(4) If there are too many interruptions, then workers may take steps to stabilise their earnings by insisting on lieu rates which convert wage systems into time-rates.
(5) The spread of the shop steward system may mean that production becomes sub-contracted and management may lose control of the shop floor.

However, there has been a revival of interest in piece-rates since the mid-seventies. One factor responsible for the increased interest has been the effect of successive incomes policies which have prevented managers granting time-rate increases. A second factor, most noticeable in the coal industry, has been the failure of time-rates to increase productivity and the tendency for national time-rate negotiations to develop into political confrontations.

Piece-rates may be usable where output can easily be measured and quality control presents no serious problems; time-rates may be used where supervision costs are low. But there are difficulties in the case of managerial staffs whose output is not easily measurable and for whom the attempt to put a time dimension on work may also be tricky. Abraham and Medoff (1980) found that human capital theory did not seem to explain the salary differences between workers in two firms. And it is also common for the pay of a manager to double when he is promoted even though there is no apparent doubling of productivity. Managing directors do not suddenly become twice as efficient as their seconds in command.

Two explanations have been put forward for the apparent differences in salary rankings. First, there is the obvious point that a manager is paid not only on the basis of his productivity, but also on the basis of that of his subordinates. Hence, the higher up the managerial ladder a person is, the more subordinates he will have under him. Secondly, the economic problem may not be to find out who is the best at a job absolutely (indeed, the notion of an absolute may be meaningless), but to find out who is the best relative to the others. All that one is trying to do is to find out who is the best managing director given that there is no obvious way of assessing abilities. Hence, the problem is solved by establishing prizes of such magnitude that many will take part in the race. And not only will the top prize necessarily bear no relation to the productivity of the person on that rung, but many of the intermediate prizes may bear no relationship to the productivity of their recipients. What the prizes do is to encourage people to compete. And although the notion of a tournament has only been applied to managers, it can be generalised. Thus, the earnings of barristers and solicitors obtained under contracts of service may exhibit great disparities because success breeds disproportionately greater rewards. Indeed, the entire labour market may be viewed as a gigantic tournament from which some contestants may be detached because their skills are measurable (Lazear and Rosen 1981).

(b)   Wage Contracts, Salary Contracts and Profit-Sharing Schemes

So far we have dealt with the distinction between service contracts and employment contracts and with time-rates and piece-rates. There are, however, other aspects to employment contracts, such as duration of the contract and method of enforcement. We have therefore to consider the following factors:

(1) the degree of risk averseness of employers and workers;
(2) the ease of access to information of employers and workers;
(3) the work–leisure preferences of workers;
(4) the existence of unemployment benefits;
(5) the methods and costs of enforcing a contract;
(6) the transaction costs associated with hiring, training and dismissing workers.

For ease of exposition we can distinguish between (1) wage contracts; (2) salary contracts; and (3) profit-sharing contracts.

Under a *wage contract* management may offer workers a fixed reward and no job security if workers are no more risk averse than they are, if unemployment benefits exist, if workers are easy to replace and if workers are willing to accept the bunching of spells of enforced leisure.

If workers are extremely risk averse, then they will prefer *salary contracts* in which they are guaranteed a fixed reward and guaranteed employment. Whether management will offer such a contract will depend upon its attitude to risk and its ability to spread risk through the capital market. It may, of course, offer such contracts to specific groups whose contribution to total costs is small and whose replacement costs are high. But the expression 'salary contract' should not be confined to white collar workers; it may be a contract offered to some manual workers.

A *profit-sharing contract* is one which guarantees employment but not rewards and is likely to be acceptable where workers can exercise some form of control over decision taking.

The three contracts we have outlined are pure types and in practice most contracts will tend to contain elements of all three. One obvious reason for composite contracts is that the quasi-rents (profits) which members of the firm earn will not be known until the goods have been sold. The second reason why composition will take place is that we have so far not considered how contracts are enforced.

(c)   Methods of Enforcement

Consider the following problem. An employer may not know in advance the productivity of a worker nor what his sales (value productivity) may be. But he must offer the worker a contract which will overcome his current work–leisure preference. On the other side, a worker may not know what his productivity will be, or if he does, he may be reluctant to disclose it in advance of a contract. Hence, a contract may be for two periods. In the first period, the probationary period, the employer is able to assess the productivity of the worker. The second period begins with the confirmation or recision of the contract and in this period there may be opportunities for cheating or reneging. Thus, at the end of the first period the employer may attempt to drive down the wage, not on the grounds that the worker's productivity is low, but because 'trade is bad' (that is, value productivity has fallen) and the worker may have difficulties in obtaining information on the state of trade, except by quitting and trying to obtain another job. An appeal to the courts may be of no avail because the courts may lack expertise. Hence the traditional reluctance of employers and workers to use arbitration. However, a trade union can provide such information and by organising a strike, force the employer to reveal the state of trade. In a similar fashion, an employer may be faced with the possibility that having installed expensive equipment in the first period, the worker attempts to capture all the quasi-rents in the second period. Lack of enforceability of contracts—a consequence of the 1906 Trade Disputes Act—could make for a low level of investment, although fluctuating exchange rates may be an equally potent factor.

Of course, some of these problems are peculiar to the *casual trades* where there may be a once-and-for-all zero sum game. In the *regular trades*, which involve a continuous non-zero sum game, no employer can afford to risk his reputation by cheating and no worker can afford to acquire a reputation for reneging on contracts. Such managers and shop stewards get sacked. But this is not to deny the importance of strikes and lock-outs as means of eliciting information in regular trades. Indeed, the underlying assumption in strikes and lock-outs is that there is no breach of contract and normal relations will be resumed once the wage has been fixed.

Regular trades are therefore characterised by an initial contract which attempts to fix payments in the light of estimates of productivity and the state of trade. The initial contract is likely to be a salary contract which implicitly assumes that at contract renegotiation, wages will be revised to take into account any profits or losses incurred as a result of the first period's activities. Past profits and losses are not, therefore, bygones; they represent that portion of quasi-rents which had not been anticipated when the members of the club or team locked themselves into a contract and became, for a while, immobile resources having no opportunity cost and analogous to Ricardian land. Of course, the size of the initial payments will depend upon attitudes to risk, but we must not assume that it is only employers who are risk averse. No employer will ever offer a worker a salary contract in perpetuity, a fact which Japanese workers discovered in the aftermath of the oil price rises of the 1970s.

(d) Indexation

Employment contracts normally stipulate a monetary reward, that is a reward in nominal terms. Workers, however, would prefer a wage which is fixed in real terms, in other words a wage which measures some bundle of consumer goods. Management, on the other hand, would prefer to fix a wage in terms of their own product, that is a wage which is linked to the selling price of the product they produce. Because of these differences of opinion there is seldom an explicit statement of the real wage which is measured by the nominal wage mentioned in the contract. Of course, some notion of a real wage is in the minds of the employer and employee, but it is only in periods of severe inflation, when governments underwrite the contract, that explicit indexation of the wage to an index of retail prices becomes common. In normal circumstances changes in the real wage are usually the subject of contract renegotiation. Thus, in Britain since the 1940s it has been common for contracts to be renegotiated annually because the costs of revision at a shorter time interval are considered to be too high.

8.12   Unemployment

The employment contract links the internal labour market to the external labour market and provides us with a starting point for a consideration of unemployment. In the absence of perfect knowledge, unemployment arises from a mismatching of demands and supplies which take time to remove because most labour markets are neither auction markets nor casual markets, in which contracts can be instantly revised at no cost. Reduction in unemployment, then, occurs through the acquisition of information, through search and through the lapsing of old contracts. By analogy, unemployment in the labour market is like the idleness of people at airports (Hall 1983). There is not a large, hard core of unemployed, but a continuous turnover. On the basis of the information available to them, people make decisions which may turn out to be wrong: they may arrive early for planes which may be held up for repairs or because of bad weather; they may quit jobs on the basis of incomplete information. And once they have quit their jobs they may lose their index of quality and reliability. The unemployed may be suspect. If they offer to work for lower wages and employers use wages as an index of quality, then the unemployed's wage offers may be rejected. In this sense they are involuntarily unemployed. Wage rigidity may therefore arise from the demand side. And from the supply side, wage rigidity may arise from the existence of staggered wage contracts in a decentralised market economy. Only in a centralised economy, as Keynes observed, might it be possible to have a once-and-for-all wage reduction which would remove unemployment overnight (Keynes 1936).

Wage rigidity is compatible with unemployment and wage increases are also compatible with unemployment. During a recession and shake-out of labour, changes in work organisation bring about differences in attitudes and quality between the employed and unemployed. Hence wages become firm-specific and bear no relationship to national wage negotiations. Thus management may increase wages in line with increasing productivity and thereby minimise labour turnover. The mistake of macroeconomics is to assume that labour is homogeneous.

References

Abraham, K. G. and Medoff, J. L. (1980) 'Experience, performance and earnings', *Quarterly Journal of Economics*, 95, pp. 703–735.

Adams, J. S. (1963) 'Wage inequities, productivity and work quality', *Industrial Relations*, 3, pp. 9–16.

Addison, J. T. and Barnett, A. H. (1982) 'The impact of unions on productivity', *British Journal of Industrial Relations*, Vol. 20, pp. 145–162.

Addison, J. T. and Siebert, W. J. (1982) 'Are strikes accidents?' *Economic Journal*, 92, pp. 387–402.

Alchian, A. A. (1977) *Economic Forces at Work*, Liberty Press, Indianapolis.

Alderfer, C. P. (1972) *Existence, Relatedness and Growth: Human Needs in Organizational Settings*, Free Press.

Andrews, P. W. S. and Brunner, E. (1975) *Studies in Pricing*, Macmillan.

Bain, G. S. and Elsheikh, Farouk (1978) *Union Growth and the Business Cycle*, Basil Blackwell.

Bain, G. S. and Elsheikh, Farouk (1982) 'Union growth and the business cycle: a disaggregated study', *British Journal of Industrial Relations*, XX, pp. 34–43.

Baumol, W. J. (1982) *Contestable Markets and the Theory of Industry*, Harcourt Brace.

Becker, C. S. (1964) *Human Capital*, Columbia University Press.

Brannen, J. *et al.* (1976) *The Worker Directors*, Hutchinson.

Brown, W. A. (1981) *The Changing Contours of British Industrial Relations*, Basil Blackwell.

Buchanan, J. M. and Stubblebine, C. (1962) 'Externality', *Economica*, 29, pp. 371–84.

Chiplin, B. and Sloane, P. (1976) *Sex Discrimination in the Labour Market*, Macmillan.

Craig, J. C. *et al.* (1982) *Labour Market Structure, Industrial Organization and Low Pay*, Cambridge University Press.

Creedy, J. (ed.) (1981) *The Economics of Unemployment*, Butterworths.

Dertouzos, J. N. and Pencavel, J. H. (1980) 'Wage and employment determination under trade unionism: the international typographical union', *Journal of Political Economy*, 89, pp. 1162–1181.

Dunlop, J. T. (1950) *Wage Determination Under Trade Unions*, Macmillan.

Elias, P. *et al.* (1980) *Labour Law*, Butterworths.

Feldstein, M. (1976) 'Temporary lay-offs in the theory of unemployment', *Journal of Political Economy*, 84, pp. 937–978.

Flanders, A. (1970) *Management and Unions*, Faber.

Freeman, R. (1976) 'Individual mobility and union voice in the labor market', *American Economic Review*, Vol. 66, pp. 361–368.

Freeman, R. and Medoff, J. (1977) 'Substitution between production labor and other inputs in unionized and non-unionized manufacturing', Discussion Paper No. 581, Department of Economics, Harvard University.

Fryer, R. H. (1973) *Redundancy and Paternalist Capitalism*, Allen and Unwin.

Gennard, J. *et al.* (1981) 'The extent of closed shop arrangements in British industry', *Department of Employment Gazette*, 88, pp. 16–22.

Georgescu Roegen, N. (1966) *Analytical Economics*, Harvard University Press.

Hackman, J. R. and Oldham, G. R. (1980) *Work Design*, Addison Wesley.

Hall, R. E. (1983) 'Is unemployment a macroeconomic problem', *American Economic Review*, 73, pp. 219–222.

Herzberg, F., Mausner, B. and Snyderman, B. B. (1959) *The Motivation to Work*, Wiley.

Hicks, J. R. (1963) *The Theory of Wages*, Macmillan.

Keynes, J. M. (1936) *The General Theory of Employment, Interest and Money*, Macmillan.

Layard, P. R. G. (1982) 'Is incomes policy the answer to unemployment?', *Economica*, 49, pp. 219–39.

Lazear, E. and Rosen S. (1981) 'Rank order tournaments as optimal labour contracts', *Journal of Political Economy*, 89, pp. 841–864.

Lerner, A. P. (1980) *M. A. P.: An Anti-Inflation Plan*, Harcourt Brace.

Lewis, W. A. (1978) *Growth and Fluctuations 1870–1913*, Allen and Unwin.

Lupton, T. (1963) *On the Shop Floor*, Pergamon.

McCormick, B. J. (1959) 'Labour hiring standards and monopolistic competition theory, *Quarterly Journal of Economics*, Vol. 78, pp. 607–618.

McCormick, B. J. (1979) *Industrial Relations in the Coal Industry*, Macmillan.

Magrath, P. (1959) 'Democracy in overalls: the futile quest for union democracy', *Industrial and Labour Relations Review*, 12, pp. 503–525.

Meade, J. E. (1964) *Efficiency, Equality and the Ownership of Property*, Allen and Unwin.

Meade, J. E. (1972) 'The theory of the labour-managed firms and profit sharing', *Economic Journal*, 82, pp. 402–428.

Meade, J. E. (1981) *Stagflation: Volume 1 Wage Fixing*, Allen and Unwin.

Medoff, J. L. (1979) 'Layoffs and alternatives under trade unions in US manufacturing', *American Economic Review*, 69, pp. 380–95.

Oi, W. (1962) 'Labor as a quasi-fixed factor', *Journal of Political Economy*, 70, pp. 538–55.

Parsley, C. J. (1980) 'Labor unions and wages: a survey', *Journal of Economic Literature*, 18, pp. 1–31.

Phelps Brown, E. H. and Hart, P. E. (1957) 'The sizes of trade unions: a study in the laws of aggregation', *Economic Journal*, 67, pp. 1–15.

Prais, S. J. (1982) *Productivity and Industrial Structure*, Cambridge University Press.

Reder, M. W. and Neuman, S. R. (1980) 'Conflict and contract: the case of strikes', *Journal of Political Economy*, 88, pp. 867–886.

Revans, R. (1958) 'Human relations, management and size', in E. M. Hugh Jones (ed.), *Human Relations and Modern Management*, North Holland.

Roethlisberger, F. J. and Dickson, W. J. (1939) *Management and the Worker*, Harvard University Press.

Ross, A. M. (1948) *The Theory of Trade Union Wage Policy*, University of California Press.

Roy, D. (1954) 'Efficiency and "the fix": informal intergroup relations in a piecework machine shop', *American Journal of Sociology*, 60, pp. 255–66.

Sampson, A. A. (1983) 'Employment policy in a model with a rational trade union', *Economic Journal*, 93, pp. 297–311.

Sargeant, T. J. and Wallace, N. (1968) 'The elasticity of substitution and the cyclical behaviour of productivity, wages and labour's share', *American Economic Review*, LXIV, pp. 257–263.

Shorey, J. (1980) 'An analysis of quits using industry turnover data', *Economic Journal*, 90, pp. 821–37.

Slichter, S. H. (1937) *Unions and Industrial Management*, Brookings Institution.

Smith, C. T. B. *et al.* (1978) *Strikes in Britain: a Research Study of Industry Stoppages in the United Kingdom*', Department of Employment Manpower Papers 15, HMSO.

Snell, M. W. *et al.* (1981) *Equal Pay and Opportunities*, Research Paper No. 20, Department of Employment, HMSO.

Turner, H. A. (1962) *Trade Union Growth, Structure and Policy*, Allen and Unwin.

Turner, H. A. *et al.* (1971) *Management Characteristics and Labour Conflict*, Cambridge University Press.

Turvey, R. (ed.) (1952) *Wages Policy Under Full Employment*, Hodge.

Wall, T. D., Clegg, C. W. and Jackson, P. R. (1978) 'An evaluation of the job characteristics model', *Journal of Occupational Psychology*, 51, pp. 183–196.

Wall, T. D. and Stephenson, G. M. (1970) 'Herzberg's two-factor theory of job attitudes and some fresh evidence', *Industrial Relations Journal*, 1, pp. 41–65.

Webbs, S. B. (1902) *Industrial Democracy*, Longman.

9
Managing Risk and Uncertainty

T. A. J. Cockerill and H. Kinloch

9.1 The Nature of Risk and Uncertainty

Just as death is the only certainty, so risk and uncertainty are fundamental facts of life. Business planning, decision making and control are carried out in an environment of risk and uncertainty and corporate success and survival depend to a great extent upon 'good luck' or the effective anticipation of future events. Whilst it is manifestly impossible to predict the future with complete accuracy, many organisations devote considerable financial and physical resources to forecasting key elements in their environment: changes in the level and composition of demand; changes in the prices and supply conditions of labour, capital, energy and raw materials; developments in production technology; and alterations in the legislative framework and climate of opinion in which they operate. This chapter is concerned with ways in which corporate bodies can identify and seek to reduce the impact of risk and uncertainty and so improve their planning and performance. Following a consideration of the nature of risk and uncertainty, we analyse the types of risk, outline ways of measuring risk and consider possible lines of response to risky situations. Finally, two case studies are given of the impact on enterprises of risk and uncertainty.

The distinction between risk and uncertainty is often said to be that risk is insurable whereas uncertainty is not. More precisely, objective probabilities—the likelihood of the occurrence of particular events following a given action—can be assigned in the presence of risk, whereas in the case of uncertainty the assignments must be made on other empirical and unverifiable grounds. The estimation of risk probabilities can be done on the basis of known mathematical or physical principles (*a priori*), as in the cases of the incidence of equipment failure or the ratio of stocks to output to avoid the inability to supply, or on the basis of the analysis of past experience (*a posteriori*), as with life or property assurance.

Estimation of the probability of an occurrence tells the decision maker only the likelihood of the event taking place; at least as important is the impact that the event will have on the organisation. Thus, the probability of a devastating explosion at a chemicals factory may be remote, but it would have an overwhelming effect on the firm if it did occur, perhaps threatening its ability to survive in the long term. Events that combine a high probability of occurrence with a high impact are those that the firm must try most hard to avoid; low probability/high impact events must also be drawn into the planning environment. Low impact events can be relegated to lower priorities, whatever their probabilities.

A further important aspect is the decision maker's and controller's attitude to risk. As discussed elsewhere in this volume, managers and other policy makers in large organisations may be essentially risk averse, endeavouring to avoid difficult situations even though corporate profits and growth, and therefore the long-term maximisation of the value of the firm, are sacrificed as a result. Where security of personal or corporate incomes is an important element in the utility function of a management team, then risk-avoiding activity may be expected. Associations and trading agreements with competitors and pressures on government to erect protective devices against imports may be manifestations of this attitude. Indeed, in so far as government seeks to raise industrial efficiency by increased competition, legislation or other action to prevent or remove barriers to trade and interfirm competitiveness may be essential elements of government policy. In such cases, increased uncertainty for suppliers in a market may be equated with increased competition. One element of the traditional market model of perfect competition is the presence of complete uncertainty as to which buyers will favour which of a wide array of suppliers.

But just as some (perhaps most) management teams can be expected to avoid risk, others may actively seek it. Inveterate gamblers are the obvious example; business investors and policy makers alike may also be prepared to risk funds, income and employment prospects in pursuit of high profits and growth through identifying market trends and developing new products and processes ahead of their competitors where the prospective payoff after adjusting for the degree of risk is attractive. The expansion of a small firms sector and the development of a range of new products and services, from which increased economic growth may flow, require individuals and groups to actively seek and accept risky and uncertain situations.

9.2 Types of Risk

There are many types of risk that impact on enterprises. Four aspects of risk are examined in this section: market, technological, factor cost and political risks.

Market Risk

The characteristics of markets in which firms operate may alter or, in planning a new venture or the redesign of a marketing campaign, a supplier may mis-specify the market which it intends to supply. These may be defined as 'demand risks'. In addition, some firms may take initiatives that impact on others. These are 'competitor risks'. The three main factors that influence the level of demand for most goods and services are income per head, price, and the intensity and nature of product differentiation—reflected in such aspects as advertising campaigns and product design and quality. Of these, suppliers have some control over the latter two, but little direct influence over the first. The growth of income per head can be crucial, depending on the responsiveness of demand to real income (i.e. the income elasticity of demand).

For suppliers of products with a high income elasticity, real income growth will be associated with rapidly expanding markets and may allow profit margins to be increased during a period of rising sales volume, giving high returns on capital employed. The demand for synthetic fibres—nylon, polyester and acrylic—had these characteristics during the first stages of those products' life cycles and it provided the opportunity for the high initial research and development expenditures to be recouped in a fairly short period. The demand for packaged foreign holidays, other leisure activities, sports cars and expensive clothing are further examples of products with high income elasticities. It follows that the failure of incomes per head to reach the levels expected by the suppliers of such products can have serious consequences. Thus, the development of the Anglo-French Concorde supersonic transport aircraft was based on the expectation that corporate and personal incomes would be sufficiently high to generate enough demand for reduced journey times by air at a premium fare to make the venture viable. This was in any case extremely optimistic, and the combination of the oil-induced recessions of the 1970s and the concurrent development of wide-bodied subsonic aircraft and severe competition in air fares on the high density routes has caused considerable financial problems for the two operators, Air France and British Airways.

Where income elasticities of demand are low, however, suppliers may suffer less during recessions; and for so-called 'inferior' goods, the demand for which *increases* as real incomes *fall*, suppliers may benefit in recession periods. It is thought that part of the buoyancy of colour television purchases during the 1970s was a result of cutbacks in discretionary leisure expenditure and decisions to improve the quality of home entertainment.

Suppliers of new or redesigned products may mis-specify the characteristics of the market. Three examples may be quoted, beginning with a classic failure.

(a) The Edsel motor car was launched by the Ford Company of the

USA in the mid-1950s. Ford developed a medium-sized sedan (saloon) car as an addition to their range which was named after Henry Ford II's son, Edsel Ford. The development costs were so high, sales so far below target and losses so great, that the model was withdrawn after a period of a few months. It is generally thought that the product's failure was the result of poor design in relation to the requirements and expectations of the market, but the main causes were Ford's marketing and distribution policies. Then, as now, the company had two main automobile divisions: Ford, the volume car operation, whose models were sold primarily on price; and Lincoln-Mercury, which catered for the less price sensitive, higher specification, sector of the market. Each division had its own separate network of dealers and distributors. The intention was to market the Edsel through both systems, but the failure occurred because typical Ford purchasers perceived the model as over-specified and too expensive, whilst Lincoln-Mercury purchasers saw a dilution in the exclusivity of the model range.

(b) Throughout the 1960s the health risks from smoking tobacco (particularly cigarettes) became increasingly apparent and publicly acknowledged. The major contributor is nicotine tar. With support and encouragement from government and the tobacco companies, ICI and Courtaulds in Britain developed a tobacco substitute (NSM) that could be used wholly or partly to replace tobacco in cigarettes. The development programme cost several million pounds and the manufacturers' policy in the early 1970s was to maintain intact their existing brand range, but in some cases to provide the alternative of a given brand with or without NSM. Sales of cigarettes containing NSM were negligible, and the initiative was dropped after a few months. The key element in this failure appears to have been potential customers' attitudes to risk. By the 1970s those who chose to smoke recognised in the main the health risks and chose to accept them. The introduction of NSM was perceived as materially altering the flavour of cigarettes, with a significant reduction in the smoker's satisfaction, that was seen as more than offsetting smokers' perceived loss of utility from the risk to health. Those who rated the health risks more highly gave up smoking.

(c) Early morning television services on a regular basis began in Britain in the opening months of 1983. There were two competing services, offered by the BBC and TV-am, a commercial company that had been awarded the franchise by the Independent Broadcasting Authority (IBA) in the face of strong competition. The beginning of services involved building new studio and office accommodation and recruiting a full range of staff for presentation, planning, programme production and news gathering and editing. TV-am started transmissions in March 1983, a date that had been announced some six months previously. The BBC responded by beginning its programmes some three weeks in advance. The size and characteristics of the potential audience were largely unknown. In the initial months the BBC captured the greater part—about 1.5 million viewers a day on average—whilst TV-am began with an average audience of about one-third of that total, which then began to decline. After a few weeks major changes in management and in programming policy were introduced. The chief elements in the difficulties of the early months appear to have been a misreading of the audience's requirements for news and programmes, an underestimation of the impact of competition from the BBC, and a disaffection among viewers caused by the interruption of programmes with advertisements.

Another threat to corporate performance and survival comes from unexpected changes in established markets. These may be the result of changes in the legislative or wider economic environment that it would have been difficult to predict (e.g. controls on imports into third countries; changes in government policy) or of the failure of suppliers to monitor and forecast trends accurately. There are many examples of difficulties in anticipation. *Burtons* built a large and successful business on the retailing and manufacture of men's made-to-measure suits. Fashion and social changes caused demand to fall rapidly as ready-to-wear casual and co-ordinated fashions for men grew in importance, and the company began to follow a policy of diversification and adjustment to customers' new requirements. *Woolworth* enjoyed considerable success as a variety chain store operator, supplying a vast range of low unit price household goods, but failed adequately to adapt to competition from specialist do-it-yourself stores, the shift away from High Street shopping to edge-of-town locations, and the strategy of many other retailing groups of developing distinctive market images. *Beer* sales in the UK have fallen since 1978, after 25 years of steady growth. The causes of the decline are uncertain, but probably include a drop in beer sales through public houses as social habits change, increased competition from other 'leisure' activities, and increases in the real price of beer coupled with a fall in consumer's real disposable incomes.

It is clear from these examples that management teams must analyse as accurately as possible the nature of their markets and compare the results with their intended product and marketing policies. They must also be constantly aware of the changes that are taking place in the market and of the factors that are influencing change. It is probably easier (and doubtless more interesting in a perverse sort of way) to record and analyse the failures rather than achievements. But there have been successes, for example fast food retailing, video cassette recorders, supermarkets and telecommunications equipment.

Technological Risk

Technological risk is associated with the development and implementation of new products and manufacturing processes and of the use of existing systems. Invention and innovation are important elements of social progress; economic growth and efficiently operating markets will not only encourage firms to market new products that appear to meet consumers' demands and offer the supplier increased profits by way of improved margins or increased volume, but will also introduce new techniques of production that will reduce costs or improve the quality of the final product.

New process and product development involves investment in basic and applied research and in raising manufacturing systems to commercial scales. The entire operation is invariably expensive and often risky. Many studies have been made of the economic significance of research and development (R and D) expenditures in evolving new products and processes and of the influence of market form upon innovation and technological progress.[1] Research expenditures are often quite modest in relation to total development costs and, although risky (since many new ideas never come to commercial fruition), the initial work can often be done at a small scale by individual inventors or by small firms. Expensive pure research can be supported by government through the universities or research establishments. The development stage is, by contrast, frequently very expensive. Polyester (a substitute for cotton), for example, cost ICI at least £25 million to develop in the 1950s, representing about £300 million at today's prices.

Research and development expenditures for successful products or processes are in the nature of investment expenditures, but are subject to high risk. Firms are generally unwilling to capitalise them, and will normally try to write them off against current income. In consequence, companies active in R and D are commonly those which are diversified, with several products at different stages of their life cycles generating adequate cash flow to fund invention and innovation. This suggests that large scale is essential to support and spread the risks of R and D, although Scherer (1980, pp. 418–422) finds that higher rates of R and D expenditures do not necessarily lead to higher rates of innovative output.

Firms faced with technological threats and opportunities can choose to be leaders or followers. A leader will bear the initial costs and risks of

---

1. For example Jewkes *et al.* (1969), Mansfield (1968), Scherer (1965).

development, but will hope to enjoy the benefits of early entry into the market. Followers, by contrast, will anticipate a reduction in risk as the problems associated with the new techniques or the product will have become apparent and alternative systems may have become available. Additionally, the market prospects will have become clearer. The choice between leadership and following the lead of others depends on several factors. First, the company's attitude to risk itself is important: is the management team stimulated or repulsed by the prospects of technical difficulties and the chances of success or failure? Second, the timing and the size of the prospective returns in relation to the initial expenses will be important. The higher the initial expenses are and the higher the rate of time discount, and the farther ahead in time are the prospective returns, the less likely will the firm be to innovate, even in a risk-free environment. Thirdly, how easily and rapidly will new techniques or products be matched by competitors? Inventions can be protected by patents, but the mere registration of an invention may alert competitors to the commercial possibilities. New techniques can sometimes be 'invented around'. Secrecy and the conscious decision *not* to patent can often be a more effective means of market protection, especially where operating 'know-how' is important for successful production.

Where technological risk is an important element of the market environment in which firms operate, it is important that they should have sufficient funds to finance innovation and be sufficiently diversified to spread the risks. British Rail's Advanced Passenger Train (APT) is an example of an ambitious project with a high degree of technological risk that did not have enough financial support to enable the difficulties that emerged to be overcome. A tilting mechanism was to be developed that would enable purpose-built rolling stock to operate at very high speeds (150 mph) over existing track. SNCF, the French railway system, by contrast, based its system on specially constructed track dedicated solely to the very high speed train (TGV),[2] thereby simplifying the technological challenge but increasing by several times the investment requirement.

Fison's pharmaceutical division had a major setback in 1982 when a new drug that was on the brink of being launched was withdrawn on safety grounds. A pyramidal structure of product development, in which there is an array of possible new products at different stages of development and testing, is one way in which overall product development risk can be reduced, but it demands large investment and a continuing commitment to R and D which may be difficult to sustain in times of strong price competition, weak markets and poor profits. One of the most dramatic examples of the impact of technological risk on a company is the case of the RB211 jet engine, developed by Rolls-Royce for the Lockheed TriStar

---

2. Train à grande vitesse.

(L10) wide-bodied airliner. Wide-bodied aircraft require high thrust engines with low weight–power ratios, and to reduce weight to a minimum Rolls-Royce intended to use carbon fibre for the turbine blades in place of tungsten alloy steel. The Lockheed contract was at a fixed price. The chief technological problem encountered with carbon fibre was its lack of lateral strength, so that turbine blades were liable to fracture if impacted by solid material drawn into the engine. The difficulty delayed the development of the engine, raised its costs, and led eventually to the replacement of carbon fibre with tungsten alloy steel, thus reducing the engine's performance. The ultimate consequence was that the company went into liquidation, obliging the government to rescue it through nationalisation.

A low probability, unexpected event, can have a high impact on a firm. The destruction of the Nipro caprolactam plant at Flixborough as a result of an explosion in 1974 halted completely the UK production of an essential chemical intermediate for the production of a major type of nylon. The two major fibre manufacturers, Courtaulds and British Enkalon, were immediately faced with shortages and a threefold price increase.

Factor Cost Risk

The main inputs of firms are materials, labour, energy and capital, and the costs of each of these may be subject to unexpected variations that can cause severe financial difficulties. Commodity prices are sensitive to small movements in the relationship between supply and demand and can be affected by poor harvests, increases in the world rate of economic activity, or the discovery of new reserves. Producer cartels have become an increasingly important feature of commodity markets since the first oil crisis of 1973 and the formation of the Organisation of Petroleum Exporting Countries (OPEC), but their strength depends upon the level of overall demand, the ease of substitution of alternative commodities, the degree of similarity (or difference) in costs between the members, and the internal consistency of their economic, social and political objectives.

International currency exchange rates have shown considerable fluctuations since the ending of explicit stabilisation policies by the leading advanced industrialised nations in 1971. Free of other influences, exchange rates should move to adjust smoothly to deficits or surpluses on the current accounts of the balance of payments of the trading nations, but in practice movements have been erratic and have also been influenced by capital movements and interventions by central banks. A sharp increase in the exchange rate of one currency against others, as occurred in the UK in 1979/80, will raise the foreign currency price of exports and reduce the price of imports in the home country. The currency appreciation may be so large and occur too rapidly to permit firms to reduce their internal costs by raising productivity or to reduce their profit margins to continue to compete effectively with their international competitors.

Likewise, a sharp currency depreciation may initially stimulate sales in both the home and foreign markets, but will increase the costs of imports of commodities and semi-manufactures and may, through its contribution to falling real wages, subsequently lead to faster inflation as a result of pressures for increased nominal wages. The management of exchange rate risk is discussed in more detail in Chapter 10.

Industrial relations disputes may affect a firm's operations through strikes or other forms of work disruption. These may depend to a large extent upon the effectiveness of the firm's relationships with its employees, but can also be affected by the overall level of demand for the product and the climate of opinion among trade unions and their members.

Financial charges depend mainly upon interest rates and the composition of a firm's asset financing. Interest rates are affected by the supply of loanable funds, mainly from the personal sector and from abroad, government borrowing requirements for public expenditure and debt servicing, and official policy towards the money supply and the exchange rate. Following a lengthy span of time after World War Two in which the UK authorities followed policies intended mainly to achieve steady or gradually adjusting interest rates, the period since 1970 has been characterised by sharp variations in interest rates in both nominal and real[3] terms. Increases in nominal interest rates raise the cost of working capital to firms and may encourage them to reduce stocks. The effect on interest charges against profits depends chiefly on the debt–equity ratio. The higher the proportion of debt in the financing of assets, the higher will be interest charges and the more sensitive profits to interest rate movements.

The impact of factor cost movements on firms depends upon the importance of each factor cost item in total costs, the magnitude of the cost movement and the extent to which competitors at home or abroad are affected.

Political Risk

Companies face political risk in both their home markets and in foreign markets which they may supply by direct exports, by production from wholly-owned or partly-owned subsidiaries or from licensees located in the country of sale or in third countries. Threats in the domestic market may come from shifts in government policy as a result of elections or

---

3. Allowing for the effects of inflation. Thus, if the nominal interest rate is 15 per cent and the inflation rate is 10 per cent, the real interest rate is 5 per cent.

adjustments to international economic and financial conditions and may involve changes in the levels of personal and corporate taxation, in monetary and interest rate policies and in policies towards imports, competition and public ownership.

The main focus of interest with political risk is, however, on cross-frontier trading activities of international companies. Investment in local market production facilities may be desirable if there is a possibility that the national government may reduce or close access to the market by imports. But the international producer is then faced with the risks of sequestration of its assets, with or without compensation, if government policy changes, or with requirements in respect of the amount of locally-produced material or components in the finished product and the number of expatriates that may be employed. Joint participation with a local enterprise, often state-owned, may be a requirement. The repatriation of debt service payments (interest and principal), dividends and royalties may be subject to regulation. Host governments may also adopt restrictive state procurement policies that confine orders only to enterprises owned and operated locally.

9.3 Assessing Risk

A firm's reaction to risk depends upon the nature and importance of the risk and on the attitudes and objectives of the management team. Strategic and policy decisions are taken in terms of situations in which a series of recurrent events occur (for example, the demand for bus or train services) and in which a single irrevocable decision will affect subsequent trading performance (for example, the choice between alternative production systems, or sales promotion campaigns). In taking such decisions, the objectives of the decision makers may be to maximise the net benefits (usually profits), taking account of the probability of each outcome, minimise risk, or aim for the maximum benefits irrespective of risk. The various approaches to risk can conveniently be demonstrated with a simple example.

Suppose the Aldcrox Car Company manufactures and sells a range of motor vehicles. One model has been in production for several years and there are signs that annual sales are beginning to decline. To deal with this, the company is considering *either* giving the existing model a face lift *or* introducing a new model. The profitability of each option over the next two years depends upon the state of the economy, as shown in Table 9.1. The company's corporate planning department has assigned the following probabilities to the likelihood of each state of the economy occurring: downturn, 0.3; constant, 0.5; upturn, 0.2.

Table 9.1   Payoff Matrix

State of the economy	Profitability of strategies (£000)	
	Minor face lift	New model
Downturn	20	10
Constant	30	20
Upturn	80	150

Expected Value

The table shows that if there is a downturn in the economy over the next two years, reducing the volume of sales and increasing the importance of price competitiveness, the firm will make a profit of £20,000 if it decides on a face lift, but only £10,000 if it launches the new model. On the other hand, the new model policy will be much more profitable in relation to the face lift if there is an upturn. No change in the level of economic activity would favour a face lift. Since one of the three states of the economy *must* come about, if each had the same probability of occurrence (0.33) the firm could simply calculate the mean of the sum of the profitabilities for each strategy and choose that which had the highest value (the new model strategy in this case). But the probabilities of occurrence are not equal for each state of the economy, so the estimated payoffs must be weighted by the appropriate probabilities, as shown in Table 9.2. The aggregated weighted payoffs are the *expected values*; the new model is still the preferred option, but its relative advantage over the face lift is less than when the unweighted averages are considered.

The Degree of Risk

Although the new model strategy yields the highest expected value, it may also be a more risky choice than the face lift, and this consideration may also be of importance to the management if the investment required is large in relation to the firm's available resources, or if the firm's share price is sensitive to fluctuations in its reported profits. The degree of risk is usually gauged by the *coefficient of variation*, defined as the standard deviation (σ) of the estimated payoffs divided by the expected value (EV). The standard deviation in turn is the square root of the probability-weighted variance of the payoffs.

Table 9.3 shows the method of calculation of the coefficient of variation for the two strategies, and it can be seen that the face lift (coefficient of variation 0.59) is less risky than the new model (coefficient of variation 1.25). A risk-averse management would be likely to select the face lift option, even though the new model offered the higher expected value.

Table 9.2 Expected Values

State of the economy	Minor face lift			New model		
	Payoff	Probability	Expected value	Payoff	Probability	Expected value
Downturn	20	0.3	6	10	0.3	3
Constant	30	0.5	15	20	0.5	10
Upturn	80	0.2	16	150	0.2	30
			37			43

Choice: New Model

Table 9.3 Risk Comparison

(a) Minor Face Lift

Outcome	Expected value	Deviation (D)	D^2	Probability (p)	$D^2 \times p$
20	37	−17	289	0.3	86.7
30	37	−7	49	0.5	24.5
80	37	+43	1,849	0.2	369.8
				Variance	481.0

Standard deviation = $\sqrt{\text{var}}$ = 21.93
Co-efficient of variation = 21.93 ÷ 37 = 0.59

(b) New Model

Outcome	Expected value	Deviation (D)	D^2	Probability (p)	$D^2 \times p$
10	43	−33	1,089	0.3	326.7
20	43	−23	529	0.5	264.5
150	43	+107	11,449	0.2	2,289.2
				Variance	2,881.0

Standard deviation = $\sqrt{\text{var}}$ = 53.67
Co-efficient of variation = 53.67 ÷ 43 = 1.25

Choice: Minor face lift

Certainty Equivalent

Faced with risky situations, individuals and firms may be prepared to accept an assured sum of money instead of proceeding to make an operational decision. Contestants in TV quiz shows who are shown (much to the audience's delight) agonising over whether to 'take the money' or run a risk, such as opening a box whose contents are unknown or answering a further question correctly, are making implicit assessments of certainty equivalents. If they choose to run the risk, the certainty value of the assured sum is insufficient to compensate for the prospect of the risky return. Similarly, a firm's owners may require a certain minimum sum of money in cash or shares in order to sell out to an alternative management and to lose the benefits but be relieved of the future risks of running the business. In the example being considered here the expected values of the two strategies will normally also be their respective certainty equivalents, since given the offer of assured but smaller sums, management could reasonably expect to do better by taking the risk of the appropriate strategy. If, however, the management team is very pessimistic for some reason, it will be prepared to accept £20,000 rather than go ahead with the face lift, or £10,000 rather than launch the new model. Certainty equivalents may be very low in relation to expected values if the risk is very high, or if the need for money is acute (consider the impecunious gambler at the roulette table).

Risk Preference

Managers may actively seek risk or may avoid it; apart from their individual psychologies, attitudes to risk will be affected by the philosophy, objectives and reward systems of the organisations for which they work. Stock options and bonus schemes may make managers more risk-oriented than if they are rewarded only by agreed annual salaries. Two opposing approaches typify the risk-averse and the risk-seeking decision-taker. It can be seen from Table 9.1 that the worst outcome for the firm as a result of choosing the face lift would be a profit of £20,000 in the event of a downturn in the economy. The worst outcome if a new model is launched would be £10,000 with an economic downturn. Risk-averse managers will choose the face lift because that maximises the return from the worst possible outcome—a strategy known as *maximin*. Risk-seeking managers will, by contrast, launch the new model because that offers the chance of the highest profit of all, £150,000. This is a *maximax* strategy.

Decision Trees

Major business decisions are in reality far more complex than in the example above. Typically a series of interacting and interdependent decisions have to be made before the final decision for producing and marketing a product can be made. The sequence of choices can be shown as branching out from one another in a decision tree, with each choice being assigned a potential profit and a probability of occurrence. The aggregated net present values of profits, weighted by their appropriate probabilities, may then be compared to indicate the most appropriate route to choose.

Figure 9.1 shows a highly simplified example of a firm choosing between the production of sunshades or umbrellas on the basis of expected profits over the next two years. It is assumed that the initial investment required for the two projects is the same in each case, so that the selection process rests solely on identifying the option that will yield the highest present value of forecast profits. Sales, and hence profits, depend chiefly on the state of the weather which in each year may be (mainly) rainy, dull or sunny. Thus, if the firm decides to produce sunshades and the weather is sunny, a profit of £6,000 will be made in year 1. Alternatively, if umbrellas are manufactured and the weather is rainy, a profit of £8,000 will be made.

In year 1 there is a 30 per cent chance that it will be rainy, a 40 per cent chance that it will be dull, and a 30 per cent chance that it will be sunny. Similarly, in year 2 the corresponding chances are: rainy, 20 per cent; dull, 40 per cent; and sunny, 40 per cent. These indicate the probabilities of the occurrence of any one type of weather and hence of the achievement of the various profit levels shown.

Several routes can now be traced out: for example, the firm may choose to manufacture sunshades and the weather may be dry in year 1 (£6,000 profits), but rainy in year 2 (£1,000 profits). Each of the possible routes for the two products are identified in Table 9.4 and the corresponding profits for the two years are expressed in terms of their present values, assuming a discount (or interest) rate of 10 per cent. The occurrence weighting is the *conditional probability*, or the product of the probabilities in each of the two years. Thus, the probability of dull weather in year 1 is 0.4 and the probability of rainy weather in year 2 is 0.2, so the conditional probability of the profits associated with a dully/rainy sequence of weather over the two years is $0.4 \times 0.2 = 0.08$. The table shows that the probability-weighted present value of profits is highest for the production of sunshades with a sunny/sunny sequence of weather (£1,447.9). Had the unweighted present values been used, the decision would have been to produce umbrellas, since the rainy/rainy sequence yields the highest profits (£15,537.2).

As with all decision techniques, the usefulness of decision trees depends upon the accuracy of profit forecasts and the probabilities assigned to each

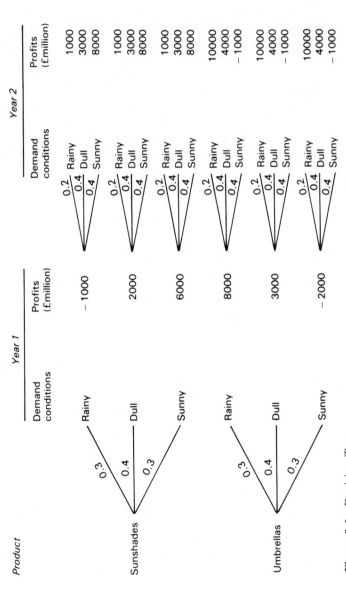

Figure 9.1 Decision Tree

Table 9.4 Decision Tree Analysis

Demand conditions	Year 1		Year 2		Profits (£) aggregate PV	Conditional probability	Probability-weighted PV
	Actual	PV	Actual	PV			
Sunshades							
Rainy/rainy	−1,000	−909.1	1,000	826.4	−82.6	0.06	5.0
Rainy/dull	−1,000	−909.1	3,000	2,479.3	1,570.2	0.12	188.4
Rainy/sunny	−1,000	−909.1	8,000	6,611.5	5,702.4	0.12	684.3
Dull/rainy	2,000	1,818.2	1,000	826.4	2,644.6	0.08	211.6
Dull/dull	2,000	1,818.2	3,000	2,479.3	4,297.2	0.16	687.6
Dull/sunny	2,000	1,818.2	8,000	6,611.5	8,429.7	0.16	1,348.8
Sunny/rainy	6,000	5,454.5	1,000	826.4	6,280.9	0.06	376.9
Sunny/dull	6,000	5,454.5	3,000	2,479.3	7,933.8	0.12	952.1
Sunny/sunny	6,000	5,454.5	8,000	6,611.5	12,066.0	0.12	1,447.9
Umbrellas							
Rainy/rainy	8,000	7,272.7	10,000	8,264.5	15,537.2	0.06	932.2
Rainy/dull	8,000	7,272.7	4,000	3,305.8	10,578.5	0.12	1,269.4
Rainy/sunny	8,000	7,272.7	−1,000	−826.4	6,446.3	0.12	773.6
Dull/rainy	3,000	2,727.3	10,000	8,264.5	10,991.8	0.08	879.3
Dull/dull	3,000	2,727.3	4,000	3,305.8	6,033.1	0.16	965.3
Dull/sunny	3,000	2,727.3	−1,000	−826.4	1,900.9	0.16	304.1
Sunny/rainy	−2,000	−1,818.2	10,000	8,264.5	6,446.3	0.06	386.8
Sunny/dull	−2,000	−1,818.2	4,000	3,305.8	1,487.6	0.12	178.5
Sunny/sunny	−2,000	−1,818.2	−1,000	−826.4	2,644.6	0.12	317.4

route. Despite the numerical results of the above example, a management team in Manchester would undoubtedly choose to manufacture umbrellas!

9.4 Managing Risk

It is clearly in the interests of management teams to reduce the degree of risk and uncertainty that confronts them. This can be done through the planning and implementation of corporate strategy. The importance of effective planning cannot be over-emphasised. Drucker (1974) defines strategic planning as 'a continuous process of making present entre-preneurial (risk-taking) decisions systematically and with the greatest knowledge of their futurity, organising systematically the efforts needed to carry out these decisions and measuring the results of these decisions against the expectations through organised systematic feedback'. Ex-pressed in these terms, planning is one of the most important business functions, and one which can only be carried out effectively by the top echelon of management. It is costly and time-consuming, but vital, and must embrace contingency alternatives to allow for environmental shifts. None of this can be delegated. It is and must remain a general management function. Once the policy has been established it is up to the managers to make it work.

Gaining knowledge of 'futurity' requires an intelligence network to collect and analyse information. On this basis the organisation can decide its strategic responses.

Information

Information, provided it is reliable and appropriately analysed, gives managers a more detailed picture of the market, technological and broader economic, social and political environments in which decisions have to be taken. Much relevant material is nowadays easily accessible from news-papers and broadcasts, official government publications, specialist jour-nals, academic studies and trade associations. More specific and detailed information can be obtained by in-house technical and market research, or by commissioning studies by consultants. It should be noted, however, that collecting and analysing technical and market intelligence is costly in terms of both direct expenditures and the time of those involved. As a con-sequence, it is important to ensure that the additional benefits obtained from intelligence activity (gauged in terms of direct profits, corporate growth or security) exceed the avoidable costs of information gathering. Otherwise, the exercise is not worthwhile. Four main aspects of informa-tion collection and analysis can be briefly described.

(a) *Demand Forecasting* The level of product demand in any period is the result of many interacting variables, the most important of which are typically: price, the price of competing products, consumers' real incomes, non-price characteristics of the product, and sales promotion policies. Information on the likely relationships between all or some of these variables and the likely level of demand can be obtained from interview and/or questionnaire data from a statistically representative cross-section of actual or potential purchasers; alternatively, it can be obtained by test marketing the product.

Past data on the level of sales and the variables that influence it can be analysed statistically to produce a forecast of future demand. The main method used for this is *regression analysis*, by means of which a line or multi-dimensional surface is obtained which best fits the array of data collected. The analysis can be done in respect of *time-series* data, in which observations recorded over time in a particular situation are used, and of *cross-section* data, in which the observations are for different firms or markets at the same point in time. The main problem with time-series analysis is that consumers' tastes and preferences may change, while the results of cross-section analyses may be affected by differences in the underlying characteristics of firms or markets. In both cases forecasts will be inaccurate if the main variables influencing demand are inadequately specified and if unexpected shocks occur to demand or supply.

(b) *Technological Forecasting* Unforeseen technological change can have a great impact on a firm through the effect on its relative competitive position. Both the range and characteristics of products and the appropriate process technologies can be affected.

Technological change can be either continuous or discontinuous. The level of risk associated with the first type is usually low, since new process developments or product characteristics can be incorporated incrementally as they occur. Discontinuous change is riskier because entire product ranges or process systems can be made obsolete. Examples of high impact, discontinuous technological change include the following: the replacement of sailing ships by steam ships; the development of steam railway traction soon after the completion of the inland waterways network; and the invention of the basic oxygen steelmaking system that replaced the lengthy, high-cost open hearth method.

Forecasting technological change is generally difficult. The Delphi technique involves the preparation of alternative scenarios prepared on the basis of projected changes in scientific and technological knowledge, market requirements and relative input costs. Trends in other advanced nations, particularly the USA, can be monitored carefully, including an analysis of patent applications and the rate at which new techniques and products are diffused through an industry.

(c) *Competitor Analysis* Many markets for manufactured products in advanced market economies are characterised by the presence of a small number of suppliers that are large relative to the size of the market—a structural pattern known as *oligopoly*. Oligopolistic competition is typified by emphasis on non-price features of products and on patterns of behaviour that reflect close interdependence of actions between suppliers. Risk can be reduced if the reactions of competitors to any initiative action on the part of one supplier can be correctly anticipated, and if likely moves on the part of competitors can be predicted.

Market actions in these circumstances depend chiefly upon the relative sizes of the competitors, their relative cost structure and their objectives. Financial analysis provides information on profit margins, return on assets, the sources and applications of funds, the financing structure and growth of assets, sources of revenue and the structure of costs. This information can help to indicate whether competitors could reduce prices to boost sales volume without damaging profitability unduly, their ability to raise additional funds for stock-building or capacity expansion, and the importance of fixed costs (including interest charges) in total costs, with implications for pricing policy in times of weak demand. The marketing strength of competitors can be gauged by assembling and analysing data on product specifications and ranges, prices and pricing policies in separate markets, and policies towards distribution channels and relations with customers, suppliers and other competitors.

(d) *Environmental Monitoring* The quality of decision making can be improved by maintaining a continuing intelligence and review system of the overall environment in which a business operates. There are four main aspects to be analysed. Information on the *economic* environment should include: the composition and growth of gross national product (GNP); inflation; employment levels and trends; earnings; productivity; fixed asset formation; stocks; the balance of payments; interest and exchange rates; and monetary and fiscal policies. For the monitoring of the *social* environment, data should be collected on: population size, composition and growth; expenditure patterns; leisure trends; family size, structure and stability; and housing patterns. Indicators of the *technological* environment include: developments in energy transformation and distribution; telecommunications technology; manufacturing systems; agricultural and mining technology; data processing; and transportation. The *political* and *legislative* environment monitoring will yield indicators of trends in popular representation, special interest and pressure groups, trends in economic, social and environmental policies and prospective legislation. An important contribution from this type of analysis is guidance on effective corporate lobbying of government.

Most major enterprises undertake environmental monitoring as part of the corporate planning process and in some the functions are grouped together in a specialised business environmental monitoring department. On the basis of the analyses of such activities, scenarios can be built up that indicate possible patterns of market, national and international development. Alternatives can be compared and evaluated by weighting them with *a priori* probabilities, and 'optimistic', 'pessimistic' and 'neutral' scenarios developed, but care must be taken to guard against undue optimism or pessimism by including together in a single scenario all the best or worst outcomes.

The writing of scenarios has increased in importance as part of the corporate planning process since the 1960s. The key elements for its successful use seem to be that only a limited number of simple scenarios should be prepared, and they should be communicated effectively to all involved decision makers throughout the organisation.[4]

Strategic Responses

The risk and uncertainty confronting firms may also be reduced by policies designed to anticipate and react to changed circumstances and to achieve more secure control of markets. This can be done by means of growth, marketing policies and relationships with competitors.

(*a*) *Growth*   Firms grow by horizontal or vertical expansion, or by diversification. Horizontal growth involves expanding a particular activity or group of activities—increasing the volume of output of motor vehicles, for example. In many cases this will result in the supplier's market share increasing, reducing the price elasticity of the individual demand curve and bringing it closer to that for the industry's demand as a whole. The scale of the producer's output, together with the share of the market, may discourage competition from potential entrants and increase the degree of interdependence with other competitors, thereby reducing the level of risk in the market.

Vertical growth is achieved through linkages with suppliers or customers. Risk can be reduced through secure access to markets; swift acquisition of information that can improve stock level management and production scheduling; the ability to maintain sales through captive outlets at times of weak demand; and access to vital raw materials and supplies at times of high demand.

Diversification into a wider field of activities offers the opportunity to spread risk. Activities that show marked cyclical fluctuations (construction, steel, shipping services) can be matched with other activities that have

---

4. See *Financial Times* (1980).

counter-cyclical patterns (e.g. some financial services) or which generate fairly steady cash flows and profits (e.g. food and drink manufacture). A portfolio of products can be developed in which the several products are at different stages of their life cycles, thus both generating cash and absorbing it for future development. Firms may also endeavour to become involved in markets with differing structural characteristics so that, for example, dominance in one highly concentrated but slowly growing sector can be set against a presence in a small, rapidly growing but highly fragmented market.

Whichever growth route is selected, expansion can be by means of either internal growth or acquisition. Internal expansion involves the building of new manufacturing capacity, the development of new products and securing access to distribution channels. This is often more costly, time-consuming and risky than a policy of growth by acquisition, in which existing manufacturing capacity, products and distribution systems can be taken over as going concerns and integrated into the operations of the acquiring firm without the risks attached to the addition of new capacity to an industry and the need to launch new products in competing with existing and well-established lines.

(*b*) *Marketing Policies* Distinguishing a product from its close competitors by its design, brand image, after-sales service, distribution channel or price can, if done successfully, attract consumer loyalty and insulate the supplier to some extent from sudden and unexpected changes in market demand. A gap in the market can sometimes be identified into which a new product can be placed on the basis of its unique combination of non-price characteristics.

Where buyer loyalty is generally low (as in some consumer markets such as soaps and detergents), overall demand stability can be achieved and potential entrants discouraged by offering and promoting a wide range of similar branded products. High advertising costs restrict the number of suppliers, and the net effect of buyers switching at each repurchase occasion is small as they are likely to purchase another brand from the same suppliers.

A firm that has developed a new product or process can protect its innovation and its control of the market by patenting the invention. Additional income from a wider market than the firm is able to supply can be obtained by licensing the invention to selected producers. When patenting is not possible, or the firm prefers to try and keep its discovery secret, the need in many cases for detailed operating knowledge will deter potential competitors.

(*c*) *Agreements with Competitors* These are designed to reduce risk and protect the market shares of existing suppliers by laying down rules on price, output and other conditions of supply. Such agreements are generally seen as being in restraint of trade and are illegal in most countries, but may in certain circumstances be condoned if it can be shown to the satisfaction of the regulatory authorities that they confer net benefits on consumers or promote the national interest. Agreements can reduce the costs of the participating suppliers by enabling them to plan production more accurately and to avoid fluctuations in demand and in inventories. At the same time, however, the intention is usually also to regulate total supply in relation to market demand in order to raise prices and profits. Markets, such as construction and heavy engineering, in which price is determined by a system of competitive bidding may be particularly susceptible to tendering agreements between contractors in order to reduce the costs of unsuccessful bidding. In the absence of formal market-sharing agreements between suppliers, the presence of a few firms in the market is likely to result in a high degree of mutual awareness and recognition which can lead to competitive behaviour that is very similar to that under a formal agreement. Particular firms may take the initiative in raising prices in the expectation that others will follow. Public discussion of the problems of an industry can also lead to concerted behaviour.

It will be apparent that some of the strategies and practices discussed above may be considered, in certain circumstances, to be in restraint of trade and to increase unduly the power of the supplier in relation to the buyer. Governments generally have introduced legislation to check such abuses (see Chapter 11). There is thus a direct association between the degree of risk and uncertainty and the level of competition in a market.

9.5 The Impact of Risk and Uncertainty

However diligently analysis, forecasting and planning are carried out, enterprises still encounter the unexpected. The business environment is complex and inter-related and more than one set of conditions may change during a particular period. Lack of preparation and failure to respond on the part of management can make the impact of such changes much worse. The impact on two enterprises of unexpected changes in their environments is examined in this section.

British Shipbuilders

The shipbuilding industry in Great Britain was nationalised in 1977 by the Aircraft and Shipbuilding Industries Act which established British Shipbuilders as a public corporation, comprising the assets of 27 shipbuilding and allied engineering companies. The eventual passage of the Act ended a long period of uncertainty that had been very damaging for the commercial prospects of the industry. Shipbuilding is one of the oldest of British industries. The modern industry stems from the effects of the industrial revolution which boosted world trade and increased the importance of the merchant marine. Imperialist expansion and the need for defensive security gave a concomitant stimulus to naval shipbuilding.

In the postwar period, the UK's share of world trade has fallen and other countries in the industrial, centrally-planned and developing economies have taken an increasing share of merchant traffic. In addition, the annual level of world trade has shown marked cyclical fluctuations. Total UK merchant shipbuilding output in 1954 was 1.5 million gross registered tons, 0.8 million tons in 1964 and 1.5 million tons in 1976, the year before nationalisation.

Successive official reports from 1950 onwards had recognised the need for a reduction in total British shipbuilding capacity, modernisation of design and construction methods and reorganisation and rationalisation of operations. With the election of a Labour government pledged to the extension of nationalisation, it was clear in 1974 that transfer of the whole or a major part of the industry's assets to public ownership would eventually be accomplished. But the Government lacked an overall majority and was able to only strengthen slightly its command over the House of Commons in the subsequent General Election later in the year. Because of the pressure of legislation and the time required to obtain the approval of Parliament, the Aircraft and Shipbuilding Nationalisation Bill was not introduced until 1976. During this time very few initiatives had been introduced in the industry and the private sector owners were naturally unwilling to embark on investment in new assets that seemed likely to be compulsorily acquired by the State in return for an uncertain amount of financial compensation. In addition, there was no guidance on the likely organisation of the industry or of the Government's strategic policy towards it. There was an immense amount of uncertainty in the industry which stultified decision making. Its effects were made worse by the impact of the world recession following the first oil crisis of 1973 which led to a sharp drop in the volume of world trade, causing the losses of the industry to increase still more.

Although the fact of nationalisation removed most of the uncertainty about the industry's future ownership, it did little to clarify the Government's attitude or the amount of financial support that could be expected. In preparing strategic plans for the whole industry, the Corporation's management faced the risks that their proposals would be rejected by government or not given the necessary political and financial support. The Corporation was set several objectives by the Act including the achievement of an efficient and competitive industry; co-operation with the merchant marine and equipment suppliers; operation within the limits of government financing; meeting the requirements of national defence; and promotion of industrial democracy.

These gave very little guidance as to the strategic policies that British Shipbuilders should follow and after preparing a detailed forecast of the world demand for shipbuilding, the Corporation put to government plans to reduce capacity and employment, whilst raising productivity and investment, and plans to increase the proportion of shipbuilding carried out in mixed yards capable of constructing a wide range of merchant and naval vessels. The scheme was drawn up on the following assumptions:

(a) that the government subsidy required would be spent as desired by the Corporation on those resources of men and material which the Corporation thought appropriate to its future;
(b) that government would support the Corporation in its efforts to use finance in a way similar to that of its overseas competitors;
(c) that government would take a strategic view of the nation's need to protect its merchant fleet and support an effective scrapping and rebuilding policy; and
(d) that the naval building programme drawn up in the light of the commitment to NATO would be followed.

In the event all of these assumptions proved to be unfounded. The Government did not give management discretion to use the agreed level of subsidy as it saw fit in order to achieve the aims of the business. Neither was it willing, because of limitations of public expenditure, to provide equity finance and credit facilities that would allow the enterprise to compete on an equal footing with foreign yards. There was also no acknowledgement of the importance of the merchant marine and a failure to support UK shipyards by encouraging British shipowners to place orders with them for new and replacement capacity and repair work. Finally, the naval building programme was not increased in line with policy statements. As a consequence, strategic policies were frustrated and had to be reformulated, investment was curtailed and there were continuing and unpredictable calls on public expenditure to fund operating losses. The Corporation's financial performance and employment levels between 1977/78 and 1982/83 are shown in Table 9.5.

There were two main failures in coming to terms with the risks in the post-nationalisation environment. The first was the insufficient time devoted by management to learning the aims, attitudes and objectives of those who would be involved in assessing the performance and activities of the enterprise—government, Parliament, the trade unions, shipowners and the general public. The second was not to define performance objectives appropriately and to persuade important interest groups to accept them. Success for the industry in the second half of the 1970s referred to its survival in the medium term, while plans were put in place for longer-term

Table 9.5   British   Shipbuilders: Financial   Performance   and   Employment,
               1977/78–1982/83

Year ended March	Turnover (£million)	Trading loss[a] (£million)	Employment (000)
1978[b]	497.0	104.5	86.7
1979	842.0	49.4	85.7
1980	813.0	109.9	78.3
1981	899.3	41.4	70.0
1982	1,025.6	19.8	66.6
1983	—	117.5	—

Source: Annual Reports and Accounts.
Notes: (a) After crediting Intervention Fund subsidy, but before interest and
          extraordinary items.
        (b) Nine months.

adjustments to market conditions and government policy. Management
generally defines success in terms of positive achievements—usually profitability and growth. The relevant indicators in the case of British
Shipbuilders were reductions in capacity and employment, containment of
losses and operation within the limits of government financing.

Antony Gibbs (PFP) Limited

The Conservative Government of Edward Heath came to power in June
1970. It took up the reins of office with the objective of setting the UK
economy to rights by removing as many as possible of the financial curbs
and controls, thus allowing greater competition amongst the financial
institutions. This was seen as the culmination of two decades of discussion
between the Treasury, the Bank of England, and the Department of Trade
on the way in which the financial sector should work. In a matter of weeks
after the Government had been in office, the Chancellor of the Exchequer,
Iain MacLeod, died. Policy is one thing, operation is another. An
argument can be made suggesting that with the death of MacLeod (the
experienced practitioner within the Conservative hierarchy), any innovative ideas were doomed to some kind of failure.

   In 1971 the Government published a White Paper on Competition and
Credit Control which, amongst other things, scrapped the ceilings on bank
lending and aimed at new techniques in monetary policy, including the use
of interest rate manipulation as a prime weapon in the control of inflation,
credit and hence the economy. The scheme was supported by the Bank of
England, but there was some passive opposition from Treasury officials
(though not Ministers). The objectives generally were laudable, but they
had unforeseen consequences. The atmosphere into which they were
introduced was one of *laissez-faire* trading and supervision. Supervision of

Table 9.6   Antony Gibbs (PFP) Ltd: Income, Profit and Employment, 1971–74

Year ending 30th June	Income (£000)	Profit before tax (£000)	Staff no.
1971	223	85	31
1972	635	73	150
1973	1,600	—	350
1974 (budget)	3,024	288	550

the financial sector, undertaken jointly and severally by the Bank of England, the Treasury and the Department of Trade, was at best confused.

Following the publication and implementation of the new competition and credit control policy, the monetary boom of 1971 to 1973 took off. There was enormous expansion in financial services generally and in the property sector in particular. Massive lending by secondary banking institutions was undertaken in an atmosphere where term of lending and interest rates were critical, but risk assessment had gone by default.

Much has been written about this period by journalists and also by judges who have had to unravel a great many of the legal consequences of the pell-mell rush for financial growth. The consequences of this growth and its impact are starkly illustrated by the experience of Antony Gibbs (PFP) Ltd, a subsidiary of a merchant bank (Antony Gibbs & Sons Ltd). Table 9.6 shows the growth of the Company from its start in July 1970 to June 1973.

The table shows a history of rapid, indeed violent, growth. Almost all (98.5 per cent) of the Company's income was derived from the sale of one particular product type sold through one distribution channel—life assurance linked income bonds sold through newspaper advertising. During the latter half of 1973 management reviewed the operating position of the Company and determined the following objectives:

(a) to generate revenue and control costs to achieve a ten per cent profit on sales;
(b) to re-organise the sales and marketing structure to achieve the targeted sales volume without increasing the numbers in the sales force;
(c) to change the emphasis of selling so that the dependency on immediate sales of bonds would be reduced and a profile of tax planning and investment advice established; and
(d) to widen the range of products and services and develop a new market for financial services.

It was recognised that this would take some time to achieve and a three- to five-year period of transition was discussed.

While this process of redefinition was taking place, a fullblown financial crisis was developing (Reid 1982). Throughout 1973 there were many signs of the turmoil to come, but so far as public awareness was concerned the first real outward sign of financial crisis occurred in December 1973 with the collapse of Cedar Holdings.

Cedar was a classic company to run into trouble. It specialised in second mortgage lending to individuals, and also in commercial property. It had expanded very rapidly and was seen from the outside to be an aggressively competitive organisation. Cedar had relied heavily on funds borrowed short term, and was now experiencing a run on those funds. The problem for the supervisors of the financial markets was that the troubles that had beset Cedar were troubles which would affect many other organisations. Thus, when officials of the Bank of England, City Institutions and the Treasury met, they knew that they were discussing not just Cedar, but a potential calamity which would affect the reputation of the City itself.

The period was also one of political change. In February 1974 a general election was called by the Conservative Prime Minister, and was fought mainly on the issue of the miners' strike. The Conservatives failed to obtain an overall majority and the minority Labour Government of Harold Wilson came to power. One of the new government's intentions was to sort out a great deal of what it saw as being wrong in the financial sector. It was also determined to increase the burden of direct taxation and reduce tax benefits. The March 1974 Budget put up marginal rates of income tax, altered the taxation laws and (much more important from the point of view of Antony Gibbs) changed fundamentally the basis of tax provisions for life assurance and estate duty.

The damage for the Company lay not in the change of policy, but in the fact that new legislation was outlined but no real guidance given. In March 1974 the Government announced the intended abolition of Estate Duty and the creation of a new tax, Capital Transfer Tax. Detailed proposals were not given until the 1975 Finance Act, with many actual elements not being clarified until much later. The Insurance Companies Act of July 1974 simply stated that 'regulations may be made' in respect of linked long-term policies. These regulations, which had significant retrospective elements covering critical issues, such as early surrender, did not appear until the Finance Act of the following year.

The consequences for the industry were serious. For Antony Gibbs (PFP) Ltd and for many other organisations, they were severe. Virtually the entire business income disappeared overnight. In a period of two days the sales force were rendered inactive, they had no real basis on which to approach new clients and nothing to sell. There was no market at all at which to aim. Some of them had some skills; the company measured its sales resource by examinations and training. But the conventional industry was also badly affected. For a period of nearly eighteen months to the end of 1975, during a period of political instability (there was another election in November 1974), the whole life assurance industry struggled and tried to cope with the consequences of the turmoil.

The firm decided, in an attempt to survive, to:

(a) lay off 75 per cent of the sales force;
(b) restructure the head office function to reduce overhead costs to a level which could be supported;
(c) shift the emphasis from selling life assurance products to selling investment and tax expertise as quickly as possible;
(d) create and design products; and
(e) consider what size of the market, if any, there was to be.

This was a situation where (unlike shipbuilding) the legislative process had not just changed the nature of the market, it had by and large removed it.

Because the company was owned by a bank and through that by a much larger financial institution, a large part of the strategy was to run inwards towards clients and contacts of the parent. This provided a stop-gap, and with the help of this, the survival strategy enabled the Company to break even in 1975 on a much reduced turnover of £1 million.

In 1974, when faced with the cliff face of government interference in the financial services sector, the management of Antony Gibbs (PFP) Ltd had to decide where to go. There were many tempting avenues. They could have decided that it was all too difficult and gone out of business; they could have taken the conclusion that the environment was such that they should shut up shop for eighteen months and wait until someone had got the act sorted out. What they in fact did was determined by what they had:

(1) A system for selling and a method of distribution.
(2) A bank of clients.
(3) Some knowledge of the financial market and, more importantly, some knowledge of the history of clients and their involvement in the market.
(4) A very clear view as to how it was thought the market should develop.
(5) Hence, a view of a small sector of the market that could be captured and developed.

These five points formed the cornerstone of the strategic planning. Most of it was done on the back of envelopes and in the heads of one or two people, but essentially it was decided to widen the base of operations of the Company, taking in financial services in general and concentrating on the areas initially where the legislative framework had not changed (e.g. investment) and on specific, continuing client needs, like tax planning and tax litigation. They knew that in doing this, while they were not *de facto* establishing a basis for continued and continuous operation, they were likely to provide enough income for the organisation to survive until such time as the legislative framework settled down. That was the short-term planning goal—to stay in business and to survive; the longer-term goal was inextricably bound into the fortunes of the parent company.

9.6 Summary and Conclusions

Risk and uncertainty are ever-present features of the business environment and are important elements in the competitive process. Probabilities can be assigned to the likely occurrence of risky events, but no prediction can be made about uncertainties. The significance of risk to the decision maker depends upon the probability of occurrence, the impact on the organisation and the decision maker's attitude to risk.

Four main types of risk have been identified in this chapter. Market risk arises when changes take place in the factors that influence demand or when a supplier mis-specifies the market he is serving. Continuing technological change, giving rise to new processes and new products, challenges existing suppliers to keep abreast of developments and gives opportunities to new competitors, possibly new enterprises or suppliers established in another market who are diversifying. Risks surrounding factor costs can arise from the volatility of the markets for commodities, finance and labour. Developments in legislation and changes in government policy constitute the main elements of political risk.

Choice in risky environments is influenced significantly by the decision maker's attitude to risk. There may be a preference or an aversion to risk. Methods available for decision making include comparisons of expected values (the probability-weighted mean outcomes); the coefficient of variation, giving a standardised comparison of the degree of risk; the certainty equivalent; and decision trees for the analysis of complex, sequential decision problems.

Corporate strategy must be formulated to take account of risk. There are two stages: planning and strategic response. Planning requires an effective intelligence system in which information from a wide range of sources is collected, collated, analysed and interpreted. This is a complex and costly operation for large organisations if carried out comprehensively. Environmental monitoring systems maintain surveillance of the economic, technological, social and political arenas in which firms operate. Information collected can be employed in demand and technological forecasting and the analysis of competitors' performances and strategies. The availability of information can turn uncertainty into risk and reduce the level of risk. The strategic responses that are open to firms to anticipate environmental changes and so reduce the impact of risk include horizontal, vertical and diversificatory growth, marketing policies and tacit or overt agreements with competitors. The two case studies illustrate clearly that whatever efforts are made to plan and forecast effectively, substantial changes in the business environment (in these cases as a result of legislative and policy shifts) can have an overwhelming impact, demanding immediate and far-reaching adaptation. The capability of management teams will be thoroughly tested in these circumstances.

Risk and uncertainty thus present a significant challenge to management. Awareness of the existing environment and of the possible patterns of development are essential for strategic planning, in which full provision for contingencies must be made. Businesses that carry out this function effectively will be efficient in terms of both their operations and their responses to the market. The incidence of risk forces existing management teams to adapt and provides opportunities for competitors. In this way it is a vital part of the competitive process.

References

Drucker, P. (1974) *Management: Tasks, Responsibilities, and Practices*, Heinemann.

Jewkes, J., Sawers, D. and Stillerman, R. (1969) *The Sources of Invention*, Macmillan.

Mansfield, E. (1968) *The Economics of Technical Change*, Norton.

Reid, M. (1982) *The Secondary Banking Crisis 1973–75*, Marathon Press.

Scherer, F. M. (1965) 'Firm size, market structure, opportunity and the output of patented inventions', *American Economic Review*, vol. 55, December.

Scherer, F. M. (1980) *Industrial Market Structure and Economic Performance*, Rand McNally.

Financial Times (1980) 'How Shell made its managers think the unthinkable', by Christopher Lorenz, 5th March.

10
Managing in the Macroeconomic Environment

Sir Douglas Hague

10.1 Time Horizons

The management team of any business is mainly interested in the way its economic environment will develop within a fairly short period. Decisions about production, marketing and personnel rarely need information looking more than twelve to eighteen months ahead, and often an understanding of what is likely to happen in the next three or four months is sufficient.

The main reason for making forecasts going further into the future is to assist in the firm's investment programme. Even here, many new assets (for example, new machinery) can be acquired within a fairly short period—say, not more than twelve months. When major investments are being made as, for example, in a new production plant, supermarket or administration block, the relevant time horizon can, however, be quite long. It is not only that in making this decision the firm will need to forecast the level of demand when the new facility comes into operation; it also needs to be assured that the demand will be adequate over a long enough period to make the investment profitable, that the necessary supplies of raw materials, components or labour will be available, and so on. Investment decisions therefore rarely require information for a period of less than five years ahead.

With a very large investment, like a large power station or petrochemical plant, it can be ten years before the new complex even begins to operate, so that some idea of likely demand fifteen to twenty years ahead will be needed. Beyond even this, a large, integrated international oil company has to plan for the development of new oil fields, for the abandonment of depleted ones and for substantial changes in its vast network of exploration, production, refining, transport and marketing facilities. Such a company will have a group of specialists who, as a matter of routine, are looking twenty to twenty-five years ahead. They will be making macro-economic, political, social and technical developments that will, in due course, have a major influence on the company's activities and development.

10.2 Two Basic Rules

The discussion in Section 10.1 allows us to enunciate a basic rule. For each type of decision the firm should look as far ahead, but only as far ahead, as is necessary for that particular decision. There is no point in spending large amounts of time (and therefore money) on macroeconomic projections which are over too short a period to be helpful in taking particular decisions, or over too long a period to be relevant at all. There may, of course, be a case for looking a long way ahead, in a general way, to create a climate of opinion about the future among the firm's management. This will reduce the degree of surprise contained in future events in the environment, and hence the degree of confusion in dealing with them within the company.

But the general rule is clear. One should use a time horizon which goes as far into the future as required by the decision for which the information will be used, and no farther (Rule 1).

Two additional rules can be derived from inspection of Figure 10.1. In Figure 10.1 we are concerned (from left to right) with the probability that particular events will occur, and (from top to bottom) with their impact on the company if they do. We can see at once that the most important area for forecasters is the top left-hand cell. There, events are both likely to occur and will have a big impact on the company if they do. Similarly, very little effort needs to be devoted to the bottom right-hand cell, where events

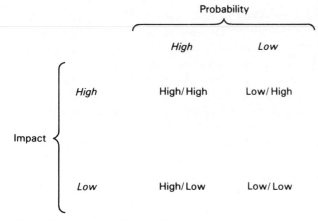

Figure 10.1 Impact–Probability Matrix

are both unlikely to occur and, even if they do, will have little impact on the business. Nor is there need to spend much effort in forecasting events which, while likely to occur, will have little impact (bottom left-hand cell). It is the top right-hand cell which is the interesting one. While the events here are unlikely to occur, they will have a serious impact on the firm if they do.

This, I suspect, is the area where many businesses slip up, both in their forecasting and in their arrangements for dealing with unlikely, but potentially serious, events. It is obviously important to devote a high proportion of one's forecasting resources to forecasting high-impact/high-probability events, but it is also important (Rule 2) to devote an *adequate* proportion of those forecasting resources to high-impact/low-probability events as well. It may, however, be impossible to predict these accurately. If so, the firm then needs (Rule 3) to devise adequate contingency plans for dealing speedily with such an event if it *does* occur. This is so even though the event appears very unlikely. A failure *either* to forecast the event *or* to make contingency plans to avert or deal with it at once if it occurs, though not forecast, will have serious consequences. The firm should lay its plans—and deploy both its forecasting and its management resources—to ensure that such serious consequences, of whatever nature, do not occur. Although I believe that firms frequently fail to do this, it is clear that the number of potential events with *really* high impact is for all companies relatively small. They can therefore be identified and prepared for at relatively low cost.

10.3   Macroeconomic Forecasting

Basic Economic Forecasts

The main concept which economists use to measure the rate of economic growth is gross domestic product. This measures total national output, including that from agriculture, industry, distribution and services, as well as the government sector, which includes the civil service, armed forces and social services (like education and health). When discussing the growth of GDP, economists usually concentrate on percentage growth in *real* terms. That is, they look at it in physical terms, adjusting money increases for inflation. Suppose, for example, that GDP in money terms has risen between two years by 15 per cent. If prices have risen by 10 per cent, then in real (physical) terms GDP is up by 5 per cent.

In discussing developed economies, economists often concentrate on the Organisation for Economic Co-operation and Development (OECD) countries, namely those in Western Europe, North America, Japan and Australasia. During the 1950s and sixties in the OECD countries economic progress was rather rapid and relatively painless. GDP rose on average by about 5 per cent (compound) per annum.

Inflation rates were low, at least before the late 1960s. Unemployment was small too. The main reasons seem to have been as follows: (a) considerable reconstruction was needed (especially in continental Western Europe) after World War Two; (b) automobile sales grew rapidly and encouraged associated developments—production of raw materials and components, of cars themselves, of roads, oil refineries, oil tankers, service stations, supermarkets, etc; (c) Keynesian demand management techniques, for most of the period, led to increased output rather than higher prices; and (d) there were moves towards freer international trade. The situation, however, was much less satisfactory in the less-developed countries (LDCs).

A golden age of economic development meant a parallel golden age for the newly-developing profession of economic forecasting. Though few of us realised the implications at the time, economic forecasting was bound to be rather simple in a situation where economic growth in most major countries was relatively steady, and where the main problem was to forecast relatively small increases and decreases in the rate of growth of GDP, as well as the turning points (upward or downward) in economic activity. We did not realise that things were going to change dramatically.

Since 1973, the situation has been very different. The increase in the price of oil in 1973–74 (and again in 1978–79) led to outright falls in the level of output in some developed countries. In the OECD countries as a whole growth rates of real GDP in 1974–79 were roughly half of those in the 'golden age'.

The oil price increases were important because they diverted income to countries (many of them in and around the Arabian Gulf) with very different spending habits from those in the OECD. It took time for money to be spent at all, though the delay was shorter after 1978–79 than after 1973–74. When the money was spent, much of it went on development projects so that construction activity was increased in the oil countries. Considerable sums were also spent on military equipment. The result was a switch in spending to goods and services that were different from those that OECD citizens had been buying in the 'golden age' or, as with construction, were in different locations, often in the Middle East. The increase in the oil price also helped to increase inflation at a time when Keynesian policies had begun to increase prices more than output.

Perhaps too much emphasis has been put on the role of the 1973–74 oil price rise. It was certainly the event which triggered world recession. Inflation was, however, already very rapid before the oil price increase, and moves to cut back inflation by reducing the rate of growth of the money supply would have been undertaken even if oil prices had never risen. The oil price increases did represent the major disruption; but they came at a time when an end to the golden age was already foreshadowed. The stimulus to economic growth from the development of automobiles was coming to an end as potential markets (especially in developed countries) were largely satiated. There was also rapid industrial develop-ment in a number of poorer countries, now termed newly-industrialising countries (NICs). These countries provide a new threat, not only to industries in developed countries which are raw material and labour intensive—like textiles, clothing, footwear and shipbuilding—but also to OECD producers of newer products, like transistor radios and simple electronics. This adds to the threat posed by Japan, which has already moved into areas like cars and electronics and is now planning to become one of the world's leading producers in information technology, bio-technology and alternative sources of energy.

Economic forecasters need to pay sufficient attention to these basic changes in the world's economic structures and to the way that they are changing opportunities and posing threats for their own business. Good economic forecasting *must* take adequate account of these important structural changes, but both economists and businessmen in developed countries seem to be giving too little attention to what is going on in the NICs. Yet that is where the most important industrial developments will take place in the next two decades.

Macroeconomic Forecasting

Within these broad trends, businesses need to forecast developments that will occur in their own economies and in those elsewhere which contain significant markets, competitors, or suppliers. Over a period, an experi-enced economic forecaster, using fairly simple techniques like studies of trends, will acquire a sense of how economic events are going to move in the relatively few sectors of the relatively few economies that are important to him.

So far as outside assistance is concerned, he can find help from two main sources. First, there is a growing number of macroeconomic forecasting models. These are now mostly computer-models with substantial data bases. Though still imperfect, they contain large amounts of statistical data on the economies of the main OECD countries in Western Europe, North America and Japan. Much information of this kind is published officially by government statistical agencies. It is relatively up to date, and appropriate selections from it are included in the data bases.

Computer-based models are constructed by fitting a number of inter-related mathematical equations to past events and using them to forecast the future. Most macroeconomic models concentrate on the next eighteen to twenty-four months, but an increasing number of forecasts are now being produced for five-year periods. While less accurate than the short-term forecasts, they are nevertheless valuable. Some models, including that of the UK Treasury, have a very large number of equations. Few have less than twenty or thirty.

As was implied above, the record of those forecasting models in the 1970s and early 1980s has not been as good as in the more settled 1960s. Nevertheless, they give managers who are interested in general economic developments in the world's major economies a good understanding of how the main elements in those economies are developing. For the less-developed countries, the forecaster is much more on his own. This is partly because the number of companies prepared to pay for forecasting in these countries is much smaller than in the major economies; partly because competent economists and statisticians are few in number; and partly because little statistical information is available about these economies.

Where they exist, economic models always provide forecasts for the main segements of economic activity: GDP, consumer expenditure, government expenditure capital investment (public and private), and exports and imports (see the following section below). There are also forecasts of general (often retail) price levels and of the important exchange rates for the country in question, almost always including the ratio between its own currency, the US dollar and the Deutschmark.

There have been two important developments with the economic models in recent years. First, it is now possible, at a fairly small cost, for subscribers to many of these models to use them for simulation purposes. That is to say, a subscribing company which wishes to test the sensitivity of a published forecast to changes in one or more of the underlying assumptions can discover the effects directly. It is possible, for example, to discover the effect of a 10 per cent higher level of private investment or of a 15 per cent lower exchange rate. At the very least, this simulation exercise shows which assumptions underlying a model appear to be the most important. The model builders, who are themselves continually trying to improve the forecasting abilities of their own models, can also carry out such exercises. Many forecasting organisations both publish periodic analyses of the accuracy of their own and other modellers' forecasts and also keep subscribers abreast of changes they are making in their own models and the reasons for them.

The second development is also to some degree associated with the advent of simulation models. This is the growth of 'clubs' formed by the users of a particular model. Clubs hold periodic meetings to discuss with those who have produced the most recent forecasts from a particular model the assumptions which underlie that forecast; to discuss with the model-builders and other club members the validity of the assumptions and forecasts; and to explore, perhaps by simulation, what effect changes in the assumptions would have. Forecasting can be a lonely activity and, not surprisingly, the popularity of such clubs for subscribers shows that they perform a useful function.

Especially in the USA and UK, an enormous amount of statistical and other information—about their own and the world's other major economies—is provided free of charge by stockbrokers and banks. Indeed, many business economists and forecasters now argue that their job requires them to do little more—when considering the national situation—than to study carefully the mass of economic information, with expert interpretation, which they can obtain cheaply in this way. It is an extremely valuable source of economic-forecasting information, for which the financial institutions concerned receive too little public thanks.

Certainly, no company can afford to ignore such a very cheap source of information; an important part of the role of the business-forecasting manager or unit must therefore be to keep abreast of what is freely available, and from whom. Similarly, business newspapers, like *The Financial Times* in the UK and Western Europe, are now the source of a great deal of economic information and comment. They not only give important clues about which financial institutions and other organisations are providing economic information services, but they can also themselves form the basis of a valuable press-cuttings service.

This section has highlighted how much economic forecasting information is now available. It has also pointed out that there are a growing number of forecasters and users of forecasts who are only too willing to discuss with others likely developments in the main OECD countries and, to a smaller extent, in the rest of the world. This means that the task of an economic forecaster is much easier than it was a decade ago. Business is much clearer about *what* is happening in the world's economies than it was, though economists seem less certain than they did in the 1960s about *why* it is happening.

An early task for anyone establishing an economic-forecasting department in a business must therefore be to become an active member of at least one of the 'clubs' or networks of forecasters that the developments outlined in this section have brought into being.

Sectoral Analysis

Because most outside economic forecasters concentrate on forecasting GDP and its main components, it is tempting to derive forecasts of the demand for an individual company's products and services from such forecasts. If this procedure appears valid and works well, it is entirely reasonable to use it. But the company should not base its more detailed forecasting projections on a broader aggregate than is actually necessary merely because that forecast happens to be available. Even though it may be more difficult, it is usually preferable to make a direct forecast based on data for the specific sectors or geographical areas for which the business needs to make projections.

Nevertheless, forecasters do not necessarily have to operate as much on their own as this implies. Many large macroeconomic models are now being used to produce forecasts for individual sectors, as well as for GDP etc. They have begun by issuing forecasts for the sales of a few industries, often including energy, automobiles, chemicals and construction, and are likely to extend the coverage steadily as time goes on. The increasing complexity of models has been achieved by the introduction of separate equations for individual sectors linked into the whole model.

Since macroeconomic forecasting models are mainly concerned with forecasting demand and prices, these are what sectoral models mainly forecast too. These variables are also, of course, usually the most important ones for the firm. But it does not necessarily follow that because sectoral equations are built into large national forecasting models, forecasting for individual sectors need be very difficult. During the early 1970s one of the most successful models in the UK forecasting registrations of motor vehicles was based on very few variables. Moreover, these did not include some of those that economic theory would have suggested as likely to be the most important. A little imagination and experimentation can often produce very good sectoral forecasts.

Given this, there is a case for the business (especially if reasonably large) to devise simple sectoral forecasting models of its own. When it does this, the company will certainly want to forecast factors other than future sales and price levels. For example, it will wish to forecast the prices and availability of raw materials and components, supplies and wages of labour, or changes in government policy. Something can be done in this direction by intelligent analysis of data and by consultation with experts— in the case of factors like government policy, with appropriate political scientists or commentators.

In constructing one's own projections for a particular sector, a good deal can be deduced from the imaginative study of past data, perhaps to the extent of using it to construct one's own simple mathematical model. My own personal heresy is that an adequate forecasting model, certainly for a single sector, will often contain fewer variables than economists or statisticians would have us suppose.

There are three main sources for the kind of information on which such analysis could be based. First, there are the firm's own records. I have been surprised in research work to discover firms which complain that they lack particular information, for example about customers and markets, when that information could have been obtained from appropriate analysis of their own records. If companies wish to go beyond that, especially in identifying new opportunities in a sector where the business has not previously operated, there is usually a good deal of published information. In countries with very detailed national income accounting systems, trends in expenditure in a particular sector, as well as in the prices of products and raw materials, will be published. More detailed information on these and other factors will often be available in published government statistics. There will also often be a trade journal for a particular sector, which will give a great deal of information about it, as will articles in more general financial and business newspapers and journals. Similarly, financial institutions frequently go beyond general analysis for the whole economy to produce periodic surveys of particular industries or sectors.

It must also be remembered that government departments and agencies, and indeed journalists, can often be persuaded to provide more information for an individual company than appears in published form. Nor should one overlook what universities and business schools can offer. A feasibility study of the possibility of moving into a new sector can often be made in a student project, while members of the business school faculty will either have, or be prepared to find out in consultancy assignments, valuable economic, commercial or technical facts.

Finally, there are the trade associations. The association for a particular trade will, again, provide basic information about the sector, though some or all of this may be made available only to members of the association. It will, however, often be prepared to go beyond this for individual members or even for non-members if they have a good reason for their enquiry. This source can be especially useful when a company is seeking information about an overseas country where the information provided by that country's government departments is limited.

In analysing information about individual sectors one will, of course, be looking for trends. But even for a whole sector, trends are unlikely to be stable for very long. An individual sector will usually experience a rapid and continuing rise in demand only when GDP per head reaches a particular level and when more urgent demands have been accommodated; for a time, demand for the new industry's products can expand rapidly. Alternatively, new technical developments may absorb a good deal of consumer spending for a period, as well as diverting demand from other industries, as happened with automobiles in the 1950s and 1960s in developed countries. These took a high percentage of the extra income which became available, as well as diverting expenditure from bicycles, motor cycles and public transport.

Even where there is a steady advance in the demand for the products of a whole sector, it does not at all follow that the demand for each individual product will behave in the same way. One of the most useful concepts for analysing the performance of the product range of a company is that of the product life cycle, shown in Figure 10.2. Here, time is shown along the

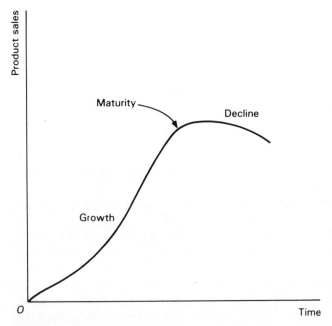

Figure 10.2   Product Life Cycle

horizontal axis, and sales up the vertical. Many individual products experience the rapid growth in sales shown in Figure 10.2 in the introduction phase for the product. This rapid growth then slows, to be replaced by a period of maturity when demand reaches a steady level. Finally, there is a phase of decline when, if the firm is well organised, it will at some stage decide to stop supplying the product (or service) altogether.

As this implies, a portfolio approach to its product range is the *sine qua non* for the profitable survival of a business which is selling a range of products or services. Each product, in its declining phase, has to be carefully monitored and the correct moment chosen to abandon its sale. Of course, not all individual products—or even product portfolios—will follow the life-cycle pattern. In such cases, it is the responsibility of the company to discover, if possible, other demand patterns (which apply to enough of its products over a sufficient period of time) on whose characteristics it can base a good overall product strategy.

Having a successful range of products or services to sell is an important factor, perhaps the most important factor, in the success of a business. So, indeed, are the firm's prices: the lower they can be relative to those of competitors without making the firm unprofitable, the bigger its market share and sales volume. Similarly, the price of raw materials and of competitive products helps to determine profitability.

It is therefore very helpful, especially for the large company with a few

major competitors, to try to model the situation of those competitors and
to work out what is happening to them, and especially to their profitability.
One can then predict their competitive moves and be able either to
anticipate them or to respond quickly and correctly to them. Companies
often deny that it is possible to do very much in this direction. They admit
that market-size and market-share information is available, but do not see
that it can be at all easy to work out the competitor's production, market,
cost and profit structures from outside. Yet a number of companies
perform such analyses of competitors successfully. Experience shows that
if a group of production people and accountants are put together and told
that they *must* estimate the cost structures of a competitor, they can do so
surprisingly successfully.

The correct identification of opportunities in a sector clearly also
requires that the company should assure itself that labour supplies of an
adequate amount and with the required skills will continue to be available.
If not, it should make arrangements to train them. Similarly, if the firm is
considering whether to establish a new plant or a new commercial or
administrative centre, it is essential to ensure that transport, communications and other important facilities are good. All possibilities of grants,
subsidies, etc. from national and local governments must be explored, and
the cheapest source of finance, whether or not subsidised by a third party,
must also be used. The data sources identified earlier in the section will
usually prove adequate for discovering the information required for this.

10.4 Responding to Fiscal and Monetary Policy

Mention of the possibility of government assistance in financing new
investment leads us to a fuller examination of the impact of fiscal and
monetary policy on the business.

Fiscal policy will, of course, affect the business by determining the way
that governments raise money and the way that they spend it. In most
developed countries a relatively small proportion of government revenue is
raised directly from taxation on company profits, but this does not mean
that tax policy has a similarly small impact either on after-tax profit or on
the business as a whole. Governments usually require companies to collect
tax from their employees by withholding part of their income, and then to
pay this directly to the revenue authorities, with those authorities making
adjustments later in the year. Perhaps more important for the company are
taxes levied on employers and/or employees in proportion to numbers
employed.

In some countries at some time subsidies to employment have been paid
either for employees of particular types or age groups, or for those working
in particular, usually depressed, areas. Obviously the correct way of taking

account of such subsidies is to deduct them from pay rates when deciding how many people the company should employ in order to reflect the true cost to the firm.

Incentives are also frequently given to investment, either as direct money payments or in the form of relief from taxation. Allowance should be made for the appropriate amounts in making investment decisions. As should always happen with investment decisions, the timing of such payments (or tax reductions) as well as the amounts in question should be correctly allowed for in the calculations upon which the decision is based. A reduction in tax payments due is just as much income to the company as a direct subsidy. And the timing of receipts must be correctly identified so that they can be correctly discounted in the investment calculation.

Fiscal policy at the national level will, of course, also affect the company. Where one or more of the company's products is subject to a value-added, sales or excise tax, a significant change in the rate of that tax can have important consequences for the company. Severe effects of this kind are less likely where taxation is levied at the same rate over a wide range of products, as with the value-added taxes currently levied in most Western European countries. These rates are rarely changed substantially; if they are, they usually affect *all* of the products taxed equally, so that there is no change in the relative price of a particular product. For that is what has a serious impact. Such changes did occur with the system of purchase tax in the UK during the 1950s and 1960s (for products like automobiles and television sets). Indeed, this was one reason for the move in the UK to a value-added tax system. Problems do remain in the UK, and in other countries, where goods like petrol, alcoholic drink, cigarettes and tobacco are subject to excise taxes instead of, or possibly as well as, value-added taxes.

It is, of course, an increase in the rate of tax which causes difficulties rather than a reduction, but there is little that the individual company can do to alter the rate of tax, though lobbying by an industry association or a national employers' association might help. Given the rate of tax, whatever it may be, all that the individual company can do is to adjust to it as best it can. Especially with duties on alcohol in the UK, consumer pressures usually lead retailers to sell off existing stocks at the price ruling before the tax increase. A policy for inventories therefore needs to be carefully worked out to allow the company to take maximum advantage of any pre-budget boom when consumers try to buy at the old pre-budget prices, and to avoid having to sell off too much of its stocks at the pre-increase price once the tax increase has been made.

General changes in fiscal policy can also affect the company substantially, though again it is when these cause falls in sales (through increases in income or commodity taxes which cause a depression in the economy) that the resulting problems are most serious for the company.

The company's response must be to predict, as far as possible, the effects of such tax changes on GDP, consumer expenditure, or whatever is the most important variable determining the company's sales. It must then proceed to calculate the expected effect on sales and cash flow and respond to this quickly and appropriately, if necessary by reducing output and therefore costs. It may, for example, reduce numbers employed and ensure that it has to borrow no more to maintain its cash position than its bankers think appropriate or than the company itself feels it can sustain, given the increase in interest payments this will imply.

This leads us to monetary policy. Monetary policy today is being used to reduce or increase the rate of growth of money GDP, when the government and/or the central bank feels that to be appropriate. Monetary policy normally works either through quantitative controls on the amounts of money which the banking system is permitted to lend or through changes in interest rates. These make it profitable for companies to borrow more or less, according to whether interest rates have fallen or risen. As with tax changes, problems arise for the company when bank loans are more difficult, or more expensive, to obtain. When more bank money is available, or where interest rates fall, the only problem for the company is the rather pleasant one of deciding, in the light of expected sales levels, the rate and directions in which it should expand.

Again, as with tax changes, the impact of monetary restrictions shows itself through a reduction in the firm's net cash flow, and therefore through a reduction in its cash balance. A company needs funds in order to maintain its working capital (to finance any excess of the amount it pays to creditors over the amount received from debtors, and to finance stocks). These comprise raw materials, components, work in progress or stocks of finished goods, whether held in warehouses or elsewhere. One problem is likely to be that in times of tight monetary policy, creditors will, like the firm itself, be seeking to extend less credit. If they succeed in doing so, this in itself will make the firm's cash position more difficult. Instead of being able to delay payments to creditors, it will have to make them earlier. It may be able to take offsetting measures by reducing the amount owed by its debtors. The difficulty, of course, is that whether an individual firm can delay payments to creditors and speed up payments by debtors will depend on its bargaining position. It should clearly attempt to do this where possible, but it may not succeed. If it does not, this will mean that the balance between amounts owed to creditors and amounts owed by debtors will worsen and itself cause the firm's cash position to deteriorate. If this happens, the company will either have to borrow more, or to reduce either working capital or long-term investment.

The problem, of course, is that the time when bigger loans from the bank would be helpful is during a period of monetary restriction, and that is when they are more difficult and/or more expensive to obtain. There are then two ways in which cash flow can be increased. First, it may be possible to reduce inventories, whether of raw materials, components, finished goods, or all three. Indeed, during a period of monetary restriction there will often be a fall in sales which, unless the firm is remarkably quick in spotting it, will cause inventories of finished goods to increase. A reduction in output, intended to bring inventories down to a level appropriate to the new, lower rate of sales, will then ease the cash position.

It may, of course, be that the firm is reluctant to match the fall in output with a reduction in employment either for social reasons or because it anticipates that when an upturn comes, it may be difficult to rehire some of those who have been dismissed. The firm will have to make its own judgement about this. At the same time, a reduction in output will mean reduced sales for suppliers just when the firm's own customers, in their turn, are reducing their purchases of its products. Here also the firm will have to make its own judgement about the best course of action, but if the monetary squeeze is severe, a reduction in the level of inventories through a reduction in the level of output will be essential, whether or not the company has to go beyond that and reconcile itself to a temporarily, or permanently, lower level of sales.

The second way of improving cash flow substantially will be to cut back on the firm's programme for investment in new capital assets. Where these were being financed by borrowing, the company may not only be unwilling to pay the higher interest rates implied by the monetary squeeze; its difficult cash position may make it unwilling to increase these borrowings in order to finance capital investment because it is either unwilling or unable to increase borrowings to carry out capital investment at all. Even if capital investment does continue, the company will be wise, if at all possible, to borrow short-term rather than long-term money. Since the essence of a monetary squeeze is that interest rates are raised, it is virtually certain that once the squeeze is relaxed, they will fall again. If the firm has to borrow at all, it will be wiser to borrow short-term money while interest rates are high, 'funding' this if necessary by longer-term borrowings when rates fall.

This allows us to lay down another general rule. When interest rates are expected to fall, the company should borrow short and, if it is a company that lends at all, lend long. Similarly, if it expects interest rates to rise, a company should borrow long and lend short. A firm may at times feel able to take such a 'view' of interest rates, and will then operate on the basis just enunciated. It must recognise, however, that when it does this it is to some extent gambling on interest rates behaving in the way it predicts. To avoid gambling, a further general rule is that the company should match the length of its borrowings against the length of time for which the corresponding assets will be held. This is why, in general, companies borrow short-term money to finance net debtors and inventories, and why they borrow long-term money to finance long-term capital investment.

These general principles are, however, simply refinements of the basic position which we have been outlining. A monetary squeeze can be met by reducing output and/or employment and/or net debtors and/or inventories and/or capital investment. As experience in Western Europe and North America in the early 1980s has shown, companies can often release a great deal of cash in this way. The difficulty, of course, is that the process of doing so causes difficulties for other companies, just as similar action by these other companies will be causing difficulties for the company itself. A further difficulty is that if the company's capital investment is reduced, it may be less able than it otherwise would have been to take advantage of an upturn in the economy when the squeeze ends.

10.5   Developments in International Trade

As a background to Section 10.6 we now consider developments in international trade since World War Two, and especially during the 1970s. Despite the effect that the increase in oil prices had on the level of activity, especially in developed countries, world trade in the 1970s was fairly buoyant. The total volume of world trade increased by about 70 per cent between 1970 and 1980, while the volume of trade in manufactured goods increased by 90 per cent. Because inflation in the 1970s was rapid, the increase in the *value* of world trade was much more rapid. The value of world trade increased by about five times; so did the trade of the centrally-planned countries (i.e. the USSR, China, the Eastern European countries, etc.). The trade of the OECD countries rose slightly less rapidly. Largely because of the increase in oil prices, the value of both the exports and the imports of the oil-exporting countries increased by some fifteen times while, with the developments outlined earlier, the trade of non-oil developing countries increased by about six times. In other words, their trade increased significantly more rapidly than the OECD countries, and a little more rapidly than world trade as a whole, and it did so mainly because of the success in exporting of the NICs.

If we look at the whole period since 1945, there have been substantial changes in the pattern of world trade. Some of these have been changes that one would expect in a world where several major colonial powers were giving their former dependencies independence and therefore the ability to choose to reduce imports from their former masters. These reductions did occur, especially in the case of British dependent territories. Similarly, there have been changes which reflect the creation of regional common markets—not least the European Economic Community (EEC)—which have led to increased trade between their member countries. Finally, the emergence of the NICs has meant an increase in the flow of trade between them and the developed countries.

There are, however, two changes in trading pattern which may seem more surprising. First, since about the middle 1960s there has been a substantial increase in the percentage of output which the OECD countries have exported and imported. For example, in the mid-1960s the UK was importing and exporting a good deal less than 20 per cent of its GDP. Today, that figure is rather above 30 per cent. Nor is the UK alone in this. The developed countries as a group have similarly increased the share of trade in GDP.

The second development has been that much of this increase in trade over the last twenty years has taken place *between* developed countries. Not only have developed countries traded more, they have above all traded more with each other. The slogan of 'trade not aid' which was supposed to signal the readiness of the developed countries to provide help to the less-developed countries during the 1950s by trading more extensively with them, remained more of a slogan than a reality.

There seem to have been three reasons for this increase in trade between developed countries. The first was the moves made towards freer trade in manufactures throughout the world, especially during the 1960s. The second was the development of the EEC, which is a free trade area and contains many of the developed, industrial countries. Increased trade between these countries was therefore increased trade between developed countries. Finally, multinational companies (MNCs) have been specialising in producing parts of products in different countries and then bringing them together in one of those countries for assembly. Thus a 'British' motor car may be assembled in the UK from components that have been made in several, mainly European, countries. The spread of this practice is the third reason for the increase in trade between developed countries which has typified the last ten to fifteen years.

10.6 Exchange Risk

The earlier sections of this chapter were concerned with an economic environment where, whatever the source of its impact on the company, by implication the transactions being considered were made in the currency of the company's own country. We must now consider what happens where other currencies are involved. The company then has to take account of yet another price—the exchange rate between its own and other currencies. This introduces a further complication.

As with so many other factors, the situation was easier in the 1950s and 1960s. Under what was known as the Bretton Woods Agreement, the value of each currency was held at or very close to a 'parity' set in terms of the United States dollar. As economic conditions in different countries moved out of line it was, of course, impossible to keep all currencies at their parity rates. Nevertheless, changes in those rates were made infrequently and then by substantial amounts. Thus the pound sterling was worth \$2.80 from 1949 until 1967, when the rate was reduced to \$2.40. Since the early 1970s 'fixed' exchange rates have been abandoned in favour of 'floating' rates which can move by small or large amounts from moment to moment. In practice central banks usually operate in a way that smooths fluctuations. Even so, changes of ten or twenty per cent between the value of one currency and another can take place within weeks. Moreover, even where the trend is upwards or downwards, there will be day-to-day fluctuations around that trend. It is much more difficult than it was in the 'golden age' to operate a business which buys and sells in more than one currency and/or lends and borrows different currencies.

This increased complexity shows itself in two ways. First, it makes business decisions more difficult to take because more than one country and currency is involved. Second, it makes actual transactions more difficult because the company has, at more or less frequent intervals, to exchange one currency for another. In Section 10.7 we consider the impact of foreign exchange risk on business decisions. In Section 10.8 we consider the problems of financing a business which operates in more than one currency.

10.7 Decision Taking under Exchange Risk

Pricing

So far as business decisions are concerned, fluctuating foreign exchange rates have their influence in two main areas. First, they affect the pricing of products which the company sells or buys overseas. Second, they influence decisions on whether to purchase assets—especially long-term assets—overseas. We consider these two types of decision in turn.

So far as pricing is concerned, the main difficulties relate to the company's own products. Perhaps the most important decision is one of principle. Most companies price their products in their own currency, leaving customers overseas to decide whether or not to buy at those prices, with whatever discount they may be able to negotiate with the company. In general this is undoubtedly the most sensible procedure. Suppose a company sells in more than one or two overseas countries. The task of altering, in each of those countries, the price which the company charges for each of its products in order to take account of the changes in exchange rates which occur under the present system would then be far too complicated. Indeed, where firms consider invoicing their customers in currencies other than their own, they usually do so by using only one other currency, usually a major currency like the dollar or Deutschmark. To do this, however, means taking a 'view' of what will happen to the exchange rate between the currency of the country where the company is based and the currency in which prices are charged.

For example, suppose that a company based in the UK expects the value of the pound to fall relative to that of the dollar. If it prices in sterling, this will mean that its sterling receipts remain constant, unless the sterling price is changed, whatever happens to foreign exchange rates. If the pound is expected to fall in value, say against the dollar, the company can *increase* its sterling receipts by quoting a fixed price in dollars. It will then receive more pounds at the fixed dollar price as the sterling exchange rate falls. But this requires the 'view' which the company has taken to be correct. If, instead of falling, the value of the pound rises against the dollar, the company will actually have lost by this decision.

Moreover, a company deciding to quote its prices in terms of another currency cannot do so sensibly for very long when exchange rates are fluctuating. If rates are changing by as much as would be required to make such a decision sensible, the company will have to time its decision to charge in another currency exceptionally well to profit from it. It would be all too easy to decide to make such a change when the increase or decrease in the foreign currency value of one's own currency had been going on for so long a period that it was just about to be reversed. The company would then lose, not gain, from the change. This is the main reason why in general companies quote prices and invoice customers in their own currencies.

This still leaves difficult decisions to be taken. First, the company must decide whether it is possible to charge different prices to home and overseas customers. If not, then overseas customers will pay the new foreign currency equivalent of sterling prices which are charged whenever the company decides that conditions within its own business, and country, require a price change. Only if overseas sales represent a major proportion of the business's turnover, will conditions overseas be taken into account in setting these prices.

Where it *is* possible to charge different prices at home and overseas, an important question will then be how frequently to adjust them. Obviously, when the company decides to change prices within its own country it is likely to change them overseas as well. If, however, exchange rates are altering, it may be necessary to make more frequent changes in the prices quoted to overseas customers. As we have already seen, a rapid fall in the foreign exchange value of the domestic currency will reduce receipts from overseas (measured in domestic currency) substantially. Given that different prices can be charged to domestic and overseas customers, the company will have to 'take a view' on how frequently overseas prices can be changed, bearing in mind the administrative costs to itself of doing this and any psychological effects on overseas customers that frequent price changes may have. This is, of course, the reason why companies in a country whose currency is unstable frequently consider invoicing in a stable currency, but we have already seen the dangers inherent in that.

When overseas prices are being changed, a basic principle underlies such a decision. Suppose that the exchange value of one's own currency has fallen. A given level of prices in domestic currency will then represent a lower foreign currency price for overseas customers. If the company is interested in increasing the volume of sales overseas, rather than their value, and/or if it is having difficulty in meeting the prices of overseas competitors, this may be acceptable. If the company is not anxious to increase overseas sales volume and meets little competition overseas, it may, however, wish to offset the fall in the foreign currency price by increasing the price in domestic currency. This decision will have to be taken in the light of the same kinds of factor as must be considered in setting domestic prices. One extra point needs to be considered, however.

Research suggests that a company deciding to change its prices following a fall or rise in the overseas value of its domestic currency often makes the same percentage change in the prices of all products to all overseas markets. Yet the cost/revenue situation for every product is unlikely to be changing in the same way; nor will the situation faced by the company in every country be uniform. There will be a limit to the time and expense which it will be worth incurring in making differential price increases between products and, where this is possible, between countries. Yet raising or lowering domestic prices by a given percentage across the board for all overseas customers and countries may well *not* be the right course to take, certainly when substantial changes in foreign exchange rates have taken place or when a considerable amount of time has elapsed since the last change in the price list for overseas customers was made.[1]

Investment Overseas

In considering the impact of foreign exchange risk on decision taking, we have so far considered only a situation where a business based in one country is exporting its products to other countries. We must now consider a situation where a firm based in one country has either already established a subsidiary overseas, *or* is considering the initial establishment or the expansion of such a subsidiary. Where a subsidiary is already established and not being expanded, foreign exchange will become an issue in two sets of circumstances. These are (1) where the company is deciding how much it

---

1. For a fuller discussion, and in particular for a check-list for issues to be considered in responding to a change in the exchange rate, see Hague *et al.* (1974).

is prepared to spend in supplementing the working capital of that subsidiary or (2) where it is considering how much of the surplus funds available in that subsidiary should be brought back to its home country. Once the budgets for cash investments between the parent company and the subsidiary have been worked out, the only question is the timing of such payments. If there is no choice because the funds are needed immediately by the subsidiary or by the parent, then the foreign exchange transaction will have to be carried out immediately at whatever happens to be the going rate of exchange (though Section 10.8 examines the possibility of using the forward market). If there *is* a choice, the company is then in a position to advance or delay payments according to the view it takes of what the future movements in the relevant exchange rate will be. In addition, it could, if it wished and if that were permissible, raise the funds for use by the overseas subsidiary in the overseas country rather than transmitting them across the exchanges. In either of these cases the issues raised become similar to those facing a firm deciding whether to invest funds in an overseas subsidiary, and whether to raise these funds overseas or at home.

The first point to be made in this respect is that, as we have already made clear, a company which advances or delays payments because it has 'taken a view' on what will happen to exchange rates is, whether it recognises it or not, gambling. Many businessmen feel that there is sufficient risk and challenge in running all the functions that go to make up a business without adding the additional risk that one may lose rather than gain in foreign exchange transactions. If this is the view that the firm takes, then the simplest way to avoid such gambling is this. Wherever possible, the company should raise the funds required to acquire business assets in the country where those assets are used. Assets and liabilities will then be matched in terms of currencies: the influence of exchange rates, if not totally eliminated, will at least be minimised. There is much to be said for this approach; since businessmen are not experts in foreign exchange movements, they should not take risks with them. If this approach is taken, then the short-term budgets and long-term investment decisions of each company will be made in a situation where costs and revenues are both denominated in the same currency.

It may well be that for one reason or another funds are not available in the country where the subsidiary is located. If so, the only way to finance overseas investment will be to use either the company's domestic currency or that of a third country. Of course, if the firm is prepared to gamble on exchange rate movements, the same issues will arise as when it decides on the movement of funds over the exchanges (whether for investment purposes or for other reasons).

If the question is simply what is the best moment at which to move funds to or from the parent firm's country, the answer in principle is simple enough. Funds should be moved out of a currency whose exchange rate has reached a peak and is about to fall; they should be moved into a currency which has just reached a trough and is about to rise. The problem, as we have emphasised throughout this section, is that spotting peaks and troughs is an extremely difficult and hazardous business. Many forecasts of exchange rate movements are available, both from the macroeconomic modellers who featured in Section 3.2, as well as from some major banks who specialise in forecasting exchange rate movements. Even these banks would admit that it is extremely difficult to predict the exact time at which a turning point in the movement of an exchange rate will be reached or the extent to which (and the period of time in which) the exchange rate will move upwards or downwards.

Where the question is *when* to move funds abroad or repatriate them, good judgement based on the kind of factor outlined above is the most one can hope for. With investment decisions, the situation is rather more complicated because, at least in theory, the parent company should be looking at the timing and amount of payments from it to the investment project and back again. Again in theory, these should be correctly dated and converted to the exchange rate which is expected to obtain at the time when payments are made. In practice, I suspect that the best procedure is usually to carry out the whole investment appraisal in terms of the currency of the country where the project is to be carried out, and then to make a separate judgement on exchange rate movements. If the company is reasonably confident that any exchange rate movement will be in favour of the country where the project is located, then perhaps the best that can be done is to view the appraisal of such a project rather more generously than if the exchange rate movement is expected to be in the opposite direction. And, as I have already emphasised, it may well be best simply to finance the project by raising local money, whether in the short term or long term.

Perhaps the most important point is this. If a country's exchange rate is expected to rise, it is likely that the rate of interest at which that currency can be borrowed will be low relative to interest rates in other countries. What must be remembered, however, is that the low interest rate will itself be an indication that the exchange rate is likely to appreciate so that the total cost of borrowing, taking the interest rate and the expected change in the exchange rate together, would be much the same as the 'pure' interest rate in a country whose exchange rate is expected to remain stable. A number of British companies were seriously caught out by this in the early 1970s. They made long-term borrowings of currencies like the Deutschmark, attracted as they were by a low interest rate. When the money came to be repaid, however, many of them found that the pound had fallen so much relative to the Deutschmark that the overall cost of the loan, taking account of both the interest rate and the change in the exchange rate, made the loan extremely expensive. Again, the principle is simple enough. One should borrow from countries whose exchange rate is expected to fall; one should lend to countries whose exchange rate is expected to rise. The problem is being certain to which group any individual country belongs.

10.8 Foreign Exchange Transactions

The implication of the preceding section is obviously that unless the company is in the actual business of speculating in foreign currency, the most sensible course is to minimise exchange risk. As we have explained, there is a good deal to be said for moving funds from one country to another at whatever the exchange rate happens to obtain at the time when the funds become available. Delaying a payment in the hope that the value of one's currency will rise, or speeding it up because that value seems likely to fall, is a course that should be taken only after obtaining the most expert advice available, which will be from one's bank or foreign exchange dealer.

There is, however, one further method of reducing risk. This is to use the 'forward' foreign exchange market. If a payment has to be made to a foreign country at a known future date, in other words if the foreign currency has to be bought at that date, it is possible to *sell* that amount of foreign currency today, agreeing to buy it back at a future date. If the foreign currency falls in value, the gain from buying it back at the date of the future transaction will roughly offset the loss on the transaction itself. The opposite procedure can, of course, be followed if the foreign currency is expected to appreciate.

As this discussion suggests, dealing in foreign exchange is an extremely specialist business. Unless a company employs a real specialist in foreign exchange, much the best advice is that it should rely on the expertise of its bank or merchant bank, explaining to that bank how it expects its net foreign exchange position to move and then discussing with the bank the best way of dealing with the expected movements. Perhaps using the forward exchange market will help, but it must be remembered that forward exchange markets operate effectively only in the world's major currencies, and even there it is not always possible to deal more than a few months ahead. It is much easier to 'hedge' transactions in this way for those in the fairly near future than for those that are not expected to take place for some time.

10.9 International Finance

The world financial system has changed significantly in the past two decades. We consider here four of the most important developments.

The first is the internationalisation of the world's commercial banks, and especially the biggest of these, many of them British or American. With rapidly growing world trade since 1960, with the industrialisation of the NICs, and with the movement towards more flexible foreign exchange rates, there have been growing banking opportunities, many of them associated with international trade or with international money movements. The world monetary system is much more international than it was twenty years ago, with foreign exchange transactions easier to arrange.

The second development is the enormous change in the distribution of world income that has been caused by the increase in the price of oil. This has led to the establishment and rapid growth of local banks, not least in the Arabian Gulf. Most of these are, as yet, not genuine international banks, and this has led them to develop strong links with the major international banks mentioned above. At the same time, the tremendous increase in the wealth of governments and some individuals in these countries has concentrated recent increases in wealth among them rather than in the OECD countries. Partly because of the reduction in industrial investment in the OECD, as a result of the structural changes in the world economic system during the 1970s, and partly because these new owners of wealth have felt a need to hold a high proportion of that wealth in a relatively liquid form, a good deal of it has gone into relatively liquid financial assets in the world's traditional banking centres, like London, New York and Frankfurt. This movement has in turn helped the growth of the world's major banks, since increased deposits in those banks have offered scope for increasing their relatively liquid assets.

This has assisted in the third development. To a large extent because governments have concentrated in recent years on borrowing the funds they require by the issue of long-term, fixed interest securities, commercial businesses have found it very difficult to obtain such finance. This has led the banks, which as we have just seen were in a good position to increase lending after 1973, to move into the supply of medium-term finance. In the past, banks have concentrated on short-term lending, especially in the UK. They lent money on what was known as the 'seed time to harvest' principle, with loans repaid once the product—whether an agricultural commodity, a mineral or a manufactured good—had been sold. To some extent, this concentration on short-term lending was more apparent than real. In practice, for example, once the transaction underlying the original loan had been completed, the bank was happy to make a further loan until the next transaction was completed, and so on. Indeed, banks would not in practice identify individual transactions, except the very largest ones. They would look at the business as a total and continuous activity. Provided the business appeared to be thriving, the amount of credit extended to it would grow roughly in line with its own turnover.

The demise, at least for a time, of the medium- to long-term fixed interest capital market so far as the private borrower is concerned has led during the 1970s to more explicit medium-term lending. While in practice short-term loans were in the past usually 'rolled-over' in the way described above, there was nothing to prevent a bank calling in short loans at very short notice. In recent years banks changed their policies. They have been keen to make medium-term loans of, say, five years, giving the borrower the certainty that the loan would not be called in within that period. This arrangement gave firms the possibility of arranging a number of medium-term loans whose termination dates could be staggered to ensure a continuing supply of medium-term finance. And, as with short-term loans, there is no reason to suppose that a credit-worthy business would fail to have the credit facility represented by these medium-term loans renewed when they expired. As a result of this, the structure of bank lending has been radically changed in recent years.

The last, and the most important, of the four developments outlined in this section has been the growth of what is known as the 'Eurodollar' market. During the 1950s and 1960s several factors led to substantial net United States payments overseas. The main ones were US aid to Europe soon after World War Two (and to other parts of the world more recently), US military expenditure overseas, and a surplus of US imports over exports at various times since 1945. The result was that large numbers of dollar deposits in American banks moved into the ownership of non-Americans. Because of controls over the interest rates which US banks could charge to US citizens, banks in a number of major centres outside the USA began to borrow these dollar deposits and lend them on terms that were rather more favourable to the lender than those permitted under US banking regulations. The result was a dramatic growth in what came to be known as the 'Eurodollar market'.

This market lent foreign-owned dollars, usually for short to medium periods but sometimes for long ones, to individuals and businesses throughout the world. Since the dollars were actually deposits in American banks, the rest of the world was using part of the American money supply to finance its own activities. Having become so firmly established, the Eurodollar markets are therefore one source of finance that all large companies should consider using, though one should remember all the qualifications about the use of foreign currency that we have expressed in Sections 10.7 and 10.8. As the name implies, the Eurodollar market began to develop first in London, with lending by British banks and by the British-based branches of large American banks. Euromarkets have, however, spread widely round the world and now thrive in a large number of financial centres. Smaller markets, known as Eurocurrency markets, carry out similar transactions in sterling, Deutschmarks and other major currencies. Again, the basis is that the loans are made using funds owned by non-residents of the country whose currency is being lent.

The speed and scale of the developments outlined in this section have been such that it would not be surprising if there were now a period of consolidation. Even so, the amount of innovative ability in the world's financial institutions is such that new developments will continually occur, though it is far from easy to predict exactly what these will be. One development, certainly, will be the increasing use of credit cards and similar instruments, though this will mainly affect individual businessmen (especially when travelling overseas) rather than companies. This development is, nevertheless, likely to be of substantial importance. So is the expected development of 'direct debiting', where suppliers are given authority to debit a customer's bank account directly at an agreed date, rather than go through the present procedure of awaiting the customer's cheque.

10.10   Conclusion

This chapter has covered a great deal of ground. Even without considering the social, political and technological environment of the business, it has indicated the number and complexity of the economic factors which good business decision taking should take into account. It has emphasised the scale and significance of the changes currently taking place in the world's economic structure, and the need for businessmen to recognise and be prepared for these. Finally, it has emphasised that the growing integration of the world's business activities has been paralleled by an increasingly international world banking system. We have insisted that it is essential that in carrying out foreign currency transactions businesses should seek the best financial advice they can. The innovations being made by an increasingly effective world banking system mean that such advice is now readily available. The aim in this chapter has been to give the background information which those in business need in order to take best advantage of specialist help, whether from firm economists, business forecasters or bankers.

Reference

Hague, D. C., Oakshott, W. E. F. and Strain, A. (1974) *Devaluation and Pricing Decisions*, Allen and Unwin.

11
The Firm and its Social Environment

J. F. Pickering and T. T. Jones

11.1 Introduction

Other chapters have shown how the firm operates in a number of different environments and markets. It relates to a capital market, to various labour and product markets and responds to competition in these markets. It also works in a macroeconomic environment which may well have a significant influence on its overall scale of activities and profitability.

In addition to these aspects of the economic environment, the firm increasingly finds itself having to take into account influences from a wider social environment. This social environment is made up of a number of elements, including local and central government, employees, consumers, environmental and other interest groups. The essence of the influences in the social environment is that they all seek to encourage the firm to take actions or at least to take into account other factors that, left to its own preferences and calculations of revenues, costs and profits, it would not have chosen. Thus corporate decision taking is also influenced by non-economic considerations. While some economists would argue that this is an undesirable trend, it is a phenomenon that cannot be ignored.

There are a number of reasons why social factors have become more significant. As individual business organisations have grown relatively larger and industrial concentration has increased, so the influence of business as an employer, supplier, user of resources, etc. and, hence, its influence on the nature and quality of life and society, has become more significant. In other words, big business is an important social institution which merits attention. This is reinforced in the light of the effects of modern technology, production methods, marketing practices and the forms of business growth adopted. Business firms are often believed to have a significant degree of independence of market forces which allows them to exploit their market power either through taking excessive profits or by pursuing non-profit maximising aspirations. Thus, management has discretion in modern markets and if it is free to pursue its own interests, then other interest groups too may also wish to influence the making of business policy. With power also comes responsibility. The presence of monopoly is one aspect of 'market failure' which is often used to justify governmental intervention. The absence of perfect and costless information and the possibility that market prices will reflect only private costs and benefits, while ignoring the potentially important public costs and benefits, are further reasons for social intervention. In addition, it is apparent that in many respects the firm is operating not only in a market, but also in a 'negotiated', environment in which bargaining takes place in relationships with customers, suppliers, government, other interest groups and sometimes even competitors.

There are also social phenomena that have contributed to the growth of societal pressures on business. The growth of pressure groups of consumers, environmentalists, etc., reflects a concern to improve information, protect the weaker and unrepresented elements in society and to draw attention to the difference between private and social interests. There has been something of an anti-business mentality in society that has no doubt contributed to these pressures, though it may be that this is more of a luxury that can be indulged in when economic conditions are buoyant than in times of economic depression when the wealth and job creating potential of business is more readily appreciated. The growth of unionisation, including white collar unionisation, is also a material factor since this has created an organised interest group ready to negotiate with management over the making of business policy. As companies have increased the overseas element of their operations both through exports and direct investment, so government has become increasingly involved—by providing export incentives and help and in monitoring the effects of any inward investment. On occasions government: business relations in international markets can quickly raise international issues between governments. This sensitivity is particularly acute where questions arise concerning the impact of multinational companies on poverty and the process of development in Third World countries or over allegations that foreign companies have attempted to influence the political situation in a country in which they are operating.

Last, but by no means least, there is evidence that those employed by business organisations are often exercised about the ethics of some business practices adopted and are anxious to have guidance concerning the appropriate ethical basis of their own actions. In other words, there is both an ethic of business and a question of ethics in business. As managers and others recognise their trusteeship of the resources they command and their accountability to society as a whole, of which shareholders are only one (albeit an important) element, so the relations of business with its social environment will remain important even if the particular pattern of emphasis is likely to vary from time to time.

In the following sections of this chapter we explore some of the areas in which the social environment impacts on business. We commence with various aspects of social responsibility, including business self-regulation; then we consider consumerism, competition policy and conclude with a discussion of ways in which governmental industrial policy affects business.

11.2   Corporate Social Responsibility

(a)   The Concept of Social Responsibility

Many commentators have endeavoured to define what is meant by the concept of corporate social responsibility (see, for example, Beesley and Evans 1978, Bowie 1982, Christian Association of Business Executives (CABE) 1974, Goyder 1961, Luthans et al. 1980, Morgan 1977, Zanisek 1979). There appear to be almost as many definitions as commentators! However, it is possible to identify a number of key features.

The firm internalises within itself social goals. This means that non-economic factors are considered which represent the concerns of interest groups other than owners and managers. The action is voluntary and goes beyond the requirements of the law. It is recognised that such action may well involve some sacrifice of profits either through revenues foregone or additional costs incurred. Indeed, the essence of the concept is that it goes beyond the expression of an attitude and actually requires action.

This does not suggest that profits are in any sense unimportant or undesirable. They are recognised as a spur to efficiency, a basis for resource allocation and a source of growth. Indeed, as Bowie (1982) has argued, in one sense it is the profitable firms that can afford to be moral. If we treat profits in this case as relating to the 'super-normal' profits identified in the neoclassical analysis, we can agree since under conditions of keen or 'perfect' competition the impact of market forces may be argued to be much more likely to achieve the socially desired outcome.

The basis for taking socially responsible decisions requires rather more attention then it has perhaps normally received. The Paretian system in economics, even if it could work effectively through perfect markets, etc., is open to criticism since it does not set bounds to the reasonableness of people's actions and it ignores the interdependence between people—as Boulding (1970) puts it, in this system 'there is no scope to weep with those that weep'. The need for a greater ethical contribution in a different branch of economics has also been emphasised by Elliott (1966), who has commented that the ranking of development projects takes place in an ethical vacuum.

> Many economists recognise the inhumanity and superficiality of [computing the productivity of alternative competing investments]. What they are looking for is some kind of ethical criterion by which they judge the possibilities presented to them.

Some of the contributions to thinking on the development of the basis of social responsibility come from a specifically Christian tradition while others approach the matter from a different perspective. However, it is of interest that there is a substantial commonality in the emphases that are made. In an important analysis of the subject Matthews (1981) argues that there should be neither complete egoism (pursuit of unbounded self-interest) nor complete altruism. Rather, there is a need for commercial morality to constrain the operation of self-interest through the operation of a moral code. This moral code would reflect an emphasis on honesty, trust, obedience to the law, personal responsibility, and an absence of malevolence and law breaking. This commercial morality would, in the view of other commentators, be based upon concepts of justice, equity, trusteeship, accountability, service and responsibility for others. In some discussions the nature of business as a means of fulfilment of human personality is emphasised, and hence the need for emphasis on the humanity of those working in it recognising that people are moral beings and require much greater consideration than to be treated as merely another factor of production.

(b)   The Content of Social Responsibility

It is unlikely that all companies will have the same attitudes to social responsibility as a concept; indeed, it is unlikely that they will all be equally affected by the same issues. However, it is clear that in broad terms a number of general issues will keep recurring for companies. The main interest groups likely to be affected and some indicators of their probable concerns are outlined below (see McKie (ed.) 1974, McAdam 1975, Beesley and Evans 1978, CABE 1974).

Employees—health and safety, payment levels and systems, pensions and sickness benefits, training provisions, working conditions, industrial relations systems, participation opportunities in decision taking and in the financial success of the company, disclosure of information.

Customers—product quality and safety, marketing practices including information and promotion, acceptance of liability, complaint handling, reasonableness of prices, maintenance of competition.

Suppliers—equity in trading relations, provision of technical and other assistance, continuity of trading.

Shareholders—maintenance of overall ethic of the business, level of profit distribution, disclosure of information, equity of treatment between different classes of shareholder.

Environmental interests—policies towards the reduction and avoidance of pollution in its various forms, conservation of depletable resources, safety procedures in the event of accidents, transportation arrangements for heavy or dangerous loads.

Community interests—relations with national and local interests, willingness to locate in areas of high unemployment, employment policies towards ethnic minorities and other disadvantaged groups, degree of participation in community projects, level of philanthropy.

If these are important areas where interest groups may be anxious to encourage the firm to increase its socially responsible efforts, what factors might motivate the firm to respond favourably to such pressures and what basis for choice might it use in deciding in which areas it should act? There are a number of factors (both 'pull' and 'push') that may bear upon the firm's decision to act responsibly.

The most persuasive 'pull' argument in favour of adopting a policy of social responsibility is the view that 'good ethics is good business', in other words that such a policy yields the prospect of economic gain to the firm. Even though, as we have defined it, social responsibility implies the voluntary sacrifice of short-run profits in the social interest, it may well be that this is rewarded through greater profitability in the longer term. A good employer may find that expenditure on training programmes and attractive working conditions is reflected in higher productivity, lower labour turnover and the opportunity to recruit better quality staff. If so, unit costs will be lower and profits higher. A firm that is motivated by 'just price' considerations may find that although short-run profit is conceded, a lower selling price acts as an entry forestalling price and so reduces the risk of disruption and a more difficult competitive environment through longer-term new entry. Equally, a firm with a better appreciation of customer requirements in terms of product quality, information, etc., may well find that repeat business is easier to obtain, thereby lowering marketing costs, and that there are lower costs of handling consumer complaints. The lower are the actual costs of adopting a socially responsible approach, the more likely are net financial benefits to accrue, and it is often the case that desirable actions have negligible incremental costs associated with them (see Pickering and Cousins 1982).

A socially responsible programme will be easier to promote within a company where it reflects the personal ethical system of major interest groups, company managers, employees or shareholders, and where it is apparent that any costs can be met from organisational slack. The incentive to act ethically may also be stronger if it is believed that this will be followed by other firms in the industry (so offering the possibility of a stable transition) and where it is recognised that socially responsible action has elements of an externality with the prospect of wider gains to firms as a result of each other's actions. This may be manifested in a larger pool of trained, skilled labour available to all firms or in a greater degree of public confidence and good will towards the products of an industry as a whole.

There are also other factors ('push' factors) operating from outside the firm, but tending to encourage it in the same direction. Respect for the law and externally stated standards will encourage socially responsible action. Some commentators argue that the law has only a limited role to play in this matter (see McKie (ed.) 1974) and, indeed, obedience to the law should be mandatory, not voluntary. However, commitment to both the letter and the spirit of the law cannot always be assumed and so it is relevant to consider this as an influence. The threat of legislation may be sufficient to encourage companies and industries to act voluntarily in order to avoid more formal regulation. The presence of other interest groups both within and outside the company may also influence corporate action, perhaps especially where this is drawn to the attention of a wider public through the media.

Within a market economy there is much to be said for the use of the price mechanism to encourage socially responsible action. If relative prices are changed or subsidies offered to reflect social preferences, the firm may be encouraged to act in the desired way while still responding to the profit motive. Equally, if externalities (such as the costs of pollution) can be internalised so that the costs fall upon the individual polluter, this will have the effect of causing the firm to respond in the socially desired manner. Economists tend to have a preference for the use of the price mechanism to influence decision taking rather than the imposition of laws or standards. This is useful where it can operate, but does not deal with all aspects of social responsibility decisions that a firm may need to make; thus other incentives will still be relevant.

We should, however, note that not all firms in all cases will be persuaded to abandon a profit oriented approach in the interests of corporate social responsibility. Firms may argue that departure from a profit orientation will weaken the stimulus to efficiency and progress and that such action would be contrary to the interests of their shareholders. The adoption of social objectives may make it more difficult to make corporate choices between alternatives and may make it difficult for managers to establish the nature of their loyalties and responsibilities. Companies may with some justification claim that it is not their duty to deal with wider social issues such as income distribution and, further, they may argue that undue paternalism may have adverse repercussions on the company concerned.

If the pursuit of social rather than economic goals does proceed in a way that weakens profits and in an environment where other companies continue to pursue economic objectives, there may be concern that the socially oriented company will lose out to its rivals and will therefore be a target for a takeover bid. In those circumstances short-run heroics may lead to longer-run social disadvantages. This serves to emphasise that socially responsible actions may be more attractive to companies where there is discretion as a result of high profitability or where all firms in an industry can be relied upon to adopt a similar philosophy. Indeed, one of the major fears is of the 'free rider' who does not adhere to appropriate standards and so gains a significant economic advantage. Where this is a major problem, legislation or at least the possibility of some industry sanctions may be required. However, care must at least be taken by public authorities and those reflecting social concerns to ensure that a free rider that is doing a useful job in promoting competition where none has previously existed is not excluded.

(c)   The Practice of Social Responsibility

On what basis might a company decide to which social issues it will respond, and to what extent should a trade-off of social gain at the expense of profits (where this is the real choice) be countenanced? Companies are likely to have a differing propensity to respond (see Beesley and Evans 1978, Hay and Grant 1974, Zanisek 1979). The spectrum tends to range from profit oriented firms responding only to the strict requirements of the law, through companies with a degree of commitment to responding to direct interest group pressures, to those which are prepared to incorporate wider social concerns within their own corporate ethic. Such variations in approach will affect and reflect not only attitudes to profit, but to all areas of social concern and management style. However, it seems likely that willingness to respond to social pressures will vary not only from company to company, but also from case to case.

Although the concept of social responsibility implies a voluntary response by the firm, there are likely to be a number of situations where some degree of external coercion, perhaps from government or from other pressure groups, is likely to occur. Here it may be very difficult to resist the pressure. Equally, there may well be cases where a common industry policy, as for example in establishing a code of practice, places a strong onus on all firms to participate. Unless it is clear that there is much greater benefit to the firm (and perhaps, in its view, to the social interest) from standing aloof from the development, it is likely that the socially related policy will be adopted.

Where there is no such strong external pressure, the incentives to adopt a social policy commitment will be less. There are, however, some criteria which the firm may apply to help it choose which social action to undertake. It is most likely to select policy commitments where there is no significant cost or where it is clear there will be a positive profit contribution.

Where some net cost and hence reduction to at least short-term profits is likely, then the firm may have a range of decision options open to it. It may decide to adopt those policies that impose a low cost on the company. It

Private returns (profits)

	Negative	Low	Medium	High
Negative				
Low				
Medium				
High				

Social Benefits (row axis label)

Figure 11.1   Comparison of Private and Social Returns from Projects

may emphasise those policies where it believes the chances of acceptance within the organisation are greatest. It may give priority to those projects where the social benefit is highest, though it may not always be easy to obtain agreement on just which projects satisfy that criterion.

The exercise of choice between alternatives may be made on the criterion that the discounted contribution to net profits should be maximised over a given time period. Different projects (as with any investment) will have different time streams over which the returns will be available. The company's choice will depend on its time horizon and its discount rate; the longer the time horizon and the lower the discount rate, the more likely it is perhaps to adopt policies with a substantial element of social benefit. An alternative way of taking into account both private and social effects of particular possibilities would be to rank projects on both criteria, as shown in Figure 11.1. Here, projects showing high benefits both to the company and socially would be most likely to be adopted by the company. Those with high private benefits but negative social effects would be likely to give greatest cause for concern to the socially responsible company. Projects with negative or low private effects but high social gains would be unlikely to be adopted by the company, unless government or some other agency was to act to increase the private rewards for such a policy, e.g. by offering a subsidy or otherwise changing relative costs and prices of the activity in question.

Given that many social responsibility projects will involve at least some short-run costs, or opportunity costs, the company will need to consider establishing a budget for such activities and ranking competing uses for those funds on the basis of one of the decision criteria considered earlier. Given that there is often some discretion within budgets, this should not be

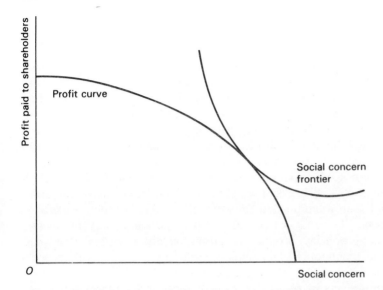

Figure 11.2   Allocation of Resources between Shareholders and Social Concerns

an insuperable problem. The decision as to how much to allocate will need to be taken in the light of prevailing moods and commitments within the company and society and in the light of a view as to just how much could be diverted from other purposes. This is indicated in Figure 11.2 where a trade-off between profits and social concern is indicated. A minimum level of payment to shareholders and a minimum level of social concern expenditure may be specified and, subject to those constraints, the optimum mix of expenditure is determined by the point of tangency between the profit curve of the firm and its social concern frontier.

It is apparent from this analysis that decision criteria for socially related expenditures are not well established. However, in the absence of external incentives and pressures to act in a particular way the firm should, by establishing a budget for such purposes and identifying ranking and choice criteria along the lines outlined here, have some basis for rational decision taking.

11.3   Applications of Social Responsibility

While socially responsible conduct manifests itself in a variety of ways, there are two aspects which merit some further attention here—the development of social audits and the growth of voluntary self-regulation by business.

(a)   *Social Audits*

The use of a social audit is defined as involving a retrospective review of the impact or contribution of the company in a recognised social dimension (Beesley and Evans 1978). Thus it implies an assessment of the contribution of a company measured in ways other than through its profitability. This assessment may be carried out by staff within the company or perhaps by independent organisations anxious to promote social responsibility as a more significant element in business decision taking (as, for example, with the various publications of *Social Audit*).

To carry out a full social audit is a very extensive undertaking since it involves identifying all areas of social responsibility that bear on the firm's actions and then attempting to measure the company's performance in those respects. This may, of course, cover the whole area of production and marketing policies, product design and safety, environmental questions, employment policies and employee relations, relations with the local community and with government, charitable contributions, etc. Measurement of the effects in respect of each of these is sometimes advocated (Linowes 1975) with socially beneficial acts voluntarily undertaken shown to the credit of the company to the value of the expenditures incurred in adopting the policy, while failure to act or socially undesirable actions are treated as detriments and count against the company. It is, of course, quite possible that by basing such valuations on the costs incurred in taking a particular action, the true social valuation is overlooked since values may bear no relation to the costs of the action. If any company's decision making was to be influenced by such procedures, an objection may be seriously raised in that they encourage firms to choose policies that maximise the cost outlays of the policy rather than maximise the real social benefits.

Those social audits that have been undertaken have often had a more limited objective and have often focused on their impact on only one interest group, especially consumers (see, for example, the Annual Review of the Code of Practice adopted by William Timpson Ltd). In a consumer oriented social audit such matters as design, quality control, packaging and labelling, marketing and competition, and after-sales service are likely to be scrutinised (Medawar 1978). The costs of collecting data on complaints or consumer satisfaction will be quite considerable, let alone the costs of undertaking other aspects of an audit.

In view of the potential scope of social audits there does seem to be a limit to the extent to which they are likely to be adopted to the full. On a more limited basis the social performance of important companies is often a matter of attention from the press, particular shareholders and other interest groups. There may be much to be said for a company voluntarily releasing information about its social performance. Indeed, disclosure may well be argued to be part of a company's social responsibility. If the social auditing process is carried out internally and kept in close touch with the on-going management system, as advocated by Beesley and Evans (1978), this should help avoid the problems discussed earlier where socially responsible company managers find it more difficult to establish just what their responsibilities are. Thus appropriate balance between commercial and social goals may be achieved.

(b) Voluntary Self-Regulation by Business

A second, and perhaps more frequent, form of specific social responsibility action involves the establishment within particular trades or industries of a form of voluntary self-regulation by business through what are known as codes of practice. In some cases these have been directly encouraged by government and its agencies, as in Britain by the Office of Fair Trading under the provisions of S124(3) of the Fair Trading Act 1973. In other cases the decision will have been taken entirely voluntarily within the industry, though perhaps in response to particular concerns expressed by others. Such voluntary self-regulation is an attempt to guide and encourage ethical practice within an industry. It has particular attractions where the desire is to reduce the impact of government regulation and where the limitations of primary legislation are recognised (especially its inflexibility).

The main purpose of a code of practice is to provide a statement of principles that should guide the conduct of business, especially by indicating standards of practice that are perhaps in excess of those that have been traditionally achieved. It is noticeable that so far, at least in Britain, codes of practice have tended to be developed in consumer goods trades and to relate to those aspects of firm conduct which impinge directly upon consumers. There seems no inherent reason why codes of practice should not be developed in other situations, e.g. to reflect environmental or employee concerns, especially if it is felt that the desired effects could be more readily obtained in this way than through legislation or bilateral bargaining, etc.

There are a number of common features of the codes of practice that are currently in operation (see Pickering and Cousins 1982, for an overview of these issues). In particular they specify the legal rights and obligations of both supplier and customer, desirable performance levels, and appropriate complaint handling procedures; they encourage improvements in the standard of trading practices (e.g. through information provision and advertising); they prohibit undesirable practices (e.g. small print exclusions and misleading pricing); and they establish conciliation and arbitration services.

The development and promotion of such codes in a trade is frequently the responsibility of the relevant trade association. The incentives to companies to adopt the code are likely to be greatest if they can envisage prospective benefits in terms of favourable publicity and consumer relations, additional sales revenue (e.g. from greater customer loyalty or discouragement of new entrants), and lower costs (e.g. of complaints handling) to offset any additional costs they may incur in establishing and operating the scheme. In addition business may feel a strong incentive to adopt a voluntary scheme in order to avoid what may be thought to be the less desirable implications of direct government regulation. On the other hand, if business feels that the costs of such self-regulation will outweigh the benefits or if it prefers direct government controls (perhaps because it thinks it is easier in this way to control 'free riders'), then it will be more difficult to obtain acceptance of, and adherence to, a code of practice.

Research evidence on the effects of such codes of practice (see Pickering and Cousins 1982, 1983) suggests that although the effects may not have been substantial in most cases, they have at least been favourable and worthwhile. Companies have not found the costs of setting up or operating codes to be generally very substantial, though they have noticed an increase in consumer complaints. They have benefited to some extent from the existence of a codified complaints handling system and from an increase in their efficiency. Moreover, they believe they have gained from increased customer confidence and from a generally enhanced competitive position. They also note a rise in the trading standards adopted by other companies and a greater cohesion amongst firms in their trade. Trade associations have by and large raised their standing and effectiveness and this has contributed to a general improvement in relations with government. Since it appears that consumers have also derived benefits, it seems that in appropriate circumstances further emphasis on voluntary self-regulation may be anticipated.

If this form of social responsibility response is to develop further, what are the key considerations that need to be borne in mind (see Bowie 1982, McKie (ed.) 1974, Pickering and Cousins 1982)? Successful codes of practice are likely to be those where there is a common ethic in the industry and a commitment to its objectives from all companies, thus ensuring wide participation. It requires standards to be set at a high level, not to represent the lowest common denominator. There is a need for adequate publicity of the existence and content of the code to those who might use it and for full and effective enforcement of its provisions. In order to achieve the full social benefits, it is important that a code should not be used as a means of cartelisation or to restrict entry from potential competitors. Equally, enforcement should use appropriate rules of justice and should not be based upon private trade courts. The temptation should be avoided to use a code of practice as a means of restricting supplier or customer choice. There is also a danger that codes may adopt prescriptive standards (how standards are to be achieved) rather than performance standards (what standards are to be achieved). The latter is preferable since it allows the individual company to determine the choice of approach and this is therefore more favourable to competition. Equally, it would be unfortunate if adoption of a code of practice were to lead to a restriction of the range of price/quality/service combinations offered to consumers and particularly to eliminate 'poor people's goods' (McKie (ed.) 1974). The preservation of choice should therefore be a prime concern in a code of practice.

In order to internalise the benefits available from a code of practice, management of an individual company will need to respond positively to the opportunities and challenges the code presents. It will need to sustain and publicise its own commitment to the code and ensure that its own personnel at least attain the ethical standards set by the code. Staff training programmes and other internal procedures will need to reflect the requirements of the code. The company will also no doubt wish to monitor its own performance standards through an internal information system rather than rely solely on the trade association's own enforcement procedures. Indeed, such an internal information system may well be of considerable benefit to the company in identifying areas where cost savings ought to be achieved or where new market opportunities present themselves.

11.4 Consumerism

(a) The Nature of Consumerism

Of all the social pressures (other than government) constituting part of the external environment in which business has to operate, the influence of consumerism has been perhaps the most long standing and most influential. Consumerism is viewed as 'a social movement to augment the rights of buyers in relation to sellers' (Kotler 1972). This reflects concern about the balance between buyers and sellers in the market place and is perhaps indicative of a general social critique about some aspects of business in general and marketing in particular. It should be recognised that this is also directed at the provision of goods and services in the public sector as in the private sector. Indeed, given the existence of monopoly positions in so much of the public sector, the case for consumerist involvement there is particularly marked.

The term consumerism also covers a wide range of activities through both governmental and non-governmental agencies. It includes the making of consumer laws; the use of other agencies of consumer protection in local and national government, e.g. through such bodies as the Office of Fair

Trading and local authority trading standards departments; independent agencies offering consumer protection and advice, such as Citizens Advice Bureaux; participation in decision taking and consumer representation, e.g. through the nationalised industries consumer councils; the activities of independent agencies providing advice and information to consumers, including (perhaps especially) the role of the comparative testing organisations, such as Consumers' Association in the UK and Consumer Union in the US. Consumerism also includes actions to improve the education of consumers and to help them take considered and informed decisions. Finally, there is much to be said for encouraging business to seek its own response to the consumer as an element of consumerism. Indeed, the development of voluntary codes of practice is an important aspect of this. With this breadth of coverage it should be apparent that consumerism is not solely about confrontation between consumers and business but should, ideally, be a much more creative process of interaction to improve the working of markets.

(b)   The Concerns of Consumerism

The growth of pressures from consumer-based groups for changes in business behaviour appears to have arisen for a number of reasons, some of which are related to specific consumer problems while others reflect wider social influences (on this and other aspects of this topic see, for example, McKie (ed.) 1974, Robertson 1978, Greyser and Diamond 1974, Mitchell (ed.) 1978, Swann 1979, Morris (ed.) 1980). As regards the specific consumer problems, attention is frequently drawn to such aspects as:

(1) *problems of product or service quality*—unsafe goods, products lacking fitness for purpose, items that are not of merchantable quality, built-in obsolescence, inferior service;

(2) *unsatisfactory marketing*—the use of deceptive advertising, misleading claims, the promotion of false values, misleading pricing through artificial price comparisons or the inclusion of hidden charges;

(3) *packaging*—that is unnecessarily expensive, deceptive as to the size of the actual contents or nutritional values, lacking information about contents, nutritional values and the dates by which perishables should be used;

(4) *terms of sale*—that purport to weaken the consumer's legal rights, meaningless warranties, etc.;

(5) *fraudulent practices*—such as the sale of under-weight items.

Within the general context of the discussion of social responsibility in this chapter, we might suggest that many of these problems reflect low ethical standards on the part of some suppliers.

The economic effects of this manifest themselves in the problems of market uncertainty since there is no consistent price–quality relationship on which consumers can rely; this means that there are also high information costs and high transaction costs facing consumers. The market is therefore not working well. Furthermore, since the consequence of the practices of which consumers complain may have been to encourage consumers to purchase more goods and services of particular types than would have been the case if the true value of the product was known or reflected in the price, a loss of consumer welfare occurs. On the other hand, it may be argued that consumer uncertainty about the quality of goods and services leads them to purchase less than they would if they had reliable knowledge of the quality of goods and services. There is then a loss of welfare both to consumers and to producers.

If the reasons advanced so far are related to the accumulated concern over particular products and services, the next group of reasons reflects wider socio-economic influences. Four key factors may perhaps be emphasised. These are:

(1) *relative market power positions*—with the individual domestic consumer having little influence over manufacturers and suppliers, a problem that has perhaps been exacerbated by the growth of concentration and the increasing remoteness of the consumer from advice from local retailers;

(2) *product sophistication*—as technical progress has proceeded, so the complexity of products increases and the ability of consumers to make effective choices is reduced; this is particularly a problem for consumers buying high unit value items which are also likely to be infrequently purchased so personal experience and learning cannot be relied upon;

(3) *economic developments*—some would argue that by increasing consumption opportunities, growing affluence has contributed to the growth of consumerism, while high rates of inflation tend to encourage particular attention to business actions in raising prices and varying the quality or quantity of products;

(4) *social trends*—a number of factors seem relevant here, namely the increasing social concern about the economic position of the poor, growing concern about the environment, doubts in some social groups about business—its marketing practices especially and perhaps the role of the profit motive, the possibility that consumerist concerns may be an effective political vote-catcher.

Not all of these concerns will remain powerful at all times; indeed, it is likely that consumerism experiences something of a socio-economic cycle. It is also possible that ethics in trading standards will vary according to the business cycle. While it would often be far too expensive for an individual consumer to undertake major actions to redress a major wrong, by externalising the action either through some voluntary grouping of consumers or through the provision of public money, remedial or enforcement action can become worthwhile in the sense that it may cost less to achieve than the group benefits it offers. Since such action benefits all consumers, with one person's gain not detrimentally affecting any other's, it is arguable that in economic terms consumer protection is a legitimate public good.

(c)   The Methods of Consumerism

Just as the agencies in consumerism are numerous and varied, so are the approaches adopted to try to improve the position of the consumer. The techniques and their outcomes can be considered under four heads—consumer information, consumer protection, consumer education and consumer representation.

Perhaps the *provision of information* to consumers is one of the least contentious aspects of consumerism. If effectively carried out it should improve the working of markets and offer particular benefits to companies that offer good value to consumers. The comparative testing organisations publish data on a wide range of goods and services. In the UK the magazine *Which?* reaches over 600,000 subscribers, while readership may be up to five times that number. This could mean that around one in seven households have access to *Which?* comparative test reports. Its prospective impact could be substantial and even if only a relatively small proportion of consumers actually allow it to influence their brand choice, given the structure of costs in manufacturing and retailing, marginal sales are likely to be highly profitable.

Emphasis has been placed on increasing the flow of useful information to consumers about products. Grading, certification and labelling schemes have been introduced in some cases, including content and care labelling and open dating of perishable items. There have been moves to provide more consistent and accessible information on pack sizes and prices, including the use of standard packs and unit pricing. True rates of interest are now required in hire purchase transactions. While research studies do not all indicate a high level of consumer use of unit prices and labelling, some do indicate this, and all report a high level of consumer approval of these developments (see Padberg 1977, McElroy and Aaker 1979). In some countries countervailing advertising has been used to refute what are believed to be misleading claims put forward by suppliers.

Action to improve *consumer protection* covers a very wide variety of areas and, as Smith and Swann (1979) show, the consumer has protection at all stages in the purchase process—in preparing to buy (through controls on information, prevention of deception, acquisition of finance), at the point of sale and in obtaining redress and enforcing the consumer's rights. Much of this protection is embodied through legislation protecting consumers against deception and misleading advertising, the imposition of unfair terms, injury from dangerous materials in food, drugs or clothing, the supply of goods that are not fit for the purpose or of merchantable quality, and exclusion clauses. Strict product liability provisions are being advocated. In addition to the growth of statute law in this respect, the development of codes of practice is, as we have noted, also important here.

Whether there has been too much legislation is perhaps debatable. There are costs involved in the legislative process and in its enforcement. There is a risk that the legislation may be inappropriate or adopt either too lenient or too severe a stance. It would be unfortunate to rule out goods or services where, given full information, there is a significant demand (assuming that there are not social grounds for prohibition). On the other hand, there are clearly areas where it is preferable that the law should specify particular prohibitions in the best interests of both consumers and reputable suppliers.

Many would argue with justification that the consumer should be encouraged to engage in self-help. The development of various forms of consumer information is an aid to self-help by improving purchase decisions in the market place. Steps to increase *consumer education* more generally both in schools and among adults and to increase awareness of the factors that ought to be taken into account in making purchase decisions are useful. Practical help in this direction comes from business, the consumer organisations and government.

The final area of consumerist action and achievement is concerned with *representation*. The consumer voice is now heard in the nationalised industries through their consumer councils; some business organisations have appointed directors or management to represent the consumer needs in the company. In some countries, class actions have been instituted on behalf of consumers against suppliers. Where this is so, the incentive to suppliers to avoid all risks must be very high and insurance costs are large. A final, but significant, way in which the consumer movement has gained representation is through the respect which it has gained for its professional and research-based approach, together with its adroitness in helping to encourage legislation in the consumer's interest. Such actions have been reflected in President Kennedy's statement of consumer rights in the US (rights to safety, information, choice and to be heard) and in the EEC's programme for consumer protection. But these are really only indicative of the fact that consumerism has established a position of significance in many countries. While there will be peaks and troughs in the level of respect and attention accorded to consumerism, it is difficult to believe its significance will materially decline.

(d)   Corporate Responses

So what, then, might be the corporate response to consumerism? In commencing this discussion we should note that there are some who would argue strongly that consumerism is detrimental to the interests of business and, indeed, of consumers (see the sources cited in Swann 1979 and Foxall 1978). They would argue that consumerist measures impose more costs than they offer benefits; that business costs are increased through having to deal with increased complaints and modifying production arrangements; that product and marketing innovation is hindered; and that there is a considerable expense in having to monitor a large number of laws.

In addition, they suggest the consumer movement's representatives do not always reflect what 'ordinary' consumers require or would benefit from receiving. Furthermore, there is a cost to the public sector of a heavy consumer law enforcement programme. Enforcement agencies may not be effective and indeed may be 'captured' by the business interests. Thus such opponents would prefer to place much greater emphasis on the operation of market forces and on the consumer's ability to act sensibly. While there is no doubt some validity in these arguments, especially if consumerism is taken to extremes, they do not seem to negate the case for consumer policies or for a positive response to them from management.

If such a positive response is to be brought about, it will take its place alongside those other areas of ethical action we have considered where an appropriate blend of corporate and social objectives is sought, though here too it seems likely that, effectively handled, such actions may also offer direct commercial benefits to the company concerned. The key to the business response is to adopt a policy that emphasises the interests and needs of the consumer, which is after all the essence of the marketing concept (see Robertson 1978 and Mitchell (ed.) 1978, especially the papers by Nelson and Rodger). To achieve this, emphasis will be placed on the importance of frankness and honesty in communications with the customer, the supply of worthwhile and safe products, the adoption of responsible and honest trading practices, and fair treatment where, as inevitably happens from time to time, the consumer requires redress. Such an approach will cover all the key activities of the company in product design, production, promotion and marketing, servicing and complaints handling. While consumers and business may from time to time diverge about what is fair and honest, the establishment of an ethical basis of trading is central to the demands of consumerism. It should also, incidentally, go without saying that business is equally entitled to look to its customers to behave ethically in return. Unfortunately, this expectation is not always fully satisfied.

It also needs to be said that there may well be occasions where legislation or other regulations are proposed which are unlikely to bring any net benefits to either consumers or to competitive and efficient businesses. (It is arguable that restrictions on the use of meaningful comparisons of promotional prices with recommended prices is a case in point here, see Pickering 1979b). They may impose such costs on business that benefits to consumers will be dissipated through higher prices or reduced choice. In such cases it is clearly incumbent upon business to make its concerns clearly known and where possible to support this with objective evidence.

A second area of business response concerns its use of research. If a consumer oriented strategy is to be adopted, consumer needs should be effectively identified and their response to the firm's offerings adequately monitored. While considerable expenditures are incurred on market research, it may be that more attention could be paid to this aspect in helping formulate a policy that is likely to have both social acceptance and the prospects of market success. Companies might also consider whether they take sufficient notice of the comparative test data produced by magazines like *Which?* This offers an influential source of comment about the strengths and weaknesses of their own brand, together with considerable information based upon extensive testing procedures about their competitors' products. To what extent is this used in further product developments?

If companies are to make the most effective response to consumerism and to get the greatest possible benefits from it, the consumer oriented nature of the policy should be built into the corporate ethos. It has been suggested that this requires that top management should be closely involved in the policy and should receive regular feedback on its effects. There should also be a senior executive, if not a board member, with particular responsibility for representing the consumer's interest to the company. There should be considerable effort to maintain an effective customer relations policy, including a helpful and fair complaints handling procedure.

There are prospective benefits to business from a creative and positive response to consumerism (see, for example, the paper by Peterson in Mitchell (ed.) 1978). In particular, greater consumer trust in a company will offer the potential for higher market shares, at lower promotional cost, and with the prospect of more ready acceptance of new products. In addition, as Peterson's company found, there were direct benefits in terms of better stock control when open dating was introduced and avoidance of store pricing errors when unit pricing was adopted.

11.5   Competition Policy

(a)   Introduction

Competition policy is a further area in which government intervenes to modify the conduct of individual companies away from practices which their own self-interest might commend towards those which are believed to enhance a wider social interest. In this case the aim of policy is to improve the working of markets by promoting competition and constraining the undesirable accretion or use of positions of market dominance. The expectation is that such policies should benefit consumers, help other businesses that might be adversely affected by monopolies or restrictive practices, and enhance wider aspects of economic performance within the economy.

Many countries have their own competition policies and while they all have similar objectives, their approach to the achievement of those objectives tends to vary. This clearly makes life difficult for management of companies trading or producing in several different countries. A number of guides to the different policies are available (see, for example, Swann 1979, Office of Fair Trading *passim*, OECD *passim*, EEC *passim*, Neale and Goyder 1981, Korah 1978). The reason for the variation in policies between countries (and through time) is no doubt partly due to difference in political attitudes and is also a reflection of the size and state of a particular economy. It also reflects the fact that it is very difficult indeed to state for certain whether monopolies and other restrictions on competition give rise to net detriments from a loss of choice, loss of efficiency, hindrance to new entry, restrictions on the growth of the efficient, and excessive prices and profits; or whether such monopolies and restrictive practices are on balance more likely to offer net benefits in terms of scale economies, innovation, stronger international performance, beneficial co-operation, and reasonable prices and profits. Much research has been carried out on these matters and while there seems to be a balance of evidence in favour of a general preference for competition, there is sufficient evidence of both a general and a specific nature to the contrary that caution is required in formulating policy, especially in the 'grey areas' where both advantages and disadvantages may arise.

There are also variations in the system of competition policy adopted. Some approaches are based on an administrative tribunal which is thought to offer the advantages of flexibility, while others use a judicial procedure when the greater regard for precedent and consistency is thought likely to offer benefits of predictability. Some measures adopt a cost–benefit or discretionary approach in which conflicting arguments can be considered and weighed up to establish where the public interest resides, while others adopt a *per se* approach which declares illegal particular situations or practices that are referred to in the legislation. Again, some elements of competition policy are form-based, where the law specifies certain situations that are to be investigated or prohibited, while other elements are effects-based, seeking to deal with any situations, whether specifically identified in the legislation or not, that affect the public interest. Finally, some approaches (as with the EEC) are based upon a general system of law, while in other cases (as in the UK) the approach is based upon specific pieces of legislation.

In this section we shall endeavour briefly to identify the key features and economic issues surrounding the main areas of competition policy—dominance, mergers, cartels and international aspects of competition policy. The focus will be very much on the arguments that business will either wish to advance or rebut. In so short a space it is not possible to distinguish in any detail between competition policy issues in different countries or to outline the detail of individual policies. The majority of the evidence will be drawn from the UK situation, but some use will also be made of experience in the EEC and other countries.

(b) The Control of Dominant Firms

While most countries have a policy towards the presence of dominant firms, there is no case where dominance *per se* is illegal. However, in some cases, e.g. the USA, monopolisation of a market is an abuse unless it arises from superior efficiency and business acumen. In other countries, provision exists for the investigation of positions of dominance and control of abuses of such positions. In the USA the Clayton and Federal Trade Commission Acts prohibit certain practices, such as price discrimination, exclusive dealing and tie-ins, if they substantially lessen competition.

The starting point for such policies has to be the establishment of the concept of dominance. As in the UK monopolies legislation, a rule of thumb may be used to indicate a minimum market share (currently 25 per cent) above which a firm may be considered to be dominant. This does not, of course, mean that all such market shares indicate dominance and a cause for investigation. Indeed, in the more recent Competition Act 1980 dealing, *inter alia*, with anti-competitive practices, no market share is referred to at all. Thus dominance has to be established through economic and business analysis of the circumstances of the particular case. In Britain, for example, there is a screening system to identify candidates for investigation. This takes into account prices, profits, behaviour, concentration levels and complaints from third parties.

Dominance is normally held to be indicated by evidence of freedom of action by the firm concerned. This is reflected by the absence of effective market controls, by a low level of commercial risk, evidence of the adoption of practices that create or sustain a dominant position, and by evidence that the firm has received the benefits of monopoly through a quiet life or high profits, etc. Thus, the approach to dominant firms requires an assessment of aspects of the structure of the markets concerned, and the conduct and performance of the firm in those markets.

Structural analysis of the existence of a dominant position must inevitably commence by establishing just what is the relevant market. If the market is narrowly defined, it is more likely that a high market share will be found to exist. Furthermore, there may be a considerable disparity in size between the market leader and his rivals. Both these factors may suggest dominance. If a broader definition of the market is adopted, as business people normally advocate and economists often resist, individual market shares are likely to be lower and dominance is less likely to be found. However, this static description of the market alone will not suffice. The scope for competition from substitute products (the cross elasticity of demand) and from producers of related products broadening their output to move into the product market concerned (the cross elasticity of supply) may materially influence the interpretation of the initial evidence, as will competition from imports. Other considerations are the scope for new entry competition and the extent to which competition has been increasing by, for example, multiple sourcing by existing customers. Potential competition will be affected by the nature and height of barriers to entry into the industry (e.g. through economies of scale, patent or technological advantages, or exclusionary arrangements adopted by the dominant firm). Assessment of the significance of the individual company's dominance will also need to take into account the exercise of countervailing buying power and the size and growth of the market. In the light of these factors it should be possible to establish whether a company has a significant dominant position or whether even if its market share is high, there are other reasons associated with that particular market which indicate that the scope to exercise market power is restricted. Unfortunately, however, the conclusions reached by the authorities do not always satisfy commentators (see, for example, Korah 1980).

The next question that is likely to be addressed concerns the economic rationale for the dominant position. How has the position arisen? It may be that it is a logical consequence of the overall enterprise and expertise of the company in successfully developing products and meeting demand in a way that its rivals have not achieved. It may be that there are significant economies of scale associated with the operations which make a more diluted market structure economically undesirable. It may reflect the rewards for technological or other skills which have given the company know-how advantages or a strong patent position. It may even be due to the breadth of product range or the strength of brand names which make effective competition from others more difficult, or it may be the effects of past acquisitions or other practices which have tended to concentrate the industry and keep it concentrated.

Whether a company has a 'natural' monopoly or not, investigation of its conduct and performance in that position is important and may give rise to various sanctions, such as fines or instructions to desist according to country, if it is concluded that the monopoly position has been abused and has worked against the public interest. While various pieces of legislation give indications of how the public interest is to be defined (e.g. Section 84 of the Fair Trading Act 1973, Article 86 of the Treaty of Rome), they tend to be rather broad and lacking in specificity. Consequently, it is in the working out of the concept in individual cases that the most effective interpretation of the content of the public interest can be achieved.

The types of practice that are likely to attract the attention of the competition authorities if used by a firm with a position of market dominance or, in the case of the UK Competition Act 1980, some degree of market power, can be considered under three separate heads: pricing, product line, and distribution policies. Of course, it must be recognised that not all practices under these heads will incur official disapproval, but there are some which will be likely to receive scrutiny. It is on these that we need to focus some attention. We commence by identifying the practices that might be questioned and then consider generally the economic objection to the practices and possible defences open to business. For a more detailed review of these issues see Pickering (1983).

Pricing Policies   A number of aspects of pricing policy may give rise to concern. Various forms of price discrimination, charging different prices in different markets where these are not justified by cost variations or, indeed, charging uniform delivered prices where varying freight costs would point to the need for different prices, may be scrutinised. Cross-subsidisation is another variant of this which may attract attention. Policies regarding the granting of discounts may also be scrutinised, especially where quantity discounts are given that are not cost-related, where there are discounts offered to particular classes of trader only and where various forms of overrider or aggregated and fidelity discounts are offered. This may apply also to the obverse case, namely the exercise of excessive buying power by a dominant purchaser. Predatory pricing involving selective price cutting in limited competitive situations or the use of selective cancellation charges may also be investigated.

Product Line Policies   Action taken by companies that may have the effect of reducing competition from competing brands (inter-brand competition) is likely to attract the attention of the competition authorities. Exclusive purchasing requirements, where a supplier may require a customer to take all his requirements from the one source, are a good case in point. Indeed, Howe (1983) comments that such practices have become virtually a *per se* violation of EEC competition law when adopted by a dominant firm. Other actions which may be thought likely to restrict competition include full line forcing and tie-in sales where a range of items must be obtained from the same supplier, the insistence on long-term contracts to take supplies from a particular source, and the use of rental-only agreements which restrict the customer's freedom of manoeuvre. Excessive promotional expenditures, restrictive patent policies, and the action by a vertically integrated company to interfere with supplies to independent companies that are both customers and, at a later stage in the process, competitors, may also attract critical attention.

Restrictive Distribution Policies   Such policies are more likely to affect competition between distributors of the one brand (intra-brand competition), although an unwise choice of policy may encourage other distributors to seek out alternative suppliers and so generate competition between suppliers too (as the makers of Raleigh bicycles discovered; see Monopolies and Mergers Commission 1981). Refusal to supply and the operation of a selective distribution system are the main manifestations of such restrictive policies; prohibitions on resale provide another example.

The listing of types of practices that may be under particular scrutiny by the competition authorities is of course indicative and not comprehensive. Further, not all instances will be investigated or opposed, depending on the form of competition policy adopted, but especial care is perhaps required in using such practices. While the details of the economic argument will undoubtedly vary in each case, there are a number of general issues that will be addressed both by those opposing a particular form of conduct and by those wishing to defend it on public interest grounds.

Opponents of a practice are likely to argue that it has an adverse effect on competition, hindering the competitive process, reinforcing monopoly positions and acting in a discriminatory manner. It favours large firms at the expense of small, forecloses markets and raises entry barriers, so excluding new competitors. Customer choice will have been restricted. The efficient use of resources will have been impaired by the weakening of the price mechanism and competitive system generally. The inefficient are protected, a wasteful proliferation of outlets or of other forms of expenditure is encouraged and customers are denied the opportunity to allocate their demand according to their own best interests. The vigour of these arguments will be strengthened if it is believed the effects of this conduct are abusive.

The defenders of particular practices will seek to emphasise that such practices can have beneficial effects and that they do so in the individual case. They will endeavour to show that competition is promoted by the practice (e.g. that new entry is helped or a previously rigid market structure is loosened up) or that the practice is subject to external competitive constraints. It may offer distinct benefits to customers and may be economically acceptable where there is a close relation between costs and prices for different activities. The practice may be justified as making a major contribution to business efficiency through better production planning, lower marketing or distribution or administrative costs. It may be fully justified by the nature of the product or service concerned; it may be necessary to enable the company to obtain a fair return on a major investment it has incurred. Finally, it may be shown that the way in which the practice operates is reasonable and not exploitative.

Besides investigating the implications of certain practices, there are elements of competition policy which are concerned with the effect of a dominant position on the overall performance of the company. This is typified by the British approach to monopolies investigations and it is evident that the operations of the National Board for Prices and Incomes in the late 1960s and the Price Commission during its later, more discretionary, phase, were also concerned with aspects of the economic performance of firms with market power. (On the issues concerned in price control policies, see Pickering 1971, 1979a.) This is therefore the area in which the regulation of business through price and profit controls, efficiency audits, etc., becomes possible. Three areas merit attention: prices and profits, efficiency, and adequacy of capacity.

Prices and Profits While these are viewed as natural indicators of performance, and indeed standard monopoly theory analyses the effects in terms of these variables, it is not easy to derive reliable measures in modern multi-product companies where the apportionment of costs between products, the effects of inflation and transfer pricing, and differences between economists' and accountants' views of costs all complicate the matter. The approach of the competition agencies tends to emphasise the desirability as far as possible of prices being set in line with those that competitive markets would bring about. Where there are no effective market forces and where the view is taken that prices and profits are excessive or pricing is exploitative and irresponsible, then some form of control on prices and profits is more likely to be proposed.

A number of factors influence the assessment of the reasonableness of prices and profits. Prices should be directly related to costs of individual items without undue cross-subsidisation. The benefits of cost savings should be shared with consumers. Trends in prices and profits are likely to be explored and particular attention may be paid to the extent to which prices and profits are kept up under recessionary conditions and where there is excess demand, since this is likely to be indicative of a failure of market forces to exercise effective control and hence a need for some other form of regulation. Assessment is also made of the reasonableness of profits. This is particularly likely to depend upon the degree of risk facing the company and its investment requirements. Evidence of modern methods of investment appraisal and inflation accounting is likely to be looked for in these circumstances.

Efficiency   In terms of both technical and overall (X) efficiency, this is important. Overall efficiency is difficult to measure objectively, but instances have occurred where managements have been criticised for being slow to respond to needs or opportunities or to make necessary internal changes. Cost minimisation has been particularly emphasised by price control agencies, while there has been general attention to questions concerning the use of advanced management techniques (e.g. scheduling). Comparisons of the productivity of labour (or indeed wider factor productivity) between plants and firms may offer reassurance about efficiency. A dominant firm's action in facilitating or hindering technical progress and product development is also likely to feature in any overall assessment of its performance.

Capacity   If a firm has the benefits of a dominant position, it is important that it should maintain sufficient capacity and be prepared to increase production where demand increases. Inadequate levels of supplies have been strongly criticised, though this does not necessarily mean that a company should maintain capacity to meet all peaks in demand since this may imply that a lot of capacity would lay idle for considerable periods. On the other hand, the persistence of excess capacity may be viewed as a sign of inefficiency or an attempt to discourage potential new entrants. This too may be open to criticism.

(c)   The Control of Mergers

Mergers are an important means by which companies may increase their market power. In contrast to expansion through competitive action in the market place, the process of merging may be held not to offer benefits to consumers, though it might to shareholders and companies' financial advisers. There are grounds for divergent views about the public interest implications of mergers. In some cases they may be beneficial; in others they may be detrimental. While many small countries tend not to have a merger control policy, presumably taking the view that the domestic market is too small to support many firms in an industry, the larger countries do have such a policy, though its form tends to vary. The USA has traditionally had a restrictive policy on mergers, prohibiting any which may lessen competition, with the effect that horizontal and vertical mergers involving quite small market shares are likely to be opposed. Conglomerate mergers are also likely to be opposed if a merger removes a potential competitor from the market. This may, however, be changing with the development of merger guidelines offering the possibility of a somewhat more pragmatic policy (see *Anti-Trust Bulletin* 1982). Other countries, e.g. Japan and to some extent Canada, also prohibit mergers that would lead to a substantial reduction in competition, while the EEC, as a result of the Continental Can judgement, has shown that Article 86 of the Treaty of Rome can be used for the same purpose.

In other countries (e.g. Britain, France, Germany) a more pragmatic approach is adopted with provision for investigation of selected cases. Such an investigation is likely to involve a cost–benefit procedure identifying potential advantages and disadvantages of merger and, if necessary, deciding on which side the balance would reside. In Britain a neutral finding is all that is required for the merger to proceed and only a small proportion of cases that the law would allow to be investigated are in fact referred to the Monopolies and Mergers Commission. In the cost–benefit approach the following issues are most likely to be considered (see Pickering 1980).

Competitive Effects   All mergers may have the effect of reducing competition, though this is most obvious in the case of a horizontal merger. This is of particular concern if the target company is a key competitive force in the market, if there is a prospect of other mergers, or if the effects of the merger would leave a major imbalance in market shares. High entry barriers would tend to reinforce the adverse effects that a merger could have on competition. Vertical and conglomerate mergers may also have adverse effects on competition by squeezing competitors who are also customers, and denying the possibility of cross entry competition if, instead of merging, the acquirer were to enter the market on his own account. Competitiveness may be lost if the merged company was weakened or if, in a conglomerate merger, the relevant subsidary was denied sufficient resources to remain a significant competitive force.

On the other hand, competition may be enhanced by merger if it strengthened the competitive effectiveness of the companies involved. Even if market shares were to increase through the merger, the persistence of effective competition from other sources (other competitors, substitutes or imports), the likelihood of effective countervailing power being exercised, threats of new entry, together with social responsibility on the part of the company concerned, may well be sufficient to avoid any adverse effects on competition.

Technical Economies   It is often claimed that mergers offer the possibility of significant cost savings through economies of scale and size. These may come in the production process through improved planning and rationalisation of production, the opportunity to achieve economies of long runs or to reduce costs by investing in improved manufacturing methods. Other facilities, e.g. in marketing and distribution, may be used more effectively, purchasing power may offer cost savings and overhead expenses may be reduced. There may be advantages of a stronger asset base and more stable earnings.

While these are good theoretical arguments it may, however, be necessary to convince the authorities that the savings claimed are realistic, that they would not take a long time to achieve, and that they could not be obtained in other ways not involving a merger.

Management and Overall Efficiency   There is a general concern that companies should be efficient in terms of their overall factor productivity. This, together with a recognition of the importance of effective management to overall business success, helps to explain why increasing attention is being paid to the managerial aspects of proposed mergers. Does the potential acquirer have a good management record, the resources to achieve a strong performance from its potential acquisition and the ability to manage the enlarged organisation? Are the managerial styles of the two organisations likely to blend? Is there likely to be any long-term threat to managerial morale and efficiency? Could the target company, if not acquired, remain independent and viable?

Employment and Regional Effects   If a merger is believed to strengthen a company and enhance its prospects of gaining orders, the effects on employment will be favourable. If, however, merger is likely to weaken either party or to cause plant closures, especially in areas of high unemployment, the effects of the merger may be deemed undesirable. The prospect of serious conflict with trade unions and employees is also a factor that may discourage clearance of a merger.

Technological Progress   What effects would a merger have on the level and direction of research and development? A merger may allow the target company access to greater technical and financial resources and encourage a greater cross-fertilisation of ideas between two research and development teams. On the other hand, the preservation of competition in R and D together with independent decision taking on lines of research to pursue may point to the desirability of keeping the companies separate.

Balance of Payments Effects   These are likely to be very closely related to the probable effects of the merger on the overall strength and competitiveness of the company. If it benefits from the merger, the balance of payments should gain either from import substitution or improved export performance. Where the acquirer is a foreign-owned company, there may be some risk of balance of payments loss through the outflow of earnings, a reduction in UK production (and hence increased imports) and a loss in export opportunities. Conversely, acquisition by an efficient foreign company may strengthen UK productive performance and offer greater and more secure export opportunities.

It will be apparent that not all factors apply with equal force in all cases. It is, however, clear that the cost–benefit approach to mergers involves consideration of more issues than just the trade-off of monopoly power against cost savings on which the economic analysis of these issues is based. It is also the case that there may be conflicting considerations within each of the separate heads of analysis identified.

Some might argue that this broadening of the factors taken into consideration, especially managerial issues, is hardly consistent with a competition policy. We would not agree. They are certainly relevant to the public interest in changes in industrial structure and performance which is what competition policy is about and they do materially affect the competitiveness of industry which should be a prime concern of such policies.

(d)   The Control of Restrictive Trade Practices

The incentive to restrict competition by agreeing on common prices, to share markets, etc., is probably strong in many areas of business. Companies may well feel that such action would be in the wider public interest as well as their own. Governments or their agencies may even from time to time encourage cartels and other restrictions on trade. But this is the area of competition policy which is subject to the most extensive regulation, both in terms of the number of countries with such controls and the severity of the policy in at least some of those countries. There are strong *per se* prohibitions in the USA, the EEC (though with provision for exceptions) and some other countries, while numerous other countries (e.g. Canada) have various provisions for prohibiting cartels where they lessen competition unduly or have other harmful effects (such as limiting production or sharing markets), or where (as in Britain) they are shown to be contrary to a more widely construed public interest.

The general case against cartels argues that by avoiding competition they cause rigidity, stultify initiatives and protect the inefficient. They are often found to be defensive in character, aiming to prevent new entry competition and to preserve the quiet life. It is often claimed that industries with strong cartels tend to have poor overall economic performance. Prices tend to be high; not only do they give a high margin of profit; often the prices are based not on the costs of the most efficient producers, but on some higher level of costs which is anyway not influenced by competitive pressures for cost minimisation. In contrast to this picture it is claimed that competition is preferable to restrictive agreements since it keeps prices lower, shifts resources towards the more dynamic companies and rewards the efficient.

When the opportunity arises to make a case for exemption from a prohibition of cartels, a number of counter-arguments may be advanced. It may be argued that short-run price competition is disruptive and may especially jeopardise small firms without large financial assets. Such competition may impair the stability and predictability of the business environment; agreements and information exchanges between firms, in contrast, may lead to better investment planning and, through the effect on profits, a higher level of desirable investment. Agreements may help to promote technical progress and greater efficiency by encouraging collaboration in research and development, information exchanges on cost savings and in achieving specialisation and standardisation in production. The competitive process may not always be the best or quickest way of bringing about a necessary restructuring of an industry and of balancing capacity to demand. An industry may need to cartelise to strengthen its bargaining power if faced by customers or suppliers with considerable market power. It may be argued that prices, profits and efficiency are satisfactory and that the benefits are shared with consumers. It may also be helpful to be able to show that no other restrictions are included which are not indispensible to the attainment of the basic objective of the agreement.

While the system of competition law to deal with cartels varies, it is clear that in many countries, whatever the system, the outcome is likely to be that certain identifiable practices, if not *per se* offences anyway, are very likely to be strongly opposed by the competition authorities. This comment appears to apply particularly to the following collective practices: price fixing agreements; collusive tendering (for which there are proposals in the UK to make it a criminal offence, see Cmnd 7512, 1979); market sharing, production restrictions and quota agreements; collective boycotts; collective agreements for reciprocal exclusive dealing or aggregated rebates; agreements to combine buying power; agreements to prohibit parallel imports; and information agreements that have the effect of restricting competition. This list probably covers the key types of restrictive agreement and in many countries it is clear that business is unlikely to make much progress persuading governments or the competition authorities to take a more lenient view of such practices. The penalties for being found guilty of participating in any of these restrictions can be very substantial indeed, as in the USA and the EEC.

There are other forms of restriction, less likely in general to have a substantial impact on competition, that in *some* systems of competition policy may receive more favourable consideration for *ad hoc* exemption. The EEC under Article 85(3) of the Treaty of Rome, for example, has provision for the grant of exemption in particular cases, while the Restrictive Trade Practices Court in Britain may not only grant exemption under s10(1) and s19(1) of the Restrictive Trade Practices Act 1976, but the Secretary of State may exempt agreements of importance to the national economy under s29 and permit the Director-General of Fair Trading under s21 to refrain from proceeding against agreements that he deems are not of sufficient significance to warrant action.

It would appear that generally speaking the types of agreement that are likely to obtain exemption are those which involve only small firms or relate to joint ventures, especially in production and research and development. Specialisation agreements may be exempt in some instances, but not all. In the UK the types of agreement which the Director-General has tended to treat as not of sufficient significance to warrant proceedings are those which, while not restricting independent decision taking by the companies concerned about prices, outputs, etc., and while not causing detriment to consumers, deal with the adoption of standard terms and conditions by trade association members, agreements to participate in codes of practice, joint venture agreements, franchise agreements and the setting of minimum standards.

There are three types of agreement or practice where the general nature of competition policy is less clear cut. Crisis cartels tend to raise major issues both for and against. There is already some tendency to allow these, perhaps partly as a western response to the Japanese use of cartels of varying forms to restructure its own industries. Where they are allowed, they tend to be for short periods of time only and with clearly specified objectives and procedures approved in advance. Export cartels tend to be excluded from some domestic competition policy systems, though cartels affecting exports within the EEC would be covered by the general Article 85 prohibition in the Treaty of Rome. Finally, concerted or parallel action, e.g. in pricing, that does not involve formal or informal agreements and is characteristic of some oligopolistic situations, has long attracted attention from the competition authorities. While in the UK this can be dealt with by a dominant firm inquiry of a 'shared monopoly' situation, it is clear that in general the competition policy authorities have not yet established how they might deal with what they suspect is often an example of tacit collusion and which they would therefore hope to bring within the controls on cartels.

Finally, in this review of policy towards restrictions on competition we should mention resale price maintenance (rpm). The collective enforcement of rpm is generally prohibited, and in many countries the individual enforcement of rpm by a single manufacturer is also subject to control, often involving prohibition. In Britain, for example, rpm has to all intents and purposes been abolished (Pickering 1974), though from time to time the Director-General of Fair Trading needs to remind suppliers of this and to emphasise that unless they can demonstrate loss leading, they may not refuse to supply a trader simply on the grounds that they fear he would cut the prices of their products.

(e) International Aspects

As international trade and, indeed, international production through multinational companies has increased, so international aspects of competition policy have become of potentially greater importance (see Swann 1979, ch. 7, Jacobs 1980a and b). While governments appear to take a much less concerned view about the activities of domestic export cartels, they are more likely to be concerned at the actions of multinational companies that affect their own domestic interests. Less developed countries are also likely to have particular anxieties about the possible existence of restrictive business practices which may affect operations in their own economies.

Clearly foreign subsidiaries operating in a particular country must honour the domestic competition laws of that country. Indeed, there may be much to be said for caution, especially in taking advantage of any dominant position that may exist, since increasing co-operation between governments on such matters may mean that action against a monopoly position in one country may give rise to similar proceedings in other countries too. But what happens when two parent companies in, say, country A, but both with important subsidiaries in country B, wish to merge? The competition authorities in A may be agreeable, but those in B may be opposed to the merger of the subsidiaries on the grounds that competition in B will be materially weakened. What happens where the relationship between parent and foreign subsidiary is such that transfer pricing procedures are used to establish high transfer prices, but low profits in the market in which the subsidiary operates? The problems of effective control by the competition authorities may be very considerable. Furthermore, the existence of international market sharing arrangements between the worldwide subsidiaries of the same parent company may leave a country with a feeling that it is losing out on markets that could be served by the subsidiary based in its own country. Thus the nature of parent-subsidiary relations may leave both countries in some difficulty regarding the achievement of effective control of multinational operations.

The prospective complications become even greater where one country, through its competition policy, seeks to exercise control over the foreign subsidiaries and even affiliates of its own national parent companies, or seeks to extend its sanctions over the foreign parents of subsidiaries operating within its domestic market. This is the problem of extraterritoriality, which has caused some tensions in international relations especially because of the claims to extraterritorial control by the US competition agencies. Some countries have found it necessary to pass domestic legislation to protect their own companies from the effects of US policy.

A further difficult area concerns the operation of international cartels. While the EEC has successfully brought some of these under control where they involved trade between the member states (and included sanctions against parent companies based in countries outside the EEC), the absence of effective international notification provisions makes it difficult to establish just where potential abuses exist that should be brought under some control. Not only are companies from within the private sector concerned in such activities, but state-owned corporations are often involved in major cartels such as OPEC.

In the view of at least some authorities the prospects of a harmonised international competition policy is a long way off. Co-operation between governments is increasing and there is clear evidence that governments are not afraid to enforce their domestic laws against the subsidiaries of foreign-owned multinationals. This is, however, an area where voluntary socially responsible action by companies would be helpful to governments. To this end various attempts have been made to construct guidelines through OECD and UNCTAD or a code of practice through the United Nations Committee on Transnational Corporations to guide business practices.

(f) Implications for Management

It should be apparent from the discussion of competition policy that this is an important, wide-ranging and complex (yet growing) area in which the social environment impinges on business. The monitoring and response to competition policy by business involves many different skills and functional specialisms. While some areas of competition policy are subject to *per se* prohibition, others are not, and the balance varies from country to country. This serves to emphasise that the voluntary exercise of social responsibility is clearly appropriate and is being encouraged by domestic and international codes of practice. Indeed, this may be beneficial to the company if it thereby avoids the costs of discretionary competition policy investigations.

There are considerable risks to companies that contravene competition laws, especially if this involves engaging in prohibited practices. Fines, personal damage suits and class actions, even imprisonment, may ensue. It is therefore extremely important that companies monitor carefully their actions in the light of the laws of the countries in which they are operating. This is clearly not easy when there is so little harmonisation on the details of the laws from country to country. It is also not easy to achieve where so many different functional activities may be involved, perhaps unwittingly in anti-competitive practices through pricing or distribution decisions, and where technical decisions and liaison are concerned. Many of these decisions are probably pushed quite well down the organisation and into operating divisions, thereby making top management surveillance more difficult. Developments in international aspects and especially extraterritoriality issues point to the desirability of clarifying the nature of the relation between parent and overseas subsidiary, especially the question whether the subsidiary is an agent of the parent or is autonomous in the national market in which it is operating.

It is to be hoped that companies will take a positive rather than negative view of sensibly developed and operated competition policy. Not only does it seek to give effect to the legitimate interests of other interest groups in society, it also provides a set of rules and conventions within which market operations can take place. This should be to the general benefit of the operation of markets and hence of the competitive process. They should offer particular benefits to efficient and enterprising companies and may provide a safeguard for those companies that have cause to complain about exploitative or discriminatory conduct by other firms.

It is, however, likely that at some time or other many major companies will have some involvement in some aspects of competition policy enforcement. Such action may be very costly both financially and in management time; they may therefore need to decide whether to fight the case at all or whether to consent to a change in their practices even if they feel they may be defensible. A comparison of the costs of fighting against the discounted benefits of retaining a practice (after allowing for the probability of being successful in the case) will guide the decision on this question. If the company does decide to proceed, it will probably need to call upon a range of specialist advisory skills in the presentation of the case (legal, economic, financial, etc.). The work may need to be carried out very quickly. It will often require an effective market analysis so that the circumstances of the company or industry and the practices concerned can be put in the appropriate context of the relevant market. The evidence presented will need to reflect the actual situation and the best estimate of the likely consequences of an adverse outcome to the case, rather than a theoretical or over-dramatised plea.

As far as possible companies will no doubt wish to demonstrate that the practices or situations they seek to defend are not only in their own interests, but actually benefit the consumer and other relevant groups, that competition is not harmed, the restrictions are reasonable and not abusive, and that the benefits are shared with other interest groups. The discussion of the three main areas of competition policy earlier in this chapter indicates the sort of economic arguments that are likely to be relevant. Companies will do well to bear in mind that much evidence about the effects of a practice or position of dominance relies upon historical data. Thus yesterday's conduct in the market place may well materially influence tomorrow's success with the competition authorities. If a case is lost and perhaps a particular practice prohibited, the selection of an appropriate business response will be a major strategic challenge. If a proposed merger is rejected, other means of growth or problem-solving will need to be sought. If a cartel has to be terminated, new forms of competition may develop and initial uncertainty in an industry may create an opportunity for the enterprising to gain a competitive advantage. The abolition of rpm raised many new issues for suppliers regarding production, distribution, pricing and discount policies (see Pickering 1974).

The administration of competition policy is an area that often involves close contacts between business and government or government agencies. In some systems there is an openness on the part of the competition authorities which business is encouraged to use in seeking informal guidance on whether particular practices may be acceptable. Since the enforcement agencies are also likely to prefer to avoid formal inquiries or court proceedings, they may be willing to negotiate with business to avoid undesirable restrictions or practices but to allow others that are not deemed harmful. It is clearly open to business to decide whether it is prepared to negotiate and respond to suggestions, but where channels of communication are open they may well be worth using. Given that there is such a variety in the system of competition policy in use and evidence of a state of flux in thinking about the desirability of alternative approaches, business may also wish to indicate to government which type of system it prefers. Is the greater certainty and predictability of a *per se* approach with the backing of judicial procedures preferable to the less predictable *ad hoc*, discretionary procedures? Would the uncertainties in this area be reduced and business policy making made easier by a greater emphasis on a structuralist approach?

The area of competition policy is one in which there is a blend between the exercise of voluntary responsibility and the imposition of responsible action through legislation. This therefore involves, as we have seen, an interaction between business and government. Such interaction also occurs in the area of government industrial policy and it is to this that we now turn.

11.6 Industrial Policy

(a) Introduction

Industrial policy is a term used to describe a further variety of ways in which governments may intervene to modify the actions of companies or to assist the fulfilment of a company's plans with the objective of improving industrial performance. The tools of such policy include negotiation and encouragement, financial incentives and controls, prohibitions and public purchasing. In some circumstances the policy instrument may include public ownership. The impact of such policies on business may affect a variety of decisions, particularly pricing, investment and location. Thus industrial policy has consequences for the firm, both in terms of the environment or rules within which the firm makes decisions and in the opportunities presented for profitable production and investment (see Royal Institute of Public Administration 1981).

(b)   Reasons for Government Involvement

There are both economic and political factors influencing the motivation of governments to intervene in aspects of business decision taking. Ultimately the two types of factors tend not to be entirely separable and it must be recognised that in a democracy the chances of a government being returned to power in an election may depend upon the success of its economic policies. There are three key reasons for intervention.

Macroeconomic Management   While, since the Keynesian revolution, governments have to a greater or lesser degree attempted to control the level of aggregate money demand in an economy, they have not been able to influence the supply side of the economy by similar action. If there is an imbalance in the movement of the monetary aggregates (influenced by government) and output and capacity (determined by the corporate sector), severe disequilibrium may result with adverse effects on inflation rates, employment levels and the balance of payments, etc. Thus governments may seek ways of encouraging the corporate sector to keep their investment and output decisions in line with overall macroeconomic objectives. Options available here may include subsidies, such as investment incentives, indicative planning and public ownership.

The incentives for such governmental intervention are strong when it is recognised that within the private sector of the economy there are a relatively small number of companies which account for a high proportion of total output, exports and investment. This concentration of wealth creating potential is also reflected in the importance attached to relatively few companies in the main sectors of the economy such as manufacturing, financial services, energy, retailing, transport and communications. Government's own success may therefore depend closely upon the responses of relatively few organisations. This provides a strong incentive for governments to seek a close relationship with and understanding of those companies. This may be achieved through the establishment of tripartite organisations (involving Government, business and unions), special inquiries in which the particular problems of a sector are discussed or through indicative planning.

Market Failure In many areas of the economy markets cannot be assumed to be working perfectly. Not only does this arise from the growth of monopoly and cartels which we considered earlier in this chapter, it is also a consequence of the attempt by firms to 'plan' their markets, the existence of externalities and the provision of public goods (see Bator 1958 for a formal analysis). In the Galbraithian analysis (Galbraith 1967) modern corporations are seen as actively attempting to plan and co-ordinate their activities in order to minimise their exposure to market forces. In this system the initiative in deciding what is to be produced comes not from the consumer, but from the large producing organisations reaching forward to control the markets they are presumed to serve and attempting to mould consumer demand to the needs of the company.

Externalities arise in the process of production or consumption and impose costs and/or benefits on third parties. These effects are not reflected in market prices or outputs. Since business is often held to be the cause of certain externalities such as pollution, noise, etc., governments will intervene to encourage business to adjust output or production methods to reduce social costs or provide social benefits. This may be achieved by taxing products with undesirable effects, subsidising the production of those offering social benefits or through legislative controls.

Public goods tend to have one or both of two key economic characteristics—non-rivalry in supply (where the supply of a product or service to an additional customer does not impose any additional cost until full capacity utilisation is reached) and non-excludability (where one individual's consumption does not reduce the amount available to another and where it is difficult to exclude any individual from consumption). These features help to explain why such facilities as bridges, rail transport, defence and public health are provided by government or with the aid of public subsidy.

Politics and Bureaucracy Politicians require policies that are sufficiently popular with voters that they offer good prospects of electoral success. If voters are concerned with economic issues, and as more areas of life become politicised, so the political influence in economic decision taking increases (Downs 1957). Although public administrators are the servants of politicians, they have considerable scope to influence the nature of government policy and its implementation. It is the civil servants who meet and negotiate with their opposite numbers in firms and so listen to the business viewpoint on policy requirements. Sections of ministries become the sponsoring agencies for particular industries. The interchange of personnel between business and government has increased in many countries. In addition, the objective of public servants may well be to maximise the size of the budget under their own control irrespective of the views of the government of the day (Jackson 1982). For all these reasons it is likely that there will be strong political and administrative pressures for a significant degree of interventionism in the approach to industrial policy.

(c) Business Demands of Governments

It should not necessarily be assumed that governments always impose industrial policy upon an unwilling business community. Business also recognises the benefits that government action can offer to it either generally or to specific companies. Thus business has also fostered its relationship with government, both at the level of national bodies, such as the Confederation of British Industry, and trade associations, to represent business interests and in the establishment of government relations departments in the major companies (Grant 1982). Such organisations will have a number of important contributions to make. They will represent business views about actual and proposed policies to government. (The availability of a central point of contact with an industry or firm will be welcomed by ministers and civil servants.) They will endeavour to influence thinking within government and will lobby for other policy commitments that will benefit business. In addition they will provide a means by which information can be collected and interpreted and policy developments anticipated that will be beneficial to the industries and firms concerned, especially in formulating corporate strategy.

In its approach to government, business will have a number of objectives and policy aspirations.

Financial Assistance   Governments may be encouraged to provide funds to business. This may be in the form of subsidies or grants or loans. The effects of such help may be to lower costs incurred by business and hence to raise profits and/or increase competitiveness relative to others (e.g. foreign suppliers) who are not helped in this way. The effect of such action may also be to raise prospective rates of return in order to make projects economically viable which, without subsidy, would not be undertaken. Companies may argue that government should provide such assistance as a compensation to them for locating in areas of high unemployment etc. which would not have been their preferred choice or as a means of matching subsidies given to other competitors. The provision of grants or loans may also be sought as a means of achieving funding that would not otherwise have been available through commercial financial markets.

Public Expenditure Governments, national and local, tend to be important customers for the output of many firms. Governments are also providers of funds for research and development in a number of key industries. Companies involved in those industries will undoubtedly seek to encourage government to maintain its level of demand in order to help sustain employment, turnover and profitability. In a number of countries governments have also been prepared to spend public money on rescuing companies that have run into serious financial difficulties and are threatened with bankruptcy. In such cases management, employees, and shareholders of the company concerned, and possibly other customers and suppliers, will hope that the government will decide that the company is of such national importance that a rescue is justified on cost–benefit criteria.

Legislative Action The law-making abilities of government may represent a significant influence on the overall social environment within which business has to operate. We have already noted the implications of competition and consumer protection policies in this respect. The nature of fiscal policy is also important, since changes in rates of corporation tax and levels of allowances directly affect profitability. Aspects of fiscal policy influence the optimal manner of financing new investments and the overall nature and complexity of laws may well affect the administrative costs incurred by firms in monitoring and complying with them. Other areas of legislation and related measures can offer protection to firms against unwelcome or unfair competition. This may be reflected in health and safety legislation (including product standards), environmental controls, tariffs and related import controls. This too may therefore affect business competitiveness and profitability.

(d) Policy Instruments

In advancing its own objectives and responding to business demands, governments have a number of available options. They may use macro-economic policies, fiscal policy (see Chapter 10) or public ownership (see Chapter 13). The areas of industrial policy as such are more narrow in their approach, but still offer a variety of alternatives. For simplicity we shall group them under two main heads: subsidies and planning.

(i) *Subsidies* Government subsidies to business come in a number of different forms (for an extensive discussion of this topic, see Whiting (ed.) 1976). There may be tax advantages such as favourable depreciation allowances or tax holidays. They may come in ways that would reduce factor costs in production through subsidies to employment and training or transport or energy costs, in the form of export subsidies, or through public expenditure to increase the quality of the economic infrastructure in which firms can operate. Cheap finance may be offered. The guarantee of orders from the public sector at specified prices, perhaps in excess of market prices, may also be seen as a form of subsidy. There may be direct grants for specific purposes, such as investment or research and development. Subsidies may be generally available or only for specific firms or industries or those operating in particular areas of a country. The subsidies may be made available on a non-discretionary basis to all companies that fall within predetermined categories or they may only be available on a discretionary basis to companies that satisfy further criteria that indicate that the prospective benefits of the subsidy would exceed the costs.

Governments may also have a variety of reasons for offering subsidies. The creation or protection of employment, investment or research and development is often advanced as a reason. Increasing competition, both international and inter-regional, to encourage the location of 'footloose' industries in one place rather than another often takes the form of competition on subsidies. Governments may use subsidies to 'correct' instances of market failure or to encourage the provision of public goods. Some industries may be the recipients of subsidies where reasons of national security, prestige or the importance of involvement in high technology activities points to the desirability of working to ensure the survival of the industry or firm concerned. Subsidies may be used to help firms offset high start-up or launch costs, or to encourage an industry to undertake necessary rationalisation. In all cases governments are likely to argue that the subsidy policy is necessary to attain agreed social objectives and that the benefits that will be obtained exceed the costs of the subsidy. However, it should be noted that there are some areas where the scope for governments to pursue subsidy policies is limited by international agreements through, for example, the General Agreement on Tariffs and Trade and through the EEC's Treaty of Rome.

If subsidies are to have their desired effect, they will do so by influencing firm decision processes in such a way that their actions are moved nearer to the social optimum. They have this effect by changing relative prices and so making some actions relatively cheaper than others (e.g. employing labour rather than capital, or building a new plant in one region rather than another). They also have the effect of lowering the total costs of an activity and so increasing the total profitable scale of potential economic activity. These are the theoretical predictions. The reality is more difficult to assess and will depend upon the form of subsidy offered and the circumstances and decision procedures of the firms affected. Some subsidies may be treated by the firm as a bonus or windfall that does not influence any specific business decision. In other cases a subsidy will have a direct influence on actual firm decisions taken at the margin. The more specific and discretionary the subsidies offered, the more likely it is that they will influence the marginal decision. Even so, as Mellis and Richardson point out (in Whiting (ed.) 1976), the particular effects of a subsidy on a company may also depend upon the form of investment appraisal undertaken and especially whether discounting procedures are adopted or not.

One area in which government policy is likely to impinge very much on some companies concerns the operation of regional policy and its effect on firms' location decisions. The desire of government to achieve as far as possible a balanced regional distribution of economic activity can be well understood and this can benefit companies by avoiding problems of congestion and labour shortage in some areas. Various forms of 'carrots' (in the form of subsidies and other incentives) have been offered, and 'sticks' have sometimes also been used in the form of planning controls (refusing permission to build in areas of high existing employment) or high taxes (a negative subsidy) for doing so.

Where choice of option is left with the company whether to respond to the subsidy and move to the government's preferred area or to remain in the area not preferred by government, decision taking will need to consider alternative net effects on profits of operating in either of the two locations (on this see Walker and Krist 1980). To move to a new location will involve some initial disruption costs plus, presumably, some on-going net increase in operating costs, including perhaps a lower level of efficiency, through additional communications costs with other parts of the organisation, suppliers and customers, etc. (although some costs, e.g. wage rates and local rates, may be lower in areas of higher unemployment). To justify a move, the value of the subsidy offered should be at least sufficient to offset the net increase in costs incurred as a result. In both cases the time stream of subsidy and costs will need to be projected and discounted back to a present value. There do seem to be cases, such as that of the motor industry, where a move to areas of high unemployment in response to government pressures or incentives has been less than successful so this is a matter that requires careful consideration by companies and governments.

Governments are also major purchasers of the outputs of a number of industries. This too offers scope for help to be given in important cases and to the extent that governments may not always buy from the cheapest available source, an element of subsidy is implied. This may occur particularly where governments are anxious to provide orders for domestic suppliers. This may be justified on the grounds of security or the need to have a national representation in an industry of particular economic significance, or the desirability of supporting an infant industry. It may be argued that even if the initial cost is higher, the whole life cost of the product from a domestic source is lower when the costs of spares and servicing are also taken into account. Governments may also be willing purchasers of the early output of a new product in order to encourage a rapid build-up of output and to encourage other purchasers.

In general terms it is likely that firms that are favoured with government orders stand to benefit. There are certain caveats that should be borne in mind. It is dangerous to allow the existence of a guaranteed order, perhaps at favourable prices, to cause a decline in efficiency or in a general market orientation. Indeed, the heavy hand of public purchasing and specification may weaken the firm's ability to make sales to other customers. If excess profits are made from supplying government, these may have to be repaid. Undue tying-up of customer–supplier relations may encourage similar reactions in other countries which restrict access to export markets. Furthermore, there is always the possibility that the existence of preferential purchasing arrangements may work to the disadvantage not only of some foreign suppliers, but also of some domestic suppliers if they are not on lists of approved tenderers or are otherwise unable to benefit from public purchasing. On balance, then, preferential public purchasing is likely to be attractive to favoured suppliers, but there are caveats that should also be taken into account.

Company rescues also involve an element of subsidy since either loans are provided or an equity stake is taken in circumstances and on terms that commerical financial markets would not support. If faced with the prospect of collapse of a major company, governments may argue that there are wider or longer-term economic considerations that point to the need for the rescue. This may well be explained in terms of a cost–benefit analysis in which it is argued that the costs of the subsidy are outweighed by the benefits obtained, especially when it is recognised that the costs to the Exchequer of the collapse of a major firm can be significant in terms of additional social security payments, export earnings foregone, etc. It was on these grounds that the rescue of Chrysler was justified (see Expenditure Committee 1975/76). Such rescues are of course likely to be strongly welcomed by management and employees of the companies concerned and their suppliers. Such action, which by definition will be selective, is less likely to be welcomed by competitors, especially if it preserves in existence capacity that is in excess of that required to meet efficiently the most likely level of demand. In wider economic terms such a rescue may constitute a misallocation of resources. A rescue of a company that, with some short-term assistance, can prove inherently viable and make a needed contribution to the output of the industry is more to be encouraged than one that simply props up a company that does not have favourable future economic prospects.

(*ii*) *Planning* The second broad area of industrial policy interaction between government and business emphasises a close interaction between the two in order to identify and implement desirable action to raise industrial performance. The term 'planning' is used as a summary description, but it involves a wider range of activities than formal planning alone.

In the UK and some other countries, especially France and Japan, a tripartite relationship has developed between business, government and the trade unions. In Britain this is reflected in the existence of the National Economic Development Council and the associated economic development committees and sector working parties. They are seen as a useful forum in which information can be exchanged and suggestions for policy development discussed. While other attempts at more formal planning, such as the proposal for government to reach planning agreements with major companies, have not come to fruition, the more informal, indicative approach to planning has continued for more than twenty years.

There is a considerable interaction between government and business in the international arena. Governments will hope that overseas operations by major domestic companies are of general economic benefit to the home country. In some situations governments may bring pressure on companies to adopt policies which reflect the particular political judgements or policies of their government. Thus refusal to supply sensitive products to a hostile country may be required. Companies may be strongly encouraged by governments to accept particular contracts for wider political or economic considerations, such as the access this allows to other exports. Governments may encourage domestic companies to transfer and license technology or to put together financial packages to help the development process in Third World countries.

Companies also have expectations of what government can do to help them in international markets. Trade missions and international trade fairs may be used for this purpose. Companies will look for financial assistance, e.g. through export credits and possibly other forms of government financial help to the customer country to encourage it to buy from one source rather than another. Indeed, there has been considerable competition between governments to offer the most attractive financial packages to enable their companies to win attractive export orders. Government aid to other countries may be tied in such a way that the value of the aid has to be spent with the domestic producers of the aid-giving country. Government protests may help to protect a firm's foreign assets from nationalisation or seizure by local interests.

Thus both government and business have some mutual interests and interdependencies in the international sphere. This is an area where government help can be very useful to companies and while we have placed it among those activities that are not primarily based upon subsidies, it should be recognised that some element of subsidisation may well be involved. While on the basis of a partial equilibrium analysis of the effects on one country such help may be valuable, the growth of international competition between governments to help their domestic companies to win overseas orders, perhaps involving considerable subsidisation and hence interference with market processes, may be less attractive in a general equilibrium context.

Governments and their agencies have tended to interest themselves in questions of the structure and performance of individual industries. Numerous reports of committees of inquiry on the problems of particular industries exist (e.g. Cmnd 2937, 1966). Often it seems the conclusions are that there are too many firms and too much productive capacity in the industry so mergers are desirable and there is a need to encourage re-equipping of the industry in order to raise productivity. The execution of such schemes is not necessarily easy and the outcome is not always what was expected. Some would argue that it is wiser to leave such developments to the effects of the competitive process rather than to intervene administratively, but others claim that direct encouragement to restructure is quicker and therefore more attractive. In some cases the incentive to act is increased by the offer of subsidies or the possibility of tariff protection. There seem to be cycles in economic opinion about the desirability of industrial concentration and examples exist of attempts from time to time to encourage a more extensive restructuring of sectors of industry. The work of the Industrial Reorganisation Corporation in Britain in the late 1960s was a good example of this (see Hague and Wilkinson 1983).

Besides an interest in industrial structure, governments also have tended to take an interest in the possibility of adopting a more entrepreneurial role in industry. An example of such activity is to be found in the work of IRI in Italy (see Holland 1972), but there are similarities in the approach of the National Enterprise Board (NEB), now the British Technology Group, in Britain (see Grant 1982, ch. 5). The key feature of these bodies is that they provide funding to business on an equity (rather than loan) basis and so exercise a role equivalent to that of a merchant bank. They are much closer to the actual management of the business and monitor its performance in terms of rates of return achieved. While some such investments are in companies that needed to be rescued, there are other examples of investments in companies and activities that were judged to deserve encouragement on the grounds that private sector financial markets would not provide funds. This applies particularly in the area of high technology activities, where shorter payback periods required in the private sector discouraged investment whereas the NEB was prepared to take a longer-term view which may well prove beneficial to the development of the economy overall.

Companies may argue that such use of public money in the private sector is unnecessary (since if the project was worthwhile, private funds would be forthcoming) and undesirable (since it raises the spectre of backdoor nationalisation and there are doubts whether the state can play an entrepreneurial role). In practice, however, many companies have seen joint ventures with the NEB as a way of setting up new enterprises and supporting underfunded activities. The evidence of returns to full private ownership of healthy companies in which the NEB had previously held a significant stake also suggests that this can be a worthwhile form of government—business interaction.

The degree and form of government involvement through industrial policy will vary from time to time according to economic needs and political judgements. It is likely that there will always be some of these policy instruments in use. Companies will no doubt therefore wish to respond in an appropriate manner to the forms of assistance available to them. Subsidies and loans should be carefully appraised for their effects on optimal business decisions in the light of corporate objectives. Where competing sources are offering incentives, the choice should be made in the context of a wide-ranging comparison of the overall, long-term, economic, and other effects of the alternatives.

This does not mean that companies would necessarily wish to encourage the maximisation of levels of government intervention. This may be considered undesirable because of the effects on the level of bureaucratic involvement and because of the diversion of resources away from the private sector in the first instance. In addition, while general subsidies may be less attractive to government because their effects are less predictable and less related to the specific objectives of the policy, non-recipients of selective or discretionary help may feel that they are at a marked disadvantage compared with those that are beneficiaries. Attention to the optimum forms of industrial policy is therefore in the interest of both business and government.

References

Bator, F. M. (1958) 'The anatomy of market failure', *Quarterly Journal of Economics*, pp. 351–379.

Beesley, M. E. and Evans, T. (1978) *Corporate Social Responsibility*, Croom Helm.

Boulding, K. (1970) *Economics as a Science*, McGraw-Hill.

Bowie, N. (1982) *Business Ethics*, Prentice-Hall.

Downs, A. (1957) *An Economic Theory of Democracy*, Harper and Row.

Elliott, C. K. (1966) 'Ethical issues in the dynamics of economic development', in D. L. Munby (ed.), *Economic Growth in World Perspective*, Association Press and SCM Press.

Foxall, G. (1978) 'Towards a balanced view of consumerism', *European Journal of Marketing*, 12, pp. 264–274.

Galbraith, J. K. (1967) *The New Industrial State*, Hamish Hamilton.

Goyder, G. (1961) *The Responsible Company*, Basil Blackwell.

Goyder, G. (1976) *The Responsible Worker*, Hutchinson.

Grant, W. (1982) *The Political Economy of Industrial Policy*, Butterworth.

Greyser, S. A. and Diamond, S. L. (1974) 'Business is adapting to consumerism', *Harvard Business Review*, September/October, pp. 38–60.

Hague, D. C. and Wilkinson, G. (1983) *The IRC—An Experiment in Industrial Intervention*, George Allen and Unwin.

Hay, R. and Grant, E. (1974) 'Social responsibilities of business managers', *Academy of Management Journal*, Vol. 17, pp. 135–143.

Holland, S. (ed.) (1972) *The State as Entrepreneur*, Weidenfeld and Nicolson.

Howe, M. (1983) 'The Competition Act: early case law', *European Competition Law Review*, 3, pp. 331–345.

Jackson, P. (1982) *The Political Economy of Bureaucracy*, Philip Allan.

Jacobs, D. M. (1980a) 'Problems arising from extraterritorial application of competition laws', *European Competition Law Review*, 1, pp. 199–212.

Jacobs, D. M. (1980b) 'Control of restrictive practices in international trade', *European Competition Law Review*, 1, pp. 63–79.

Korah, V. L. (1978) *EEC Competition Law and Practice*, ESC Publishing, Elek.

Korah, V. L. (1980) 'Concept of a dominant position within the meaning of Article 86', *Common Market Law Review*, 17, pp. 395–414.

Kotler, P. (1972) 'What consumerism means for marketers', *Harvard Business Review*, 50, pp. 48–57.

Linowes, D. F. (1975) 'Let's get on with the Social Audit', in R. L. Heilbroner and P. London (eds), *Corporate Social Policy*, Addison Wesley.

Luthans, F., Hodgetts, R. M. and Thompson, H. R. (1980) *Social Issues in Business*, Collier Macmillan.

McAdam, T. W., (1975) 'How to put social responsibility into action', in R. L. Heilbroner and P. London (eds), *Corporate Social Policy*, Addison Wesley.

McElroy, B. F. and Aaker, D. A. (1979) 'Unit pricing six years after introduction', *Journal of Retailing*, 55, no. 3, pp. 44–57.

McKie, J. W. (ed.) (1974) *Social Responsibility and the Business Predicament*, Brookings.

Matthews, R. C. O. (1981) 'Morality, competition and efficiency', *The Manchester School*, pp. 289–309.

Medawar, C. (1978) *The Social Audit Consumer Handbook*, Macmillan.

Mitchell, J. (ed.) (1978) *Marketing and the Consumer Movement*, McGraw-Hill.

Morgan, E. (1977) 'Social responsibility and private enterprise in the UK', *National Westminster Bank Review*, May.

Morris, D. (ed.) (1980) *Economics of Consumer Protection*, Heinemann.

Neale, A. D. and Goyder, D. G. (1981) *The Anti-Trust Laws of the USA*, Cambridge University Press.

Padberg, D. I. (1977) 'Non-use benefits of mandatory consumer information programs', *Journal of Consumer Policy*, 1, pp. 5–14.

Pickering, J. F. (1971) 'The Prices and Incomes Board and private sector prices', *Economic Journal*, 81, pp. 225–241.

Pickering, J. F. (1974) 'The abolition of resale price maintenance in Great Britain', *Oxford Economic Papers*, 26, pp. 120–146.

Pickering, J. F. (1979a) 'The Price Commission and the investigation of proposed price increases', *European Journal of Marketing*, 13, pp. 228–246.

Pickering, J. F. (1979b) 'Recommended prices, the consumer's economic interest and public policy in Britain', *Journal of Consumer Policy*, 2, pp. 97–109.

Pickering, J. F. (1980) 'The implementation of British competition policy on mergers', *European Competition Law Review*, 1, pp. 177–198.

Pickering, J. F. (1983) 'The economics of anti-competitive practices', *European Competition Law Review*, 3, pp. 253–274.

Pickering, J. F. and Cousins, D. C. (1982) 'The benefits and costs of voluntary codes of practice', *European Journal of Marketing*, 16, pp. 31–45.

Pickering, J. F. and Cousins, D. C. (1983) 'Corporate reactions to voluntary codes of practice: results of a survey', *Journal of Consumer Policy*, 6, pp. 37–54.

Robertson, A. (1978) *Strategic Marketing*, Associated Business Programmes.

Smith, P. and Swann, D. (1979) *Protecting the Consumer*, Martin Robertson.

Swann, D. (1979) *Competition and Consumer Protection*, Penguin Books.

Walker, G. and Krist, H. (1980) *Regional Incentives and the Investment Decision of the Firm*, University of Strathclyde Studies in Public Policy, No. 55.

Whiting, A. (ed.) (1976) *The Economics of Industrial Subsidies*, HMSO.

Zanisek, T. J. (1979) 'Corporate social responsibility in a conceptualisation based on organisational literature', *Academy of Management Review*, Vol. 4, pp. 359–368.

Anti-Trust Bulletin (1982) Symposium on merger guidelines.

Christian Association of Business Executives (1974) *A Code of Business Ethics.*

Cmnd 2937 (1966) *Shipbuilding Inquiry Committee*, Geddes Committee, HMSO.

Cmnd 7512 (1979) *A Review of Restrictive Trade Practices Policy*, HMSO.

Commission of the European Communities (*passim*) *Annual Reports on Competition Policy.*

Expenditure Committee (1975/76) *Public Expenditure on Chrysler UK*, HCP596, HMSO.

Monopolies and Mergers Commission (1981) *Bicycles*, HCP67, HMSO.

Office of Fair Trading (*passim*) *Annual Report of the Director General of Fair Trading*, HMSO.

Organisation for Economic Co-operation and Development (*passim*) *Annual Reports on Competition Policy in OECD Member Countries.*

Organisation for Economic Co-operation and Development (1978) *Comparative Summary of Legislations on Restrictive Business Practices.*

Royal Institute of Public Administration (1981) *Allies or Adversaries.*

12
Managing Multinational Organisations

Peter J. Buckley

12.1 Introduction

The simplest definition of a multinational firm is one which owns outputs of goods or services in more than one country. Such a firm adds value by producing in more than one national economy. The addition of value may involve increasing the quantity of goods, enhancing their quality, or improving their distribution, both spatial and temporal. Such a firm therefore faces decisions on at least some elements of the 'marketing mix'—price, product, promotion and distribution.

Often this all-embracing definition of the multinational firm is felt to be inappropriate to the task at hand. Usually this is in the context of describing the institutional power of the 'world's largest firms'. In such situations definitions are employed which emphasise the scope of such firms; for instance, any company having x per cent foreign content of either sales, earnings, assets or employment is considered a multinational firm (Aharoni 1971).

Multinational firms most usually control assets abroad through the medium of foreign direct investment. The act of foreign direct investment involves bringing income-generating assets under the control of a foreign corporation through purchase or through the creation of new assets. There are other methods of controlling foreign assets such as control through key inputs—normally technology—through management or other key workers (in, for instance, management contracts), or through joint ownership even if exercised by a minority stake. The element of control distinguishes direct foreign investment from portfolio foreign investment, which is usually carried out by individuals, not firms.

Several types of foreign direct investment can be distinguished. Horizontal direct investment occurs when the firm carries out the same stage of production abroad as in the parent country. The assembly of cars by

Volkswagen in Brazil as well as in the Federal Republic of Germany is an example. Vertical foreign direct investment occurs where the firm adds a stage in the production process. Thus Dunlop's purchase of a rubber plantation would be vertical direct foreign investment. Such vertical extension of the firm's operations can be backwards, towards raw materials, or forwards towards markets. Immediately we can see that there exists a wide variety of motives for the multinational expansion of the firm, including economies of scale, control of raw material supplies and control of markets. Finally, conglomerate diversification internationally occurs where the firm purchases or creates activities abroad which are unrelated to its domestic operations, e.g. when a metals producer buys a hotel chain abroad.

The control of assets and operations abroad, often on a vast scale, poses a number of problems in the economic management of the multinational firm.

12.2   The Internationalisation of the Firm

(a)   The Motives

Three main classes of motives for foreign direct investment can be identified: (1) market oriented investments; (2) cost reducing investment; and (3) vertical foreign investment aimed at reducing the cost of raw materials or other key inputs. Very rarely is a foreign investment decision taken for a sole overriding purpose. More often the motive is mixed, often even unclear.

There are a number of secondary or supporting motives which may come into the calculation. These can include (1) the investment climate of the host country (its tax regime, political stability, cultural closeness to the investor, provision of infrastructure); (2) the firm's response to an external approach, perhaps by the host government, the firm's local agent or distributor, or from a customer, supplier or even a competitor; and (3) factors related to the source country, such as difficulties at home, underemployed resources, attempts to diversify risk, insurance against problems at home ('multiple sourcing'), the difficulties of supplying the market by other means, or as a response to a foreign investment by a competitor in the firm's home market.

The foreign investment decision is rarely taken for a single reason and rarely is it taken at a single moment of time. Rather it is the result of cumulative pressures and opportunities impinging on the firm. The process of foreign investment is akin to the building of a commitment in the firm.

(b)   The Process of Internationalisation

The first foreign investment decision will be very different from subsequent investments. Initially a national firm is likely to be very risk averse as regards foreign involvement which is often seen as a leap into the unknown. Consequently, inexperienced foreign investors often require a strong simulus even to begin to consider internationalisation (Aharoni 1966). Such stimuli can be internal to the firm, such as an executive with an interest in foreign expansion, or external, such as an opportunity presented by the firm's agent for instance. Such a stimulus will usually initiate a search for information, both general indicators on the host country and then on-the-spot investigation. Careful consideration is then made by key decision makers before the decision to go ahead (or not) is made. In observing this management process, it may never be obvious at what point 'the investment decision' took place. Far too frequently among inexperienced investors far too little assessment and investigation takes place, often leading to disastrous outcomes (Newbould *et al.* 1978). One particular error is often the failure to specify clear performance targets for the new subsidiary.

(c)   The Route

It is unusual for a firm to go immediately to a foreign direct investment in a country without passing through a number of intermediate stages as illustrated by Figure 12.1. From home activities only, such intermediate stages may be direct exporting, foreign agency representation and a foreign sales subsidiary before embarking on a full production subsidiary. It has been found that there is a direct positive correlation between the number of stages in the route and the ultimate success of the foreign subsidiary (Newbould *et al.* 1978). This is because of the learning effects permitted at each stage of the longer route and because the intermediate stages allow the firm to withdraw before too much damage occurs. The full route (5 in the diagram) allows learning on the requirements of the foreign market in the exporting phase, learning on methods of doing business in the host country and dealing with local people directly at the agency stage, learning on laws, taxes, controlling operations directly, selling, stockholding and promotion at the sales subsidiary stage; all in advance of having to cope with production problems abroad at the final stage. Foreign licensing or some other contractual arrangement may of course also be included as replacements or supplements for some of the above intermediate stages.

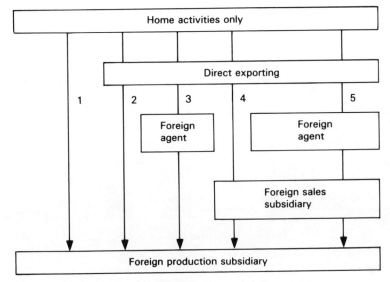

Source: Reproduced from Newbould *et al.* (1978) p. 45.

Figure 12.1   Routes to a Foreign Production Subsidiary

(d)   The Timing of the Move Abroad

The timing of a firm's move abroad is a very difficult management decision because it involves so much uncertainty and it is also very difficult to model adequately. The Product Cycle approach to foreign direct investment suggests that the switch to foreign investment should occur according to the following cost-based formulation (Vernon 1966):

Invest abroad when $MPC_x + TC > ACP_A$

where MPC_x is marginal cost of production for export
    TC is transport cost
    ACP_A is average cost of production abroad.

The argument here is that marginal costings are appropriate for exports because domestic production would be undertaken anyway whilst the foreign unit must bear the full average costs of production.

A fuller model of the switch to foreign investment is given by Buckley and Casson (1981). Essentially two types of cost, fixed and variable, attach to the different forms of foreign market servicing—licensing, exporting and foreign direct investment. As the market grows the variable cost declines and so the switch occurs from low fixed to low variable cost modes, typically from exporting to direct investment (see Figure 12.2). This model is complicated when set-up costs are also included. Key variables in the

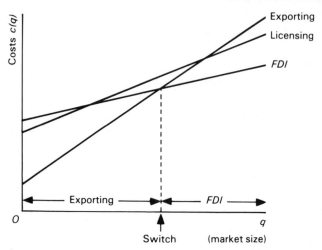

Source: Reproduced from Buckley and Casson (1981) p. 80.
Note: In this example, licensing is never the preferred alternative.

Figure 12.2   The Timing of a Foreign Direct Investment

timing of the move abroad are therefore the costs of servicing the foreign market, demand conditions in that market and host market growth.

A major complicating factor in the move abroad is the action of competitors. This oligopolistic reaction among large firms has been analysed as a major influence on foreign direct investment (Knickerbocker 1973). Amongst the largest multinational firms Knickerbocker found that entry into particular host country markets was grouped in time around a three year peak. The important influences on this were: (1) industry structure—the more concentrated the industry, the more leader-follower behaviour occurred; (2) industry stability—rivalistic investment behaviour was directly connected with the break-up of industry stability under pressure from new entrants; and (3) the smaller the number of alternatives open to the firm, the more likely they were to engage in oligopolistic reaction. Interestingly, low technology firms are defensively more active than high technology ones.

12.3   Market Servicing Policies

The market servicing policies of multinational firms are the set of decisions about which production units should service which markets and what methods or channels shall link production to markets. We can thus speak of a market servicing network. There are three main modes of market servicing: exporting, licensing (and other market contractual arrangements) and foreign direct investment.

(a) Influences on the Pattern of Market Servicing

The market servicing network of a particular firm will be subject to a number of important influences. First, the size of firm is important. The larger the firm is, the more likely it is to service the market via investments into markets linked by flows of internal exports of intermediate goods, semi-finished products and technology and information flows. An interesting tension is important here between plant level economies of scale, which dictate concentration of production at one point (plus worldwide exporting), and firm level economies of scale (including the internalisation of research results), which dictate foreign investment (Buckley and Casson 1976). Second, the industry of operation will be important. Influences arising from the nature of the product (transportability, perishability) influence location, and so will the nature of integration in the industry.

Third, the nationality of the firm in question influences market servicing (Buckley and Pearce 1979, 1981). Japanese firms, for instance, are low on multinationality of production ratios (foreign production divided by world-wide sales), preferring to concentrate production in Japan and export worldwide. Multinationals from small countries such as Switzerland, Belgium and Holland are very high on this ratio. Obviously one major influence on this pattern is home market size, but cultural influences too are relevant because cultural closeness is a major cost-reducing factor for foreign investment.

A set of factors involving the firm's response to external markets will also determine the pattern of foreign market servicing. In many industries a 'presence factor' occurs. The act of investing in a country will increase the demand which the investor faces through increased local knowledge of its products, improved contacts and an enhanced ability to influence local demand. Further, the act of investment enables the firm to 'piggy back' products other than the ones it actually manufactures in the host country. Thus a production subsidiary for a particular product can be used to sell the rest of a firm's range in the country. Where particular products require extensive after sales activities or where control of the distribution network is vital, then investment will be favoured over other modes of doing business abroad. It should be noted also that it is often a mistake to equate market with country. A country may well be made up of more than one effective market (for instance, most European multinational firms investing in the USA have at least one base on the East Coast and one on the West) or, less usually, a market may encompass more than one country.

Fifth, government policies may influence the pattern of market servicing. Regrettably, these will often pull in different directions. A source country government will usually wish to encourage firms of its nationality to export rather than have a presence in foreign markets in order to improve its balance of payments and to maintain or increase home employment. Host governments will, however, wish to reduce their imports and will attempt to encourage inward investment or licensing to encourage inflows of technology and increase employment. Multinationals, as so often, are therefore subject to contrary pressures from the environment.

Sixth, the goals of the individual firm may affect market servicing policy through a desire for diversification, the need to avoid a decline in the home market, as a reaction to competitors, or a desire for growth for its own sake. These non-conventional goals tend to favour investment rather than the other forms. Seventh, the influence of least cost location will encourage sourcing policies to change as input and marketing costs vary. Finally, the experience of the firm is an important determinant. First time and naive foreign investors will be more risk averse in foreign investment policies than experienced multinationals, for whom the costs of doing business abroad are far smaller.

The market servicing network and its obverse—the sourcing network for inputs—represent at any moment in time a snapshot of a dynamic management process. Changes in the internal management and external environment will cause the firm to adapt its policies. Involvement with any particular market is not fixed but is a process of incremental change. Moreover, the strategy of a firm in market servicing cannot be deterministic but must be responsive to external changes. The essence of a market servicing strategy is responsiveness.

(b) Exporting in a Firm's Foreign Market Servicing

As Figure 12.1 showed, exporting is often the primary means of penetrating a foreign market. It is regarded as a cheap and low risk method of foreign selling, but the fixed costs of a low volume of export sales can be prohibitive despite the fact that there are tax advantages to be gained in many countries. The main problems of exporting are the costs of product adaptation and the difficulties caused by barriers to trade.

Research on exporting (ITI Research 1975, Khan 1978, Buckley 1982) suggests several elements are important in export success: (1) the need for export sales specialists within the firm; (2) the need to concentrate on the firm's most important foreign markets rather than amass haphazard unco-ordinated foreign sales; and (3) the importance of selection, training and control of foreign intermediaries and effecting feedback from the foreign market. Proper representation in the foreign market is vital, and the need to protect export markets by defensive investment in sales or production subsidiaries leads to a deepening involvement and further internationalisation.

(c)   Licensing and Other Contractual Arrangements Abroad

On the face of it, foreign licensing appears to represent an ideal situation, combining the technological and possibly management skills of the multi-national firm with the local knowledge of the host country partner. The relatively small use of licensing, which represents only six per cent of the UK's total foreign sales (Buckley and Davies 1981), is a result of the management difficulties of effecting the firm to firm transfer of technology and skills which impose heavy costs, as compared to the internalisation of such resources in the multinational firm's subsidiaries (Buckley and Casson 1976). The first problem concerns the identifiability of the advantage to be transferred, which is related to the degree of embodiment of the technology. If the technology is embodied in a machine or brand name then transfer is easy. Often, however, the skills of multinational firms are diffuse and involve heavy transfer costs. Second, licensing technology involves heavy policing costs, for the licensor needs to ensure that the licensee does not use technology 'in ways which have not been paid for'. Third, the licensor runs the risk of creating a competitor. Fourth, there exists a buyer uncertainty problem (the buyer does not know what he is acquiring until he has obtained it, and once he has acquired it he will not wish to pay for it) which inhibits the market for licences or at least increases the cost by requiring insurance clauses in contracts. Fifth, there may be no local firm which can profitably absorb the knowledge, particularly in less developed countries.

However, there are a number of situations where licensing may be appropriate. First, it may pay multinationals in highly concentrated industries not to compete directly through subsidiaries in the same market, but to cross-license their products to each other (for instance, in the pharmaceutical industry). Second, licensing may be the best form of market servicing in the presence of barriers to the other methods. Government policy may prevent exporting and may insist on local host control. Small firms may find it difficult to raise the capital and management for a direct investment but require a local presence. Finally, licensing is often a way to exploit small, residual markets at low cost.

(d)   Direct Investment in Market Servicing

Direct investment has been considered above. Three situations occur where management chooses direct foreign investment (Buckley and Dunning 1976). First, firms produce when the market growth or profit potential is favourable relative to other forms of market servicing. Second, firms produce abroad where their competitive strength is greater than indigenous firms (Hymer 1976, Kindleberger 1969). Third, multinational firms are better seekers of the most profitable and fastest growing activities than are host country firms.

One form of direct investment is worthy of further investigation. This is cost-reducing offshore production.

(e)   Offshore Production

Offshore production is the situation where one stage in an integrated production process is located abroad in order to reduce costs. The offshore plant (or foreign feeder plant) is usually located in a cheap labour country and the final output is sold in an advanced country, usually in the multinational firm's home market. A typical offshore process is shown in Figure 12.3.

In the electronics industry the most popular countries for offshore investment are Singapore, Malaysia, Hong Kong, Taiwan and South Korea; for servicing the US market Latin America is popular, particularly Mexico; and for the European textiles market, North Africa.

The decision process leading to the establishment of an offshore plant is usually prompted by a threat to the home market from a low cost producer (Moxon 1974). The threatened firm either has to reduce costs or phase out the product. Frequently offshore establishment is the optimum way to cut costs. Successful establishment offshore is dependent on several character-istics of the product: (1) large inputs of relatively unskilled labour; (2) a high value to low weight ratio in order to keep transport costs down; (3) low tariffs in the reimporting country; and (4) a standardised product and process. Initial problems of offshore plants, such as inadequate throughput and difficulties of management at a distance, together with the inherent risks, have receded as managements have learned to cope, and offshore production is a rapidly increasing component of international investment.

12.4   Foreign Investment Entry Strategy

The management decisions involved in setting up a subsidiary in a foreign country have two important dimensions—the buy or build decision and the ownership decision.

(a)   Greenfield Ventures versus Takeovers

A priori, there are strong arguments either to build a new foreign plant from scratch on a greenfield site or to acquire an existing firm or part of a firm. The proponents of greenfield entry support their case by reference to

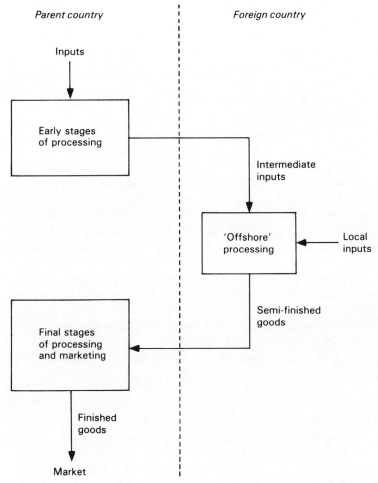

Figure 12.3 Schematic Representation of a Typical Offshore Production Process

the following arguments. First, greenfield ventures can be a cheaper form of entry because the scale of involvement can be precisely controlled and the facility can be expanded exactly in line with achieved market penetration. This argument is likely to be particularly strong for smaller firms who face difficulty in raising the capital necessary for a takeover. Second, building a new plant means that there is no risk of inheriting problems. Third, the most modern techniques of production and management can be installed. Fourth, there is likely to be a welcome by the host government for greenfield ventures which are seen as increasing activity, employment and competition. Positively, this may entail financial assistance and negatively, there is less risk of anti-trust action. Fifth, the choice of location is open to the entrant and a least cost site, including possible regional grants, can be chosen. Finally, where no suitable takeover victim can be found, greenfield entry can be a second best solution.

There are counter arguments in favour of entry by takeover. First, takeovers permit rapid market entry and allow a quicker return on capital and learning procedures. In cases of strong competition, the pre-emption of a rival firm's move may dictate takeover entry. Second, cultural, legal and management problems, particularly in the difficult start-up period, can be avoided by assimilating a going concern. Third, the major advantage of a takeover is often the purchase of crucial assets. Such assets may, in different circumstances, be products, management skills, brand names, technology and distribution networks. Fourth, takeovers do not disturb the competitive framework in the host country, and they avoid competitive retaliation.

There are, however, several potential drawbacks to the takeover mode of entry. The entrant is faced with the task of evaluating the worth of the assets to be acquired. This involves a costly and difficult assessment of the synergy between these new assets and the firm's existing operations. Second, there may be severe problems of integrating a previously independent unit into a larger entity; and third, the search for the ideal victim often involves heavy costs.

Almost every entry decision involves giving a different weighting to the above factors. Of particular importance in determining the outcome are the specific skills of the entrant and the environmental circumstances in the host country.

(b) Ownership Strategy

The arguments for 100 per cent equity ownership of a foreign subsidiary rely heavily on the fact that control by the parent is total and that there can be no conflict over potentially contentious issues of company policy such as dividend payments, exports, the distribution of new investment and internal transfer prices. In cases where the parent firm can supply all the necessary inputs for a subsidiary, these costs of interference need not be borne. Further information, both technical and competitive, is not leaked to outsiders who may not fully share the goals of the parent firm. Finally, some types of strategy are incompatible with joint ventures, notably those based on rapid and sustained innovation, on rationalisation and on control of key inputs.

The arguments for joint ventures are more circumstantial and depend on finding a joint venture partner with complementary resources. The argument that unique resources are contributed by the local partner is usually the most important reason for joint ventures. These resources may be local knowledge, contacts, or marketing expertise. Second, the entrant company's outlay is reduced and the risk of loss correspondingly diminished. This reduction of risk is an important reason why joint ventures, which can be easily reversed, may be a good way of effecting initial entry. Finally, in many countries some element of local shareholding is made a condition of entry, e.g. India, where the normal ceiling on foreign equity is 40 per cent, but where this can be increased to 74 per cent on technology considerations where the project is for the home market and 100 per cent for export oriented units (Indian Investment Centre 1981).

The success of the decision to enter a joint venture will of course depend on the choice of partner. There are many cases on record where a good agent or distributor has become a poor joint venture partner. It is clearly difficult to appraise a prospective partner in advance, but on such an appraisal may depend the success of the foreign venture.

12.5 Management in Multinational Firms

Management in multinational firms is essentially a response to the same issues facing national firms: how to make a profit; how to control operations; how and in which direction to grow; how to respond to a changing environment and so on; but it is complicated by operating in more than one country and by differing national business frameworks. Consequently, each functional area of the firm—financing, marketing, production, research and development (R and D)—must be organised so as to respond to global operations.

(a) Organising the Multinational Firms

Organisationally, the multinational firm must respond to global challenges in a way which allows the maximum control of policy by top decision makers with maximum flexibility of response to changing circumstances. This means the creation of an efficient communications network within the firm. Reporting relationships between managers are therefore vital. Channels of reporting relationships internationally can run along functional lines, where the heads of divisions (finance, marketing, production) have worldwide responsibilities, along product group lines, or the firm can be organised geographically (Middle East division etc.). The organisational problem then becomes the effective co-ordination of these major divisions across the other specialism, e.g. in a product division structure to co-ordinate the sales of different product groups. Some multinational firms have thus adopted multiple reporting channels (sometimes referred to as matrix structures). Here the danger is that the organisational procedures may become disoriented.

An alternative response to global organisation, particularly utilised by smaller multinationals, is the International Division structure, where all non-domestic activities of the firm are grouped together and reporting is directly between the Chief Executive of the company and the Chief Executive of the International Division. Such a structure is useful in giving impetus to an internationalisation drive, but does not allow the firm to benefit fully from synergy between national and international operations and often leaves foreign activities dependent on the domestic product division.

Personnel problems in multinational firms can be severe. Expatriate executives are far more expensive than when employed at home and pose problems in promotion, pensions, emoluments and reintegration at home (Brooke and Gilling-Smith 1983). Recruitment of local executives can be difficult and risky but may be forced on the company by indigenisation plans, by which local governments demand that a fixed proportion of executives must be host country nationals. Cultural differences amongst executives often require careful handling by top management. A training programme which matches these personnel needs is a vital component of a multinational's operations.

(b)   Planning in the Multinational Firm

It has become commonplace that structure should follow strategy, and the setting of strategy at the highest levels—the management plan— is a vital weapon in the economic management of multinationals. Three elements are of major importance: (1) control of operations; (2) decision making by the people best equipped to judge the impact of the decision; and (3) the communication of information to facilitate good decisions.

The management plan should thus incorporate well-defined targets which can be measured. Multiple targets which are comprehensible to decision makers should include a time-scale for their achievement and an action programme to tackle key problems and take advantage of opportunities. Such provisions prevent the plan being vague and give clear guidance to managers.

The key issue of devolving responsibility to the managers of foreign subsidiaries whilst retaining control of policy in headquarters is an issue which troubles all multinational firms, however organised. It is essential that group support must be given to the manager on the spot who must actually make operational decisions.

(c)   Financial Planning in the Multinational Firm

Multinational operation complicates financial management by posing extra problems, but it also opens new opportunities. The possibilities for exchange loss or gain increase with multinationalisation. Exchange loss is the risk of loss to a firm exposed to devaluation in the value of a currency which the firm is contracted to receive in the future or from an appreciation in the value of a currency which the firm is contracted to deliver in the future. Exporters and importers are so exposed, but multinationals are more vulnerable because of their larger trading across exchanges and because their net assets will be differentially affected in different currency areas. Consequently, a hedging policy designed to minimise these effects is necessary for a risk averse multinational. Of course, a more aggressive policy attempting to play the foreign exchange market is a possible alternative, but no such scheme has yet been perfected and many multinational firms have lost money in the attempt.

The differential cost of money worldwide enables multinational firms to reduce the costs of raising capital, and the use of internal indebtedness (e.g. a subsidiary borrowing from the parent firm) allows flexibility in its utilisation. However, each subsidiary of the firm must adapt to local financial practices and institutions. The reconciliation of local subsidiaries into an overall consolidated balance sheet can be a difficult and expensive task.

Financial planning in the multinational firm must face the issue of taxation. A spectrum of policies is possible, from an outright policy of attempting to reduce taxation payments wherever possible to ensuring simply that the same profits are not taxed twice. A large amount of information on tax regimes and double taxation agreements between countries is necessary in international taxation planning and a great deal of uncertainty prevails because of the impact of changes in any of the variables affecting taxation.

The problem of withdrawing funds from abroad is a unique financial problem faced by multinational firms. A variety of channels is available including dividends (usually taxed at source and as income to the parent), royalties and management fees to the parent (often tax-deductible in the host country), repayment of loans and interest on intra-company debt, and transfer pricing on intermediate goods and services.

The issue of transfer pricing is the most controversial issue multinational firms face. The manipulation of internal prices of goods and services to move funds around the world can achieve several objectives. Included amongst these are the following: (1) to maximise post-tax profits; (2) to artificially affect declared profit levels; (3) to transfer funds in the face of changes in currency parities; (4) to avoid government restrictions; and (5) to impose control on foreign subsidiaries. However, such artificial prices affect the incomes of the countries between which the transaction occurs and multinationals are therefore distrusted by governments who believe that they cannot control their own economies in the presence of multinational firms. Despite the existence of constraints by customs and revenue authorities, exchange control authorities and specialist transfer price checking firms employed by some countries, suspicion remains. The practice also has drawbacks from the firm's point of view. A loss of efficiency can occur from operating non-market prices. A costly control system may be necessary and mistakes in transfer pricing may be expensive. The practice will continue, however, whilst potential gains in tax avoidance and profit potential remain.

The existence of different tax and trading regimes internationally poses the problem of evaluating the performance of foreign subsidiaries. Whilst it is generally agreed that the same standards of performance (return on sales, performance relative to a budget) are required from individual foreign subsidiaries, allowance must be made for the impact of local conditions and possibly the impact of transfer pricing on individual subsidiaries. Evaluation of performance at a distance remains a grey area in many multinational firms.

(d) Marketing in the Multinational Firm

International marketing involves an important decision on worldwide standardisation versus adaptation of the products to individual market needs. In general adaptation will yield revenue advantages. It is, however, dangerous to make generalisations, particularly in equating market with country. India, for instance, though a very poor country on the usual indicators, has a proportionately small, but in absolute terms large, industrial sector. Most Third World countries have a minority of high income earners whose consumption patterns approximate to those of advanced countries. Consequently, multinationals are often able to segment national markets profitably.

Studies of international marketing point to the importance of non-price factors in selling. Quality, variety, reliability and meeting delivery dates are frequently adduced to lead to success in penetrating foreign markets. Information needs are correspondingly greater in foreign markets and careful pre-entry market research remains an important contributor to success.

(e) Research and Development

Economic theories of the multinational firm stress the relationship between research intensity and multinationality of the firm. The supply of technolo-

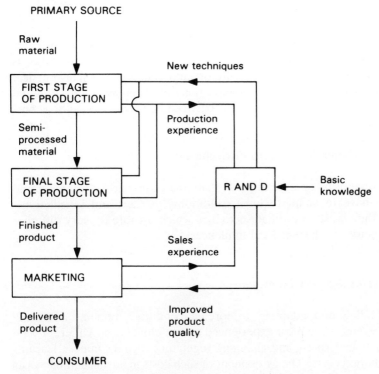

Source: Reproduced from Buckley and Casson (1976) p. 34.
Note: Successive stages of production are linked by flows of semi-processed materials. Production and marketing are linked by a flow of finished goods ready for distribution. Production and marketing on the one hand are linked to R and D, on the other hand by two-way flows of information and expertise.

Figure 12.4   The Integration of R and D into the Management of the Firm

gical advances internally exploited and marketed within the structure of the firm gives an explanation for the growth of integrated multinational firms (Buckley and Casson 1976, Hood and Young 1979, Dunning 1981). The management of R and D is vital for internationalisation, and exploiting the advances of internal research provides a motor for growth of the firm. The information flows between R and D and the other main functions are extremely important. Figure 12.4 illustrates the two-way communication necessary for management to integrate fully the fruits of research into the management process. It is often argued that the most successfully managed multinationals are those whose managements understand the implications of current research.

(f)   Global Decision Making

The management of multinational firms requires a careful monitoring of the international environment. Responsiveness to local conditions is perhaps the most important attribute of successful management practice. This section has shown the crucial importance of communication within the firm not only between countries, but between departments and divisions.

12.6   The Relationship with the Environment

Multinational firms operate in more than one economic environment and therefore have to adapt to local conditions, markets and jurisdictions. Further, they must co-ordinate activities which operate on very different bases because of different local influences.

(a)   The Host Country Environment

Understanding and adapting to foreign conditions remains a difficult problem even for the most experienced multinational firm. Different ways of conducting business and changing regulatory regimes impose learning and adaptation costs. The assessment of such costs in advance of entry can be problematic. In particular, multinationals are faced with the assessment of political risk, which is usually discounted in the home environment. Political risks arise from discontinuities in the business environment which are difficult to predict. War, revolution, nationalisation, expropriation, devaluation and the imposition of controls are obvious manifestations. Collection of information is necessary to evaluate foreign projects and a variety of screening models exist. Prior contact with the market is an important source of knowledge of host country conditions.

In many host countries, notably those of the Third World, multinationals are regarded with suspicion and they are often made the scapegoat for many internal problems of economic management. Concern on the part of host countries is expressed with regard to the balance of payments impact of multinationals, their effect on the host country's economic structure, their technological impact and their alleged inflexibility towards national planning. Indeed, it is frequently the case that foreign investors are more responsive to government policy than are local firms, and the alacrity with which multinationals respond to regional incentives is an example of this. However, the vague threat posed to national sovereignty and the achievement of national goals dictates that the management of multinationals must be sensitive to local aspirations and must avoid at all costs political interference or standards of behaviour below those of their best local competitor (see Balasubramanyam (1980) for a study of multinationals in the Third World).

(b)   The Source Country

The relationship between the multinational firm and its source country can also be fraught with difficulty. The most serious accusation thrown at multinationals is that they create unemployment by 'exporting jobs'. The growth of offshore production in particular has heightened the tension. In defence, multinationals put the view that foreign investment increases job provision in the home country by providing an outlet for intermediate and capital goods in the foreign unit and preserving jobs which would otherwise disappear in the face of low cost foreign competition. Studies of the balance between job preservation and job loss conducted in the USA have been inconclusive, as have investigations of the balance of payments impact of outward direct investment.

(c)   International Organisations

Because of the difficulty of controlling multinational firms at the national level, demands have grown that they should be internationally (or supranationally) regulated. To effect this a number of codes of conduct and other regulatory provisions now impinge on the management of multinational firms.

The United Nations (UN) has established two institutions to investigate and ultimately to regulate multinationals. These are the Commission on Transnational Enterprises, a policy-making body responsible to the Economic and Social Committee of the UN, and the Centre on Transnational Enterprises, whose function is to collect information, assist governments and commission research. Currently the UN is drawing up a code of conduct to harmonise policy on multinationals and to lay down standards of behaviour. The Code follows the OECD Code of Conduct on multinationals produced in 1976, which addresses standards of behaviour by multinationals, requires extra information from multinationals, and prescribes voluntary curbs on their power (OECD 1976). Codes on restrictive trade practices (UNCTAD), on principles for employment (ILO) and the EEC Code for Companies with subsidiaries in South Africa already exist, as do guidelines on baby foods and pharmaceuticals. In addition to the forthcoming UN Code, UNCTAD is proposing a code on the international transfer of technology, and EEC regulations on disclosure and employment are under discussion.

Clearly managements in multinationals must be aware of these codes and adopt policies which do not conflict with them for the sake of public relations, if nothing else. The impact of international regulation is likely to increase and therefore to impose management costs on multinationals much more heavily in future.

12.7 Conclusion

The economic management of multinational organisations has additional dimensions not faced by the national firm. Adaptation to differing local conditions, extra information requirements, control problems, organisational problems and problems of liaising with external decision makers are all exacerbated by international operations. However, with these problems come opportunities for growth, stability, diversification and cost reduction, leading to higher profitability. The principles of sound economic management do not differ between national and international firms, but the extra dimensions of the latter pose interesting challenges.

References

Aharoni, Y. (1966) *The Foreign Investment Decision Process*, Harvard University Press.

Aharoni, Y. (1971) 'On the definition of a multinational corporation', *Quarterly Review of Economics and Business*, Autumn, Vol. 11, No. 3, pp. 27–37.

Balasubramanyam, V. N. (1980) *Multinational Enterprises and the Third World*, London, Trade Policy Research Centre.

Brooke, M. Z. and Buckley, P. J. (eds) (1983) *Handbook of International Trade*, Kluwer.

Brooke, M. Z. and Gilling-Smith, D. (1983) 'Organisation and staffing', in Brooke and Buckley (eds), *Handbook of International Trade*, Kluwer.

Buckley, P. J. (1982) 'The role of exporting in the market servicing policies of multinational manufacturing enterprises: theoretical and empirical perspectives', in Czinkota, M. R. and Tesar, G. (eds), *Export Management: An International Context*, Praeger.

Buckley, P. J. and Casson, M. (1976) *The Future of the Multinational Enterprise*, Macmillan.

Buckley, P. J. and Casson, M. (1981) 'The optimal timing of a foreign direct investment', *Economic Journal*, March, Vol. 91, pp. 75–87.

Buckley, P. J. and Davies, H. (1981) 'Foreign licensing in overseas operations: theory and evidence from the UK', in Hawkins, R. G. and Prasad, A. J. (eds), *Technology Transfer and Economic Development*, JAI Press.

Buckley, P. J. and Dunning, J. H. (1976) 'The industrial structure of US investment in the UK', *Journal of International Business Studies*, Fall/Winter, Vol. 7, No. 2, pp. 5–13.

Buckley, P. J. and Pearce, R. D. (1979) 'Overseas production and exporting by the world's largest enterprises', *Journal of International Business Studies*, Spring/Summer, Vol. 10, No. 1, pp. 9–20.

Buckley, P. J. and Pearce, R. D. (1981) 'Market servicing by multinational manufacturing firms: exporting versus foreign production', *Managerial and Decision Economics*, December, Vol. 2, No. 4, pp. 229–246.

Dunning, J. H. (1981) *International Production and the Multinational Enterprise*, Allen and Unwin.

Hood, N. and Young, S. (1979) *The Economics of Multinational Enterprise*, Longman.

Hymer, S. H. (1976) *The International Operations of National Firms: A Study of Direct Investment*, MIT Press.

Khan, M. S. (1978) *A Study of Success and Failure in Exports*, University of Stockholm.

Kindleberger, C. P. (1969) *American Business Abroad*, Yale University Press.

Knickerbocker, F. T. (1973) *Oligopolistic Reaction and the Multinational Enterprise*, Harvard University Press.

Moxon, R. W. (1974) 'Offshore production in less developed countries', *The Bulletin*, Institute of Finance, New York University, July, Issues 8–9.

Newbould, G. D., Buckley, P. J. and Thurwell, J. (1978) *Going International—The Experience of Smaller Companies Overseas*, Associated Business Press.

Vernon, R. (1966) 'International investment and international trade in the product cycle', *Quarterly Journal of Economics*, May, Vol. 80, pp. 196–207.

Indian Investment Centre (1981) *Foreign Investment in India: Opportunities and Incentives*, New Delhi.

ITI Research (1975) *Concentration on Key Markets*, Royal Society of Arts, BETRO Trust.

OECD (1976) *Declaration on International Investment and Multinational Enterprises*.

Further Reading

For a thorough treatment of the management policies of multinational firms see:

Brooke, Michael Z. and Buckley, Peter J. (eds) (1983) *Handbook of International Trade*, Kluwer.

For the economics of multinational enterprise see:

Caves, Richard E. (1982) *Multinational Enterprise and Economic Analysis*, Cambridge University Press.

Dunning, John H. (1981) *International Production and the Multinational Enterprise*, Allen and Unwin.

Hood, Neil and Young, Stephen (1979) *The Economics of Multinational Enterprise*, Longman.

13
Public Enterprise Management
T. T. Jones and T. A. J. Cockerill

13.1 The Growth of Public Enterprise

State ownership of industry increased substantially in Britain after 1945 as it did in several other European countries. Direct involvement by government with industry had been mainly confined in the inter-war period to posts and telecommunications. In the first six postwar years coal, electricity, gas, railways, the steel industry, the Bank of England and significant parts of road passenger and freight transport and air services were nationalised. Between 1964 and 1979 the steel industry was nationalised for the second time and the shipbuilding and aerospace industries and part of the oil industry were taken into public ownership.

Public ownership in each of these cases was accomplished by means of an Act of Parliament, vesting the assets of the enterprises acquired in a public corporation, comprising members appointed by the responsible minister. Compensation, where appropriate, was paid to the former owners. This pattern of organisation for public ownership is unique to the United Kingdom and was intended to permit the corporation to formulate and implement corporate policies on a commercial basis, subject only to broad strategic guidance from the minister and free from persistent monitoring and inquiry from Parliament. In practice, many difficulties have arisen in formulating and implementing corporate policies that meet the varied objectives of managers, workforces, customers, suppliers, Government and Parliament.

There are at present 51 public corporations in the UK. Of these, 17 are defined for purposes of public expenditure planning and parliamentary scrutiny as nationalised industries on the basis that they derive the majority of their revenue from the sale of goods and services and are not dependent on Parliament for the supply of the majority of their funds. It should be noted that although they are described as 'nationalised industries', in several cases this is inaccurate since the enterprises are not responsible for the whole of the output of the sector in which they operate.

State influence and control of industry extends beyond the nationalised industries and has increased over the past twenty years as successive governments have provided finance in the forms of grants, loans and equity to private sector enterprises and have become involved with policies to improve the efficiency and performance of industry by means of restructuring sectors or increasing the level of domestic and international competition. In some cases (e.g. Rolls-Royce, British Leyland) virtually the whole of the share capital is held by the state. These enterprises, however, remain limited companies and do not fall within the scope of this chapter, although many of the issues raised are relevant to them.

By far the greater part of the importance of the public corporations within the economy is attributable to the nationalised industries. Public corporations account for 11 per cent of the overall output of goods and services in the economy (gross domestic product), 8 per cent of employment, and 18 per cent of fixed capital formation[1]. They are by any standard a major component of the economy. The turnover, profits, employment and capital expenditures of the main nationalised industries in the most recent accounting year are given in Table 13.1. The electricity supply industry in England and Wales is the largest organisation in terms of the value of annual turnover; the industry is bigger still if the two Scottish bodies are included. The National Coal Board (NCB) has the largest number of employees. British Telecom accounts for the largest capital expenditure.

As important economic entities, efficient and profitable operation is as important for these enterprises as for those in the private sector. But account must also be taken of the wider economic and social obligations of publicly-owned enterprises and of the objectives and involvement of government. These aspects increase the complexity and uncertainty of management decision making. It is the framework in which these decisions are made, in terms of economic principles, institutional procedures and government policy, that is the concern of this chapter. The next four sections outline the organisation and objectives of public enterprise in the UK. Then four major aspects of economic decision making and control are analysed: pricing, investment, financing and financial control. Finally, the role and influence of government is considered.

13.2 Economic Rationale for Public Ownership

Public ownership of industry in Britain has been undertaken for a complex set of reasons, not all of them rational. They include economic, social, political and technological motives. The economic justification for public

1. Central Statistical Office (1982).

Table 13.1   Key Statistics for Selected Nationalised Industries, 1981/82

Industry	Year ended	Turnover (£million)	Net profit (loss)[a]		Capital expenditure (£million)	Employment (number)
			Historical Cost basis (£million)	Current cost basis[b] (£million)		
National Coal Board	31.3.82	4,727.5	(423.5)	(646.5)	736.1	218,500
Electricity (England and Wales)	31.3.82	8,056.5[c]	972.3	(80.1)	1,169.8	146,655
British Gas Corporation	31.3.82	5,235.3	510.4	143.6	515.1	104,700
British National Oil Corporation	31.12.82	5,751.7[c]	76.6	13.0	262.9	2,323
British Steel Corporation	31.3.82	3,443.0	(358.0)	(392.0)	164.0	103,700
Post Office	31.3.82	2,496.7	128.7	96.2	75.6	178,038
British Telecommunications	31.3.82	5,708.0	457.8	476.0	1,456.1	245,882
British Airways Board	31.3.82	2,241.3	(118.4)	(149.0)	167.0	42,012
British Railways Board	31.12.81	2,655.8	(34.3)	(61.0)	170.1	227,252
National Bus Company	31.12.81	618.4	5.5	(20.5)	34.0	53,172
British Shipbuilders	31.12.82	1,025.6	(13.9)	(41.0)	32.8	66,613

Source: Annual Reports and Accounts.

Notes: (a) After crediting revenue grants and deducting depreciation, interest and taxation.
  (b) As compared with historical cost profit/loss, adjustments are made to increase depreciation charges to the current value of fixed assets, for the effect of price changes on stocks consumed within the year (cost of sales adjustment), and for additional working capital needed as a result of changes in the input prices of goods and services used and financed (monetary working capital adjustment).
  (c) Sales.

ownership is not itself unambiguous or free from political influence or controversy. At one extreme a literal interpretation of the supremacy of the freely functioning market economy would deny the need for state intervention or ownership in industry. Consumer choice, expressed in relation to incomes and relative prices, would require suppliers to meet the revealed pattern of demand, competition between suppliers ensuring that the demand was met at least cost and in the most efficient manner. Corporate failure would reflect inefficiency on the part of suppliers either in terms of their costs of production or in their ability to meet the appropriate pattern of demand. At the other extreme the stimulus of the profit motive and the supremacy of consumer choice are replaced by the primacy of decisions taken by the state in the interests of the nation about the allocation of scarce economic resources between alternative uses, decisions such as the production of capital or consumer goods, and whether for civil or military applications. Allocation is accomplished by a system of planning that is centralised to a greater or lesser degree.

Public ownership in Europe has typically developed as much for reasons of pragmatism as for dogma. Market conditions have often not led to a swift and effective readaptation of supply to meet a changed pattern of demand. Vital sectors of the economy have become unprofitable and have lacked vital investment funds, obliging governments to intervene. Certain economic motives for nationalisation can nevertheless be discerned. They may be discussed separately, but are inter-related.

(a) Externalities

These are costs and benefits flowing from an activity that affect economic actors (workers, firms, governments, consumers, taxpayers) other than those who initiate the action. The smoking factory chimney that pollutes the atmosphere and is a health hazard is the classic example. In an unregulated market there will be no incentive for firms to take account of the wider effects of their actions; if they are to do so, the consequences of their actions must in some way be internalised, by taxation or legislation. Public ownership may be considered appropriate where industrial activity is potentially dangerous (mining, nuclear power), where employment levels can be maintained or increased, where the development of regions can be promoted, or where the provision of a good or service (electricity, communications, social services) needs to be provided to a wide section of the community. It is usually difficult to measure the net benefits of such externalities and to compare them with the private costs of supply; it is also not always plain that supply is made more effectively through a publicly owned enterprise than through other forms of enterprise operating under legal or fiscal obligations.

(*b*)   *Market Failure*

The cost conditions prevailing in an industry and limitations on the supply and price of financial capital may prevent an industry's complete adjustment to the prevailing pattern of demand, and hence make it unable to supply its output at the least resource cost. Inappropriate market structures may be characterised by excess capacity at the going level of price, a fragmented supply structure with many small firms and plants, and low profitability that prevents the replacement of assets or the introduction of best-practice techniques of production. Three main factors that may cause market failure may be discussed briefly.

Firstly, the presence of economies of scale may require for efficiency the presence of a limited number of suppliers in the market. Scale economies are reductions in real unit costs that result from increases in the scale of operation. They are present in many manufacturing processes and are frequently represented in public sector enterprises (e.g. steel, electricity generation, railways, civil aviation). Competitive processes in the free market can result in a fragmented industrial structure in which the average sizes of firms and plants are too small to reap the full benefits of economies of scale. Restructuring by merger may be inappropriate or difficult because of the large amounts of financial capital that are needed and the risk of monopolisation once the process is completed. Government may regard it as better to achieve the restructuring by means of a public enterprise in which the impact of monopolisation can be regulated.

Secondly, restructuring may not occur of its own volition within an industry if demand is low in relation to installed capacity, and if fixed expenses form a high proportion of total costs. In these circumstances the avoidable costs of additional output are low, and competition between suppliers will drive price down towards the level of avoidable costs, resulting in substantial losses. There will be no incentive for suppliers to leave the market, or for prices to improve, until the costs of capital asset replacement drive firms into liquidation. Again, in these circumstances, public ownership can be used as an arm of industrial policy to enable the industry to cope with inevitable decline.

Thirdly, technical change may demand the wholesale re-equipment of an industry or the development of new products in order to enable it to compete effectively in world markets. If the scale of the investment required is large, the level of risk high, and the present and prospective profitability of the industry is low, it may not be possible to raise sufficient funds from the capital markets, or the interest premium charged may be prohibitive. Examples of industries in which the rate of technological progress has been rapid and in which substantial funds for re-equipment and product development have been required are steel, gas and microelectronics. Public ownership, together with the supply of additional funds, is one means by which new technology can be incorporated.

(c)   Resource Allocation

A fundamental rule of welfare economics is that scarce resources will be efficiently allocated within and between industries if price is set equal to marginal cost $(P = MC)$. Marginal cost is usually considered to be the variation in total cost with respect to a change in output at the industry's planning horizon (that is, *long-run* marginal cost). The equation of price and marginal cost will occur spontaneously only under conditions of perfect competition, and these scarcely if ever prevail in markets. Industrial markets may be stereotyped as containing elements of monopoly because of the relative sizes of suppliers, or because of consumers' ignorance or susceptibility to advertising, and it is thus axiomatic that with a negatively sloped demand curve, profit-maximising policies in which marginal cost and marginal revenue are equated will result in price exceeding marginal cost.

The public enterprise may choose, or be required by policy, to follow an allocatively efficient pricing policy. Where there is excess capacity in the industry in relation to the prevailing level of demand, this will result in accounting losses (since price will not cover full costs). Where there is a shortage of capacity, marginal costs will be rising steeply in the region of prevailing demand, and prices will be high in relation to average costs, generating cash surpluses. Only where the industry is in a state of long-run equilibrium, with capacity just matching demand at the prevailing price, will a policy of pricing based on marginal cost result in full costs (including 'normal' profit) being just matched by revenue. Marginal cost pricing may not be appropriate if such policies are not followed elsewhere in the economy (and in a mixed economy they are not). Governments are also sensitive to the impact on public opinion of high reported losses or profits.

Governments may also be concerned to regulate the impact of monopoly suppliers, either through the level of prices charged or the failure to supply the market. Monopoly conditions may arise because of cost conditions (e.g. economies of scale), the need to avoid wasteful competition (e.g. competing railway companies), or the existence of a limited source of supply (e.g. water). Public ownership is one means by which optimal pricing policies and the regulation of monopoly can be achieved.

The economic factors described above have without doubt been significant elements in the extension of public ownership in Britain. But nationalisation is ultimately a political act, and political considerations have been the most important elements in the process. One objective has been to extend the influence of the government into the leading and strategically important enterprises in the nation with the intention of influencing economic growth, incomes and employment. Another, associated, purpose has been the desire to influence the division of economic resources between capital and labour and to secure employees' rights within their enterprises. Thirdly, and within an international context, it has been seen as desirable to support strategically important industries (steel, shipbuilding, aerospace).

13.3   Features of Public Corporations

Public corporations that derive most of their revenue from the sale of goods or services, as constituted in the UK, differ from public limited companies in the private sector of the economy in four main ways.

(a) They have statutory duties, enshrined in their nationalisation acts, which impose obligations that may conflict with a strict interpretation of their commercial interests, and that are wider ranging than the legal obligations of private sector companies.

(b) There is no provision for an annual meeting of shareholders, through which the board of a limited company is held accountable, although the responsible minister represents the interests of the nation as owners.

(c) Public corporations, once established, cannot be liquidated, other than by act of Parliament. Thus there is no direct influence on managers from the possibility of bankruptcy, falling share prices, or the threat of takeover.

(d) External finance (loans and equity) is supplied with the approval of the Treasury and is derived almost entirely from general taxation or borrowing. The influence of financial institutions—banks, insurance companies and pension funds—that is important in private sector companies is absent for public corporations.

There are, in addition, other features of public corporations that distinguish them from companies in the private sector. Several of the nationalised industries are of strategic importance and cannot be subjected to the unrestrained impact of market forces. Some (electricity, gas, posts, telecommunications, railways) are endowed with considerable market power, as a result either of legislation or the economics of supply. Lastly, the trade unions have had considerable negotiating power in the recent past in some of the corporations, deriving in part from the previous features. These characteristics taken together may be expected to influence both strategy and decision taking in the publicly owned sector of industry.

The Secretary of State of the responsible department, as the representative of government and ultimately of the nation as the owner of the enterprise, is given powers by the Nationalisation Act to influence and control the corporation. These are generally as follows:

(a) To appoint the members of the corporation and its chairman ('the board')[2]. The powers of appointment, and of re-appointment, are among the most important instruments of sanction and control that the Secretary of State possesses.
(b) To approve capital investment. This is usually exercised over the totality of the corporation's proposed investment programme and over large individual projects.
(c) To approve financing. External finance is supplied annually with the agreement of the Treasury. Approval is given in the plans for public expenditure published each year for progressively reducing proportions of total finance required for up to three years ahead, but these are subject to revision in the light of changed circumstances.
(d) To set financial targets. These have been set more or less continuously since 1961 and refer to a rate of return on capital, specified generally in relation to capital employed, but in certain cases to turnover. Corporations' prices and current costs are influenced by the target set.
(e) To give general or specific directions. This is essentially a reserve power of the Secretary of State to require the corporation to undertake some action that may fall outside the pursuit of commercial objectives. General directions may relate to any matter, but must be considered and approved by both Houses of Parliament. A specific direction is confined only to matters specified in the Act. It is perhaps not surprising that very little use has been made of these powers.

In addition to the statutory powers bestowed on the responsible Secretary of State by the Act, it has generally been the case that Ministers have found it necessary to bring influence to bear on corporations beyond the powers contained in the Act. These non-statutory influences have had considerable impact upon the strategies and performance of public corporations, and they are considered below in more detail.

13.4   Corporate Objectives

The economic decisions taken within public enterprises are governed by the objectives of management. Decisions will be different, and have different economic impacts, from those taken in private sector organisations if the objectives of management teams in public enterprises differ. It

---

2. Strictly speaking, there are neither directors nor a board in a public corporation, which is composed of its members in whom the rights of possession of the assets are vested by the Act. Customary usage nevertheless refers to the board.

is usually assumed in the private sector that the main objective of management is to maximise the present value of the firm:

$$V = \sum_{t=1}^{t=n} \frac{\pi}{(1+r)^t}$$

where π equals profit, r is the rate of interest and t the number of time periods. This objective is modified if the managerial utility function is more complex and includes elements such as corporate growth and size, managerial remuneration or discretionary expenditures. The behaviour and performance of public enterprises will differ significantly from that of a comparable undertaking in the private sector only if the utility functions of the managerial teams are significantly different.

There are grounds for believing that the utility functions of public sector managers may be different. In the first place they will be aware in most cases that they have an implicit obligation to serve a wider public, so that untrammelled pursuit of maximum profits may be avoided and attention paid to increasing output beyond the level prescribed by profit maximisation. Secondly, as Millward (1978) has suggested, managers of public enterprises may regard the environment in which they work as relatively risk-free, government being expected to underwrite losses. State capital may be seen as a free good, since if interest charges cannot be met from revenue, the expenses can be met by raising more capital, or outstanding debts can be written off. Consequently, there will be a tendency to greater capital expenditures and a higher capital–output ratio than in the private sector. Finally, because of the (assumed) lower risk environment and the lack of appeal to the best and most highly motivated executives, the efficiency level of public enterprises will be lower, and their costs higher, than in the private sector.[3] The validity of these arguments has not been thoroughly tested; it seems reasonable to suggest that the managerial objectives of most state enterprises may be slightly different from those of characteristic firms in the private sector, and that this may lead to rather more emphasis on output and rather less on profitability. It is unlikely, however, that this has very much influence on the basis of decision making.

13.5 Organisational Structure

The nationalised industries are generally large organisations even by the standards of the private sector, and are to be found in the 50 largest

---

3. This seems to be the view of Mrs Thatcher, who is reported as having told the Board of British Railways that if they were any good as managers, they would be working elsewhere.

companies in the UK. In a similar way to large private corporations, they therefore need to find a way between the benefits of central control and the advantages of decentralised decision making in individual profit centres. Williamson has characterised corporations as either being of U-form or M-form structure, that is either unitary or multidivisional, with the former being typical of small to medium-sized firms and the latter being typical of large companies (see Chapter 3). The M-form enterprise is considered to be a successor to the holding company, where acquired subsidiaries are left to run more or less autonomously with little or no central co-ordination or contact between subsidiaries.

Williamson (1971) considers that business behaviour is a function not only of market circumstances, but also of the internal organisation of an enterprise which influences internal efficiency, decision-making processes and the processes of internal compliance. Organisational form is thus an important variable in explaining the performance of individual enterprises.

In the U-form organisation each operating unit performs a specialised function for all product lines of the firm, while in the M-form firm each operating division performs all the specialised functions for an individual product. In the U-form firm, expansion leads to control loss and the increasing presence of X-inefficiency. It also alters the nature of the strategic decision-making process, as decisions tend to depend upon the relative power of the functional executives whose managements are unable to see, or to identify, the overall objectives of the enterprise. These problems are overcome by the M-form of organisation which removes from executives operational decisions and allows them to concentrate on long-term strategic decisions because they are not attached to any particular division and its promotion at the expense of others.

While Williamson's analysis is concerned with private sector corporations, similar considerations apply to public corporations which are to a great extent prime examples of the division of ownership from control and of organisations run by professional managers without the threat of takeover or bankruptcy.

In line with Williamson's view of the link between size and organisational form, many public corporations tend to be multidivisional organisations because of their size. In addition, despite the restricted remits given to public corporations in terms of their range of activities, many of the corporations do produce a range of goods or services which lends itself to a divisional structure based on products rather than geography, though many exhibit both features. Despite the supposed advantages of the M-form, public corporations exhibit a wide variety of organisational forms, combining U-form and holding companies with many exhibiting features of all types of structures. All, however, have a number of common characteristics, including boards of directors and a pyramidal management structure with varying degrees of divisional management (the individual plant, power station, coalmine, etc. at the base). Each corporation also tends to own subsidiary companies, either wholly or jointly, with private interests and with limited company statutes; these could thus be declared bankrupt without parliamentary approval. This ability has been of particular importance in relation to the role of the National Enterprise Board in promoting industrial development and in not being tied for too long a period to unsuccessful ventures.

The board members of the corporations, including the chairman, are appointed by the minister for a period of three to five years. The boards generally do not include representatives of interest groups, such as workers and consumers, though in certain cases trades union and consumer members have been selected by the minister. In terms of structure there are two types of board: executive and policy. Executive-type boards have a majority of full-time members who hold executive responsibility for one functional area of the enterprise, while policy-type boards contain a majority of part-time members, with the full-time members not having specific functional duties. Examples of the former type of boards are the NCB and the CEGB and examples of the latter include British Steel and the National Bus Company. Comparisons with large private enterprises of similar size tend to show that public corporations have smaller boards, but with a greater part-time proportion of members. Ministers have in certain cases found it extremely difficult to recruit people acceptable to them who are willing to serve as board chairmen, partly because of the low salaries as compared with the private sector, and partly because of the intrinsic difficulties of running large organisations with a mixture of commercial and social obligations. While the chairmen of nationalised industries tend to become public figures, the recent trend has been to appoint strong chairmen who are expected to give strong leadership. Some of the characteristics of board size and board members in 1980–81, including the ratio of full-time to part-time members, are given in Table 13.2.

The classification of public corporations into U-form and M-form is difficult because of the particular features of each enterprise. The National Coal Board and the Post Office tend to exhibit many features of the U-form firm, with board members having functional management responsibilities, though each has a divisional structure based on geography below board level. In the case of the NCB each colliery is both a profit centre and a decision-making centre, though the degree of autonomy enjoyed by the colliery manager depends to a great extent on the profitability of his pit.

The British Steel Corporation and British Shipbuilders exhibit features of M-form organisation, with policy-type boards below which there is a management executive committee. Lower still are divisions based on products which, in the case of British Shipbuilders, are composed of the original private sector companies.

The National Bus Company exhibits an M-form organisation which

Table 13.2 Comparison of Public and Private Boards and Board Members 1980/81

	Public corporations	Large private companies
Size of board	12.5	15.5
Full-time/part-time ratio	0.37	1.93
Length of service (months)	38.5	52.2
Age (years)	56.4	57.5
Salary(£)	15,800	41,200
Number of appointments	4.1	6.9
Independent school (%)	44.8	62.4
'Oxbridge' university (%)	26.4	44.6
Relevant qualifications		
Industry (%)	33.6	30.9
Function (%)	28.0	40.9
Prior experience (%)	65.5	72.9

Source: Jones, T. T. and O'Brien, P. M. (1982) *The Composition, Background and Salaries of Board Members of Nationalised Industries*, UMIST, Department of Management Sciences, Occasional Paper.

might be described as a holding company. It has a board with a majority of part-time members and a strongly decentralised system based on geographical regions comprising a small number of individual bus companies. These are responsible for stage carriage services while another division, National Travel Ltd, is responsible for long distance services and holidays.

An unusual feature of most of the public corporations is that they either own wholly or jointly a number of limited liability companies. In the National Bus Company, for example, all the individual bus companies are private companies, while in the Steel Corporation a whole range of private companies at home and overseas are owned by the corporation as part of its commercial operation.

The organisational structures of nationalised industries have not been static, but have evolved over time to suit the particular circumstances of the industry. In some instances, where the change involves more than one statutory corporation, change requires an Act of Parliament to alter the basic structure of the industry's organisation. For example, as a result of technical change in the discovery of natural gas, it was thought desirable to change the structure of the gas industry from a federal one, consisting of area boards which manufactured and sold gas with the Gas Council as a central coordinating body, to a unitary one in the form of the British Gas Corporation. The change was intended to cope with the problems of building and operating a national distribution system and organising the monopoly buying of gas from the North Sea producing companies.

Electricity was reorganised in 1957 from a national structure (the British Electricity Authority) towards a regional structure. However, while in

Scotland two corporations were established (producing and distributing electricity), in England and Wales a tripartite structure was established consisting of the CEGB whose task is to produce electricity, area boards whose task is to sell electricity and an Electricity Council which plays a co-ordinating role. A White Paper in 1977–78 proposed legislation to reorganise the industry on the lines of the Gas Corporation, but a bill was thought unlikely to obtain a parliamentary majority and was never brought before Parliament.[4]

13.6 Pricing

(a) The Theoretical Basis of Nationalised Industry Pricing

Many nationalised enterprises dominate the markets in which they operate and as a consequence have a considerable measure of discretion over the prices they charge. Following narrow commercial objectives in the short run would lead them to charge what the market will bear and to maximise profits by setting prices and outputs at levels which bring marginal cost and marginal revenue into equality. However, as discussed in 13.2(c) above, the efficient allocation of resources within the economy as a whole would require them to set price equal to marginal cost. Alternatively, governments may require them to cover their costs, making neither surpluses nor deficits. The pricing policy of a public corporation thus depends to a great extent upon the objectives it is set.

The possible price–output–profit positions for the three types of policy are shown in Figure 13.1 for both decreasing and increasing cost enterprises. Where costs are decreasing, as in (a), the profit-maximising state firm would produce an output of OQ_P and charge a price of OP_P, earning profits of P_PCDE; the state firm attempting to break even, and adopting average cost pricing, would charge OP_a, produce OQ_a, and earn no economic profits; while the firm charging prices equal to marginal cost would charge OP_m, produce output OQ_m, and make a loss of $FGHP_m$. Where costs are increasing, as in (b), profit maximising leads to a price of OP_P, output of OQ_P, and profit of P_PHJK; breaking even would lead to a price of OP_a, and output of OQ_a, while the marginal cost pricing firm would charge OP_m, produce output OQ_m, and earn profits of P_mLMN. Therefore under decreasing costs, profit maximising results in the highest price and smallest output, average cost pricing produces a lower price and greater output compared to profit maximising, while marginal cost pricing leads to the lowest price and largest output. Marginal cost pricing,

---

4. For detailed studies of the organisation and performance of individual national-ised industries, see Pryke (1981).

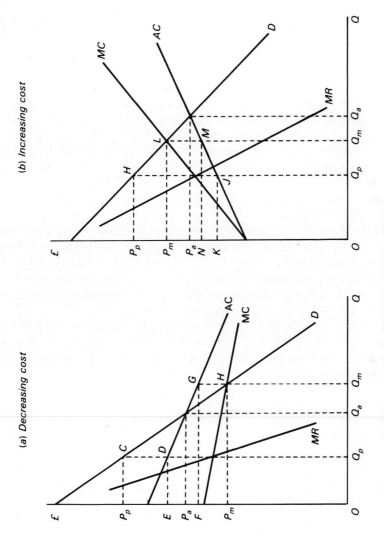

Figure 13.1 Pricing in Decreasing and Increasing Cost Industries

therefore, leads to the best use of existing capital but results in a financial loss. Where costs are increasing, profit maximising again produces the highest price and smallest output, marginal cost pricing the next highest price and a larger output compared to profit maximising, while average cost pricing produces the lowest price and largest output and is therefore politically attractive. Marginal cost pricing remains optimal in economic terms because the costs of producing the last unit of output are covered and the consumer pays the resource costs of producing it.

This traditional analysis assumes that capital is given and that marginal cost is equivalent to changes in variable costs. In the long run, however, capital is not something that can be ignored (as it can be in the short run) because investment expenditure is a major component of the long-run marginal cost of an additional unit of output. This long-run capital element needs to be included in the market signal to indicate the long-run price of the product to its consumers. If, for example, the short-run price of a fuel was substantially below that of the long-run marginal cost price compared to competitive fuels, consumers could mistakenly install equipment for heating, cooking, etc., in the belief that they were making the right long-run decision.

From the point of view of the producer, a short-run price set below long-run marginal cost encourages consumption and indicates a need for a greater volume of investment than is necessary. The divergence between long-run and short-run marginal cost can be reconciled when the concept of capacity and investment is introduced, the firms being in equilibrium when short-run and long-run marginal cost are equal.

In Figure 13.2 the firm facing demand curve DD_1 has a choice of three plant sizes represented by curves $SRMC^1$, $SRMC^2$ and $SRMC^3$. For each plant size short-run marginal cost OP_3 is constant up to capacity output. Long-run marginal cost OP_2 is constant throughout and equal to short-run marginal cost plus long-run capacity cost, which is BC. If plant 1 already exists, then the short-run marginal cost price that equates demand and supply is OP_1 which is greater than long-run marginal cost. If plant 3 exists, then the price charged is OP_3 which is equal to short-run marginal cost, but is less than long-run marginal cost. With plant 2, price is OP_2 which is equal to both short-run and long-run marginal cost. The analysis, however, depends on the acceptance of rationing by price along the vertical sections of the short-run marginal cost curves. If this is accepted, it can be concluded that with the right size plant short-run and long-run marginal cost are equal; if short-run marginal cost is greater than long-run marginal cost, expansion of capacity is needed, and if $LRMC$ is greater than $SRMC$, contraction is called for. The pricing rule thus also incorporates an investment rule.

Another criticism of the traditional analysis of marginal cost is that it is timeless. Costs are streams of expenses through time, so that costs at any

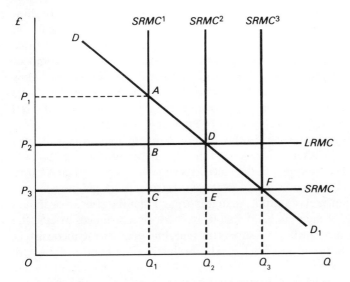

Figure 13.2 Short-Run and Long-Run Marginal Cost Pricing

point in time depend upon additions of capacity, scrappings and the variable costs of plants remaining together with the potential costs of future plants. The long-run marginal cost of a unit of output is therefore the difference between a time stream of costs with the new plant minus a time stream of costs without the plant discounted to the present time.

Economists have recommended marginal cost pricing as a first best solution for public enterprise because it is the pricing rule consistent with the achievement of a Pareto optimum position for an economy. A Pareto optimum position is one from which an economy can move only at the expense of making some group worse off. It is thus a position of maximum welfare and is reached when the marginal rate of substitution is equal to the marginal rate of transformation between all sectors of the economy, or the ratio of the prices of any two goods (which influences consumer behaviour) is equal to the ratio of marginal costs (which influences the behaviour of firms). Thus the general rule, explained in the appendix to this chapter, is derived that price should equal marginal cost or that all prices should bear the same relationship to marginal cost. Its recommended use in the real world must be made, however, in the context of the general theory of the second best which suggests that there is no particular reason for recommending marginal cost pricing as a first best solution when it is not used in every sector of the economy. The argument must therefore be made on more pragmatic grounds than the general theory of welfare economics.

The second best case for marginal cost pricing will depend to some extent upon the general cost structure of each industry and its relationships with other sectors of the economy. The main argument for marginal cost pricing is that it relates the cost of producing the marginal unit to the price the consumer pays. This avoids problems of cross-subsidisation and of encouraging consumers to buy excessively goods that are priced below marginal cost when average costs of production are rising. Where unit costs are falling, marginal cost pricing allows the more intensive use of fixed costs, but brings with it the problem of financing losses.

Where there are variations in the level of demand either within the day or by time of year, then marginal cost may be an appropriate method for setting prices. For example, in the electricity industry where demand varies by both time of day and time of year, and short-run marginal costs vary directly with the level of output, then it is argued that the consumer should cover the costs of meeting his demand. In these circumstances pricing the good or service according to short-run marginal cost is not inconsistent with long-run marginal cost pricing. This is illustrated in Figure 13.3 where the demand and cost curves refer to equal time periods, say of twelve hours, and the rule for equilibrium is that the sum of the short-run marginal cost prices should equal the sum of the two-period long-run marginal costs. Thus, night-time demand (D_n) is charged P_n, which is equal to short-run marginal cost or CQ_d. Daytime demand D_d, given the size of the system $SRMC^1$, must cover the system's entire capital cost plus its own short-run marginal cost. Thus the price of daytime electricity is equal to CQ_d $(SRMC)$ plus AC, which is equal to twice the single period long-run marginal capacity cost (BC). Hence price can vary between periods and be consistent with the long-run marginal cost pricing rule.

(b)   Pricing in Practice[5]

Following the major postwar period of nationalisation, governments did not give to the corporations any specific pricing rule. On the basis of the break-even target, the tendency was to use average cost pricing. After long debate about the merits of alternative pricing guidelines, the Government in the 1967 White Paper (Cmnd 3437, 1967) put forward the view that corporations should use marginal cost pricing. It said:

> The Government will ensure that the industries follow economically intelligent pricing policies designed to ensure the optimal utilisation of resources in the short and long run . . . Prices, if they are to contribute towards a more efficient distribution of resources (para. 17) . . . should be derived with reference to the costs of particular goods and services provided, that is, the consumer should pay the true costs (para. 18).

---

5. See also Turvey (1971), Webb (1973).

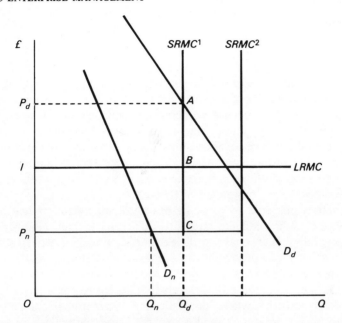

Figure 13.3 Peak Load and Off-Peak Pricing

Therefore prices need to be reasonably related to costs at the margin and in general to be in line with long-run marginal cost, although short-run marginal cost may be applied where excess capacity exists.

In practice the allocative rules relating to prices were applied with reluctance and only spasmodically in most industries. In the late 1960s the National Board for Prices and Incomes (NBPI) tried in a series of reports on applications for price increases to apply the principles and encourage their adoption in the industries. With the demise of the NBPI, such prompting disappeared and generally with it any attempt to apply marginalism to prices, except in the case of electricity, but even there it was mainly confined to the Bulk Supply Tariff which covers CEGB supplies to the twelve area boards, and in part to day and night tariffs for ordinary consumers.

The failure to use marginal cost pricing was recognised in the 1978 White Paper (Cmnd 7131, 1978) which marks the abandonment of marginal cost pricing as a major operational guideline for the industries. Instead, the Government

sees its main role as determining the overall financial target, and hence the general level of prices charged by (the) industry (para. 67) . . . (but) . . . it is not sufficient for the industries to set the general level of their prices to cover their costs. Within the overall level of prices, the industries should pay attention to the structure of prices and its relation to the structure of costs . . . Arbitrary cross-subsidisation between different groups of consumers ... should be avoided. [However,] it is primarily for each nationalised industry to work out the details of its prices with regard to its markets and its overall objectives, including its financial target.

Thus marginal cost pricing is not given the prominence it once had because of the difficulty of measuring the marginal unit of production as a consequence of the inter-relatedness in production or consumption of various goods. For example, the withdrawal of service from a branch railway line may reduce revenue on the mainline system by more than the cost savings because of system interdependence. The insistence on trying to separate services that are in some sense not separable has been called the disease of 'vulgar marginalism' (Nove 1973).

In practice, marginal cost pricing has not been widely applied but the principle has influenced the structure of pricing in many industries. In electricity, telephones, coal and the Post Office prices have been set more in line with costs of production which has meant time-of-day pricing in electricity and telephones, first- and second-class postal tariffs, and prices for coal related to different cost levels in different regions.

In other industries where domestic and international competition is important prices are determined by market forces particularly in times of excess capacity. Thus in steel and shipbuilding, excluding warships, international competition sets price levels which the British enterprises have to match if sales are to be made.

In other industries where joint costs are important, such as rail, it is difficult to identify a meaningful concept of marginal cost because supply is in terms of train loads, but demand is in terms of single seats. Thus within a given timetable, the short-run marginal cost to meet the demand for an extra seat is very low. To maximise revenue British Rail attempt to segment the market and charge prices that particular markets are willing to pay. The result is a multitude of specific fares not specifically related to costs. In practice, therefore, prices are influenced by many factors including the degree of market power, cost structures and the extent to which costs have to be covered or profits made. Thus such practices as full cost pricing, value for service pricing, marginal cost pricing and charging what the market will pay all play their part in the price-fixing process.

13.7 Investment

Public corporations are major investors in capital equipment in the UK. Over the past twenty years they have on average accounted for about 20 per cent of gross investment each year, while only accounting for some 10 per cent of gross domestic product. To undertake such a relatively large proportion of investment requires the corporations to obtain resources from other sectors of the economy to finance it. In times of relatively full employment this may thus displace more productive investments in other sectors of the economy, so it is important that the corporations utilise acceptable criteria in evaluating the worth of their investments and that the rates of return do not decline below that in the economy as a whole.

Government in the nationalisation statutes was given responsibility for taking a long-term view of the industries' development and also control of major investment decisions and borrowings. The major control mechanism since 1961 has been a system of annual investment reviews and a five year rolling programme agreed between the corporations, the sponsoring departments and the Treasury. In practice it is extremely difficult for government departments to carry out their own evaluation, or 'second guess' the benefits of a particular programme, but they can examine particular projects in the context of investment programmes for other public corporations and in terms of their relative importance for the community where limited investment funds are available. In addition the Government can request the industries to use particular methodologies and particular criteria in evaluating investment.

The 1961 White Paper (Cmnd 1337, 1961) recognised that a serious misallocation of investment might arise insofar as the public sector used different criteria to those used in the private sector. It did not, however, provide any specific guidance; this was not forthcoming until the 1967 White Paper (Cmnd 3437, 1967). This recommended the use of discounted cash flow techniques and the use of a discount rate which was not the cost of borrowing the funds used, but one based on 'the average rate of return in real terms looked for on low risk projects in the private sector in recent years' (para. 10). In addition the Treasury published investment appraisal procedures based on DCF techniques, for use by the industries as part of a 'general policy of treating the nationalised industries as commercial bodies which provide goods and services on an economic basis'. Where, however, social costs and benefits were considered important, the sponsor department would carry out a cost–benefit study and take responsibility for the final decision. The prime objective of public corporation management in appraising projects should therefore be the maximising of private benefits using accounting costs and prices.

When marginal cost pricing is the recommended pricing procedure, it has already been observed that given a known level of demand, there is an appropriate level of capacity. If, in Figure 13.2, the plant size in existence is that shown by $SRMC^1$, then with demand curve DD_1 the short-run marginal cost price would be OP_1. Thus the price is greater than long-run marginal cost, indicating that investment should take place and plant size be expanded to $SRMC^2$. If plant $SRMC^3$ already exists, then a short-run marginal cost price of OP^3 which is less than long-run marginal cost indicates that disinvestment should take place and plant size should be contracted to $SRMC^2$. Thus, given a predicted level of demand for each future year and a marginal cost curve relating to differing levels of output in future years, there will exist a marginal cost price for each desired level of output in future years and hence for desired levels of plant and machinery. From this plan will emerge the necessary levels of investment.

In investment practice this desired programme is obtained by maximising the net social benefits discounted by an appropriate rate to the year of decision less the initial investment expenditure and then undertaking all investments with positive present values, that is to the point where social benefits (demand) is equal to marginal cost. Thus the present value of any investment is given by

$$PV = -K_0 + \sum_{t=0}^{n} \frac{B^t - C^t}{(1 + r)^t}$$

where K_0 is the capital expenditure in year 0, r is the discount rate and t represents the year. Discounted cash flow analysis allows a choice to be made between alternative projects on the basis of the present values of the projects using constant prices. When all projects have been evaluated the enterprise should undertake all independent projects with a positive present value. Where projects are mutually exclusive, a series of eliminations will previously have taken place and the preferred projects included in the final list.

The discount rate plays an important role in investment appraisal using DCF techniques because it enables money values at different points of time to be added together in an acceptable way. Its effect is to reduce the weight given to benefits in later years and to take into account time preference and the ability of capital to earn interest if invested in (say) a building society. If £100 is invested for one year at 10 per cent, then after one year it will be worth £110. Thus in a reverse manner £110 in year one is worth only £100 in year 0, assuming a 10 per cent discount rate. Thus, to the private individual or company the discount rate is either the cost of borrowing the money to undertake the investment or, alternatively, if the investment is financed from retained earnings, the return it would earn in an alternative risk-free investment, e.g. in long-term government bonds.

Similar considerations apply to nationalised industries and it has been argued that the appropriate rate of discount for their projects is either the cost of long-term government debt, because this is what it costs the government to borrow, or alternatively the return earned on investments in other parts of the public sector or, perhaps more appropriately, the rate of return on marginal projects in the private sector. This discount rate is referred to as the social opportunity cost rate.

Some economists have argued in favour of using the social time preference rate of discount. This rate would represent society's preference for consumption now compared to consumption in the future. This will differ from the cost of borrowing in the public sector or the marginal rate of return on private sector projects because of such factors as divergencies between private and social costs and benefits, differences between borrowing and lending rates, problems associated with uncertainty, and the myopia of individuals who do not consider the future important and do not consider the needs of future generations. If individuals have a high rate of preference for consumption now, then the government as the custodian of the interests of future generations might wish to lower the discount rate to ensure that a greater level of investment is undertaken.

The chosen discount rate for appraising nationalised industry investment is one based on social opportunity cost. The 1967 White Paper (Cmnd 3437, 1967) recommends that major investments should be evaluated using DCF techniques and a test discount rate which 'must be sufficient to ensure that the resources are efficiently used and represents the minimum rate of return to be expected on marginal low risk projects undertaken for commercial reasons' (para. 9). The rate chosen was 8 per cent, which the Treasury regarded as the minimum rate of return earned by large private companies after allowing for the different tax and investment allowances available to private firms. This was later raised to 10 per cent at a time when the private rate of return was falling. This in real terms was a very high rate of return and in fact was used only for a minority of projects which were in some sense regarded as 'new' and independent of the existing system.

In practice much of the investment of public corporations is in the form of replacement investment designed to maintain the productive system. As such it was not subject to formal appraisal because it was considered to be essential.

The 1978 White Paper (Cmnd 7131, 1978) abandoned the test rate of discount system on the grounds that it had never been used by the industries in the way intended. In addition the 'TDR system had neither provided nor stimulated the development of an adequate way of relating the cost of capital to the industries' financial objectives' (para 59). In place of the test rate of discount was instituted the required rate of return (RRR) which again was to reflect the opportunity cost of capital in the private sector. This was set at 5 per cent in real terms and would apply to all investments by the corporations, including replacement and environmental, and whether revenue earning or not. This 5 per cent return is based on the *ex post* experience of the private sector and reflects what has been achieved rather than the *ex ante* or desired rate of return on revenue earning projects which will be expected to earn a higher rate of return.[6]

---

6. See also Heald (1980).

The top line in the DCF investment calculation, the benefits and costs, is an important part of any investment exercise. While the investment costs of the project are known with a reasonable degree of certainty, the potential net benefits which occur further into the future are much less predictable, being dependent on future levels of demand, costs of materials, etc.

The first question that must be considered in relation to net benefits is the extent to which external or social costs and benefits should be counted. The public corporations are in many ways commercial organisations and in that respect they restrict themselves to considering revenues and costs arising from the corporations' commercial activity. However, the corporations are public concerns and therefore may have social and economic obligations to consider. When this is the case investment decisions should then be viewed in a social cost–benefit framework. For example, decisions concerning investment in underground railways and airports have been specifically viewed in this way. The problem for the corporation arises when such projects are socially desirable but commercially unacceptable, so that their implementation depends upon the provision of continuous operating subsidies.

A second consideration for many public corporations in calculating net benefits is that some are integrated systems and any investment project must take into account the consequences for the costs of the system as a whole. In electricity, for example, a new power station displaces all existing stations in the merit order and creates a saving in system fuel costs. Likewise the investment programme of the Post Office in mechanised sorting offices can only achieve full benefits when the system as a whole is completed.

A third consideration is risk. This has normally been taken into account in investment appraisal through sensitivity analysis in calculating net benefits or through using a higher discount rate for riskier projects or some combination of both. Sensitivity analysis calculates benefits and costs with alternative values of key variables to check how sensitive the results of the projects are to such changes. It has been generally accepted that public sector investments have been generally risk free compared to private sector projects because of their involvement in public utility-type industries, the monopoly power that many hold, and the fact that as public corporations they are organisations which are unlikely to go bankrupt because of government guarantees. However, in practice many public sector investment projects have shown themselves to be extremely risky because market forecasts have been wrong, thus reducing revenue, because the planned equipment has not worked (e.g. the Advanced Passenger Train), or the equipment has taken longer to build and become operational (e.g. advanced gas-cooled nuclear reactors which have taken two to three times longer to construct than originally envisaged).

Thus compared to a private company the elements in the investment decision may in certain circumstances be distinctly different. This is particularly true in areas where the projects are considered to have wider social and economic effects. Then the decision is viewed less from narrow commercial considerations and more from society's point of view. Where such considerations come to the fore, the cost–benefit framework of appraising net benefits should be used, whereas in the case of commercial considerations the more traditional business valuation techniques are appropriate.

13.8   Financing

The capital assets of nationalised industries, in common with those of other commercial enterprises, are financed by retained profits and funds raised externally. Additional external finance will be required in years in which total revenue from sales is less than total cash outgoings as a result of expenditures on operating costs, interest, taxation, and capital expenditures.

The estimated net external financing requirement of the nationalised industries taken together in 1982/83 was £2,253 million[7], or about 25 per cent of the projected public sector borrowing requirement of £9,000 million for the year[8]. The funds were needed to meet the difference between the industries' internally generated funds of £4,159 million, and the estimated capital expenditure requirements of £6,412 million, almost the whole of which was for fixed asset formation in the UK. The enterprises' internally generated funds arise from: net operating profits (after interest, dividends and tax), depreciation and other net receipts. It is normally the case that the nationalised industries, taken together, have a net external financing requirement each year, although in recent years some have been significant generators of cash surpluses (e.g. electricity and gas).

The amounts of external finance supplied to nationalised industries are regulated in four ways. Each corporation has statutory maximum borrowing limits set by Parliament which can be increased only by amending the primary legislation. These limits govern all long-term finance. Secondly, the supply of finance is authorised by the appropriate Secretary of State with the approval of the Treasury, the annual total required being voted by Parliament. Thirdly, each corporation's capital expenditure programme must be authorised by the appropriate Secretary of State. Lastly, the total annual amount of funds in each case is governed by an external financing

7. See Cmnd 8789 (1983).
8. HC 216 (1983).

limit (EFL) that is set in cash terms before the start of the financial year to which it relates.

External finance is obtained from the following sources:

(*a*) *Loans from the Secretary of State*   These are provided through the National Loans Fund, the government account with the Bank of England through which most loans to public bodies are made. Loans are usually long term, extending for up to seventeen years, although recently funds have been lent for a shorter duration as part of efforts to increase the range and flexibility of finance. Repayments of the loan, together with interest due, are made at regular intervals. The rate of interest is fixed at the time of the commencement of the loan and remains unchanged for the duration; it is thus a matter of some significance to the corporations whether they borrow at times of high or low interest rates. Interest payments rank as a prime charge on the corporations and thus appear as an item on the profit and loss account, being deducted from the annual operating profit (or added to the loss).

(*b*) *Public dividend capital*   All long-term financing for nationalised industries was supplied as fixed interest loan capital until the mid-1960s. As a result, the corporations were burdened with regular interest payments that had to be met out of current operating income. When losses were made, additional loan capital was provided that raised interest costs and added to the corporations' indebtedness. It was acknowledged that companies in the private sector had access to equity finance that was irredeemable and the dividend payments on which could be varied with the state of trade. The ability to vary dividends was especially important for businesses that were faced with cyclical movements in demand and output, and hence in profitability.

Those state enterprises that were in direct competition with other companies in the domestic or international markets were recognised to be at a disadvantage as a result of the heavy burden of fixed interest debt that they were obliged to carry. On grounds of comparability, first BOAC (one of the constituent enterprises of British Airways), then BSC, National Girobank, British National Oil Corporation and British Shipbuilders, were provided with part of their capital as Public Dividend Capital (PDC). Finance provided in this way is non-repayable, but a dividend must be agreed annually with the Secretary of State. The expectation is that, taking one year with another, dividend payments will amount to the same total as if the funds had been provided as fixed interest loans. In years of poor profits or losses, the Secretary of State may authorise dividend payments to be waived. In the event, the recipients of PDC have at times made substantial losses, so that dividend payments in aggregate have been very small. In some cases (BA, BSC, British Shipbuilders) PDC has amounted to little more than an interest free, non-repayable loan to finance operating losses and capital investment, which has relieved the impact of interest charges on the profit and loss account. The financial position of BSC had deteriorated so badly by 1978 that the Government took advantage of the provisions in Section 18(1) of the Iron and Steel Act 1975 to meet the whole of the financing requirements of the corporation with 'New Capital' which, like PDC, is non-repayable. More than £2.5 billion has been provided to BSC in this form to date and no dividends have been paid.

(c) *Foreign and market borrowing and leasing* Foreign currency loans are from time to time used to supplement borrowing from the Secretary of State. They increase the flexibility of financing since they may be taken for shorter periods than is normally the case with NLF loans, and are particularly attractive when interest rates are lower abroad than in the UK and when it is more likely that the sterling exchange rate will rise than fall, thus reducing the sterling value of the repayments. The Treasury provides cover against adverse exchange rate movements in return for a premium. The benefits for nationalised enterprises in raising foreign loans are in general very small. Foreign borrowing requires the permission of the Secretary of State and is usually done to assist government economic and financial policy by increasing foreign currency reserves at times when the pound is under pressure in the foreign exchange markets, and by reducing the impact of increases in the public sector borrowing requirement on the growth of the money supply.

Short-term domestic borrowing by means of bank loans and overdrafts and commercial bills may be used to finance increases in working capital requirements; such borrowing does not count against the statutory borrowing limits. Leasing of assets has increased in importance in the nationalised industries over the last decade, as indeed it has in private sector industrial companies. The surplus funds of financial institutions are used to purchase tangible assets which are then leased back for use by the corporations, thus reducing their capital expenditures and the call against public expenditure.

(d) *Government grants* These are paid to eight of the seventeen public corporations defined as nationalised industries for public expenditure planning purposes, and are provided as operating grants to meet certain expenses charged against revenue, as deficit finance to compensate for revenue shortfalls against costs, and as grants for certain capital expenditures. Grants account for the greater part of total external finance for nationalised industries (£1,829,000 or four-fifths of the total in 1982/83), and more than 90 per cent is accounted for by the British Railways Board and the NCB.

Grants are paid for several reasons. Following the UK's accession to the European Communities in 1973 and the Railways Act of the following year, BRB was given a public service obligation (PSO) 'to operate their railway passenger system so as to provide a public service which is generally comparable with that provided at present . . ."[9] This obliges the Board to operate uneconomic rural, cross-country and urban services, for which it receives compensation. NCB receives grants for operating high-cost pits as well as for other operating deficits and essential investment. The electricity supply industry in England and Wales is compensated for being obliged to purchase coal from the NCB at prices above those in the world market. An Intervention Fund has been established to make up the difference between British Shipbuilders' costs of merchant shipbuilding and the level of contract price that it is possible to obtain given the conditions of severe competition in the world market. Grants are in general treated as revenue items in the accounts of the nationalised industries, with the effect that operating losses are reduced and profits increased. They have no effect on the balance sheet.

The general policy of the Treasury and the sponsoring departments is clear on the conditions under which the several types of finance are to be provided to the nationalised industries. In practice, however, changing circumstances and differing economic and political pressures have meant that both long-term finance and operating grants have on occasion been provided to relieve short-term operating losses, with the consequence that the true performance of the enterprises and the extent of managerial responsibility have been obscured. While it is readily acknowledged that both the degree of market power and the level of risk vary between the enterprises, factors which ideally should be reflected in the pattern of financing, it is nevertheless the case that the present capital structures of the enterprises show an almost random diversity. Thus, as Table 13.3 shows, the proportion of total net assets financed by long-term loan capital differs very much between the corporations, with consequent effects upon the amounts of interest charged to their profit and loss accounts and thus to their comparative rates of return. While the greater part of the NCB's capital is made up of NLF finance, BSC has a preponderance of PDC-type finance, and British Gas and the electricity industry have repaid most of their loan capital.

One of the causes of this variety is that long-term finance, both loans and PDC, have been used to fund operating losses. This increases the amount of nominal capital outstanding on the balance sheet in relation to the true value of the assets. In time a large-scale financial reconstruction, in which past loans and losses are written off, becomes inevitable.

Although operating grants are intended to finance specific activities, the existence of joint costs in several of the industries means that the amount of grant becomes difficult to control if trading conditions or efficiency deteriorate; the problems of British Rail since 1968 are an example of this.

In the absence of stock market sanctions through falling share prices and

---

9. Department of Transport (1983).

Table 13.3 Asset Financing of Selected Nationalised Industries, 1981/82

Industry	Year ended	Loans from Secretary of State	Foreign loans	Equity	Reserves[a]	Other[b]	Capital employed (£million)
					Percentages of capital employed		
National Coal Board	31.3.82	71.0	22.5	—	2.2	4.4	3,552.7
Electricity (England and Wales)[c]	31.3.82	12.0	2.1	—	84.6	1.1	32,605.4
British Gas Corporation	31.3.82	—	1.6	—	92.8	5.6	10,955.4
British National Oil Corporation	31.12.81	—	—	—	38.8	61.2[d]	913.3
British Steel Corporation	31.3.82	—	22.8	105.0[e]	(32.0)	4.3	2,494.0
Post Office	31.3.82	14.1	0.8	1.7	83.4	—	1,267.0
British Telecommunications	31.3.82	36.2	5.7	—	43.3	14.8[f]	8,437.8
British Airways Board	31.3.82	5.5	100.8	23.8	(53.1)	23.1	756.6
British Railways Board	31.12.81	37.0	7.5	—	48.0	7.5	1,242.2
National Bus Company	31.12.81	69.9[g]	—	—	30.1	—	230.4
British Shipbuilders	31.3.82	—	13.8	171.3	(85.3)	0.3	264.5

Source: Annual Reports and Accounts.
Notes: (a) Including retained profits.
(b) Short-term loans, deferred liabilities, deferred taxation, leased assets, etc.
(c) Central Electricity Generating Board and twelve regional boards.
(d) Including proceeds from advance oil sales.
(e) New Capital, under Section 18(1), Iron and Steel Act 1975.
(f) Long-term liability to Post Office Staff Superannuation Scheme.
(g) Including capital debt.

the threat of takeover or liquidation, and with the economic, social and political importance of most of the nationalised industries, there is a considerable risk that finance to support unprofitable and inefficient operations, without any pressures for rationalisation, may be regarded as inexhaustible. It was in an attempt to guard against this that financial targets, pricing and investment guidelines and, most recently, external financing limits were introduced. It is plain, however, that these instruments have been only partially successful and there is a real need for agreement on the economic, financial and social objectives of the enterprises and the manner in which their activities are to be financed. Until that is achieved the assessment of performance and the identification of the responsibilities of management and of government will be very difficult.

13.9   Financial Control

Financial control over the nationalised industries is exercised by government in three main ways: by the setting of rates of return, of real unit cost targets, and of external financing limits. These controls are intended to work together coherently to take account of the trading and financial prospects of the enterprises, of their investment requirements, and of government financial and economic policy.

(a)   Financial Targets

The setting of targets to provide financial objectives for the nationalised industries was first proposed in the 1961 White Paper (Cmnd 1337, 1961) and reinforced in the 1967 policy statement (Cmnd 3437, 1967). Financial targets are usually expressed in terms of a rate of return of profits net of taxation, interest and depreciation on net assets over a period of two to three years ahead. In recent years the targets have been set in terms of current cost accounting procedures to give a requirement for a rate of return in real terms. These naturally imply a higher rate of return in terms of historical cost accounting. The ratios relate to the surplus of income over costs properly chargeable to revenue account as a proportion of net capital employed and are thus not directly related to the cash position of the enterprises which may be intending to raise additional capital funds from outside the business. Profits may be related to turnover rather than to assets for enterprises (such as the Post Office) that are inevitably labour intensive and have a relatively small asset base. As first conceived, the targets set were intended to reflect the mean rate of return in the private sector of the economy, adjusted for any special factors governing the trading and financial position of the enterprise (such as social service obligations) so that managerial decision making and control would be carried out in a commercial environment. In this way it was intended that the risk of a misallocation of resources between the public and private sectors and within the public sector itself would be avoided. The main problems have been that in the absence of other controls or targets, enterprises with a degree of market power could attain their profitability targets by raising prices or reducing the standards and quality of service rather than by constraining costs. Targets have been of little use for enterprises that incur losses or are subject to intense international competition and cyclical movements in demand. Governments have also tended to use the targets more for purposes of macroeconomic policy than for the achievement of efficient resource allocation at the microeconomic level. Thus high rates of return have on occasion been set for those enterprises that could raise their prices and generate additional funds to support public expenditure. Governments have also from time to time failed to set targets, particularly when wishing to hold down prices in the nationalised sector as part of counter-inflationary policies, the results of which were to raise the deficits of public enterprises.

(b)   Real Unit Costs

Real unit cost targets have been introduced as a means of encouraging increases in the efficiency of resource usage primarily in enterprises for which competitive pressures are thought to be weak. They are defined as the ratio of annual operating expenses to a measure of output (often revenue) expressed in constant prices. The targets usually call for a specified percentage reduction in real unit costs over a period of years. Real unit cost targets were first applied to the Post Office in 1978 and have since been extended to several other nationalised industries. Enterprises may seek to achieve their targets by increasing the volume of output relative to a constant real level of costs, by reducing the real level of costs (e.g. by employment reduction) relative to a constant level of output or, as is usually the case, by a combination of the two. Government may specify quality of service standards so that cost reductions cannot be obtained by materially altering the nature of the output. Enterprises may meet difficulties in reaching their targets if factor input prices rise faster than their final output prices or the general index of prices that is being used as a deflator.

(c)   External Financing Limits

In common with enterprises in the private sector, public corporations require external finance for capital expenditure to fund operating losses and to meet extraordinary items, such as the costs of plant closures and associated redundancy charges. For an enterprise operating in a non-inflationary steady state and able to charge prices sufficient to meet the full costs of operations, there would be no demand on external funds. Asset replacement would be met from depreciation and the remaining net cash flow would be divided between interest payments, dividends and retained profits. Where there is scope for profitable capital investment, however, additional funds in the form of equity or loans will be sought.

Before 1976 all capital expenditure by nationalised industries was included in the total of public expenditure, even though the greater part was financed internally by enterprises from their revenues. These expenditures, like all others within the public sector, were planned and controlled on a rolling five year basis through the annual Public Expenditure Survey Committee (PESC) exercise. Expenditure was estimated on a volume basis, assuming constant prices. The effects of inflation were generally met by increasing the cash amounts of expenditure to allow the volume of capital formation to be broadly maintained. High and accelerating inflation rates in the mid-1970s caused sharp increases in cash demands under this system, and a consequent increase in government borrowing.

In order to control the cash levels of public expenditure a system of cash limits covering the whole of the public sector was introduced in 1976/77. The definition of public expenditure in relation to the nationalised industries was changed so that only their external financing requirements were included in the total and these were subjected to cash control by the setting of external financing limits (EFLs).

EFLs are announced by the Treasury each year in November for the following financial year and are set after discussions with the industries and their sponsoring departments. They take account of the revenue prospects of the industries, their capital expenditure plans and cash needs, the scope for cost savings, and the general circumstances of public expenditure. Details of the nationalised industries' capital expenditures for the ensuing year and of their financing, including the application of the EFL, are given in the public expenditure White Paper and the Financial Statement and Budget Report, published at the start of the year to which they relate. Table 13.4 shows the details for 1983/84.

Taken together, the nationalised industries were forecast to meet about two-thirds of their total capital requirements of £6.9 billion from internally generated funds (profits, interest, dividends, depreciation, etc.), requiring net external finance of £2.6 billion. The NCB, BRB, South of Scotland Electricity Board and BSC have the biggest requirements for external finance, amounting to almost the whole of the net financing requirements for all the nationalised industries. Four of the industries are expected to generate cash surpluses; Electricity in England and Wales has the largest

Table 13.4 Forecast of Financing Requirements of the Nationalised Industries 1983–84 (£million cash)[a]

Industry	Capital requirements			Internally generated funds					Government grants for revenue and capital purposes	External finance		
										Net borrowing from		
	Fixed assets in the UK[b]	Other[c]	Total	Current cost operating profit[d]	Interest dividends and tax[e]	Depreciation etc[f]	Other receipts and payments[g]	Total		Government (NLF PDC etc)	Market overseas and leasing	Total external financing limit
National Coal Board	800	11	811	−526	−417	601	42	−300	549	563	−1	1,111
Electricity (England & Wales)	1,395	−42	1,353	464	−537	1,627	111	1,665	11	−300	−23	−312
North of Scotland Hydro-Electric Board	43	2	45	27	−62	68	4	38	—	10	−3	7
South of Scotland Electricity Board	432	−99	332	12	−147	180	4	49	—	291	−8	283
British Gas Corporation	885	107	992	458	−162	663	41	1,000	—	—	−8	−8
British National Oil Corporation[h]	—	—	—	2	−1	—	—	1	—	—	−1	−1
British Steel Corporation[i]	217	8	225	−93	−67	160	30	30	—	233	−38	195
British Telecommunications	1,997	152	2,149	1,146	−563	1,468	2	2,053	—	196	−100	96
Post Office	130	−35	95	72	−3	64	5	138	—	−34	−9	−43
National Girobank	9	2	11	9	−3	6	—	11	—	—	—	—[k]
British Airways Board	229	16	245	165	−125	200	—	240	—	9	−4	5
British Airports Authority	152	6	158	47	−3	80	1	125	—	33	—	33
British Railways Board	337	−124	213	−1,066	−94	203	210	−747	979	−5	−14	960
British Waterways Board	4	4	8	−36	−3	1	—	−38	40	1	—	42
National Bus Company	59	2	61	−62	−25	78	4	−5	66	—	1	67
Scottish Transport Group	19	—	19	−7	−5	12	—	—	20	−4	3	19
British Shipbuilders[j]	90	70	160	−38	—	39	9	10	42	108	—	150
Civil Aviation Authority	26	3	29	14	−17	11	—	8	5	13	4	21
Total	**6,823**	**81**	**6,904**	**589**	**−2,235**	**5,462**	**463**	**4,279**	**1,712**	**1,113**	**−201**	**2,625**

Source: Cmnd 8789, The Government's Expenditure Plans 1983–84 to 1985–86, HMSO, February 1983.

Notes: (a) No figures are included for BIDB on account of its impending privatisation. Figures for BNOC take account of the disposal of its former exploration and production activities in November 1982.

(b) The capital value of leased assets is included.

(c) Includes fixed assets abroad, net investment in UK companies, net investment in long and medium-term financial assets and changes in working capital (including stocks and work in progress).

(d) Some industries use historic cost as the basis of their main accounts. Because of this, and the exclusion of Government grants for revenue purposes, the figures in this column may differ from those for operating profit in those accounts. For BGC the operating profit is after charging £553 million for the gas levy.

(e) The total figure for interest alone is −£2,007 million. That for taxation is −£225 million.

(f) Includes cost of sales adjustment, monetary working capital adjustment and other items not involving the movement of funds.

(g) Includes proceeds from sales of fixed assets (where not credited to the special sales of assets) and other capital receipts.

(h) Given the uncertainties of oil trading, BNOC's trading results are likely to fluctuate. Its capital requirements are expected to be substantially less than £1 million annually.

(i) The prospects for BSC in 1983–84 are under review.

(j) The BS figures are provisional pending decisions on the industry's corporate plan.

(k) National Girobank has been set an EFL of £−½ million for 1983–84, to take account of the reduction in the National Insurance Surcharge announced in the Autumn Statement.

surplus, namely £312 million. The special gas levy removes, in addition, £553 million from BGC.

In some cases, as will be apparent from the table, nationalised industries are net providers of cash to the Treasury. This is shown for those industries with *negative* EFLs: in 1983/84 (in descending order of contribution) this was the case for Electricity (England and Wales), the Post Office, British Gas, and BNOC. The enterprises in these cases are covering the whole of their operating costs, debt service charges, taxation, and capital expenditure requirements from revenue and generating, in addition, a cash surplus. The greatest contribution in recent years has come from Electricity. Substantial amounts have been provided also by British Gas, but the introduction of the gas levy has had the effect of reducing the apparent surplus generated by means of the negative EFLs.

Cash generated by the nationalised industries is used either to repay outstanding long-term debt, with the effect of reducing interest payments, (e.g. British Gas) or is used for the purchase of short-term government securities (e.g. the Post Office). In either case it has the effect of reducing the total amount of external finance for the nationalised industries that counts against the total of public expenditure and, hence, it also reduces the public sector borrowing requirement. The Treasury also recognises that corporations may be in long-term surplus and have repaid the whole of their long-term debt. In such circumstances legislation will be required in order that funds can continue to be extracted by government.

Once an EFL has been set, there are several ways in which management can respond.[10] If internally generated funds are expected to run below the target for the year with unchanged policies, management may raise prices, endeavour to reduce operating costs, or cut back on planned capital expenditure.

The scope for increasing internal cash flow through price increases depends upon the elasticity of demand and on any government counter-inflationary policies that may be in force. Despite the apparent monopoly positions of several of the nationalised enterprises, few in reality are able to undertake unilateral price increases without having a significant effect upon their volume of sales; for those operating in the segment of their demand curve where elasticity is greater than unity, price increases will generate less, rather than more, revenue. Where market conditions allow, enterprises within a particular sector may be able to raise prices generally in parallel, for example in the energy industries at a time of rising oil prices; and where the comparable prices of one enterprise are significantly below those of its most important competitors, price increases without loss of volume of sales may be possible, for example the increase in gas prices following the decision to increase the net generation of cash from the

10. See also Redwood and Hatch (1982).

British Gas Corporation. But in circumstances other than these, individual initiatives on price to remedy cash flow deficiencies are very difficult.

Reductions in operating costs are another possible response to binding EFLs. Most of the nationalised industries are capital intensive, with fixed overheads forming a significant fraction of total costs. In the short run, therefore, the chief way in which cost reductions can be achieved is through increases in labour productivity, with subsidiary contributions possible from reductions in discretionary current expenditures. Increases in productivity are very difficult to achieve at times of stationary or falling demand, when the pressure from restrictive EFLs will be greatest. The system also precludes effective permanent reductions in the number of employees through redundancy, since the cost of these falls on the EFL in the year in which they take place.

Because of the difficulties in conserving cash through price increases or reductions in operating expenses in the short term, it is inevitable that most of the burden falls upon capital expenditure. Cash outgoings can be reduced by liquidating stocks, thus reducing working capital needs, and by cutting back on fixed capital formation. It is likely that since the introduction of EFL controls in 1976/77, they have had their greatest impact on capital expenditures; and from the point of view of the commercial development and performance of several of the enterprises, it is in this respect that they have been most damaging. Reductions in stocks may impair the ability of the enterprise to respond to increases in demand when the market improves in the future, or even to meet the full range of customers' requirements at the present low level of sales. Part of the well-known difficulties of the British Steel Corporation are probably due to this factor. Reductions in fixed capital spending can be obtained by delaying prospective projects, or slowing down the pace of schemes that are currently underway. In both cases the real rate of return on the schemes is likely to be reduced, perhaps even falling below the point at which the project is economically viable, as the revenue receipts from the projects are pushed back in time, while the investment costs are increased through the effects of inflation and the sub-optimal pattern of asset formation that may be imposed. The need for short-term cash saving is one factor underlying the tendency for public enterprises to underspend in some years in relation to their authorised capital formation.

EFLs have been described as 'a crude and indiscriminate method of control' for the nationalised industries. More colourfully, one chairman has described their effect as 'trying to run a business with a piggy bank'. They reflect the concern of the Treasury with the impact of nationalised industries' financing requirements upon the public expenditure total in the short term. They do not distinguish between current and capital expenditures and, indeed, may lead management to rob their capital expenditure budgets to support operating cash shortfalls.

13.10   Corporate Planning

The principles, policies and procedures influencing pricing, investment and financial conditions are vital elements in planning corporate strategy for public corporations as they are for all large enterprises. Corporate planning developed as a distinct and important function within the nationalised industries from the end of the 1960s and later became a statutory requirement for some. The process involves setting the objectives, selecting appropriate courses of action and establishing monitoring procedures for the whole enterprise. There are typically three levels at which planning is carried out: for the year ahead (the annual operating plan); for the medium term, covering usually the next five years (the development plan); and for the long-term period of ten or more years ahead (the strategic plan). Each level of planning is concerned essentially with the same features considered over different time-scales: assumptions about the general economic environment during the period of the plan; the level of demand; price trends; competitors' actions; capacity availability; investment; personnel and financial requirements.[11]

Preparation and adoption of a plan can be of great value in informing and involving the many divisions and functional areas that comprise most nationalised industries and in monitoring their performance against the plan. Cost or profit centres within the business can be given definitive targets against which to work in full knowledge of the obligations laid upon other parts of the enterprise. Moreover, it may be hoped that through publication and discussion of the plan, staff and unions may be better informed about the financial position of the enterprise and its prospects for the future. Corporations may also wish to publicise their plans in order to gauge and respond to government policies and public opinion—the type and capacity of electric power generating stations, for example. In many cases they will be given close scrutiny. In addition, the comprehensive nature of the plan may be helpful in seeking to justify the economic case for new investment.

Although the elements of corporate plans are similar to those of any large commercial enterprise, there are several factors to be taken into account when preparing them that are distinctive for nationalised industries and which may impact on the eventual outturn.

(a) It can be difficult to frame and agree objectives for the enterprise when there are non-commercial aspects to be considered, such as the political sensitivity of price increases, and the effects on the level of employment or on the balance of payments. Governments in the past have sometimes been reluctant to agree precise objectives and

---

11. See Harris and Davies (1981), Kingshott (1975).

have on occasion imposed obligations on nationalised industries at short notice.

(b) Despite official statements setting out the economic case for marginal cost-based pricing, there has been little or no guidance for enterprises as to how far this should in fact be put into practice. Persistent losses are likely to be met with pressure to raise prices, if the market will bear it, whereas prices that generate large surpluses may be considered politically embarrassing.

(c) External finance in the form of loans, grants or equity may be more easily forthcoming from government if the enterprise is seen as a vital part of the industrial economy, providing social benefits that exceed the cost to the Exchequer through the provision of goods, services, employment opportunities, export sales or orders for capital goods. On the other hand, pressure to constrain the level of public expenditure can result in essential investment being cancelled or delayed. Changes in the overall prospects of the economy can result in policy adjustments at very short notice.

(d) There may be uncertainty about the forms in which external finance will be supplied by government. Revenue grants can be treated as turnover, but loans impose future burdens on the profit and loss account by way of interest charges. Additional equity may be used in part to finance operating losses, but the balance sheet will become distorted, with capital far exceeding the true value of the assets employed. Governments may then be reluctant to authorise a financial reconstruction.

(e) Financial targets may or may not be set by government. Where these lead to the generation of large surpluses (e.g. gas and electricity), there may be uncertainty about how the funds are to be applied. Whereas a firm in the private sector could acquire financial assets or undertake new investment or acquisition, nationalised industries are likely to be obliged to pass some part of their funds to central government.

(f) Corporate plans cannot usually allow for diversification to reduce the risk of the business or to develop more profitable areas of business. This can impose serious problems in the formulation of objectives for those enterprises that are in persistent loss-incurring situations.

(g) Despite the dominant position that several of the public corporations occupy in their markets, they may not be able to use to the full their commercial power in competing with private sector firms. Strategic planning may be complicated because of uncertainty about the extent to which government will allow them to respond to competitive threats.

13.11   The Role and Influence of Government

The organisational form of the public corporation was proposed by Herbert Morrison[12] as a means of establishing within the public sector of the economy commercially oriented enterprises that recognised at the same time their vital contribution to the public interest. The minister, through his statutory powers and with reference to the statutory duties imposed on the corporations, would be able to ensure that the public interest was adequately met, while at the same time avoiding undue interference by Government or Parliament in the day-to-day matters of operation and decision taking.

It is hard to say to what extent it was believed that such a system would work successfully; it is apparent that interventions by ministers have been considerable, have tended to increase in number and significance through time, and have had a generally damaging effect on the economic and financial performance of the corporations. Interventions have in general been of a non-statutory nature, have concerned macroeconomic matters and wider political objectives, and have occurred under governments formed by both of the main parties. Below are listed the main areas in which interventions have taken place.

(a) *Prices*: Proposals for price increases by the nationalised industries have been reduced either by direct ministerial intervention or by reference to a prevailing statutory or voluntary price code intended to reduce inflation. Restraints were imposed between 1970 and 1974 and between 1976 and 1978. The financial structures and perform-ances of several enterprises were considerably weakened as a result of these initiatives, particularly during the first period, and distor-tions were caused to other parts of the economy, for example as a result of the subsidisation of customers by prices that were lower than would have been charged otherwise and that were supported by subventions from public expenditure.

(b) *Incomes*: Wage and salary settlements have been influenced in a similar manner with the intention of supporting counter-inflationary policies. This has been achieved by direct instruction, by reference to independent boards (e.g. the National Board for Prices and Incomes), by limiting the amount of external finance available, and by 'moral suasion'.

(c) *Investment*: Capital expenditure projects have been cut back or delayed, with the intention of controlling the annual cash require-ments of enterprises and reducing the impact on the public expendi-

---

12. Herbert Morrison (1888–1965): Minister of Transport 1923–31, Minister of Supply 1940; Secretary for Home Office and Home Security 1940–45; Lord President 1945–51; Foreign Secretary 1951; Life Peer 1959.

ture total. Delays have sometimes occurred because of disagreements between industries and their sponsoring departments (e.g. the British Steel Corporation, 1969–73, and the British Railways Board, currently, in the matter of further electrification).

(d) *Employment*: Pressure has been brought to bear to maintain employment levels, or to reduce the rate of reduction of employment. This has been so especially in the cases of the NCB and BSC.

Where, as in coal and the railways, the long-term maintenance of an industry has been regarded as necessary, grants have been paid to support operations. Government has also provided direct assistance with certain capital projects, for example the early construction of the Drax *B* power station. But for the interventions discussed above, no direct compensation has been paid to enterprises to offset their financial consequences, save in relatively minor cases (e.g. the obligation of the CEGB to buy coal from the NCB at above-market prices). Costs have typically been met by increasing the capital subventions to the enterprises, with a consequential impact on their balance sheets, frequently eventually requiring capital write-offs and financial reconstructions.

The difficulties posed for the boards of public corporations by their statutory relationships with government and the persistent involvement of ministers and civil servants on a non-statutory basis were identified by the House of Commons Select Committee on Nationalised Industries in a report in 1973 (HC65, 1973/74). The Labour Government of the day responded by referring the issue of the control of the nationalised industries to the National Economic Development Office (NEDO) for investigation.

The main recommendations made in the subsequent report (NEDO 1976) were the following:

(a) Each enterprise should have a policy board established as the overall controlling body and composed of representatives of the main interest groups concerned with the industry, that is, senior managers, employees, customers, and civil servants (as representatives of the minister) together with some independent members. The policy board would be headed by a president, whose term of office should be lengthy (five to seven years). The board would be responsible for overall strategy, taking into account any matters affecting the public interest including those indicated by the minister. The hope was that by this means direct ministerial involvement in the affairs of the corporations would be avoided.

(b) Corporation boards, headed by the chairman, should be made up of full-time senior managers and should be concerned with day-to-day planning and control within the broad outlines of the strategy set out by the policy board.

   (c) In circumstances where it proved impossible to reach agreement between the policy board and the minister, he should have powers to issue specific directives to the corporation. Payment of compensation for the financial effects of any obligations placed on the enterprise was a necessary corrolary.

   (d) To aid effective economic and financial control, NEDO proposed that enterprises should agree with ministers efficiency indicators to reflect the progress and performance of the business and should publish them in their annual reports; standards of service should be specified in appropriate industries; prices should be set, taking into account the resource costs of providing the output and also the market and investment environments in which the enterprises operated; non-commercial obligations should be identified and published; the terms and conditions on which finance is made available should take account of the relative riskiness of investment opportunities; and there should be firm ground rules for providing subsidies and for capital write-offs.

Concern was voiced in some quarters that the implementation of the proposal for policy boards would inject another layer of bureaucracy and authority into an already over-loaded system, but there can be little doubt that NEDO's recommendations, if implemented, would have gone far to clarifying and improving relationships between government and the nationalised industries and laying a sound basis for a more commercial orientation on the part of boards. The Government, replying in a White Paper in 1978, proposed only modest changes in the directions proposed by NEDO, the effects of which would have been broadly to have maintained the *status quo*. Thus, the proposals for efficiency indicators and specific directives were accepted, and the intention was expressed to widen representation on corporation boards. Resource-related pricing policies were to be pursued more vigorously, and the test discount rate (TDR) would be replaced by the requirement to earn a specified real rate of return (RRR) on the whole of proposed new capital expenditure in order to increase the effectiveness and appropriateness of investment decisions. There was also to be more flexibility in the types of finance provided to the nationalised industries. The proposal for policy boards was, however, firmly rejected on the grounds that it would 'slow down the process of decision making and would confuse responsibility and accountability' (Cmnd 7131, 1978).

The 1978 White Paper remains the most recent formal statement of government policy towards the nationalised industries, but it has been overtaken by events. The Conservative Government elected in June 1979 came to power with a manifesto commitment to reduce the size of the public sector and the extent of public ownership and to introduce market disciplines and commercial policies to the nationalised industries. Despite difficulties, steps have been taken to introduce private capital into some enterprises, to establish joint ventures between public and private enterprises, to transfer assets to private ownership, and to extract financial surpluses from those industries in favourable market environments for the relief of the public sector borrowing requirement and general taxation. It has, nevertheless, been necessary to continue substantial financial support for those enterprises that face intense international competition (steel) or provide vital products or services (coal, railways). The Competition Act 1980 widened the powers of the Monopolies and Mergers Commission to enable it to undertake efficiency audits of the nationalised industry upon reference from the Secretary of State for Trade, and several reports have been published.[13]

It remains the case that ministerial involvement in nationalised industries, beyond the levels envisaged in the nationalisation acts, continues to complicate and frustrate managerial responsibility and strategic planning. Principal obligations currently placed on boards include: sale of profitable or potentially profitable assets to private sector interests (gas, railway hotels, North Sea oil distribution, shipyards); generation of financial surpluses to relieve government borrowing (electricity, posts, oil); and the continuance of loss-making operations for purposes of maintaining employment (coal, steel). Until 1979 enquiries by the Select Committee on Nationalised Industries provided a forum in which the industries could bring to the attention of Parliament and to a wider public the nature and commercial impact of ministerial involvement in their activities, as well as increasing the degree of accountability of boards, ministers and civil servants. The introduction of the system of departmentally-based select committees in the Parliament that first met in June 1979, and the failure to re-appoint a nationalised industries' select committee, has meant that scrutiny of policy towards public enterprise has been fragmented among several committees and in consequence has lost coherence and incisiveness. There are no signs at present that a stable and effective system of relationships between ministers and the boards of the enterprises they sponsor is likely to be developed.

13.12 The Task for Management

Despite the measure of agreement that exists on the economic principles on which public enterprises should be established and operated, and the recognition of these principles in legislation, institutional procedures and

---

13. For example, Cmnd 8046 (1980); HC 315 (1981); HC 339 (1980); HC 515 (1980).

stated policy, the preceding sections of this chapter indicate that the successful formulation and implementation of corporate strategy in nationalised industries is very difficult. Many forces influence pricing decisions—the need to generate internal cash flow; the opportunity cost of resources; the nature of the market; the strength of competition; financial targets; government expenditure and borrowing targets; and counter-inflationary policies. Demonstrating the financial and economic justification of capital projects is often insufficient to guarantee their authorisation or completion. Schemes may be initiated or terminated for a variety of reasons, including political, social and short-term macroeconomic needs. Financing methods are labyrinthine in their complexity, offering ample scope for the costs of non-commercial obligations imposed, or assistance provided, by government to be obscured. Financial control is designed to act mainly as a short-term regulator and makes long-term planning and execution of policy difficult. Corporate planning must thus encompass a wider range of factors than in most large private sector enterprises, for account must be taken of the direct effects of government policy towards the nationalised industries and efforts made to anticipate shifts in policy and to develop contingency plans accordingly.

In these circumstances public enterprise managers must first recognise that inevitably their life is lived in a goldfish bowl. There is intense public interest in the policies and revealed performance of the enterprises. The nature of the political environment is such that both losses and profits are condemned. To cope with this it is vital that enterprises should set their own realistic long-term objectives and design strategy to achieve them. At the same time, the political climate must be continuously monitored, and close contact maintained with government. Operational plans must be capable of modification to suit changed circumstances in the market and in government policy. Only by this means can some of the risk and uncertainty be removed from the business.

Over the longer term, representation can be made for a more stable relationship between the public corporations and government, and the public's attention drawn to the impact of any non-commercial obligations that may be imposed. Inevitably, however, the task will be taxing and frustrating, but with some compensation from the opportunity to work in a vital sector of the economy. Dr Johnson's aphorism about a woman's preaching applies as well to public enterprise management: 'It is not done well; but you are surprised to find it done at all.'[14]

---

14. Boswell's *Life of Johnson*, Vol. 1, p. 46, quoted in OUP (1979).

Appendix: Marginal Cost Pricing

The marginal cost pricing rule is derived from the Paretian rules for an optimum allocation of resources. The allocative rule requires that the marginal rate of transformation and the marginal rate of substitution between any two goods be equal to each other and to the ratio of their prices.

The marginal rate of transformation between the two goods (MRT_{xy}) can be shown to be equal to the ratio of the marginal products of labour (MPL), so that symbolically

$$MRT_{xy} = \frac{MPL_y}{MPL_x}$$

A move along the transformation curve means moving resources from the production of, for example, good X to the production of good Y. The additional units of the good Y will require additional units of labour and capital, so that

$$\Delta Y = \Delta L \cdot MPL_y + \Delta K \cdot MPK_y$$

Likewise, the change necessitated by the reduced production of good X is given by

$$\Delta X = -(\Delta L \cdot MPL_x + \Delta K \cdot MPK_x)$$

Combining the two expressions, it can be shown that

$$\frac{\Delta Y}{\Delta X} = \frac{MPL_y}{MPL_x}$$

When capital is in fixed supply, an increase in output will require further employment of the variable factor, labour. If the wage (W) is the cost of the additional labour (ΔL), then the cost of the extra labour is $W \cdot \Delta L$. This is also the change in total cost since capital is fixed. The change in cost per unit of output is

$$\frac{W \cdot L}{\Delta X} \cdot \frac{W}{\Delta X / \Delta L}$$

But $\Delta X / \Delta L$ is the marginal product of labour, while the increase in cost per unit of output is the marginal cost, thus we have

$$W / MPL_x = MC_x$$

If inputs are being varied together, then the same argument holds, the marginal cost of the good in equilibrium being given by W/MPL_x or by R/MPK_x, where R is the cost of capital.

Using the relationships $MRT_{xy} = MPL_y/MPL_x$ and $MC_x = W/MPL_x$, then $MPL_x = W/MC_x$. Similarly, the $MPL_y = W/MC_y$. Together these relationships give

$$MRT_{xy} = MC_x/MC_t$$

If both firms operate so that they produce the ouput at which marginal cost is equal to prices, we have $MRT_{xy} = P_x/P_y$. Thus firms should operate in such a way as to respond to changes in market or shadow prices by changing their output until marginal cost is equal to price. Since we assume that consumers face the same prices as the producers, the MRT_{xy} will be equal to MRS_{xy}, so that marginal cost pricing observed in all sectors of the economy is a sufficient condition to ensure Pareto optimality.

References

Harris, D. J. and Davies, B. C. L. (1981) 'Corporate planning as a control system in United Kingdom nationalised industries', *Long Range Planning*, Vol. 14, February, pp. 15–22.

Heald, D. (1980) 'The economic and financial control of the nationalised industries', *Economic Journal*, Vol. 90, No. 358, June, pp. 243–265.

Kingshott, A. L. (1975) 'Planning in a nationalised industry', *Long Range Planning*, October, pp. 58–65.

Millward, R. (1978) *Public Ownership, the Theory of Property Rights and the Public Corporation in the UK*, Salford Papers in Economics 1978–I, University of Salford Department of Economics, mimeo.

Nove, A. (1973) *Efficiency Criteria for Nationalised Industries*, Allen and Unwin.

Pryke, R. W. (1981) *The Nationalised Industries: Policies and Performance since 1968*, Martin Robertson.

Redwood, J. and Hatch, J. (1982) *Controlling Public Enterprise*, Martin Robertson.

Turvey, R. (1971) *Economic Analysis and Public Enterprises*, Allen and Unwin.

Webb, M. (1973) *The Economics of Nationalised Industries*, Nelson.

Williamson, O. E. (1971) 'Managerial discretion, organisation form and the multi-divisional hypothesis', in R. Marris and A. Wood (eds), *The Corporate Economy*, Macmillan.

Central Statistical Office (1982) *National Income and Expenditure 1982*, HMSO.

Cmnd 1337 (1961) *The Financial and Economic Obligations of Nationalised Industries*, April, HMSO.

Cmnd 3437 (1967) *Nationalised Industries: A Review of Economic and Financial Objectives*, November, HMSO.

Cmnd 7131 (1978) *The Nationalised Industries*, April, HMSO.

Cmnd 8046 (1980) *British Railways Board: London and South-East Commuter Services*, Monopolies and Mergers Commission, HMSO.

Cmnd 8789 (1983) *The Government's Expenditure Plans, 1983–84 to 1985–86*, February, Vol. 2, Table 3.4b, HMSO.

Department of Transport (1983) *Railway Finances*, Report of a Committee Chaired by Sir David Serpell, HMSO.

HC 65 (1973) *Capital Investment Procedures*, First Report from the Select Committee on Nationalised Industries (1973/74), HMSO.

HC 339 (1980) *Severn and Trent Water Authority, East Worcestershire Waterworks Company and South Staffordshire Waterworks Company*, Monopolies and Mergers Commission (1980/81), HMSO.

HC 515 (1980) *Inner London Letter Post*, Monopolies and Mergers Commission (1980/81), HMSO.

HC 315 (1981) *The Central Electricity Generating Board*, Monopolies and Mergers Commission (1980/81), HMSO.

HC 216 (1983) *Financial Statement and Budget Report 1983–84*, HMSO, March.

NEDO (1976) *A Study of UK Nationalised Industries*, HMSO.

OUP (1979) *The Oxford Book of Quotations*, Oxford University Press.

14
The Management of the Small Firm

D. A. Littler, J. F. Pickering and T. A. J. Cockerill

14.1 Introduction

At the time of writing, the creation and development of small firms is seen as an important element of overall economic policy, especially for promoting employment and reviving a lagging mature economy. This contrasts markedly with the received wisdom of an earlier period where belief in the benefits of size and scale as a basis for effective performance in domestic and international markets initiated much greater attention to large units and the encouragement of mergers.

Undoubtedly there are a variety of explanations for the present emphasis on the economic importance of small firms. The disappointing performance of large firms and their failure to increase size of plant in line with increasing size of organisation (Prais 1976) has shown that technical arguments on scale economies alone are not sufficient. Furthermore, it has to be recognised that economies of scale are much more significant in some industries than others. The case advanced by Schumacher (1973) that 'small is beautiful' was undoubtedly influential. The Bolton Committee Report on *Small Firms* (Cmnd 4811, 1971) helped to focus attention on the importance of small firms and resulted in some government action through the allocation of special responsibility for small firms to a minister within the Department of Industry and the establishment of advisory and counselling services for small firms.

More recently, the problems of economic recession and of the apparent secular decline of major British industries where large firms predominate have made the issue even more pressing. It has been argued that there is perhaps a close association between industrial decline and the existence of bureaucratic management in large firms which impedes adaptation and change. In contrast small firms are believed to be more flexible and entrepreneurial and especially important in helping the development of a significant presence in the new technologies which must take up at least some of the reduction in employment and output from the decline of the long established staple industries. Thus it is not surprising that increasing attention should be paid to small firms by business people, researchers and by government.

The primary purpose of this chapter is therefore to attempt to identify those aspects of the management of small firms where the approach may be different from that likely to be adopted in larger organisations. First, however, it will be helpful to consider some of the characteristic features of small firms.

14.2 The Characteristics of Small Firms

(a) The Concept of a Small Firm

The term 'small firm' is singularly inexact. It embraces diverse forms ranging from the single proprietor business such as hairdressers, independent garages, printers—who employ at most only a handful of workers (many of them part-time)—to furniture makers, clothing manufacturers and engineering workshops that employ many personnel with differing skills. This variety of activity and size presents definitional problems since a firm that may be large in terms of employment or turnover or capital employed in one type of activity may be very small in another. Small retailers, for example, may employ fewer people than small manufacturers. In order to deal with this the Bolton Committee established different definitions of a small firm for different sectors. These are set out in Table 14.1 with equivalent turnover figures for 1982 added. While this definition

Table 14.1 Bolton Committee Definitions of 'Small Firm'

Corporate activity	Specific definition
1 Manufacturing	200 employees or less
2 Construction	25 employees or less
3 Mining and quarrying	25 employees or less
4 Retail trade	Turnover of £50,000 p.a. or less (£290,000)
5 Wholesale trade	Turnover of £200,000 p.a. or less (£1,160,000)
6 Motor trades	Turnover of £100,000 p.a. or less (£580,000)
7 Miscellaneous (mainly hairdressers, shoe repairers and laundries)	Turnover of £50,000 p.a. or less (£290,000)
8 Road transport	5 vehicles or less
9 Catering	all except multiples and brewer-managed public houses

Note: The figures in parenthesis are the March 1982 equivalent values of the Bolton Report definitions as estimated by the Department of Trade.

indicates a very large population of small firms, it has been argued that the definition may in some cases have been set rather on the low side (Bannock 1976), as even larger units still have many of the critical operational characteristics and problems of small firms.

It is also not possible to offer a definition of a small firm based on a legal concept. Although it is perhaps unlikely that a small firm would be a publicly owned company with its shares quoted on a stock exchange, some small firms may be limited companies while others are unlimited; some may have an issued share capital while others may not; some may be partnerships while others are sole proprietorships.

(b) Origins of Small Firms

The origins of small firms are also likely to vary. For some, their foundation is now a matter of some considerable history and the business has been handed down within a family for a number of generations. Present-day small firm creation comes from a number of sources. The establishment of professional practices such as accountants, solicitors, independent service agencies, hairdressers, etc. will reflect the desire of an individual or small group of people to use their training and skills independently. The creation of some small businesses may come about as a result of economic necessity as people become redundant and find that other jobs are hard to obtain, or decide that they would wish to be in command of their own futures. Bannock (1981) has argued that it is not unusual to find the generation of new businesses increasing at times of recession and higher unemployment. Individual initiative in small-scale business with low entry barriers can also be a feature of economic activity by some members of socially disadvantaged groups (e.g. some ethnic minorities). New firms also tend to arise for reasons of 'technological pull' where employees of existing organisations are conscious of a market opportunity which they wish to develop independently. This may be due to difficulties of obtaining acceptance or commitment to a new idea or technological opportunity within a large firm or it may be that the desire for independence together with a new concept encourages the creation of a small firm to pursue it. In some areas of high technology, especially areas of electronics, this has become an important phenomenon. Finally, small firms arise as a result of the decision of larger companies to hive-off particular activities (see Chapter 2 above for a discussion of this). The opportunity may present itself to the existing management team to buy the activity and run it as a separate company.

(c) Key Features of Small Firms

Any analysis of the approach to managing small companies needs to consider the ways in which they differ from larger organisations. A number of important characteristics may be identified in this context. First, it follows from what has already been said about some of the origins of small firms that the motivation of owners of small firms may well be different from those in large organisations. The separation between ownership and control is less likely to exist and the purely pecuniary motivation of owners of large firms will be tempered by other motivations in the case of small firm owner/managers. This is supported by the survey evidence collected by the Bolton Committee which showed that 85 per cent of small firms were controlled and most owned by one or two people, with a further 13 per cent being owned by three, four or five people. In addition, in 81 per cent of the manufacturing firms the chief executive was the original founder of the business. The view that the desire for independence rather than direct monetary reward was a prime motivation was confirmed by Golby and Johns (1971):

> This need for 'independence' sums up a wide range of highly personal gratifications provided by working for oneself and not for anybody else. It embraces many important satisfactions which running a small business provided: the personal supervision and control of staff, direct contact with customers, the opportunity to develop one's own sense of personal achievement and pride—psychological satisfactions which appeared to be much more powerful motivators than money or the possibility of large financial gains.

While this independence may offer advantages in terms of a greater commitment to the long-term success of the business and a willingness to put money back into it, there can be potential disadvantages as well. Small firm entrepreneurs tend to have learned through experience rather than from a formal management education, although the Bolton Report showed that a significant minority had a degree or accountancy or further technical qualifications. The experience of such people is often restricted to the firm itself and this may be a disadvantage in an era where the ability to import new ideas and practices is a material influence on a firm's success. The desire for independence may account for a reluctance to seek outside assistance where necessary. It may also limit the potential of firms to grow if an increase in the financial base of the firm would involve a dilution of ownership or some loss of control. This no doubt helps to explain why small firms have low external borrowings.

The nature of ownership and control in the small firm tends to mean that decisions can be taken quickly and flexibly since the owner–manager is in complete control of his business and does not have to refer investment or other plans to some remote parent company board. He also does not have to carry the central overhead charges that would fall on subsidiaries of larger organisations. However, this also means that there is not ready-made access to specialist advice from within the company. This problem is also compounded by the fact that the absence of a full managerial structure means that the scope for devolution of authority is limited, except perhaps for supervisory tasks. This serves to emphasise the extent to which the performance of the small firm is dependent upon the genius and health of one person. While this offers potential benefits, it also clearly carries with it risks as well (see Boswell 1972).

If there are organisational characteristics of small firms that can be readily identified, the same is true of their economic characteristics. Almost by definition, small firms are likely to have small market shares and to lack buying and marketing power relative to their larger competitors. They will therefore lack control in the market place of the form that at least some commentators believe is available to large firms. It is also apparent that small firms have a greater degree of vulnerability. The evidence suggests (Ganguly 1983) that on average about 9 per cent of small firms fail each year (in the sense of being deregistered for VAT purposes). In any given year over 50 per cent of small firms can be expected to fail within the next ten years. It would appear that the critical period is in years 2–4 from the year in which a company is formed. Beyond this time the failure rate drops markedly. There is also considerable variation in failure rates between sectors, with the lowest failure rates in agriculture and the highest in transport.

14.3   The Economic Contribution of Small Firms

(*a*)   *Contribution to Economic Activity*

There are some 1.4 million small firms in Britain at the present time. On the basis of statistics of company registration for VAT purposes the total number of companies has been rising. This seems to be attributable primarily to new firm formation amongst the small firms sectors (Figure 14.1). The contribution of small firms to overall economic activity has declined. According to Rothwell, the contribution of small firms to net output has fallen from 42 per cent in 1924 to 25 per cent in 1968 (Rothwell and Zegveld 1982). But their economic contribution remains important and in some industrial sectors, according to Table 14.2, small firms still account for the majority of employment and output. Small firms are still very important in such industries as leather goods; paper, printing and publishing; clothing and footwear; miscellaneous metal goods including cutlery and jewellery manufacture; and the production of engineers' small tools. Even in instrument and mechanical engineering, small firms remain important. In general it is likely that small firms will be most likely to arise and survive in those activities where economies of scale and size are not substantial, where craft or specialised skills are important, where capital

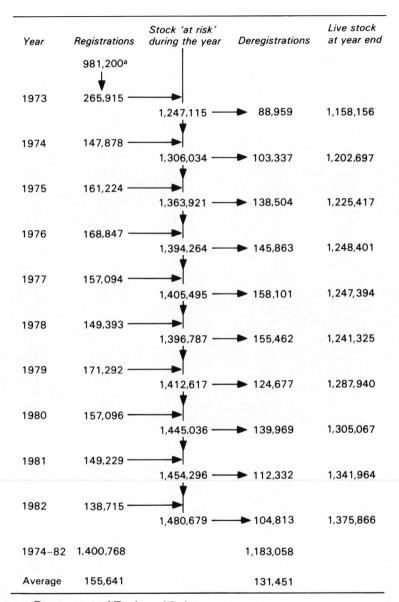

Year	Registrations	Stock 'at risk' during the year	Deregistrations	Live stock at year end
	981,200ᵃ			
1973	265,915			
		1,247,115	88,959	1,158,156
1974	147,878			
		1,306,034	103,337	1,202,697
1975	161,224			
		1,363,921	138,504	1,225,417
1976	168,847			
		1,394,264	145,863	1,248,401
1977	157,094			
		1,405,495	158,101	1,247,394
1978	149,393			
		1,396,787	155,462	1,241,325
1979	171,292			
		1,412,617	124,677	1,287,940
1980	157,096			
		1,445,036	139,969	1,305,067
1981	149,229			
		1,454,296	112,332	1,341,964
1982	138,715			
		1,480,679	104,813	1,375,866
1974–82	1,400,768		1,183,058	
Average	155,641		131,451	

Source: Department of Trade and Industry.
Note: (a) Businesses which had registered by the time VAT was introduced on 1 April 1973.

Figure 14.1 Flow of Stock of Businesses Registered for VAT, 1973–82

Table 14.2   Contribution of Small Firms in Various Industrial Sectors

	Standard industrial classification order	Enterprises as percentage of total	Employment as percentage of total	Net output in £million as percentage of total
III	Food, drink and tobacco	94.50	15.34	11.69
IV	Coal and petroleum	87.60	10.17	9.00
V	Chemicals and allied industries	91.89	12.38	11.00
VI	Metal manufacture	93.22	13.66	14.00
VII	Mechanical engineering	96.12	27.98	26.00
VIII	Instrument engineering	95.57	28.60	29.00
IX	Electrical engineering	93.62	11.37	11.00
X	Shipbuilding and marine engineering	97.04	13.10	16.00
XI	Vehicles	92.49	7.00	6.00
XII	Metal goods not elsewhere specified	97.50	43.50	42.00
XIII	Textiles	92.53	22.19	20.00
XIV	Leather, leather goods and fur	97.85	61.18	60.00
XV	Clothing and footwear	96.03	38.22	38.00
XVI	Bricks, pottery glass, cement	95.00	20.31	17.00
XVII	Timber, furniture, etc.	98.56	60.63	58.00
XVIII	Paper, printing and publishing	97.34	31.30	27.00
XIX	Other manufacturing industries	95.46	30.00	27.00

Source: Report on the Census of Production 1978 (1979) Business Monitor, HMSO.
Note: A small firm is taken to be less than 200 employees.

requirements are not high and where specialised market 'niches' can be found. Given their overall greater labour intensity than for large firms, they have a special role to play in filling any shortfall in jobs caused by technological progress.

It is sometimes argued that Britain suffers because its small firm sector is smaller and less effective than that in other countries (e.g. Bannock 1976, Prais 1976). Because of definitional problems, it is difficult to establish accurately the relative size of the sector in different countries, and certainly more qualitative assessments of effectiveness and vitality are very difficult to establish with confidence. Table 14.3 uses as a definition of small and medium sized firms those with 1–499 employees. From this it would appear that the UK has a roughly similar contribution from small firms to employment as France, West Germany and Italy, but rather less than that in the USA, Japan and the Netherlands. However, structural and cultural

Table 14.3 Contribution of Small and Medium Size Firms to Employment in Selected Countries (%)

USA	Japan	France	West Germany	Italy	Netherlands	UK
58.2	54.4	40.3	43.4	43.7	56.0	44.3

Source: OECD, DST1/SPR/80.15, Paris, May 1980

differences may well influence the ability to draw direct comparisons and it has been a matter of concern that the small firms sector in Britain has tended to decline faster than in other countries.

In addition to their absolute contribution to employment and gross domestic product, small firms offer other significant economic and social advantages. By virtue of their local ownership they offer the possibility of a greater involvement in the local community. This may well mean greater attention to local needs and interests where investment or other decisions are involved. Small firms may benefit from a greater community interest and commitment to their needs. They also offer a degree of choice that would not exist if small firms were to be less significant. Breadth of choice also implies increased competition. This is beneficial not only to the final consumer, but also to intermediate purchasers, such as other firms, who may wish to keep multiple sources of supply or cover for their own integrated activities. Indeed, large firms benefit greatly from access to small firms as suppliers of specialised components, materials and services which the large firm (because of its own overhead structure) would find uneconomic to supply internally. The small firm's flexibility is especially beneficial to larger organisations who may use it also to augment output in times of high demand.

(b) Contribution to Innovation

The development of any economy relies heavily on invention and innovation. It may be argued *a priori* that small firms face considerable and possibly insuperable problems if they wish to invent and especially to innovate. Where such activities require large scale in terms of staff, equipment or other resources, the costs may be in excess of those which the small firm can afford and the risks will be greater than those faced by large firms who may be able to afford a portfolio of such projects, at least some of which may succeed. Statistics of expenditures on research and development or the number of qualified scientists and engineers employed do not suggest that small firms are very important sources of innovative effort, though it may be that R and D activities are only separately identified and costed in large firms.

However, studies of the contribution of small firms to innovation do offer some impressive results. The early work by Jewkes indicated that small firms and individual inventors were responsible for about 50 per cent of the inventions and innovations studied (Jewkes *et al.* 1969). Freeman's study for the Bolton Committee (Freeman 1971) showed that small firms had been responsible for about 10 per cent of the major innovations between 1945 and 1970 in 50 different industries. If anything, this proportionate contribution was higher towards the end of that period than in the earlier years. Freeman found that small firms were proportionately more important sources of innovations in such industries as scientific instruments, electronics, carpets, textiles, machine tools, paper and board, leather and footwear, timber and furniture. These tend to be industries where small firms account for rather higher proportions of economic activity. They are probably also industries where ideas and personal skills are more important than expensive research laboratories as sources of significant developments.

More recent information from the Science Policy Research Unit Innovation Databank indicates that in the decade 1970–80 the share of small firms in innovations has increased still further. If anything, it might be expected that given the potentially high costs and risks in turning an invention into an innovation, small firms are less likely to be successful innovators than inventors. However, the fact remains that small firms do make a significant, and seemingly increasing, contribution to the innovative process. Indeed, it may be that given the reluctance of large firms to innovate unless a considerable volume of sales can be foreseen, small firms may now be more important sources of innovation too.

The National Science Foundation (1976) suggests also that small firms are much more productive in turning R and D expenditure into useful innovations than larger organisations, so this aspect of the economic contribution of small firms ought not to be undervalued, though this seems to be more applicable to the USA than to Britain.

(c) Contribution to Economic Development

A further aspect of the economic contribution of small firms comes from their contribution to economic growth overall. There are two dimensions to this. First, the small firms of today are quite likely to be a critical source of the large firms of tomorrow. Some major firms had humble, and quite recent, origins. Marks and Spencer started from a market stall in Leeds and Tesco from a barrow in the East End of London. Sinclair Electronics started in the 1960s as a small company and now has a high share of the market for personal computers. Xerox Corporation grew out of a small manufacturer of photographic papers which had taken on the rights to the

Carlson invention of 'electrophotography'. Often the most successful small firm is one which sees an entrepreneurial opportunity—a new market segment to reach, a more competitive spirit, a new or superior product.

The possibility of a fundamentally new product is the second dimension to the contribution of small firms to economic growth. Out of such developments come new industries and the possibility of structural change in the composition of economic activity within a country to fill some of the gaps caused by the decline in some staple industries.

The new industry will be founded on a new technology, such as the slow combustion engine in the case of the automobile industry, the transistor in the case of the electronics industry, and the microprocessor in the case of the emerging information technology industry. In the early stages of development the technology is often what might be termed 'fluid', with several competing product designs, and its development and the manufacture of the products will generally take place in small and relatively inefficient units. Innovation will tend to focus on changes in the product and in the development of new products. Demand will often be initially quite low, but will expand, particularly as a result of reductions in price with the gaining of experience. New firms will be attracted into the industry, thereby increasing competition. There will be further capital equipment developments, increases in production efficiency and eventually the emergence of a dominant product design. Economies of scale become important and production is increasingly concentrated in larger units. Demand, however, continues to expand.

Eventually the industry matures as demand stabilises or the rate of increase in demand declines whilst competition intensifies, particularly from Third World countries. By this stage production is highly capital intensive and concentrated in large units. The emphasis of innovation is on incremental changes in manufacturing technology. The product itself often assumes commodity status and will therefore have a high price elasticity of demand.

It has been suggested that the fortunes of the total economy can be analysed in terms of the growth and development of major industries. Rothwell and Zegveld (1982), for example, have described a model of post-war evolution that is based on this view. Developed economies can be regarded as being in the 'mature' phase, with the backbone of their industrial structure consisting largely of industries which have reached the late stages of the cycle of development. The current maturity of these staple industries has, of course, produced significant adverse social consequences. The effective strategy for these mature companies is not to look to the Third World markets since they are often able to satisfy their own demand; indeed, the latter's ability to produce more efficiently is part of the problem. These 'mature' firms might seek to develop new businesses based on the new technologies, although there is evidence that many large companies may not be particularly effective in doing this (Littler and Sweeting 1984).

An alternative approach would be to attempt to generate new industries based on high technology and to develop further the service sector. In both cases small firms can have a significant role. The US semiconductor industry has been widely quoted as an example of the small firm's importance in the seminal stages of the industry. The discovery of the transistor effect in the Bell Telephone Laboratories in 1947 led, in turn, to Shockley's description of the field-effective transistor with a central electrode consisting of a reverse-biased junction. Shockley left to form his own company. In turn, eight of his employees left in 1957 to establish their own company. This marked the beginning of what has been termed 'Silicon Valley'. These eight workers were backed by the Fairchild Camera Corporation and formed Fairchild Semiconductor in September 1957. Not only did this company grow rapidly, but it spawned many other companies. Although the production of basic transistors later became the prerogative of the large firm, in accordance with the model advanced above, small firms still have an important role to play in the development of specialist devices, and particularly in the development of software.

14.4   Managerial Issues in the Small Firm

So far we have identified the economic significance of small firms and some characteristics which may have a particular bearing on the way in which they are managed. In the remainder of this chapter we consider some ways in which decision taking in small firms may be subject to different considerations from those which apply to the general run of companies or to those other special cases considered in chapters 12 and 13. We approach this by outlining first the ways in which small business activities can start and be financed, then consider the question of managerial objectives and organisation, followed by the implications for particular functional activities, and finally we consider the impact of the wider economic environment on small business activities.

(a)   Starting a Small Business

Control of a small business can be taken by acquiring a going concern or by setting up an entirely new enterprise. In the first case trading relationships with customers, suppliers and competitors will be well established, the approximate level of demand will be known and there will be no net addition to the number of suppliers in the market or to the overall level of capacity. In the second instance the firm must estimate either the share of the market it can take from competitors who are already established and who may retaliate through price cuts or changes in the quality of service offered, or, if the good or service to be provided is new and has no close competitors, the initial level and rate of growth of demand.

Entry into small business ownership and management can be accomplished in seven main ways.

(1) *Inheritance of a family business* This has probably been the most common means of acquiring a small business over the past two hundred years. Assets are transferred from one generation to another and no initial cash premium is required on the part of the new owner, although there may be a considerable tax liability arising from estate duty. The new owner may be anxious to take control and to introduce new and improved methods of operation, marketing and financing, and will in many cases have had experience of working in the business before the inheritance. But there may be difficulties, with ingrained attitudes and long-established practices on the part of management and employees as well as with products or services that are losing their relevance to changing patterns of market demand. In some cases the new owner may be too sanguine or complacent about the business and make use of its financial resources for unrelated activities, interests or pastimes. The Victorian epigram, 'from clogs to clogs in three generations', is a caution against this type of attitude.

(2) *Purchase of a going concern* Many small retail or service enterprises, such as newsagents or sub-post offices, are acquired in this way. They cater for a stable and established market, risks are low, the business premises may also be used for family accommodation, and revenue can be increased through extended opening hours whilst costs are kept to a minimum by the willingness of the proprietor and often members of the family to work without direct remuneration. In some cases such a business can provide a second income to supplement that of the main income earner. The purchase price of the business will usually include an amount to reflect the intangible value of 'good will' arising from the opportunity to serve a stable and loyal local demand.

(3) *Professional services* These include the services of (usually) highly trained specialists, such as doctors, dentists, solicitors, accountants and estate agents, who in general function as unincorporated entities receiving fees or as partnerships. The practice may be set up as a free-standing enterprise, perhaps after a period of training and experience with another similar enterprise, or may be run as an adjunct to salaried or contractual work with a larger organisation (e.g. medical consultants in private practice). Both the initial costs of establishment and those of continuing operations can be relatively low and covered immediately by fee income,

whilst the size of the market is well known and stable. Entry into these sectors usually depends upon the possession of appropriate qualifications, membership of professional associations, and any national or local policies or understandings governing the number of practitioners.

(4) *New ventures* Net increases in the total of small businesses are brought about by the formation of new incorporated or unincorporated enterprises. As has been shown above, the failure rate is high among these, especially in the first few years, but they are the seed-bed from which viable, enduring and, in some cases, large-scale enterprises are developed. New enterprises may supply existing products or services to existing markets in which there are already other competitors with established links to clients and suppliers. Entry in these conditions will be easier, the faster is the growth of overall demand and the lower the level of influence of existing firms over the market. Another entry route is to supply existing goods or services to a newly emerging or newly defined segment of the market. Here insight and flair on the part of the entrepreneur coupled with effective market research and planning are very important. The supply and fitting of certain types of replacement automotive components—exhausts, shock absorbers, and batteries—is an example of the scope for new entry through redefinition of the market. These components were traditionally supplied by repair garages offering a full range of servicing and mainten-ance facilities, often in association with franchised dealerships for the sale of motor vehicles. High gross profit margins are charged by these outlets on replacement components as a means of cross-subsidising new vehicles sales and the provision of a comprehensive range of services. Scope thus existed for specialist firms to supply a limited range of the most frequently required replacement components at lower prices as a result of bulk purchasing, volume operations and the avoidance of the overheads associ-ated with repair garages. The quality of the service was also changed by providing drive-in on-demand facilities, often by using the premises of garages or petrol filling stations that had withdrawn from the market.

A third route is to develop and market new products or services. In some cases there may be the opportunity to provide goods or services to meet changes in demand, habits or tastes and for which there are few, if any, barriers to entry. Examples are health clubs, sportswear, specialist interest publications, popular entertainers and peripheral equipment for complex technology, such as audio and video cassettes and some types of computer software. Entry and exit may be swift in such sectors; success depends chiefly on the skill and ability to recognise shifts in the pattern of demand and to co-ordinate a response. Equally important may be the ability to identify how transitory a particular fashion may be and when is the best time to leave. In other circumstances the development of new products may be complex and involve extensive research and technological knowledge and ability. This aspect of technological innovation will be considered separately.

(5) *Product innovation*   In some areas of high technology, particularly electronics, research undertaken by large enterprises may provide scope for 'spin off'; new products are produced and marketed on a small scale by those involved in their discovery. The initial requirement is a high level of funding for research and development to support work that may be lengthy and uncertain in its outcome. Once the product has been successfully developed, manufacture and the evolution of derivatives may be controlled more effectively in a small organisation (Burns and Stalker 1958). The inventors may resign their appointments to set up on their own to manufacture and market the product. They have the advantages of knowing the precise specifications of the product and the problems that have been met in its development, but they may meet difficulties from their previous employer because of patent ownership or ill will. Sometimes the larger firm may be willing to take a stake in the new enterprise if it believes that manufacture can be organised and controlled more effectively on a small rather than a large scale.

Fostering interactions between high technology firms, both large and small, and between them and the professional skills available in universities and other centres of research can be important for successful innovation, and this is one of the intentions behind 'science parks' and other similar initiatives. Rather than finance being required at the initial stages of research, it may be needed at later stages of commercial development. Many new products and processes have been discovered by individual inventors working independently (Jewkes *et al.* 1969), the advances depending on individual insight and flair rather than on large-scale research. The support of large firms or of government agencies may be needed when the manufacturing system is to be scaled-up to commercial output rates, and the product put on the market.

(6) *Buy-outs*   A separately definable part of the business of a diversified enterprise may be purchased by its management team, often in association with other employees. Much of the merger-based corporate expansion that took place in the 1960s and early 1970s led to the growth of large enterprises with a wide spread of activities, some of which were not closely related to the main areas of activities and for which specialist management skills were required. In some cases, also, failing activities were supported and returned to a position of independent financial viability. Recession, a slowing down of growth by merger and reappraisals of corporate objectives and strategies have led in some cases to the separable and peripheral activities becoming suitable for sale. Where the existing management teams are knowledgeable about the business and are capable of devising and implementing realistic business plans, they may be able to raise finance

to acquire the share capital of the business. The involvement of other employees in the share subscription can offer prospects of a close identity between management and workers with the overall commercial aims of the new company. The attractions for the diversifying enterprise are that it can become free of the responsibility of providing specialist resources for a minor part of its business and can divert finance to other parts of the business where it can be more profitably employed. Buy-outs are not restricted to private sector enterprises. In one notable recent case the management and employees of the National Freight Corporation, involved mainly in road haulage in the UK, acquired the assets of the business from the government.

(7) *Specialist products or services* Businesses of this kind provide existing products or services in a form to meet the needs of a specialist sector of the overall market. Examples are caterers, equipment hire, painters and decorators, and plumbers. In many cases they operate in markets in which the demand from individual clients is infrequent (e.g. house painting, wedding receptions), but in which the aggregation of demand over a given market (say a town) can provide a fairly steady flow of contracts or orders. The activities undertaken are usually labour-intensive, depending upon a degree of skill and technical knowledge. The suppliers of these products and services often enjoy the benefits of independence in planning and carrying out their work.

Given the high failure rate of new businesses, it is clearly vital that any prospective entrant, whether by acquisition or by starting a new venture, should ascertain to the greatest extent possible the likely viability of the project. In the first phase of the evaluation three aspects are important:

(a) *The market segment* The entrant must decide whether to try to compete in the entire market, which may embrace a wide range of related products or services and cover a large geographical area, or whether to confine activities to a more narrowly defined segment. Success may depend in part on the ability to identify a unique market segment that others in the industry have not yet sought to exploit.

(b) *Ideas* Successful new products or services or the identification of market segments depend upon creative flair and insight. These abilities may be the entrepreneur's own upon which the business can be built, provided that he has the necessary level of technical skills or that these are not important. In other circumstances the new venture's success may depend on the incorporation of the ideas of others, either through close monitoring of technological, economic, social and political developments, or through acquiring knowledge and know-how by employing specialists or by purchasing a franchise.

(c) *Skills* These may be important for using ideas to exploit a market segment. Many new ventures are founded on the technological skills of the founder, but he may find day-to-day management and the control of a stable, mature organisation irksome, denying him the opportunity to expand his field of research and interest. In these circumstances a chief executive with a breadth of business knowledge may be more able to launch and manage the enterprise successfully.

Finance is critical to small businesses. They may be financed by personal wealth, reserves, profit and depreciation cash flows, trade credit, short- and long-term loans from banks and other institutions, equity and government grants and tax concessions. Enterprises acquired by inheritance do not require the existing capital assets to be refinanced, and operating costs, including interest charges, can normally be met out of revenue. Funds to meet short-term variations in activity can be obtained from trade creditors (by negotiating deferred payment terms from suppliers) and bank overdrafts. Longer-term needs for expansion can be met from reserves or bank loans. In times of recession the level of distress lending by banks tends to increase, as enterprises endeavour to remain in business until demand and prices recover.

Personal wealth, property mortgages and bank loans tend to be the main sources of finance for the acquisition of small existing businesses, whilst a partner's own liquid wealth, often supplemented by bank loans, is important for beginning in the professional services sector. Innovative enterprise, which promises a substantial flow of future profits, will be suitable for equity finance which may be supported by venture capital from merchant banks, acting individually or as a consortium. Venture capital can be provided initially as loan capital, perhaps with interest or principal repayments deferred, with the option of conversion to equity at a later date. The development of the Unlisted Securities Market has removed some of the barriers to equity finance for small- and medium-sized firms, particularly those with growth prospects. These sources of finance may also be supplemented by bank loans of the conventional type.

Buy-outs can be financed by employee share purchases and by loan finance of a venture capital type from a consortium of institutions. Government agencies and the central bank can be instrumental in arranging and co-ordinating such lines of finance. It may in addition be possible to negotiate with the vendor the transfer of the assets at a favourable price to the purchasers, especially if the opportunity cost to the vendor is less than the market price. Provision of an adequate reserve in the accounts of the new enterprise can help with the need for finance in the initial period of independence and when new asset formation is proposed. Specialist operators finance their activities from their own past savings, bank overdrafts, property mortgages and from working capital obtained from trade credit from suppliers and advance payments (payment on account) from clients. Such businesses may be very vulnerable at times of low demand and high interest rates.

Whatever the sources and types of finance used to start a new business, it is most desirable to set up an accounting system that keeps the initial finance separate from working capital and the current revenue and expenditure associated with operations. By so doing, the trading performance of the enterprise and its ability to remunerate its capital employed can be clearly identified and monitored.

Once the initial review of the scope for the new venture has been made and the prospects for its success evaluated, the management team must give detailed consideration to the market strategy, the organisation of production and the raising of finance. Table 14.4 gives a checklist of the main points to be considered. Where external finance is to be raised from banks, finance houses or from equity investors, it will be necessary to draw up a business plan, and these points will form the main structure of it. In any case it will help to clarify strategic thinking and to emphasise possible areas of difficulty if adequate time is spent in evaluation and appraisal. In addition to outlining the marketing and production policies and the finance required, the business plan should give brief details of the business and its objectives and should provide a projection of the likely cash flows over the first three or four years of operation and of anticipated profitability. It will also be helpful to indicate how the proposed range of products and services could be developed to meet the needs of the market as it grows and matures.

(b)   Managerial Objectives and Organisation

It is apparent that small firms have a number of characteristics in respect of which they differ from large firms and which have a material bearing on their activities. When we consider the organisation and objectives of small business, it is clear that the nature and attitudes of the owner–manager have a major influence.

Owner–managers of small businesses are likely to have a strong preference for independence. This may explain why they set up their own firms, often at the expense of a loss of income compared with their previous salaried occupations (Gibb and Ritchie 1982). While some recent thinking on the implications of the separation of ownership in large firms has suggested that large firms are not necessarily so responsive to a strong profit orientation (though others would challenge this), it may be that owners of small firms are even less profit oriented, preferring the quiet life. They may be less likely to respond to market signals where the profitability

Table 14.4   Outline Checklist for a New Venture

1 Market research
    1.1 Is the business concept sound?
    1.2 What will be the likely reaction of existing firms to new entry?
    1.3 What is the potential demand?
    1.4 What segment of the market is to be aimed at?
    1.5 Are there many or few buyers?
    1.6 What is the enterprise's likely market share?

2 Production analysis
    2.1 What plant and equipment will be needed?
    2.2 Who are the likely suppliers (new or second-hand)?
    2.3 How familiar is the management team with the technology?
    2.4 What is the likely initial capital requirement?
    2.5 What is the ratio of fixed to variable costs?
    2.6 What is the level of unit variable costs?
    2.7 How do total average costs vary at different levels of production?

3 Finance
    3.1 What financial investment is required and from what sources can it be obtained?
    3.2 What are working capital requirements?
    3.3 What is the cash flow profile for the first few years?
    3.4 Can sufficient finance be obtained to support the firm until profitability is achieved?

4 Marketing
    4.1 What advertising and promotion needs to be undertaken and what will be the cost?
    4.2 Will personal selling be a feature? What sales team will be required and what will be the role of the entrepreneur?
    4.3 How will the product be distributed?
    4.4 What is the appropriate pricing policy?

5 Evaluation
    5.1 What rate of output is required to break even?
    5.2 What is the probability of achieving this (a) initially, (b) eventually?
    5.3 When will profitability be attained?

of particular activities declines. While large organisations may be assumed to have an interest not only in profits but also in growth, Birley (1982/83) argues that, given their desire for independence, owners of small firms will accept and indeed possibly seek the lowest growth consistent with survival, especially if this is a way of preventing others taking an equity stake in the company. However, towards the end of their working life she suggests their attitudes may change, and in the interests of the continuity of the business they may be prepared to accept wider share participation and a greater orientation to growth.

Much is made of the way the personal characteristics of the owner–manager influence the way the company is organised and run. The possibility of greater flexibility and speed of decision taking, together with a more entrepreneurial outlook, is recognised as an advantage to small firms from the control of one person. However, a number of possible disadvantages are suggested as offsetting this (see, for example, Boswell 1972). It is suggested that owner–managers are resistant to change and tend to become complacent. They are not necessarily effective managers, at least so far as ability to cover effectively all the functional and strategic areas of management are concerned. With an increasingly complex environment (legally, economically, etc.), their shortage of time and lack of skills may become especially apparent. Whereas an autocratic style may have been of value in the early stages of the life of a company, the later reluctance to delegate may lower the quality of decision taking and may hinder the speed of response to new opportunities. Decision taking, especially in the search for finance and premises, has been described as limited and myopic (Gibb and Ritchie 1982), though theories of sequential, problem oriented, search suggest this may also be true of large firms too. The performance of the firm in the short run is highly dependent upon the health, vigour and continuing skills of the entrepreneur, while in the long run its performance will depend upon the management succession. If this is kept within the owner's family, there is no guarantee that his successors will be as effective as he had been in developing the company, thus the prospects for second and third generation small companies may be particularly uncertain.

Small firms are also subject to important economic influences which affect their performance. It follows, almost by definition, that a small firm lacks control in the market place and so may be particularly at risk from economic fluctuations. A small firm is unlikely to have much of a portfolio of products and markets and this makes the economic risks greater than that of a large firm which may at least be able to spread risks and average out returns from its wider range of activities. It is, as Mitchell (1980) argues, the uncertainty and higher exposure to risk that often makes small firms marginal units rather than a lack of profitability as such. Small firms are subject to the constraints that the lack of economies of scale imposes. This may mean that unit costs are higher due to a smaller volume of output. Bound up with this is the question of indivisibilities in that investments in plant or particular skills require a large scale of activity to allow the investment to be fully utilised. The implication of this is that incremental growth is often not an option to the small firm wishing to grow; it needs the step change in the scale of its activities to justify its investment and, inevitably, the risks from such a change in scale can be considerable. Associated with this is also the problem of the difficulties in obtaining access to the necessary financial resources for growth. While this is partly a question of the extent to which small firms search for funds and of the willingness of institutions to lend funds to small firms, the economic risks that we have identified must also influence both the demand and the supply of funds for growth.

practices and lower labour turnover. In addition, some costs associated with the labour force are avoided by small firms since they are exempt from some aspects of employment legislation (Storey 1983). However, the evidence does not all point in the one direction. The greater vulnerability of small firms to gains and losses in particular orders tends to give rather less security in work patterns and earnings and, unless carefully handled, this can be a source of difficulty. It has been suggested (Curran and Stanworth 1981) that small firms find it difficult to recruit the more able staff; there seems to some extent at least to be a different labour market for small firms than for large. The quality of staff problems may be compounded by the greater difficulty which small firms have in releasing staff, once employed, for training.

These are therefore features of small firms which do indicate the importance of positive personnel policies. Careful and considered recruitment policies are required, perhaps following on from a greater effort to extend the field of potential candidates beyond those who would normally contemplate applying to a small firm. Work scheduling (as well as better marketing) may be required to offer greater stability of hours and earnings to employees, and careful consideration needs to be given to ways of training and developing staff. Wage payment levels and systems will need to take account of the marginal productivity of the workers concerned and not simply assume that all workers in an industry, with large and small firms and with greater or lesser degrees of capital at their disposal, are equally productive.

Finance is often considered to be the main problem to the small firm. While it is clearly important, the analysis of issues in other functional areas should serve to emphasise that it is not the only one. However, small firms often suffer from cash management problems which can cause bankruptcy in a very short time if not carefully handled. The need here is for close monitoring of cash flows and insistence on not allowing undue credit to customers. While some large customers may deliberately 'pay long but charge short', often it seems that small firms are too slow in submitting accounts. Thus efficient accounts control is an important key to a successful small firm. In circumstances where a firm is stretched, adequate working capital and the sympathetic help of the bank manager or other source of financial help becomes most important. Funds are, of course, also needed for expansion of the business. Here too there are problems for small firms. There are naturally some firms that have no desire to expand and would not borrow for fear of losing their independence. Such companies were identified by Boswell (1972) as prosperous, slow growing and conservative. They may face future difficulties.

Other companies may seek finance to allow new investment, but may experience various difficulties in obtaining the requisite funds. The supply of funds for small firms may be limited. High taxation reduces the likelihood of ploughing back sufficient profits to provide the desired investment funds and the decline in the number of 'Aunt Agathas' also reduces the supply of funds within the family. Some schemes to help investment set minimum levels which are above the aspirations of many small firms. While the banks are now more oriented to providing funds for small firms, it is still the case (as the Wilson Committee (1979) pointed out) that there are a significant number of viable enterprises that are denied access to sufficient funds. The gap in the financial market identified by the earlier Macmillan Committee of the 1930s still remains. The banks are also open to criticism for a slow, bureaucratic, unhelpful and unduly risk averse approach to the provision of funds to small business (Binks 1979). Even if the supply is available, the costs may act as a strong disincentive. The management time spent in seeking funds does not rise in proportion to the size of loan sought, so small firms are likely to spend proportionately more time and money in making applications (Johnson 1978) and may find a lower success rate due to lack of experience, lack of past financial history, or absence of appropriate market and investment appraisals to persuade potential lenders of the viability of the project. The size of the security required by those advancing funds may be unreasonably high relative to the size of loan, and rates of interest charged are also likely to exceed those charged to large borrowers. Steps can, of course, be taken to mitigate these influences. Greater care and effort may be spent in producing a case for financial help with the aid of professional advisers. More use might be made of financial expertise in guiding the company and ensuring that financial control and management accounting are appropriate to the requirements of the company. The range of potential sources of financial help can be increased to make much greater use of equity capital or venture capital (Walbank 1983), though the corollary of this is that owner-managers will need to be prepared to accept some participation by others in the fortunes of the company. This may, however, often prove desirable and a necessary basis for the development of the business.

(d)   Small Firms in the Wider Environment

The potential contribution of small firms is now well recognised by governments, financial institutions and others and developments are taking place in the wider environment which should increase the prospects of success for small firms in general. There has been some reversal of the trend decline in the contribution to the economy of small firms, and economic conditions (due to changing relative factor costs, changing techniques, changing patterns of consumer demand) suggest this may continue. There is, however, a risk that, as with 'bandwaggon' developments, expectations may be raised too high. Certainly a lot of dependence is being put on the abilities of very diffuse managements of small firms to develop their overall strategies, improve their functional management performance and respond to the wider environment opportunities, so that they do make a significant economic contribution.

There have, in recent years, been considerable efforts to create an environment more responsive to the needs of small firms, both to encourage their formation and to assist their growth. The sources of finance have expanded and the nature of available financial assistance has broadened to increase the availability of risk capital through equity finance and venture capital funds as opposed to development capital. Government has offered various forms of financial help through such measures as the business expansion scheme offering tax relief on the cost of shares purchased in unquoted and new companies; the loan guarantee scheme where the Department of Industry guarantees a high proportion of loans to small firms for between 2 and 7 years; investment interest relief; and the small engineering firms' investment scheme which exists to encourage the development of new products, processes or investment in new technologies. Governments have also helped through legislation by imposing less onerous requirements on small firms in such areas as employment law and planning controls and on information requirements (Storey 1983). Efforts have been made by both public and private sectors to offer a greatly improved infrastructure within which small firms may operate. The development of enterprise zones offers cost savings and saves time in dealing with government regulations. Science parks offer companies access to factory units, technical expertise and support facilities. In other areas 'starter factories' are being established to help small firms. Advisory services are now available from many sources—government, development agencies, financial institutions, universities and consultants—which should help to raise the overall quality of small firm performance. It is significant that applications for finance from aid schemes for small firms usually exceed the amount of public money allocated, but this is sometimes after extensive publicity.

There are, however, a number of questions that must arise about these developments and their implications for the management of the small firm and the making of policy for the small firm sector. It is important to be satisfied that sufficient small firms have the motivation and enterprise to take advantage of the opportunities offered. The issue is probably not so much about new business formation, but about the growth and development of small firms. This may involve a change in attitudes of those traditionally managing small firms, an increase in their functional management performance and a willingness to see some dilution in their levels of ownership and control. Often small firms seem open to criticism for adopting an unduly protectionist stance. In these circumstances a wider range of measures and increased government expenditure will be unlikely to stimulate growth.

It has been calculated (Bannock 1976) that of 58 recommendations made by the Bolton Committee, 56 proposed some governmental action. Such an emphasis seems to underestimate the importance of the extent to which small firms can help themselves. This applies also in the field of competition policy. While some degree of co-operation between small firms may actually help competition, it is difficult to believe that in general legislative measures aimed at helping small firms by weakening competitive pressure are to be welcomed. They are unlikely to be in the long-term interests of dynamic small firms, though it is important to ensure that large firms do not hinder the growth of competition from small firms.

It is perhaps inevitable, however, that our final comments will focus upon the role of government policy, where there seems to be a danger of an undue proliferation of measures, and the need to assess both analytically and empirically the effects of policy instruments. While some (e.g. Bannock 1976) would argue that recent measures are merely removing some of the discrimination which has traditionally existed against small firms, others (e.g. Storey 1983) argue that there is evidence of an unjustified and possibly economically undesirable use of subsidies in favour of small firms. Clearly policy should aim to avoid undue interference with market processes, except where it is clear that such action may improve the operation of the market and produce an outcome which would enhance social welfare. In this case the likely response of the small firms at whom the policy is aimed is critical. What is the evidence on the required scale of assistance to encourage birth or growth of firms? What sort of help is to be preferred by small firms? For example, it may be argued that the cash flows of firms are helped by grants rather than tax relief. Does the competition between different local development agencies help to increase the stock of small firms or does it merely lead to a redistribution of a given supply? These are the sort of questions that need greater attention as efforts are made to use public policy instruments to so influence management decisions in the small firm sector that social welfare is enhanced.

References

Adams, A. (1982) 'Barriers to product innovation in small firms', *European Small Business Journal*, 1, pp. 67–86.
Bannock, G. (1976) *The Smaller Business in Britain and Germany*, Wilton House.
Bannock, G. (1981) *The Economics of Small Firms*, Basil Blackwell.
Bennett, D. (1983) 'Small firms and the law of competition in the EEC', *European Small Business Journal*, 1, No. 2.
Binks, M. (1979) 'Finance for expansion in the small firm', *Lloyds Bank Review*, October, No. 134, pp. 33–45.
Birley, S. (1982/83) 'Corporate strategy and the smaller firm', *Journal of General Management*, 8, No. 2, pp. 82–86.

Blois, K. J. (1975) 'Supply contracts in the Galbraithian planning system', *Journal of Industrial Economics*, 24, pp. 29–39.

Boswell, J. (1972) *The Rise and Decline of Small Firms*, Allen and Unwin.

Burns, T. and Stalker, G. M. (1958) *The Management of Innovation*, Tavistock Publications.

Cannon, T. and Willis, M. (1983) 'The smaller firm in overseas trade', *European Small Business Journal*, 1, No. 3, pp. 45–55.

Curran, J. and Stanworth, J. (1981) 'The social dynamics of the small manufacturing enterprise', *Journal of Management Studies*, 18.

Curran, J. and Stanworth, J. (1982) 'The small firm in Britain: past, present and future', *European Small Business Journal*, 1, pp. 16–25.

Davies, J. R. and Kelly, M. (1971) *Small Firms in the Manufacturing Sector*, Bolton Committee Research Report, No. 3, HMSO.

Freeman, C. (1971) *The Role of Small Firms in Innovation in the United Kingdom Since 1945*, Bolton Committee, Research Report, No. 6, HMSO.

Ganguly, P. (1983) 'Lifespan analysis of businesses in the UK 1973–82', *British Business*, 12th August, HMSO.

Gibb, A. and Ritchie, J. (1982) 'Understand the process of starting small businesses', *European Small Business Journal*, 1, pp. 26–45.

Golby, C. W. and Johns, G. (1971) *Attitude and Motivation*, Bolton Committee, Research Report, No. 7.

Jewkes, J. *et al.* (1969) *The Sources of Invention*, Macmillan.

Johnson, P. (1978) 'Policies towards small firms: time for caution?' *Lloyds Bank Review*, July, No. 129, pp. 1–11.

Littler, D. A. and Sweeting, R. C. (1984) 'New business development in mature firms', *Omega 11*, No. 6.

Lydall, H. (1958) 'Aspects of competition in manufacturing industry', *The Bulletin of the Oxford University Institute of Statistics*, November, Vol. 20.

Mitchell, J. E. (1980) 'Small firms: a critique', *The Three Banks Review*, June, No. 126, pp. 50–61.

Pickering, J. F. (1975) 'Co-operation and the small business', in A. J. Burkart and S. Medlik (eds), *The Management of Tourism*, Heinemann.

Prais, S. J. (1976) *The Evolution of Giant Firms in Britain*, Cambridge University Press.

Rothwell, R. and Zegveld, W. (1982) *Innovation and the Small and Medium Sized Firm*.

Schumacher, E. F. (1973) *Small is Beautiful*, Blond and Briggs.

Storey, D. J. (1983) 'Small firms policies: a critique', *Journal of General Management*, 8, No. 4, pp. 5–19.

Walbank, M. (1983) 'Equity sharing policies in new venture funding', *European Small Business Journal*, 1, No. 3, pp. 12–28.

Cmnd 4811 (1971) *Small Firms*, Bolton Committee, HMSO.

Economists Advisory Group (1983) *Co-operative Marketing and Joint Trading for Small Firms*, prepared for London Enterprise Agency and National Westminster Bank.

National Science Foundation (1976) *Indicators of International Trends in Technological Innovation*, National Science Foundation, Washington.

Wilson Committee (1979) *The Financing of Small Firms*, Interim Report of the Committee to Review the Functioning of Financial Institutions, HMSO.

Subject Index

Author Index